JUVENILE DELINQUENCY AND JUVENILE JUSTICE

JUVENILE DELINQUENCY AND JUVENILE JUSTICE

Jack Klempner
Avila College, Kansas City

Rodger D. Parker
University of Missouri-Kansas City

A GROLIER COMPANY

Franklin Watts
New York / London / Toronto / Sydney

Library of Congress Cataloging in Publication Data

Klempner, Jack.
Juvenile delinquency and juvenile justice.

Includes bibliographical references and index.
1. Juvenile delinquency—United States.   2. Juvenile justice, Administration
of—United States.   I. Parker, Rodger D., joint author.   II. Title.
HV9104.K56   364.3'6'0973   80–27194
ISBN 0–531–05419–5

Franklin Watts
730 Fifth Avenue
New York, New York 10019

To Jeanette and Jennifer

Acknowledgments

We wish to express our appreciation to some of those who contributed to this book. Forrest and Ellie McDonald provided the original inspiration. James Paul Burns and Ward Brady read and critiqued part of an early version of this work. Avila College and the University of Missouri–Kansas City provided essential resources.

CONTENTS

INTRODUCTION

Textbooks are written for a variety of reasons, including a desire for money, acclaim, and career advancement. We plead guilty to these motivations, but none of them, singly or even grouped together, would cause us to go through the agony of authorship. We believe that our primary motivation has been an eagerness to discuss the nature of the juvenile justice system; to analyze its genesis, evolution, and current tarnished state; to examine its functional limitations; and to suggest possibilities for its improvement. We have tried to present all sides of the issues and to avoid sociological, psychological, and political prejudices. Nevertheless, we have made no attempt to disguise our own biases, for they have been, in the final analysis, the greatest stimulant for this book.

Most people are unable to work actively in a controversial field for any length of time without developing a few opinions, viewpoints, or biases. And both of us have worked in the area of juvenile justice as practitioners, as researchers, and as academics. One spent about a year and a half as a probation officer in southern California, between undergraduate and graduate school. The other worked for more than five years as a juvenile court officer in Detroit. We came together at Avila College in Kansas City, Missouri. When we discussed our ideas about teaching criminal justice and started to share war stories, we discovered that our views on, and experiences in, juvenile justice were remarkably similar. Over time the idea of writing a book that would convert our experience, knowledge, and views into meaningful form took root and has now reached fruition.

So that the reader will have some awareness of our biases and views, we will state some here:

1. There is little or nothing that the criminal justice system presently does that can be demonstrated to have any significant effect upon the rate of crime.

2. There is little or nothing that the juvenile justice system presently does that can be demonstrated to have any significant effect upon the rate of delinquency.

There are two things that the juvenile justice system does do quite effectively:

1. It gives the public the feeling that something is being done to solve the problem of juvenile delinquency.
2. It provides employment for the people who work in the juvenile justice system.

Some people who read this will probably regard us as pessimists or cynics or worse. We regard ourselves as pragmatists. We want to improve juvenile justice, to make it more humane while making it more effective and more efficient. But no improvement will be made as long as people think that the present system works. We also do not wish to discourage idealistic students who may be preparing for careers in some areas of criminal justice administration. They must retain their ideals, but they also must be prepared to see reality and attempt to improve the system, for there is plenty of room for improvement.

Over the past two decades, in fact, the reputation of the juvenile court system has declined rapidly. The principles, rules, and goals of the system have also changed rapidly, partially in response to that decline and partially in response to the failure of long-established theories of delinquency. Moreover, current approaches to reform tend to be highly polarized. Conservative reformers, for example, argue for a war on delinquency and a return to retributive justice. Liberal reformers, on the other hand, are trying to reduce the scope and power of the juvenile justice system in an effort to secure "the rights of children." Given these contradictory trends, the future of the juvenile court is in serious doubt. Clearly, then, a real need exists for fresh ideas, insights, and reforms. Improvement should not be impossible.

A limit must be placed on the amount of subject matter covered in a book, or the authors run the risk of becoming trivial, of producing a mere compendium of facts. Thus, we have not attempted to provide a comprehensive overview of the juvenile justice system. Rather, we have tried to be simple without appealing to the simple-minded. We have also tried to avoid academic jargon wherever possible, for we have no special disciplinary interests to promote. Our main purpose, after all, is to provide the reader with the opportunity to understand the perplexing nature of juvenile crime and juvenile justice.

JUVENILE DELINQUENCY AND JUVENILE JUSTICE

1
CHILDREN, CRIME, AND JUSTICE: THE BEGINNING

Many intelligent, well-read people consider juvenile delinquency to be a twentieth century phenomenon. They believe that the industrial revolution with its concommitant urbanization, specialization, depersonalization, and commercialism produced the modern "degeneracy" that built up to an explosion of juvenile crime. History, however, tells us another story. Indeed, examining only modern society and culture to determine the origins of "delinquent" behavior is an exercise in futility, for every generation since the dawn of history has denounced youthful misbehavior, declining moral and ethical standards, and violations of societal norms.

Even a modest understanding of the delinquency problem, therefore, requires a context that only history can provide. Historical understanding, of course, will not solve the problem of contemporary juvenile crime, but it will provide a more rational and less emotional perspective for an analysis of it. Accordingly, this chapter will begin with a brief description of the ways in which other western cultures have described and circumscribed juvenile misbehavior. This will be followed by a detailed history of early developments in American juvenile justice.

JUVENILE CRIME IN TIMES PAST

Confucius, Hammurabi, and Socrates, among others, at different times and in different societies bemoaned the declining condition of youthful behavior. Laws passed specifically to regulate juveniles existed in ancient Sumeria, the Roman Republic and Empire, medieval Germany and Sweden, Celtic Ireland, and Anglo-Saxon England, and throughout most of western Christendom. Indeed, young people have been stealing and drinking, fighting and fornicating, menacing and murdering for as long as historians have been recording the activities of humankind. Nevertheless, "delinquent behavior" as defined by contemporary society has not always been illegal, nor has it always been called delinquency.

Until as recently as the nineteenth century certain youthful behavior, which we now consider dangerous, antisocial, destructive, or grounds for incarceration, was, if not entirely acceptable, certainly no cause for alarm. For example, "illicit sex" between teenagers informs many of the great romances of literature. Achilles and Deidamia, Acis and Galatea, Paris and Helen of Troy, Daphnis and Chloë, and Romeo and Juliet were all in their teens. Moreover, heavy drinking was never confined to adults, and well into the nineteenth century few considered juvenile alcohol abuse a problem.

Concern over drugs likewise is a modern bogey even though opium use began 4,000 years before the birth of Christ. Moreover, as late as the eighteenth century, European children often carried arms, and many schools in England suffered mutinies that were quelled only by bayonet-wielding troops.

The permissiveness of earlier societies concerning juvenile sex, drinking, and violence existed because their image of children differed considerably from our own. Contemporary American society is much more sensitive to the concept of childhood than were previous western cultures. Because of the unique circumstances existing in past societies, an extended childhood beyond sexual awakening would have seemed ludicrous. In general an individual's status changed from childhood to adulthood in the twelve- to fourteen-year age range. After that, the person merely experienced varying stages of maturity. This helps explain why, in addition to having the freedom to drink, brawl, and lust, some young teenagers were hanged for picking pockets or stealing apples. They had the same freedoms and therefore paid the same penalties as adults.[1]

Even those who were perceived to be less than adult did not have the same blessings and status that modern children do. Until the thirteenth century, for instance, parents abandoned or killed their children as easily as they did stray dogs and cats. Indeed, as late as the eighteenth century the deliberate murder of infants through either infanticide or ritual sacrifice was not uncommon. Although cultural prescriptions began to change in the eighteenth and nineteenth centuries, newborn infants continued to be farmed out to wet nurses. Contracting small children out as apprentices and servants also continued to be widespread, even in America. Clearly, for the people of the past, indifference and detachment characterized most child-parent relationships.[2]

Although the nuclear family as we know it today—with its protective umbrella of emotional interdependence and extended security—did not exist in America during the seventeenth century, the Puritans governed childhood behavior closely. Obedience to authority was their goal, for without it, given the nature of their wilderness settlements, they would not have survived. A type of corporate bonding prevailed, a bonding that produced a sense of responsibility for the behavior not only of individuals and their immediate families, but also for that of neighbors and the society at large. Accordingly the home, church, and community provided the controlling structure within which children functioned. The family provided punishment, education, and health care first. If the family failed, the community would take over.[3]

By the end of the seventeenth century families appeared to be losing their ability to keep youthful behavior under control. Numerous colonial laws threatened parents with punishment for failing to instill the proper fear of God, love for hard work, and obedience to authority in the minds and hearts of their children. At the same time other laws appeared that, if enforced, would have "put to death . . . any child above sixteen years old" who struck a parent without deliberate provocation. Those children who proved to be beyond family control the government removed and placed in other homes. Youths with severe discipline problems were apprenticed to tough masters who had reputations for breaking even the most willful troublemakers. When these solutions failed, "misguided children" found themselves in the common jails where they mixed and mingled with adult criminals who frequently used, abused, and otherwise molded youthful rebelliousness into overt criminal behavior.[4]

As the eighteenth century unfolded, the number of punishable offenses for youths grew to include running away from masters, incorrigibility, lying, swearing, fighting, and cheating. Adults, for the most part, could not be punished for committing any of these offenses. Thus, colonial laws reflected a shifting of American attitudes toward childhood and unlawful behavior. While Europeans continued to regard almost anyone over the age of fourteen as adult and considered most of the above "offenses" to be part of growing up, Americans believed that youthful misbehavior threatened the future. They maintained that America had been blessed by God for a special destiny and mission, that Americans were thus God's chosen people, and that the future greatness of America, as well as the hopes of mankind, rested on the shoulders of its youth. Accordingly, the behavior of American children had to be superior to that of children anywhere else, and any child who deviated from God's master plan had to be "enlightened and corrected."[5]

The best way to ensure that children did not stray was to put them to work. Thus, juvenile delinquency as it is known today, even with an expanding list of juvenile crimes, did not exist in colonial days. Colonists throughout America considered the young a vital part of the labor force. Most children began to work by the age of twelve, and many at an even younger age. Moreover, parents rarely objected to apprenticing or even indenturing their children, for they believed it was healthful for a child to work outside the home. Unless children learned the uplifting and saving graces of work at an early age, they and the country's future were in grave peril. Indeed, social stability, economic profitability, and America's destiny were all at stake.[6]

Nevertheless, youths managed to break the law, and punishments had to be meted out. Most colonists, however, considered delinquent behavior to be the product of idleness and associated it with "urban scum" and others at the bottom of the social scale. Hence, systems developed to inculcate these "pitious wretches" with the proper middle-class virtues of honesty, frugality, and industry. Although the colonists lived under English common law, which prescribed harsh punishments including death for serious offenders over the age of seven, capital punishment rarely occurred. Instead, the colonists preferred corporal punishment, such as public whipping.[7]

EARLY INSTITUTIONS
FOR JUVENILES

As delinquency came to be associated increasingly with the crimes and conditions of poor children, some special institutions for juvenile delinquents were founded. The few that opened in the late eighteenth century were organized to promote virtue and industry. The boys and girls who attended such institutions worked ten hours a day at shoemaking, tailoring, and housekeeping. The object was not so much to punish as to create useful and productive members of middle-class society. Thus, at the beginning of the nineteenth century criminal responsibility of children was determined not only by traditional principles of English common law, which leaned toward the protection and benefit of the defendant, but by middle-class values as well.[8]

Jails

As the nineteenth century began to unfold, the term *juvenile delinquency* had become a euphemism for the crimes and conditions of poor children. Most Americans commonly accepted as fact the notion that poor families did not have the capacity to raise their children properly. Dissatisfaction with the justice dispensed to juveniles was also pervasive. Vagrant and delinquent youths either were locked up with a conglomeration of adult criminals and misfits who schooled them for future crimes or were acquitted because of the reluctance of juries to condemn them to death or incarcerate them with depraved adults. Accordingly, reformers began to organize to prevent juvenile delinquency and to ensure that the "dregs" of society had a chance to develop into useful, productive, and well-behaved citizens.[9]

Because of their zeal to moralize and protect, reformers looked at youthful behavior in a new light. They saw immorality in every form of conduct that did not fit ideal middle-class morality. Thus behavior that had been accepted as normal through the ages now seemed depraved and corrupt. Deviance, nonconformity, and immorality materialized where it had never been seen before, and the range of acceptable childhood conduct narrowed considerably. Moreover, the reformers, who tended to be members of the middle and upper classes, believed that to preserve the proper structure and order in American society and to ensure its destiny, children must be stringently safeguarded. Consequently, they devised a new definition of childhood.[10]

In accordance with this new definition, children had to receive an extended moral, physical, and intellectual education before they could be considered adults. Ignoring, abandoning, or exploiting children no longer would be acceptable. The moral welfare of a child became paramount. The home and school, therefore, assumed a profound new responsibility and importance. And an extended childhood guided and shaped by a nuclear family replaced apprenticeship training and early adulthood. Because this childhood ideal was particularly suited to the attitudes and aspirations of the middle and upper classes, however, members of the lower classes and of minority groups were often ignored, misunderstood, or castigated for their socioeconomic condition.[11]

As the population grew during the nineteenth century, the country became urbanized, and the social control of small middle-class communities dissipated. At the same time "depraved neighborhoods" and "deprived families" received most of the blame for juvenile delinquency. Reformers believed, however, that youthful victims of corruption and dissolution, who in turn victimized society, could be saved and that America's future greatness could be preserved in the process. Accordingly, they created child-care institutions to serve as superparents and as community surrogates. If lower-class families and neighborhoods were unable to provide the necessary educational, moral, and spiritual foundations to produce "ideal" children, then child-care institutions would do so in their stead.[12]

The reformers considered juvenile delinquency along with intemperance and gambling to be but symptoms of the more pervasive disease of pauperism. Consequently, to combat the many facets of pauperism and to instill the proper middle-class values in young offenders, the New York Society for the Prevention of Pauperism (SPP) was formed in 1817. Unsuccessful in its campaign to suppress drinking and gambling, the society soon began to direct most of its efforts to the prevention of pauperism in the next generation. Thus investigations began to determine how and why destitute children wound up in jail. The SPP was one of the first groups to call attention to "those unfortunate children from 10 to 18 years of age, who from neglect of parents from idleness and misfortune have . . . contravened some penal statute without reflecting on the consequences and for hasty violations, been doomed to the penitentiary by the condemnation of the law."[13]

Houses of Refuge

The SPP found the condition of juveniles in prison and the extent of delinquency in New York appalling. As a result, the society issued a report in 1822, based largely on the success of the London Philanthropic Society in isolating the children of prisoners and other destitute and delinquent children. The report called for "the erection of new prisons for juvenile offenders" and demanded that society open its eyes to a dangerous and unconscionable situation. As a consequence of this report, the first house of refuge opened its doors in New York City in 1825. This marked the beginning of the process of separating juvenile delinquents from adult criminals.[14]

Founded by the Society for the Reformation of Juvenile Delinquents, the New York House of Refuge, along with refuges founded in Boston and Philadelphia in 1826, defined institutional treatment of juvenile offenders for the next twenty-five years. Two types of children were admitted to these refuges: those convicted of crimes and sentenced to incarceration and those who were merely destitute or neglected and who were thus considered to be in imminent danger of becoming delinquent. The refuge founders believed that their institutions would fill the void left by inadequate parental and societal control. They hoped to discipline the homeless, vagrant, and destitute children of the poor, while avoiding the cruelty and degeneracy of prison. Correction and reformation were the principal goals.[15]

In order to save children from lives of crime the refuge founders attempted to teach them middle-class values. Neatness, manners, frugality, and punctuality were all stressed, but the virtue of hard work received the strongest emphasis. By teaching juveniles how to work, the houses of refuge hoped to exorcise the demons of lower-class sin and depravity. At the same time the future security of life and property, as well as the continued prosperity of America, would be assured.[16]

Once it received a child, a house of refuge was given a wide latitude of authority. Although parents objected on occasion, they usually failed to gain release of their children. In effect, the refuges had the same powers over their charges that natural parents had over their own children. Convictions in state and local courts removed juveniles from normal parental power. Then the parental power, or *parens patriae,* of the state was conferred on the refuges. In the process the state had taken a bold step in the direction of providing welfare for its children.[17]

To demonstrate its surrogate parental control and to inculcate the proper middle-class values, the New York House of Refuge designed a system of rewards and deprivations. A jury composed of peers and the institution's superintendent, Joseph Curtis, determined infractions of the rules and imposed discipline. Whipping, solitary confinement, reduction of food, and the silent treatment occurred frequently. Children who committed the most serious offenses wore leg irons. When not being punished, the boys made goods to be sold, and the girls did domestic work; the house kept all earnings for upkeep and maintenance. Children could be apprenticed and released to the custody of masters, but all inmates could be recalled at any time should further "character building" appear necessary.[18]

Most of those in attendance at houses of refuge, because of the prejudices and attitudes of the time, were immigrant youths. Indeed many new aliens, if destitute enough, were automatically labeled criminals, and their children were incarcerated as a matter of course. In 1829 some 58 percent of the refuge house inmates were children who had been born in another country. White female transgressors and blacks of both sexes also suffered from the prevailing intolerance. Girls suffered from the relatively recent hysteria concerning promiscuity, and black children, if admitted to refuges at all, were treated much more harshly than whites.[19]

Precisely because so many of the inmates of the refuge houses were excluded from mainstream middle-class American life, both the philanthropists who founded the houses and others who visited them declared them successful. To be sure, periodic riots, internal management schisms, and reports of wretched treatment and conditions eventually caused a number of reform attempts. The managers, however, continued to claim success, in part because their original expectations had been severely limited, and in part because they viewed failures within the system—given the inmate population—as natural. Likewise, any inmates who "reformed" were seen as the direct result of refuge care and discipline.[20]

These claims of success did not go unheeded. By 1850 many other states and cities either had opened or planned to open similar houses of refuge. Inevitably, each of these new institutions[21] lauded the first refuges and expressed the continuing and ever broadening concern over the number of children in jail, a number that at mid-century in some areas approached 33 percent of the prison population. All of these new houses invariably stated that one of their primary goals was to teach their inmates the middle-class values of thrift, honesty, industry, and individual responsibility.[22]

Reformatories

In spite of the claims for success, the older houses of refuge had failed, and so too would the new ones. These institutions incarcerated too many children, reinforced the growing tendency to equate poverty with lawbreaking, and never came close to serving as surrogates for the community. Indeed, they could not possibly have fulfilled all of the responsibilities placed upon them. As a consequence, certain municipal and state governments began to found and administer public institutions for juvenile delinquents. These new "alternatives for wayward children" were called reform schools rather than houses of refuge to emphasize the need for proper education. To underscore this concern, states began to commit school truants to the new reformatories. Nevertheless, even though the proliferation of reform schools over the next fifty years called attention to the failures of houses of refuge, those who ran these newer institutions continued to focus their attention on the deviant activities of certain lower-class children whom they labeled "juvenile delinquents."[23]

The Massachusetts State Reform School, founded in 1847, was the first of the new experiments. In spite of its emphasis on education, it functioned much as had earlier houses of refuge. Boys fifteen or younger who had been deemed "salvageable" were admitted, and after a one-year "sentence" were often bound out as servants or apprentices. Moreover, although the boys spent half of their days in school, the rest of the time they performed rigorous workshop routines with little or no recreation.[24]

Other reformatories, however, managed to depart somewhat from the refuge system. Massachusetts, for example, introduced the cottage plan, or family plan, to America. This new system, based on European precedents, divided children into small "families" of thirty to forty and separated lesser offenders from repeaters. Each family had its own separate building, or cottage, and its own work and school routines. This concept seemed especially suitable for girls who needed a "strong mothering environment." Accordingly, in 1856 Massachusetts opened its State Industrial School for Girls, which was the first girls' reformatory and the first to adopt the cottage plan.[25]

Cottage reform schools for both sexes soon sprang up all over the country. Supporters of this new system argued that refuges and congregate reform schools corrupted innocent children by mixing them with older more experienced and less reformable offenders. They also asserted that depraved urban environments, where most reformatories and refuges were located, provided temptations, seductions, and lures that a rural setting avoided. Thus, these reformers promoted the methods of the Ohio Reform School, founded in 1857, for it followed the cottage plan and was located in the country, thus embodying all of the positive ideas of reform during the period.[26]

Placement Services

Other reformers had also embraced these concepts. In 1853, for example, a group of philanthropists had founded the New York Children's Aid Society, which provided placement services in the country rather than institutionalization. Rural life and family ties, these reformers believed, could resurrect malformed youngsters. Environment rather than innate depravity explained juvenile delinquency, they believed. Moreover, there were simply too many urban waifs for institutions to handle, and the reformatories and refuges that did exist did not appear to be helping much. The philanthropists argued that, by collecting vagrant and destitute slum children and "placing them out" with farm families in the country, delinquency could be cleared up. Accordingly, the Children's Aid Society and similar organizations sent many groups of children out into the West to be "purified," until it became increasingly difficult to find placement homes.[27]

Managers of congregate reformatories and houses of refuge countered the arguments of these philanthropists by pointing out that "criminal children" could not be reformed. Transplanting "thorns and thistles" from one environment to another, they said, did not produce corn and wheat. Thorns and thistles remained what they had always been, and so too did urban delinquents. Moreover, the managers argued, even if some children did behave differently on the farm, once they returned to the cities they often degenerated again. In spite of these arguments, however, the work of such organizations as the Children's Aid Society modified the programs of both the older refuges and the ever increasing number of new state and municipal institutions for juvenile delinquents.[28]

The Contract System
and the Ship Schools

Other conditions also forced changes in juvenile institutions. For example, post–Civil War inflation and competition for funds from orphanages, almshouses, insane asylums, and other institutions caused state and local governments to cut back financial support. As a consequence, to make up for lost revenues, reformatories had to rely on the "contract system." This meant contracting out the labor of boys to large workshops for money, which was used to operate reformatories. The contract system had existed for some time, but now it took on a more negative character. Boys in refuges or reformatories earned thirty cents a day on jobs that normally paid four dollars. Not surprisingly, workingmen protested that this kind of competition was clearly unfair and exploitative. Given these protests and the wretched conditions of reformatory workshops, school officials found it difficult to defend the contract system as a necessary means of developing habits of industry and productivity.[29]

The 1860s also saw another kind of exploitative experiment—the ship schools. Not really reformatories or refuges, ship schools were supposed to provide the necessary regimentation, as well as training, for the merchant marine. The reformers behind this scheme argued that male juvenile delinquents would respond positively to military life and that life at sea would purify as surely as a rural environment. The schools accepted boys up to the age of sixteen and attempted to teach them the rudiments of seamanship while they worked aboard actual ships. The experiment failed, however, because of disciplinary problems, exorbitant operating costs, and the economic depressions that put adult seamen out of work.[30]

EARLY INVESTIGATIVE BOARDS

The accumulation of problems and criticisms that plagued post–Civil War reformatories, refuges, and similar operations eventually stimulated some local and state governments to investigate all such institutions. Accordingly, Boards of State Charity were created to inspect, report on, and recommend improvements for reform schools, asylums, and almshouses. As a result of this activity, private and public orphan asylums were created, and children were removed from almshouses. This greatly reduced almshouse populations during the last quarter of the nineteenth century but proportionally raised the populations of the newly established state and county orphan asylums. The investigative boards had hoped to reduce or even eliminate state expenditures for pauperism. Instead, however, their findings and recommendations produced more public institutions.[31]

Despite the inconsistencies between the state boards' goals and results, these investigations provided the basis for a modern methodological approach to the study of crime, poverty, and delinquency. They also furnished greater understanding of the complex and interrelated causes behind poverty and criminality and clearly pointed out the need for systematic and differentially organized remedial treatment programs. In the process the state boards also demonstrated the need for expertise in exploring, analyzing, and solving the problems involved.[32]

The state boards came to the conclusion that removing children from the "poisoned moral atomosphere" of the almshouse and then dumping them indiscriminately in reform schools and other institutions solved one problem and created another. Frequently, innocent children became surrounded by and accustomed to "guilty, morally depraved, and corrupting" types who converted basically decent children into criminals. Consequently, in 1886 the National Conference of Charities and Correction proposed that state governments operate separate institutions for four classes of children: felons, minor offenders, truants, and the homeless, and that job training replace the contract labor system. These recommendations met with resistance from many reformatories, however, and many of the abuses, including the contract system, continued well into the twentieth century.[33]

Reform schools and houses of refuge had not, of course, caused the problem of juvenile delinquency, nor had they come close to controlling it. Indeed, throughout the nineteenth century youths became involved in criminal behavior whether reformatories, refuges, or committees of philanthropists existed in their locales or not. Moreover, when such institutions did appear in the western states, they almost invariably resembled the older eastern institutions and were thus bound to fail in precisely the same ways. Certainly the presence of institutions for delinquent and dependent children in the newer states did not significantly alter the juvenile crime rate.[34]

JUVENILE CRIME IN THE SOUTH

Curiously, juvenile delinquency did not present much of a dilemma to southerners. In fact, no special provisions existed for youthful offenders until the end of the nineteenth century. This condition can be explained in part because southerners had a high tolerance level for such activities as drinking, fighting, sex, and truancy, which other areas of the country had classified as juvenile delinquency. Moreover, given the primitive condition of most southern penal institutions, authorities seldom sent children to jail and quickly pardoned those who did go. In addition, apprenticing out orphans and illegitimate children to individual householders remained in effect in the South long after such practices had been abandoned elsewhere. As a result, throughout the nineteenth century, the South appeared to have the problem of juvenile delinquency under control. When the institutional approach the rest of the country followed was adopted in the twentieth century, however, the South immediately fell victim to an epidemic of youth crime.[35]

ALTERNATIVES TO REFORMATORIES

Meanwhile, in the rest of the country toward the end of the nineteenth century, reform schools began to emphasize the importance of physical conditioning. Former military men who had been placed in charge of several reformatories introduced army drill into the daily routine in order to build up the moral and physical fiber of "underdeveloped" delinquents. Such activities frequently took the place of the declining contract system and reinforced the authoritarian control that reformatory administrators believed to be essential. An increasing number of reformatories also had turned to the cottage plan with agricultural routines. Like military discipline, working the soil was supposed to produce heartier physiques, enlightened minds, and higher morality. What apparently occurred on some of the farms, however, was a wide variety of sexual activity, including buggery with the livestock.[36]

By the turn of the century the reformatory concept had been fairly well discredited. Homer Folks, the secretary of the Children's Aid Society of Pennsylvania, summed up the accumulated criticisms when he pointed out that reformatories offered parents a golden opportunity to avoid "sacred responsibilities," corrupted innocent children, stigmatized any who had ever been committed, made individual treatment impossible, and constituted a world that was totally dissimilar to that outside. As alternatives to reform school, Folks advocated widows' pensions, mothers' aid, and juvenile court and probation legislation— all reforms designed to aid children outside institutional settings.[37]

Educators also hoped to provide assistance to children outside the reformatory network. Indeed, they avoided identification with such schools and promoted themselves as experts serving the needs of all children. Accordingly, many public school systems created special schools to deal with truants and behavior problems. As a consequence, those children who in the past had been caught in the seemingly inextricable web of institutional care now found a way to escape. Reformatory officials attempted through the creation of the National Conference on the Education of Truant, Backward, Dependent and Delinquent Children in 1904 to alter the reputation of their institutions. But, for the most part their efforts failed. The image of the reform school as a last resort where cruel punishment was commonly dispensed fit the reality too closely.[38]

Alternative plans to juvenile incarceration, therefore, began to appear across the country. Several states, for example, followed the advice of charity and children's aid organizations and passed probation laws designed to keep children out of reformatories. Other states created industrial schools that provided training, food, and shelter on a day-care basis. (This concept proved so popular that many reformatories began to call themselves industrial schools or training schools.) And several new children's agencies designed to protect and help children rather than control their behavior were founded. All of these new private philanthropies, in spite of their desire to aid youths in trouble, squabbled constantly over the best way to reform delinquents. The arguments were and still are familiar. Should probation be invoked immediately? Or should a period of incarceration be required?[39]

Most philanthropists, juvenile delinquency "experts," and state board officials, however, did agree on one fundamental point: reform schools did not reform children. Something had to be done to confront the problem of juvenile delinquency without resorting to incarceration. The faith and optimism of an earlier group of reformers, a faith that had produced the asylum, the penitentiary, and the reform school, had vanished. Thus, by the late 1890s the concept of reformatories serving in the capacity of *parens patriae* had run aground. Indeed, evidence abounded which demonstrated that, instead of reforming, these schools abused delinquent children. Instead of parenting, they imprisoned. Instead of caring for vagrant and dependent children, they created new criminals. Clearly, American society, an industrialized, urbanized, commercialized, and specialized society, needed a new method of dealing with the problems of its youth. The juvenile court idea seemed to be the answer.

NOTES
CHAPTER ONE

1. Wiley B. Sanders, ed., *Juvenile Offenders for a Thousand Years* (Chapel Hill, N. C., 1970), p. xviii. Also see LaMar T. Empey, *American Delinquency: Its Meaning and Construction* (Homewood, Ill., 1978), pp. 42–43.

2. See Lloyd de Mause, ed., *The History of Childhood* (New York, 1974), pp. 25–59; Elizabeth W. Marvick, "Nature Versus Nurture: Patterns and Trends in Seventeenth Century French Child Rearing," in ibid., pp. 259–302; Joseph Ellick, "Child Rearing in Seventeenth Century England and America," in ibid., pp. 303–50.

3. See Peter Laslett, *The World We Have Lost: England before the Industrial Age* (New York, 1965), p. 21; Bernard Bailyn, *Education in the Forming of American Society* (Chapel Hill, N. C., 1960), p. 16; John Demos, *A Little Commonwealth: Family Life in the Plymouth Colony* (New York, 1970), pp. 146, 183–84; Joseph M. Hawes, "The Treatment of Delinquent Children," in Thomas R. Frazier, ed., *The Underside of American History* (New York, 1978), pp. 127–28.

4. Ibid.

5. *Two Hundred Years of American Criminal Justice*, an LEAA Bicentennial Study (Washington, 1976), p. 62.

6. Ibid. Also see Frank R. Donovan, *Wild Kids: How Youth Has Shocked Its Elders— Then and Now* (Harrisburg, Pa., 1967), p. 121; and Ivy Pinchbeck and Margaret Hewitt, *Children in English Society*. 2 vols. (London, 1969), Vol. I, pp. 131–33, 310–11.

7. *Two Hundred Years of American Criminal Justice*, p. 63.

8. See Robert M. Mennel, *Thorns and Thistles: Juvenile Delinquents and the United States 1825–1940* (Hanover, N. H., 1973), pp. xxvi–xxv. Also see William Blackstone, *Commentaries on the Laws of England*, 4 vols., 12th ed. (London, 1795), Vol. 4, 23; *Two Hundred Years of American Criminal Justice*, p. 62; Robert H. Bremner et al., eds., *Children and Youth In America: A Documentary History*, 2 vols. (Cambridge, Mass., 1970), Vol I, pp. 37–39, 307; and Anthony M. Platt, *The Child Savers: The Invention of Delinquency* (Chicago, 1969), pp. 188–89, 202.

9. Mennel, *Thorns and Thistles*, p. 8; Donovan, *Wild Kids*, pp. 145–48.

10. Mennel, *Thorns and Thistles*, p. xxvi; Empey, *American Delinquency*, p. 10; and Ruth Shonle Cavan and Theodore N. Ferdinand, *Juvenile Delinquency*, 3d ed. (New York, 1975), p. 5. Also see Society for the Diffusion of Knowledge upon the Punishment of Death and the Improvement of Prison Discipline, London, *Report of the Committee of the Society for the Improvement of Prison Discipline and the Reformation of Juvenile Offenders* (London, 1818).

11. Empey, *American Delinquency*, pp. 48–68. Also see Phillipe Aries, *Centuries of Childhood* (New York, 1962); de Mause, *The History of Childhood*, pp. 47–48; and Peter Laslett, *Household and Family in Past Time* (Cambridge, 1972); J. H. Plumb, "The Great Change in Children," *Intellectual Digest* 2 (1972): 82–84.

12. Empey, *American Delinquency*, p. 94.

13. See *Two Hundred Years of American Criminal Justice*, p. 63; and Mennel, *Thorns and Thistles*, pp. 10–11.

14. New York Society for the Prevention of Pauperism, *Report on the Penitentiary System in the United States* (New York, 1822), pp. 59–60. Also see Sanders, *Juvenile*

Offenders for a Thousand Years (Chapel Hill, N. C., 1970), pp. 70–90; and Mennel, *Thorns and Thistles*, p. 11.

15. Ibid., pp. 3–4; *Two Hundred Years of American Criminal Justice*, p. 63.

16. Mennel, *Thorns and Thistles*, pp. xxvii, 18; and Joseph M. Hawes, *Children in Urban Society: Juvenile Delinquency in Nineteenth Century America* (New York, 1971), p. 153. Also see New York Society for the Reformation of Juvenile Delinquents (SRJD) *Annual Report* (1826), pp. 3–4.

17. *Two Hundred Years of American Criminal Justice*, p. 64; and Hawes, *Children in Urban Society*, p. 153.

18. *Two Hundred Years of American Criminal Justice*, pp. 63–64.

19. Ibid. Also see Joseph Curtis, *Examination of Subjects Who Are in the House of Refuge in the City of New York* (Albany, 1825), pp. 3–17; and Mennel, *Thorns and Thistles*, p. 17.

20. Ibid., pp. 29–30.

21. Among the institutions that opened at mid-century were those in New Orleans; Westborough, Mass.; Rochester, N. Y.; Philadelphia; Cincinnati; Pittsburgh; Lancaster, Mass.; and Lancaster, Ohio.

22. Mennel, *Thorns and Thistles*, p. 30.

23. Empey, *American Delinquency*, p. 94; Michael Katz, *The Irony of Urban School Reform* (Cambridge, Mass., 1968), pp. 177–78. For a bibliography of various writings on reform schools and the juvenile court, see Augustus Kuhlman, comp., *A Guide to Material on Crime and Criminal Justice* (New York, 1929), pp. 547–62, 592–604. Also see Mennel, *Thorns and Thistles*, p. 31.

24. *Two Hundred Years of American Criminal Justice*, p. 65.

25. Ibid. Also see Mennel, *Thorns and Thistles*, p. 52.

26. Ibid., pp. 55–57; and *Two Hundred Years of American Criminal Justice*, p. 65.

27. Ibid., pp. 65–66. Also see Edward Cropsey, *The Nether Side of New York* (New York, 1972); Louisa Harris, *Behind the Scenes or Nine Years at the Four Courts of St. Louis* (St. Louis, 1893); James D. McCabe, *The Secrets of the Great City* (Chicago and Philadelphia, 1868); and Helen Campbell, *Darkness and Daylight* (Hartford, Conn., 1891).

28. Second Convention of Managers and Superintendents of Houses of Refuge and Schools of Reform, *Proceedings* (1859), pp. 38–44.

29. Mennel, *Thorns and Thistles*, pp. 59–61. Also see New York Assembly, *Documents* (1871), IV, Doc. 18, 125, 131, 163, 164, 168, 181; Pennsylvania House of Representatives, *Documents* (1876), "Evidence Taken by the Committee of the House of Representatives to Investigate the Management of House of Refuge," pp. 12–13, 225; Cleveland, Ohio, Directors of the Workhouse and House of Refuge and Correction, *Annual Report* (1876), pp. 17–18. For a summary of state investigations of prison labor, see U. S. Commissioner of Labor, *Annual Report* (1866), pp. 287–368.

30. *Two Hundred Years of American Criminal Justice*, p. 66.

31. See Aaron I. Abell, *American Catholicism and Social Action: A Search for Social Justice, 1865–1950* (South Bend, Ind., 1963), pp. 18–23; Bradford Pierce, *A Half Century with Juvenile Delinquents* (New York, 1869); George I. Chace, "The Proper

Functions of Boards of State Charities and Correction," *Proceedings* (1882), p. 26. Also see Mennel, *Thorns and Thistles*, p. 65–68; and Gerald N. Grob, *The State and the Mentally Ill* (Chapel Hill, N. C., 1966), pp. 180–81.

32. Chace, "The Proper Functions of Boards of State Charities and Corrections," p. 20. Also see Mennel, *Thorns and Thistles*, p. 68.

33. See William P. Letchworth, "Classification and Training of Children, Innocent and Incorrigible" in National Conference of Charities and Correction (NCCC), *Proceedings* (1883), p. 16; and Mennel, *Thorns and Thistles*, pp. 68–69. Also see William P. Letchworth, *Technological Training in Reform Schools* (Buffalo, 1884), pp. 34–37; C. A. Gower, "Industrial Training in Juvenile Reformatories," NCCC *Proceedings* (1888), pp. 229–34; Bernice Fisher, *Industrial Education: American Ideals and Institutions* (Madison, Wis., 1967).

34. Iowa Legislative Documents, II, *Report of the Iowa State Reform School* (1870), p. 15; Kansas Public Documents, II, *Report of the Board of Trustees of State Charitable Institutions* (1888), p. 7; and Minnesota Executive Documents, *Report of the Minnesota State Reform School* (1869), p. 288. Also see Mennel, *Thorns and Thistles*, p. 74.

35. Edgar W. Knight, *A Documentary History of Education in the South before 1860*, 5 vols. (Chapel Hill, N. C., 1949–53), Vol. IV, pp. 62–148; George Washington Cable, *The Silent South* (New York, 1885) pp. 155–56; Sanders, *Juvenile Offenders for a Thousand Years*, pp. 410–13.

36. Mennel, *Thorns and Thistles*, pp. 103–5; C. B. Adams, "The Advantages of Military Training to Delinquent Youth," National Conference on the Education of Truant, Backward, Dependent and Delinquent Children (NCET), *Proceedings* (1904), pp. 40–41; and F. H. Nibecker, "Education of Juvenile Delinquents," *Annals* of the American Academy, Vol. 23 (1904), pp. 75–84.

37. Homer Folks, "The Care of Delinquent Children," NCCC *Proceedings* (1891), pp. 137–39; Walter I. Trattner, *Homer Folks: Pioneer in Social Welfare* (New York, 1968), pp. 114–19. Also see Mennel, *Thorns and Thistles*, pp. 111–12.

38. See H. W. Charles, "The Problem of the Reform School," *Proceedings* of the Conference for Child Research and Welfare, I (1910), p. 56; Charles Olds Keeler, *American Bastilles* (Washington, D. C., 1910), pp. 8–9; Roy Lubove, *The Professional Altruist: The Emergence of Social Work as a Career 1880–1930* (Cambridge, 1965), pp. 22–54; Mennel, *Thorns and Thistles*, pp. 106–12.

39. Mennel, *Thorns and Thistles*, pp. 112–15. Also see Folks, "The Care of Delinquent Children," pp. 140–44; and Sanders, *Juvenile Offenders for a Thousand Years*, pp. 440–43.

2
THE TWENTIETH CENTURY: THE JUVENILE COURT AND BEYOND

O ver the last three decades of the nineteenth century enormous pressures had been building for the creation of some form of juvenile court system.[1] When that step was finally taken, it marked a revolution in American juvenile justice that continues to affect us today.* How the new juvenile court became the new superparent, not only in concept but in practice, and how the court has evolved will be discussed in this chapter.

THE FIRST JUVENILE COURTS

The first juvenile court came into existence in Chicago in 1899. Its purpose was primarily to protect children from the more severe punishments meted out in adult criminal courts and to serve as an alternative to incarceration in juvenile institutions. It is ironic that a state without reformatories of any kind should have been the first to create a juvenile court.[2]

Illinois had tried to initiate a juvenile court in 1895, but because of constitutional questions concerning the rights of children, the attempt had been postponed. Local jurists and reformers answered these questions, however, by creating a new adjudicating mechanism, a noncriminal court of equity that, by definition, did not have to concern itself with the rights of accused children. What they established was an entirely separate court system for children who committed criminal offenses. They also supplied a children's judge who attended to no other business and whose jurisdiction included cases of dependency and neglect as well as of delinquency. In addition, the jurists and reformers preferred placing children on probation either at home or in foster homes. Consequently, they combined existing probation legislation from Massachusetts with several New York laws providing for special trial sessions and separate detention facilities for delinquents.[3]

Those jurists and reformers hoped to extend the parental powers that reformatories had enjoyed to the entire juvenile court process. They also hoped to emphasize the traditional familial concerns of guidance, structure, and education rather than punishment. To be sure, the court maintained the power to send children to other discredited institutions should the need arise. Nevertheless, the fundamental idea, as expressed by the founders themselves, was "a return to paternalism." As such, the Illinois Juvenile Court represented both

*See Chapter Eleven for an analysis of the present-day revolution in juvenile justice.

a restatement and an expansion of the *parens patriae* doctrine, and the concept became extremely popular.[4]

By 1925 all states except Maine and Wyoming had juvenile court laws, and by 1945 every state had them. They were not all alike, however. Outside large urban areas the juvenile courts often involved little more than a country court judge setting aside some time to deal specifically with children in trouble. Usually there were no probation officers, and no attempt was made to provide separate facilities for incarcerated youths waiting for trial. In cities, on the other hand, full-time juvenile court judges monitored detention centers and youth shelters, and a probation staff provided necessary resources for the normal functioning of the court. Nevertheless, even in cities, judges generally had the power to send serious offenders to jail.[5]

In spite of the claims of their founders, juvenile courts—whether rural or urban—usually concentrated on "salvageable offenders" and left the more difficult cases to the adult criminal system. Moreover, habituating the child to subservient modes of conduct became the standard operating procedure. Developing the individual's capacity for love and understanding did not have much of a chance. Protestant children's aid societies and their middle-class women supporters were largely responsible for this condition.[6]

THE CHILD SAVERS

Beginning in the 1870s and 1880s a "child-saving" movement began, and the child savers were mostly women—well-educated, politically oriented women with genteel backgrounds. They viewed themselves as altruists and humanitarians dedicated to rescuing those who were less fortunately placed in the social order. Nevertheless, the programs supported by the child savers, including the juvenile court, diminished the civil liberties and privacy of youth. Indeed, the juvenile court system, as created and promoted by the child savers, tended to facilitate efficient categorization and storage of social rejects rather than to protect children from the physical and moral dangers of an increasingly industrialized and urban society.[7]

To be sure, the child savers' goal was treatment rather than retribution. But they should not be considered libertarians or humanists. They did not inaugurate a new form of justice; the juvenile court system merely refined and systematized policies that had been developing for some time. They assumed that adolescents had to be dependent and thus created a court that imposed sanctions on premature independence and unacceptable lower-class behavior. Although they had a paternalistic attitude toward youth, they backed up their commands with force. Furthermore, they founded correctional programs that ultimately required long periods of incarceration, excessive military discipline, and long hours of labor.[8]

The primary concern of the child savers was to see to it that poor and minority people adhered to middle-class morality, but the reformers refused to educate their charges. Moreover, differences in treatment of the sexes persisted. The child savers often equated female delinquency with sexual offenses and sexual offenses with mental incapacity. Accordingly, the juvenile court invariably sent "delinquent" girls to reformatories so that during their child-bearing years they would be protected. At the same time society would be protected from the production of "depraved" babies destined to be criminals.[9]

The child savers believed that the code of moral values that had made America great had been under attack by the forces of urban life and industrialism and by the influx of immigrant cultures. The juvenile court and other child-saving creations, therefore, represented a defense against "foreign" ideologies and a proclamation of cherished values. Consequently, juvenile court laws defined the place of children in society as different from that of adults. They also clarified and strengthened the states' "parental" role, created rules for an "ideal childhood" and punished infractions of those rules, organized a bureaucracy to implement and enforce these standards, and designated persons and organizations to serve as surrogate parents for children defined as delinquent.[10]

The most influential "parental" figure in the first courts was the judge. Benjamin Barr Lindsey, judge of the circuit court of Arapahoe County, near Denver, Colorado, fit this image perfectly. He took his task seriously and managed to secure the passage of a juvenile court law that punished parents who neglected their children. But many others involved in the new court systems recognized that caring judges and good intentions did not necessarily mean success. They believed that delinquency would continue to plague America unless a professional probation bureaucracy assumed a role equal to that of the judge. Consequently, most of the new courts quickly established extensive probation networks.[11]

For all its support and publicity, however, the probation system did not work. Indeed, juvenile delinquency in Chicago increased in proportion to the proliferation of probation officers. Probation failed in part because the officers served the judges rather than the delinquent children. They were able to investigate the families, friends, school, and activities of the youths and then present this information in court without regard for due process safeguards because children were no longer subject to criminal law. Evidence of guilt, as a result, was rarely presented in the courtroom. Moreover, once found guilty, the youths were placed under the supervision of the people who had provided the information and testimony that had convicted them.[12]

Probation also failed in part because many probation officers felt superior to the children of immigrant families. Accordingly, religious and ethnic tensions often flared up between the court representatives and the children they were ostensibly trying to aid and protect. In addition, probation officers vacillated between friendly advice and counsel and threats of force. In fact, juvenile court judges and probation officers alike exhibited attitudes, prejudices, and behaviors that were indistinguishable from those of refuge and reform school officials.[13]

CRITICISM OF THE JUVENILE COURTS

Some early critics of the new institutions argued that in addition to merely dressing up old reformatory practices in new clothes, the juvenile courts were unconstitutional. Children, they pointed out, faced prosecution for crimes and thus were entitled to protection against unfair loss of liberty as guaranteed by the Constitution. Other critics lamented that parental powers of the state had been increased rather than decreased and that the first amendments to the juvenile court laws demonstrated the persistence of blaming parents for delinquency. A third group of critics, nascent social workers and expansionist reformers, believed that the court would be effective only if it developed further its constituent parts and utilized social service agencies and resources in the community. Still others argued that the court had become overburdened with cases of neglect and dependency, thus preventing delinquency from receiving the attention it deserved.[14]

Nevertheless, even among the critics, hope remained that the juvenile court could provide a crucial service for delinquents and the community at large. It simply had to define its goals, capacities, and limitations more clearly. Then, as now, most courts operated under broad definitions of delinquency, which implied that the courts were panaceas for every type of youthful trouble from truancy to murder, from abandonment to abuse. Much of this power had been granted because there were no alternative judicial and social agencies that might have provided services for dependent mothers and children. Some reformers, as a result, hoped to create family courts that would have power over adult breakdowns in family structure and authority. The domestic relations courts, which Buffalo initiated in 1910 and which dealt primarily with cases of nonsupport and desertion, began the family court movement. Accordingly, for the next twenty years family and domestic relations courts enlarged the juvenile courts' scope and impact by performing part of their function under different organizational guises.[15]

DELINQUENCY THEORIES

Since the early nineteenth century, reformers had believed that juvenile delinquency could not be prevented solely by family government. Thus, they had developed a diverse assortment of institutions, from community organizations to juvenile courts, in an attempt to provide special treatment and services for neglected, abandoned, abused, dependent, and delinquent children and their families. This had been done to "protect society" from its worse elements and to foster behavior and attitudes more conducive and less inimical to middle-class values and standards.

During the search for the proper institutions to serve the needs of the community, several theories concerning the origins of delinquency surfaced, found acceptance for a while, and then were discarded in the face of contradictory evidence or more popular theories. Throughout most of the nineteenth century negative philosophies concerning the ability of society to reform delinquents dominated. These included the theories of phrenology, evolutionary psychology, anthropometry, and eugenics. By the 1920s, however, the progressive spirit had persuaded child experts, social workers, psychologists, psychiatrists, and sociologists that the future need not be so bleak.

Physiological Theories

Before the Civil War many Americans believed that it was possible to determine potential human behavior and character by measuring and analyzing the shape and protuberances of the human skull. They called this the "science" of phrenology. After the war, however, the emerging disciplines of child and educational psychology with their Darwinian concepts soon produced more acceptable explanations.[16]

Experimental Psychology

Granville Stanley Hall, born and trained in Germany, founded the first laboratory of experimental psychology in 1882 at Johns Hopkins University. Hall maintained that childhood, youth, and adolesence formed separate evolutionary stages of life and that these stages had their own values, which often differed from and were hostile to adult values. Hall and those who followed his precepts believed that most delinquents were not innately evil and inferior. Urbanization and commercialization, he claimed, had frustrated a natural, if primitive, pursuit of joy among children. As a consequence, youths broke laws in order to express themselves, to release pent-up frustration, and to find adventure. To support these conclusions, Hall and others began to use the techniques of observation and verification that the sciences of criminal anthropology and physiology had introduced.[17]

Scientific observation and the accumulation of empirical evidence, however, did not guarantee accurate results. Indeed, Cesare Lombroso, the Italian professor of legal medicine who dominated late nineteenth century criminology, concluded after "exhaustive scientific experiments" that criminals looked different from the rest of mankind. His book, *L'Uomo delinquente* (1876), asserted that the habitual criminal constituted an abnormal anthropological type who exhibited anatomical, physiological, psychological, and social stigmata. This type of "criminal man" had not properly evolved. He represented, instead, a regression or devolution to a more primitive, presocial type of subhuman.[18]

A few American pioneers in juvenile criminology, such as Arthur McDonald and Thomas Travis adopted many of Lombroso's methods and ideas and developed a system of anthropometry, which attempted to measure "physically unsuccessful" children. Some of these "scientific investigators" asserted that operating upon children to correct their abnormal physiology would solve the juvenile delinquency problem. Other criminologists, such as Franz Boas, agreed with G. Stanley Hall and argued that environmental problems, not physiological abnormalities, caused delinquency, but structural-deficiency concepts continued to influence analysts and investigators well into the twentieth century.[19]

Hereditarian Theories

Hereditarian theories of crime and delinquency, however, predominated turn-of-the-century thinking. Like the other theories, these tended to reflect the prejudices and preconceptions of the times rather than demonstrate the accumulated wisdom of systematic scientific investigation and knowledge. The widespread acceptance of the theory of eugenics is a case in point. Eugenics, defined as the science of improving human breeds, gave what appeared to be scientific authenticity to hereditarian explanations of crime and delinquency. As such, eugenics had special appeal to members of the xenophobic middle classes and those who lived in cities with newly arrived southern and eastern Europeans. It is interesting to note in this connection that most of the eugenics studies to which nativists referred when arguing for immigration restriction demonstrated the heredity of crime, pauperism, and feeblemindedness in old American families.[20]

Eugenics became so widely accepted during the first decades of the twentieth century that many criminologists equated children of "faulty stock" with juvenile delinquency. Intelligence tests, which appeared during these years as a tool to measure the mental abilities of children, reinforced eugenic theories. Designed to detect mental incapacity, they reflected the examiners' prejudices rather than objective reality, and they served their purpose well, for juvenile delinquents scored consistently low. Moreover, by 1936, thirty-five states had laws that allowed doctors to sterilize "defective" delinquents; Oregon even permitted castration. Although such sterilizations were finally declared unconstitutional, at least 45,000 of them had been performed by 1946.[21]

Eugenics, psychometrics, Lombrosian criminology, and the evolutionary psychology of G. Stanley Hall had one major source of commonality. They all shared negative conclusions about the future of juvenile delinquents. To be sure, "scientific studies" of criminals and delinquents ostensibly used empirical observation and measurement. But their uniformly pessimistic conclusions about the possibilities of reforming "defective" children created a distinct class of delinquents forever branded as "unsalvageable."[22]

The Progressive Movement

Not everyone shared the dark visions of these scientists. Indeed, during the first decades of the twentieth century child welfare was one of the major concerns of the Progressive reform movement. Humanitarian progressivism dominated political, economic, and social thought during these years, and if it had a central theme, that theme was concern for the child. The campaigns that Progressives mounted for health, education, better working conditions, and a richer environment all focused on the child.[23]

It is true that Progressives usually promoted the same middle-class values and virtues that other reformers advocated, but they never gave up on the possibility of reforming delinquents. Children, even those in trouble, embodied hope for America's future. Consequently, in 1898 Progressives established the New York School of Philanthropy, the first school to train professional social workers, and later they supported the juvenile court movement. Then in 1912 they persuaded Congress to create the United States Children's Bureau, which investigated and reported on a wide variety of subjects relating to childhood, including child labor, dependency, juvenile delinquency, and infant mortality. Most of the studies concluded that the best way to prevent delinquency and to ensure a better future for wayward children was to improve juvenile court systems.[24]

The Progressive movement promoted the concept of the "child expert." Thus, in addition to supporting the expansion of juvenile court facilities, Progressives urged the creation of state agencies, youth boards, and the increased utilization of social workers. Accordingly, in 1917 the New York School of Philanthropy became the New York School of Social Work, and in 1924 the University of Chicago established the School of Social Services Administration. These efforts were intended to produce professional social workers who had been trained to identify and aid families and children who needed psychological, institutional, and legal assistance. Social workers dispensed advice, economic assistance, educational and medical information, and adjunct juvenile court services as each case required.[25]

Although Progressives generally supported juvenile court programs, they also hoped to free the courts of some of their most oppressive burdens. For example, the Progressives who promoted social-work training believed that the caseworkers produced would be able to locate more appropriate community agencies and then be in a better position to direct children and families to them. Ultimately, the Progressives maintained, the community, rather than the juvenile court, had to take responsibility for reform. [26]

The Progressives were not alone in believing that the juvenile courts' responsibilities had to be shared. Certain psychologists, such as William James and William Healy, also promoted this idea. These men were as optimistic about the future as the Progressives. James, for example, considered the job of psychologists to be the discovery of those circumstances that produced an individual's misfortune. Once those circumstances had been ascertained, a program of treatment, counseling, and adjustment could begin to reverse that misfortune. [27]

Psychologists and psychiatrists had been actively assisting children in trouble since the early 1890s when Dr. Walter E. Fernald and Dr. Walter Channing began to provide clinical and outpatient services for their patients in Massachusetts. Most of these children were either feebleminded or insane, but the emphasis that the psychiatrists placed upon the social, emotional, and psychological genesis of mental problems was easily transferable to less severely disturbed youths. As a consequence, clinics and special schools for the emotionally disturbed began to appear all over the country, and they received and treated referrals from juvenile courts, social agencies, and private families. One of the primary goals of the new clinics was to dispense treatment while avoiding institutionalization, if at all possible. [28]

William Healy shared these views and incorporated them into his Juvenile Psychopathic Institution, which was founded in 1909 in Chicago. He and Dr. Thomas Salmone of the National Committee for Mental Hygiene were largely responsible for the movement to establish child guidance clinics in communities throughout the country. These clinics formed the nucleus of the mental hygiene movement of the 1920s. By 1931, of the 674 psychiatric clinics that existed, 232 had been established specifically to help children. During these years, considerations of the social dimensions of crime and poverty persuaded many social workers and psychologists such as Healy that juvenile delinquency was caused primarily by family disorders and conflicts. Thus, in order to understand and solve the delinquency problem, psychological studies of the individual delinquents' attitudes toward their families and environment had to be undertaken.[29]

Many of the new family and social-work experts, such as Virginia P. Robinson and Jessie Taft of the Pennsylvania School of Social Work, were women. This helps explain the new approaches to female delinquency taken after World War I. Concern over prostitution and premarital pregnancy among young women caused the development of new programs at many girls' reform schools like Miriam Van Waters's El Retiro in Los Angeles. During the 1920s and 1930s Waters led a movement that emphasized education, cultural appreciation, and inmate self-government. Believing in community reintegration as soon as possible, Waters attempted to find respectable jobs for her girls, maintained a halfway club and alumnae house, and generally created a sense of self-worth in her charges. She distrusted criminally oriented juvenile courts that tended to indiscriminately institutionalize girls with family problems or problems of a sexual nature.[30]

The Chicago Sociologists

Miriam Van Waters and other social workers had much in common with academic sociologists from the University of Chicago who had been critically examining problems of juvenile delinquency during the 1920s. These sociologists viewed youth crime as basically a social problem and considered family and group behavior crucial. They attached little importance, however, to the psychologists' contention that delinquency could be traced to mental problems, maintaining instead that a child's behavior was the product of environment and of social interaction with peers. Thus the sociologists focused primarily on urban gang delinquency.[31]

The Chicago sociologists argued that the deterioration of neighborhoods that had traditionally been the homes of successive waves of immigrant groups had promoted the formation of delinquent gangs. Middle-class families and businesses, as well as cultural, religious, and political organizations had moved away from the city's core. Consequently, the normal socializing institutions no longer existed in the old neighborhoods. Urban landlords and speculators had taken advantage of those left behind, refusing to improve the living conditions, and holding on to properties in order to take advantage of commercial redevelopment of those areas. Given the degree of disorganization in such communities, the sociologists asserted, it was not surprising that central city neighborhoods became slums and well-springs of organized crime, drug pushing, prostitution, and gambling. Families disintegrated with the neighborhoods, and pimps, crooks, and hustlers became the new role models. Delinquent gangs evolved naturally out of these conditions, and they blended in well with the criminal elements and corrupt politicians who dominated the areas.[32]

The Chicago sociologists claimed that in socially disorganized neighborhoods, crime and delinquency became reflections of normal group patterns rather than of aberrant ones. Indeed, members of delinquent gangs were for the most part psychologically normal and sought only traditional sociability and acceptance from their peers. Delinquency occurred when the gangs emulated the perverse nature of the slum community organizations around them.[33]

The autobiography, *The Jack Roller*, compiled over a five-year period by Clifford R. Shaw, one of the Chicago sociologists, reinforced these views. Describing the life of a teenager who mugged drunks and homosexuals, Shaw's book depicted how easily even a bright and well-meaning youth could fall victim to adverse cultural norms. By introducing the concept of "differential association," Shaw also demonstrated that even in the worst of disorganized neighborhoods some youths remained nondelinquent and, in fact, joined groups or gangs that had legitimate pursuits. Identification with one type of group or the other, and cultural sanctions for such identification, determined whether or not an individual would ultimately become a delinquent.[34]

Shaw and the other Chicago sociologists believed that when the machinery of spontaneous social control broke down, delinquency resulted. Thus, in order to control the problem of youth crime, community organizations had to be rebuilt and made effective once again. The sociologists believed, however, that the prevention of delinquency was only one part of the greater struggle to humanize the city. Robert Park, for example, maintained that the real problem was achieving a social order and a social control in the city to replace the natural order and control of the family, clan, and tribe—all of which had dissipated under pressure of modern urban society.[35]

The Chicago sociologists concluded that group life in slum areas had to be reconstructed and socialized, and they organized programs of crime prevention and delinquency prevention around these conclusions. William Healy and other psychologists had stressed clinical therapy over liaison with community groups and organizations. Miriam Van Waters and other social workers had promoted reevaluation of the treatment and status of delinquent girls and boys so that such youths could be successfully placed back into the community. Nevertheless, even though they had differing approaches to the problem of juvenile crime, all of these analysts and theorists agreed that the trend of identifying children as delinquent had to be reversed and that wayward youths needed to be reintegrated into their families and communities. Such anti-institutional conclusions and efforts were humane and rational. They were also exceptional and unacceptable to large segments of the community. Indeed, they still are.[36]

DELINQUENCY IN THE 1920s AND 1930s

The American public rejected the conclusions of experts for a variety of reasons. Most people feared, as they do now, the presence in their communities of anyone who had been identified as delinquent or criminal by institutions of justice. Hence the significance of definitions and the labeling process. Most Americans also believed in the 1920s that a juvenile crime wave had been sweeping the country. Hysterical newspaper accounts that were even more sensational than the stories are today reinforced and added to those beliefs. Almost every issue of every magazine, from *The Ladies Home Journal* to the *New Republic*, had something to say about wayward youth.[37]

Aroused by popular clamor, the Children's Bureau began a study of the records of juvenile crime in fourteen cities from 1913 until the mid-1920s. The bureau concluded that the rate of delinquency had actually fallen and that the social and recreational agencies for youth, which the Chicago sociologists had helped set up across the nation, had been largely responsible. Nevertheless, the police, the popular press, legal agencies, and juvenile institutions pontificated at length on the "juvenile crime wave" sweeping the country.[38]

The depression of the 1930s brought with it an end to the juvenile delinquency hysteria. This is somewhat paradoxical given the generally accepted belief that poverty created delinquency. Moreover, juvenile courts and other youth agencies designed to curb crime had been drastically reduced by budget cuts. As a consequence, the hundreds of thousands of youths who had left their homes to wander aimlessly across America in search of sustenance never became part of delinquency statistics, as such youths probably would today. Nor did this vagrancy create hordes of banditti pillaging, plundering, and marauding. America's youthful hoboes merely found alternative life-styles.[39]

Those who remained at home in these economically oppressed times did not turn to a life of crime either. For the most part these children did not feel oppressed by poverty as much as they did by "hard times," which they believed would inevitably pass. Accordingly, the financial difficulties drew many families closer together. On farms, in small towns, and in cities, working- and middle-class families faced difficulties, shared problems, and overcame obstacles together. This and fewer broken homes acted as powerful deterrents to delinquency. Moreover, the federal government created the Civilian Conservation Corps and the National Youth Administration to provide alternatives to unemployment and rootlessness for young people.[40]

DELINQUENCY AFTER
WORLD WAR II

The events of the 1930s seemed to support the theories of the Chicago sociologists and other Progressive experts of the 1920s. Families, communities, and youths themselves had taken care of the delinquency problem. But by 1940 this lesson had somehow been lost, ignored, or misinterpreted. For in that year the American Law Institute approved a model Youth Correction Authority Act that provided guidelines for state governments to implement an administrative integration of institutions and agencies responsible for handling juvenile delinquents. Also in 1940 the White House held its fourth conference on children, entitled "Children in a Democracy." The conference was meant to demonstrate that the future of American democracy depended upon the welfare of its children. Once again Americans had voiced their belief in a mission and destiny that only their children could carry out and preserve. Accordingly, as had past reformers and child savers, they placed their faith in institutions to weed out and incarcerate undesirables while rehabilitating those who could adopt middle-class values, virtues, and mores. Thus the institutionalization of American youth began again, and so too would another wave of juvenile delinquency.[41]

The rate of delinquency skyrocketed during the war years of 1941 to 1945, and the trend continued into the postwar period to become the object of concern, investigation, frustration, and outrage that it remains today. Throughout these years, Chicago-trained sociologists continued to stress the social origins and nature of juvenile crime. But, with few exceptions, they did not gain the opportunity to implement preventive programs. Instead, during the 1950s the teachings of psychologists John Dewey, Carl Rogers, and Erich Fromm, among others, gained prominence. The government also stepped in and passed the Federal Youth Correction Act of 1950 to improve techniques for the treatment and rehabilitation of youthful offenders. Two years later the government created the Department of Health, Education and Welfare, which included a Children's Bureau. That bureau in turn established a Division of Juvenile Delinquency in 1954.[42]

NEW TRENDS OF THE 1960s AND 1970s

In spite of these efforts, however, the rate of juvenile crime continued to increase. As a consequence, research and preventive programs emphasizing psychological approaches to the problem, federal government organizations, and state institutions for children came under considerable pressure to develop more effective methods. Accordingly, in the early 1960s a number of new programs were introduced, and institutions that had resisted change for nearly a century had to transform their philosophy, purpose, and structure. One of the most important steps in this new direction occurred in 1961 when John F. Kennedy created the President's Committee on Juvenile Delinquency and Youth Crime and subsequently persuaded Congress to pass the Juvenile Delinquency and Youth Control Act.[43]

Robert F. Kennedy chaired the President's Committee, and he channeled funds to foundation projects such as the Ford Foundation's "gray areas" program and Mobilization for Youth, a community redevelopment project on the Lower East Side of New York City. These and later federal programs promoted the theories of those Chicago sociologists who had postulated that delinquency could be attacked and perhaps prevented by altering the "loser" perception that ghetto children had of themselves. The programs' administrators believed that if a decent standard of living could be attained legally in the existing economic structure, ghetto children would not be seduced as readily into a life of crime.[44]

What President Kennedy had begun Lyndon Baines Johnson attempted to continue. Declaring his war on poverty, Johnson established VISTA, Volunteers in Service to America, which had evolved out of the Peace Corps concept. He also started the Neighborhood Youth Corps, the Job Corps, Upward Bound, and several other programs that were founded upon the principle that poverty and joblessness caused most crime and delinquency. Consequently, these programs and others trained and paid youths as nonprofessional aides, community organizers, and community agency workers. Peer counselors and workers on loan from schools and recreation centers worked with youth gangs. Storefront youth centers came into existence. And social service agencies began to employ more minority youth and those with specific language skills to help relate to social service clients.[45]

Crime control and economic opportunity concepts became so widely accepted during the 1960s that delinquency prevention ideas lost ground to broader antipoverty programs such as the Community Action Program in the Office of Economic Opportunity and the Model Cities Program. Strengthening neighborhood and local organizations also gained support in state plans like the California Youth Authority's probation subsidy program and by the President's Commission on Law Enforcement and Justice, which was created in 1967.[46]

Many state training schools picked up on these trends in the 1960s and began to shift from punitive custodial programs to those that attempt to provide marketable skills for incarcerated youths. Moreover, in 1969 the Federal Bureau of Prisons opened the Robert F. Kennedy Youth Center at Morgantown, West Virginia. This center's skillfully designed therapeutic and training programs emerged as model programs for the rest of the nation.[47]

Juvenile Delinquency and the Supreme Court

The trend away from institutionalization, which had begun in the 1960s, continued into the 1970s. For example, in 1972 the State of Massachusetts Youth Services Department closed its juvenile reformatories and placed most of the children in community-based work and educational programs. A series of landmark Supreme Court decisions concerning the rights of juveniles, however, probably affected the potential institutionalization of delinquents during these years more than anything else.[48]

In 1966, for instance, the Court ruled in *Kent* v. *United States* that juveniles had the right to proper hearings before waiver decisions could be made. Sixteen-year-old Morris Kent, the central figure in this ruling, had been charged in 1961 with robbery and rape in Washington, D. C. The judge of the juvenile court had subsequently decided, without a hearing and without consulting Kent's attorney, to waive jurisdiction on the case; that is, he had ordered that Kent be sent to an adult criminal court to stand trial for offenses "too serious" to warrant the protection of the juvenile court. Had Kent been adjudicated as a juvenile, the maximum sentence would have been incarceration and treatment in a reformatory or training school until he reached the age of twenty-one. An adult criminal court, however, could have imposed the death penalty. Although Kent did not receive the maximum sentence, he was found guilty and sentenced to a term of thirty to ninety years in prison.[49]

The Supreme Court, when it heard the case in 1966, had to decide whether or not Kent had been unfairly denied the protection of the juvenile court. The justices ruled that such protection had indeed been denied, and they suggested for the first time that constitutional principles might be applicable to juvenile court procedures. The Court also intimated that, given an appropriate case, it would consider the constitutionality of other juvenile court procedures. Shortly thereafter the Gerald Francis Gault case proved to be just such a case.[50]

Gerald Gault, a fifteen-year-old, had been adjudged delinquent for making an obscene telephone call that had largely involved questions concerning "cherries" and "bombers." The complainant did not appear at the trial, and the judge never informed the defendant or his parents of right to counsel, the privilege against self-incrimination, or in fact the precise charges against the boy. The juvenile court found Gault guilty, nevertheless, and committed him to the state industrial school until he was "cured," or until his twenty-first birthday, whichever came first. An adult found guilty of the same offense would have received, at most, two months in jail or a fifty-dollar fine.[51]

Gault's parents appealed to the Supreme Court of Arizona, but to no avail. The United States Supreme Court, however, reversed Arizona's ruling in 1967 and stated that juveniles had the right to counsel, to confront the accuser, and to cross-examine witnesses. The Court's decision implied that the juvenile justice system had not satisfactorily met the obligations imposed on it by the *parens patriae* doctrine. Confidentiality had been "more rhetoric than reality," the adjudicatory process had been "confusing and antitherapeutic," and the institutions to which youths had been remanded after disposition had not rehabilitated. In short, the Supreme Court castigated the juvenile court system for its failure to implement the humanitarian ideals of its founders and ordered that "the essentials of due process and fair treatment" must be extended to all children.[52]

The extensions of juvenile rights continued in 1970 when the Supreme Court ruled in *In re Winship* on the amount of evidence necessary to find a youth delinquent. Adults can be found guilty only if guilt beyond a reasonable doubt has been established. Children, however, before the Winship decision, could be found delinquent according to juvenile court laws and codes if the preponderance of evidence made it seem likely that they had broken the laws in question. According to the traditional *parens patriae* arguments, troubled children should not be denied the help of the juvenile court merely because some doubt existed as to their guilt. The Supreme Court, however, decided in *Winship* as it had in *Gault*—that the traditional juvenile court philosophy did not work. The Court ruled that, because a delinquency disposition could incarcerate youths for extended periods of time in reformatories or training schools, juveniles should not be found guilty on evidence that would be insufficient to convict them if they were adults.[53]

The courts were clearly catching up with others who had been attempting to deinstitutionalize juvenile justice. Indeed, after *Winship* the Supreme Court appeared to be on the verge of ruling that children had exactly the same rights as adults in criminal proceedings. Then, in 1971 in the case of *McKeiver* v. *Pennsylvania*, the Court ruled that juvenile courts do not have to provide jury trials. In so ruling, the Court indicated that even after *Kent*, *Gault*, and *Winship*, it intended to allow some procedural informality to remain in the juvenile justice system. The justices reasoned that without such latitude the goal of providing helpful, regenerative care and treatment would be unattainable.[54]

In spite of the Supreme Court decisions and reforms, which altered the basic philosophies, programs, and processes of the juvenile justice system, serious problems remained in the early 1970s. States continued to apply *parens patriae* protection ambiguously, and procedural informalities that would be unacceptable in criminal court remained the norm in juvenile courts. Juvenile crime also continued to increase, and studies showed that youths committed an ever larger share of all crimes. Moreover, teenagers became involved in a greater percentage of burglaries, auto thefts, violent crime, and major property crime than members of any other age group.[55]

Discrimination against blacks, Mexican-Americans, Puerto Ricans, American Indians, and poor whites also remained a problem in all types of reformatories, training schools, and institutions. Sexual abuse and physical attacks by peers and occasionally by staff members continued to be problems as well. In addition, the problem of status offenses—acts that would not be considered criminal if committed by adults—received much attention. Moreover, in some states juveniles continued to be incarcerated with adult offenders. And no general agreement on the definition of juvenile delinquency, or even on what age constituted a majority, existed.[56]

The general quality of organized care for delinquent children, which was abysmally low, was widely publicized during the early 1970s. Social commentators, journalists, reformers, jurists, lawyers, and scholars all pointed out that failure of treatment had all too often been the norm and that children continued to serve jail sentences. In spite of a few significant reforms, these critics argued, an overall lack of coordination and consistency in juvenile court operations and approaches to solutions had limited any significant changes. Because of this continuing confusion and the related publicity, Congress held hearings on juvenile delinquency and juvenile justice in 1974. Findings from these inquiries called attention to understaffed and overcrowded institutions, inadequate protective facilities, and a lack of technical assistance for states and cities.[57]

Juvenile Delinquency and Congress

Congress focused on two separate but related needs: protecting society from juvenile crime and providing the most effective management and care for juveniles in trouble. As a result of its investigation, Congress enacted the Juvenile Justice and Delinquency Prevention Act of 1974, which created the Office of Juvenile Justice and Delinquency Prevention. Within a short time the office developed four special emphasis funding programs to combat various problems related to juvenile delinquency. The first program attempted to develop community-based alternatives to traditional forms of institutionalization. The second initiated a diversion program that was designed to help offenders find alternatives to the juvenile justice system. The third program was designed to reduce the number of serious crimes by juveniles. And the fourth devoted all of its resources to the prevention of delinquency.[58]

Data collected from these programs and other recent studies indicated that the greatest amount of progress was made when juveniles had little or no contact with the juvenile justice system; in other words, wayward youths who avoided the vortex of the juvenile court had the lowest recidivism rate. Accordingly, the Office of Juvenile Justice ruled that any state receiving Juvenile Justice Act funds had to develop and utilize alternative shelter facilities, programs, and services. Special diversion programs and drug education projects across the country also began to receive federal funding.[59]

The new legislation and subsequent programs represented the first unified attempt to provide a national program of juvenile delinquency prevention and control within the criminal justice system. The act called for a nationwide program of leadership and coordination and asked for new solutions to the dilemmas posed by juvenile crime. To further these efforts the Law Enforcement Assistance Administration (LEAA), which had been created when Congress enacted the omnibus Crime Control and Safe Streets Act of 1968, formed the National Advisory Committee on Criminal Justice Standards and Goals in 1975. This committee, in turn, gave birth to the Task Force on Juvenile Justice and Delinquency Prevention, which then developed and published in 1976 a comprehensive set of national standards for juvenile justice and delinquency prevention.[60]

Many of the new programs and developments in the study and prevention of delinquency followed concepts first promoted by William Healy, the Chicago sociologists, and other pioneers of the anti-institutional approach. These concepts gained an increasing number of followers during the late 1970s in part because of the indictments that youths who had been through the juvenile justice process made of that system. The ultimate authorities on whether the system worked or not, juvenile delinquents told stories of drudgery and debasement and of institutions and juvenile courts that smothered decent instincts while encouraging further crime and deviance.[61]

THE CURRENT STATE OF JUVENILE JUSTICE

The demoralization of America following the Vietnam War and the Watergate scandals deepened an already active suspicion and hostility toward government institutions, including the juvenile court. Finding little evidence to support juvenile court accomplishments, many penologists, judges, lawyers, and reformers concluded that such institutions did not work either as treatment centers or as custodial institutions. As a consequence, community treatment of juvenile delinquents—in the form of group homes, halfway houses, temporary shelters, and probation—became increasingly accepted as alternatives to incarceration. And a juvenile court abolition movement began.[62]

As the 1980s begin to unfold, it is generally recognized that for the past century and a half the juvenile justice system in America has been dominated by well-meaning but class-conscious and often bigoted social groups. The principal result of this situation has been to stigmatize certain youths who have lived in the socioeconomic squalor of urban slums. This process of defining and labeling one youthful sector of American society has been a conscious effort to create outcasts and negative role models in order to save other children from future crimes and deviance. At the same time, those "misfits" caught in the web of the juvenile justice system were supposed to be either rehabilitated and reoriented, thus facilitating their return to society, or incarcerated and kept off the streets until such time as adult criminal courts could assume responsibility for them. Unfortunately, because of the stigmatization inherent in the juvenile justice system, more youths have been caught in the treadmill leading to inevitable adult criminal status than most defenders of juvenile corrections programs have ever acknowledged.[63]

To be sure, many juvenile courts and juvenile justice systems have over the years reformed their programs and policies somewhat to accommodate growing skepticism concerning their efficacy. Nevertheless, the basic rationale of treatment based upon stigma and separation has remained the prime moving force behind juvenile justice in America. Moreover, a strong punishment-rather-than-treatment movement is gaining ground. Enough investigations have been undertaken and enough evidence exists, however, to suggest that a sustained and broad-based commitment to revitalize family and community government at the expense of institutional systems is the ultimate answer. But, as this is being written, although significant changes have taken place, no such commitment has been made.

NOTES
CHAPTER TWO

1. See Willard Motley, *Knock on Any Door* (New York, 1947), pp. 27–78; Robert M. Mennel, *Thorns and Thistles: Juvenile Delinquents and the United States, 1825–1940* (Hanover, N. H., 1973), pp. 116–25; and Frank R. Donovan, *Wild Kids: How Youth Has Shocked Its Elders—Then and Now* (Harrisburg, Pa., 1967), p. 21.

2. Donovan, *Wild Kids,* p. 20; and *Two Hundred Years of American Criminal Justice,* an LEAA Bicentennial Study (Washington, 1976).

3. See Mennel, *Thorns and Thistles,* pp. 127–28; Also see Julia Lathrop et al., *The Child, the Clinic, and the Court* (New York, 1927), p. 292; Timothy D. Hurley, *The Origin of the Juvenile Court Law* (Chicago, 1970), pp. 17–21; Grace Abbott, *The Child and the State,* 2 vols. (Chicago, 1938), Vol. II, pp. 330–32; and *Proceedings* of the Illinois Conference of Charities (1898) in Board of State Commissioners of Public Charities, *15th Biennial Report* (1898), pp. 282, 336.

4. See Herbert H. Lou, *Juvenile Courts in the United States* (Chapel Hill, N. C., 1927), pp. 1–11; Bernard Flexner, "The Juvenile Court—Its Legal Aspect," *Annals* of the American Academy, Vol. 36 (1910), pp. 49–56; Robert H. Bremmer et al., eds., *Children and Youth in America,* 3 vols. (Cambridge, Mass., 1976), Vol. II, pp. 507–11; Hurley, *The Origin of Juvenile Court Law,* p. 56; and Mennel, *Thorns and Thistles,* pp. 131–32.

5. Mennel, *Thorns and Thistles,* pp. 132–33.

6. U. S. Congress, *Children's Courts in the United States,* 58th Cong., 2d sess. (1904); and Mennel, *Thorns and Thistles,* p. 199.

7. Anthony M. Platt, *The Child Savers: The Invention of Delinquency* (Chicago, 1969), pp. 3–14; and *Two Hundred Years of American Criminal Justice,* p. 66.

8. Platt, *The Child Savers,* pp. 3–14, 176.

9. Ibid., p. ix. Also see LaMar T. Empey, *American Delinquency: Its Meaning and Construction,* p. 68; and Mennel, *Thorns and Thistles,* p. 172.

10. Platt, *The Child Savers,* p. 177. Also see Empey, *American Delinquency,* p. 93.

11. Julian W. Mack, "The Juvenile Court: The Judge and the Probation Officer," National Conference of Charities and Correction (NCCC), *Proceedings* (1906), pp. 123–25; and Mennel, *Thorns and Thistles,* pp. 135–38. Also see *New York Times* (March 27, 1943).

12. Mennel, *Thorns and Thistles,* pp. 139–40. Also see Emily E. Williamson, "Probation and Juvenile Courts," *Annals of the American Academy* 20 (1902): 259–67.

13. Mark H. Haller, "Urban Crime and Criminal Justice: The Chicago Case," *Journal of American History* 57 (1970): 629; Edith Jones, "Probation in Practice," *Charities* 27 (1907): 983; Louise de Koven Bowen, "The Early Days of the Juvenile Court," in Lathrop et al., *the Child, The Clinic, and the Court,* p. 309. Also see Mennel, *Thorns and Thistles,* pp. 142–44.

14. See Margaret K. Rosenheim, "Perennial Problems in the Juvenile Court," in Margaret K. Rosenheim, ed., *Justice for the Child* (New York, 1962), pp. 1–21; Edward L. Lindsey, "The Juvenile Court from the Lawyer's Standpoint," *Annals of the American Academy* 52 (1914): 145–47. Also see Mennel, *Thorns and Thistles,* pp. 144–47.

15. See Charles W. Hoffman, "Social Aspects of the Family Court," *Journal of Criminal Law and Criminology* 10 (1919): 409–22; Willis B. Perkins, "Family Courts," *Michigan Law Review* 17 (1919): 378–81; Jacob T. Zukerman, "The Family Court— Evolving Concepts," *Annals of the American Academy* 383 (1969): 119–28. Also see Mennel, *Thorns and Thistles*, pp. 148–50.

16. See John D. Davies, *Phrenology: Fad and Science* (New Haven, Conn., 1955).

17. See Dorothy Ross, *G. Stanley Hall: The Psychologist as Prophet* (Chicago, 1972); and John and Virginia Demos, "Adolescence in Historical Perspective," *Journal of Marriage and the Family* 31 (November, 1969). Also see Mennel, *Thorns and Thistles*, pp. 80–83; and Jane Addams, *The Spirit of Youth and the City Streets* (New York, 1909), pp. 6, 69.

18. Cesare Lombroso, *L' Uomo delinquente* (1876); Lombroso, *The Female Offender* (New York, 1903); and Lombroso, *Crime: Its Causes and Remedies* (Boston, 1912).

19. See Arthur MacDonald, *Laboratory for the Study of the Criminal Pauper and Defective Classes*, 60th Cong., 2d sess., House Report 2087 (Washington, D. C., 1909), p. 2; Thomas Travis, *The Young Malefactor* (New York, 1908), pp. 209–11. Also see Mennel, *Thorns and Thistles*, pp. 86–90; Thomas F. Gassett, *Race: The History of an Idea in America* (Dallas, 1963), p. 421; and John Higham, *Strangers in the Land* (New York, 1965), p. 125.

20. See Arthur H. Estabrook, *The Jukes in 1915* (Washington, D. C., 1916); Henry H. Goddard, *The Kallekak Family* (New York, 1912); Charles B. Davenport, *Heredity in Relation to Eugenics* (New York, 1911); F. W. Blackmar, "The Smokey Pilgrims," *American Journal of Sociology* 2 (1897): 485–500; Florence Danielson and Charles B. Davenport, *The Hill Folk* (Cold Spring Harbor, N. Y., 1912); and Elizabeth S. Kite, "The Pineys," *Survey* 31 (Oct. 4, 1913): 7–13, 38–40. Also see Mennel, *Thorns and Thistles*, pp. 92–94.

21. See J. B. Wallace Wallin, *Problems of Subnormality* (New York, 1917); James B. Miner, *Deficiency and Delinquency* (Baltimore, 1920); Gardener Murphy, *Historical Introduction to Modern Psychology* (New York, 1949). Also see Mennel, *Thorns and Thistles*, pp. 94–100.

22. Mennel, *Thorns and Thistles*, pp. 78, 100–102, 158.

23. See Robert H. Wiebe, *The Search for Order 1877–1920* (New York, 1967), p. 169.

24. See Dorothy E. Bradbury, *5 Decades of Action for Children: A Short History of the Children's Bureau*, Publication 400 (Washington, D. C., 1966); and Mennel, *Thorns and Thistles*, pp. 151–55.

25. See Donovan, *Wild Kids*, p. 21; and Mennel, *Thorns and Thistles*, pp. 151–52.

26. See Louis C. Wade, *Graham Taylor, Pioneer for Social Justice, 1851–1938* (Chicago, 1964), pp. 161–85; Harry L. Lurie, ed., *Encyclopedia of Social Work*, 15th ed. (New York, 1965), pp. 309–19; and Sophonisba P. Breckinridge, ed., *Family Welfare Work in a Metropolitan Community: Selected Case Records* (Chicago, 1924).

27. See Adolph Meyer, "Thirty-Five Years of Psychiatry in the United States and Our Present Outlook," *American Journal of Psychiatry* 8 (1928): pp. 9–10, 21; Helen

L. Witmer, *Psychiatric Clinics for Children* (New York, 1940), pp. 10–27. Also see Mennel, *Thorns and Thistles*, pp. 158–59.

28. See Adolph Meyer, "What Do Histories of Cases of Insanity Teach Us Concerning Preventive Mental Hygiene during the Years of School Life?" *Psychological Clinic* 2 (1908): 95; and C. Jarrett, *The Kingdom of Evils* (New York, 1922). Also see Mennel, *Thorns and Thistles*, pp. 159–61.

29. See George S. Stevenson and Gesses Smith, *Child Guidance Clinics: A Quarter Century of Development* (New York, 1934); William Healy, "Psychoanalysis of Older Offenders," *American Journal of Orthopsychiatry*, 5 (1935): 27–28; and Franz Alexander and William Healy, *Roots of Crime: Psychoanalytic Studies* (New York, 1935). p. 3. Also see Mennel, *Thorns and Thistles*, pp. 163–71.

30. See Grace Abbott, *The Child and the State*, 2 vols. (Chicago, 1938), vol. 2, pp. 432–37; Edith N. Burleigh and Frances K. Harris, *The Delinquent Girl* (New York, 1923); Miriam Van Waters, "Where Girls Go Right," *Survey Graphic* I (1922): 361–76; Burton J. Rowles, *The Lady at Box 99* (Greenwich, Conn., 1962), p. 95; Margaret Reeves, *Training Schools for Delinquent Girls* (New York, 1929); and Miriam Van Waters, *Youth in Conflict* (New York, 1925). Also see Mennel, *Thorns and Thistles*, pp. 169–80.

31. Mennel, *Thorns and Thistles*, pp. 179–87. Also see Robert E. L. Fares, *Chicago Sociology 1920–1932* (Chicago, 1970), pp. 123–30.

32. See Robert E. Park and Ernest W. Burgess, eds., *The City* (Chicago, 1925), and Mennel, *Thorns and Thistles*, p. 188.

33. See Clifford R. Shaw and Henry D. McKay, *Social Factors in Juvenile Delinquency* (Washington, D. C., 1931), pp. 4, 387; and Frederick M. Thrasher, *The Gang* (Chicago, 1927), pp. 50–55.

34. Clifford R. Shaw, *The Jack Roller: A Delinquent Boy's Own Story* (Chicago, 1930), pp. 47–73. Also see Mennel, *Thorns and Thistles*, pp. 192–93; and Donovan, *Wild Kids*, p. 183.

35. See Robert E. Park, "Play and Juvenile Delinquency," *Playground* 18 (1924): 96; and Solomon Kobrin, "The Chicago Project—A Twenty-Five Year Assessment," *Annals of the American Academy of Political and Social Sciences* 322 (1959): 20–29.

36. Mennel, *Thorns and Thistles, pp. 193–95.*

37. See Donovan, *Wild Kids,* p. 188.

38. Ibid., pp. 189–91.

39. Ibid., pp. 218–20.

40. *Two Hundred Years of American Criminal Justice*, p. 68.

41. Ibid., p. 69; and Mennel, *Thorns and Thistles*, p. 196.

42. Donovan, *Wild Kids*, pp. 265–68; *Two Hundred Years of Criminal Justice*, p. 69.

43. Mennel, *Thorns and Thistles*, pp. 196–97; and Ruth Shonle Cavan and Theodore N. Ferdinand, *Juvenile Delinquency*, 3d ed. (New York, 1975), p. 399.

44. Mennel, *Thorns and Thistles*, p. 197; and *Two Hundred Years of American Criminal Justice*, p. 69.

45. Ibid.

46. Mennel, *Thorns and Thistles*, p. 197.

47. Cavan and Ferdinand, *Juvenile Delinquency*, p. 399.

48. Mennel, *Thorns and Thistles*, p. 198; *Two Hundred Years of American Criminal Justice*, pp. 70–71.

49. *Kent* v. *United States*, 383 U.S. 541 (1966); also see Daniel Katkin et al., *Juvenile Delinquency and the Juvenile Justice System*, (North Scituate, Mass., 1976), pp. 271–72.

50. Ibid.; and *In re Gault*, 387 U.S. 1 (1967).

51. Ibid.; also see Katkin, *Juvenile Delinquency and the Juvenile Justice System*, pp. 272–74, 291–92, 352–53.

52. *In re Gault*, 387 U.S. 1 (1967); and Katkin, *Juvenile Delinquency and the Juvenile Justice System*, pp. 272–74.

53. *In re Winship*, 397 U.S. 358 (1970); and Katkin, *Juvenile Delinquency and the Juvenile Justice System*, pp. 275–76.

54. *McKeiver* v. *Pennsylvania*, 403 U.S. 528, (1971).

55. *Two Hundred Years of American Criminal Justice*, p. 71.

56. See Thomas R. Frazier, ed., *The Underside of American History*, 3d ed., (New York, 1978), p. 128; and *Two Hundred Years of American Criminal Justice*, pp. 66–71.

57. Mennel, *Thorns and Thistles*, p. 198; and *Two Hundred Years of American Criminal Justice*, p. 71.

58. Ibid.

59. Ibid., p. 73.

60. Ibid., p. 72.

61. Mennel, *Thorns and Thistles*, p. 196.

62. Ibid.; and Cavan and Ferdinand, *Juvenile Delinquency*, p. 399.

63. Mennel, *Thorns and Thistles*, pp. 199–200.

3
DEFINING DELINQUENCY AND THE DELINQUENT

To understand delinquency—its nature, causes, and consequences—we must define it. But defining delinquent behavior is not an easy task. Although many definitions have emerged since the concept of delinquency appeared in the nineteenth century, such definitions often complicate rather than clarify the problem. Indeed, most of them reflect the deeply rooted prejudices and subjective assumptions the definers had toward delinquent children in particular and toward criminals and poor people in general.

Delinquency definitions have caused poor urban children—usually blacks or members of some other minority group—to be identified in terms of their deviant and criminal activities. At the same time they have fixed the parents of these children for the major share of the blame and castigated lower classes as the breeding grounds for "defectives." Thus, for the most part, definitions of delinquency have focused attention on behavioral aberrations that do not conform to the accepted standards of white Anglo-Saxon Protestant middle-class America. How this process occurred, how it has subsequently colored and distorted our perceptions and explanations of the delinquent and juvenile delinquency, and how the juvenile justice system has been plagued by inappropriate definitions of the problem will be the subject of this chapter.

EARLY DEFINITIONS OF DELINQUENCY

In order to understand the difficulty of defining delinquency and the delinquent it is necessary to examine briefly how Americans have attempted to explain and combat delinquency.[1] The first step is to remember that acts that went unpunished or were accepted as normal behavior in preindustrial, agrarian America became punishable offenses in modern urbanized America.[2] For example, until the nineteenth century, swearing, sexual activity, heavy drinking, quitting school, leaving home, wearing arms, and fighting were generally considered normal activities for "young lads" over the age of twelve.[3] Toward the end of the nineteenth century, however, such behavior came to be considered abnormal, deviant, or delinquent.

A survey of reform schools taken in 1880 by the United States Commissioner of Education is revealing. According to this study, some reformatories admitted only those children convicted of an imprisonable offense. Others, however, admitted "deviant" children who had been accused only of mischievous behavior, idleness, or resisting parental control. Still others admitted those who had simply been neglected or deserted. And some institutions accepted any children without conditions as long as someone paid the bills.[4] In short, the reformatories of the late nineteenth century did not operate within the context of a commonly accepted standard or definition of delinquent behavior. In fact, the confines within which deviant behavior was measured throughout society were extremely broad.

A New Concept of Childhood

Although the precise nature of delinquency had eluded the reformatory personnel as well as the rest of American society, the new concept of childhood had not. And it would be this "discovery of childhood" that would inevitably lead to more uniform definitions of delinquency and the delinquent.[5] Largely a product of white middle-class values, experiences, and expectations, the concept of childhood had led nineteenth century Americans to view childhood as a vulnerable time of innocence and incapacity. As a consequence, the harsh realities of adulthood—realities often confronted during the early teen years in previous eras—had to be postponed to ensure proper physical, moral, and intellectual strengthening. The home and the school were supposed to mold the child and guide him or her through the most "dangerous" period in life. If such protection was not provided, a child would be in danger of succumbing to crime, vice, and violence.[6]

Because standards of behavior for children had been so rigidly defined and because any violation of these standards signaled deviance, however, the chances of a child being considered delinquent increased immeasurably. Not only were children of every class and every ethnic group expected to conform to the rules of middle-class childhood, but even middle-class children found their behavior much more rigidly restricted. Accordingly, when children overstepped the new boundaries of acceptable behavior and when the informal controls of home, school, and neighborhood were blamed for the deviations, formal legal rules had to be written to control the problem. As a result, "delinquency" received legal definition, and a new juvenile justice system emerged, a system that attempted to enforce conformity to the formal legal rules, as well as to the informal social rules, of childhood. Anyone who violated these rules was defined as delinquent.

Violations of the middle-class rules of childhood, not surprisingly, occurred most often among lower-class youth. Thus the "invention of delinquency" provided a label for these dependent children of low status: it identified them as delinquents and thereby confirmed the expectations of middle-class reformers. The child savers responsible for the juvenile court and other institutions for delinquent children (see Chapter Two) believed that they were helping troublesome adolescents whom they considered sick or pathological. Nevertheless, the paternalism of the reformers, as Anthony Platt has observed, did not alter "the subjective experiences of control, restraint, and punishment."[7]

THE STATUS OFFENSE

Ever since the late nineteenth century most Americans have accepted the prejudices and assumptions of the child savers. Accordingly, the notion that poverty, disrupted families, and lower-class ignorance and immorality inevitably lead to crime continues to be a truism.[8] Defining juvenile delinquency and the delinquent as problems exclusively of the underclass,* however, is a serious mistake, for it has always been and still is unfair to force lower-class children to behave precisely according to middle-class rules. Moreover, it is equally unfair to impose the label "delinquent" upon a youth of any class who breaks laws that can be broken only by children.

Laws that only children can break are called "status offenses." In other words, a status offense is behavior that is permissible if performed by an adult but impermissible if performed by a child. The special status bestowed upon children in the nineteenth century, although it protected them from full accountability for criminal acts, also imposed upon children certain legal restrictions that did not apply to adults. For example, ideal children were expected to obey their parents and other figures of authority, to attend school, and to refrain from drinking, engaging in sexual activity, and staying out late. In general they were

---

*The underclass refers to all those individuals who for reasons of race, ethnic origin, poverty, or other factors beyond their control are outside the mainstream of middle-class American life.

expected to comport themselves as children never have throughout history.

Currently almost half of the states define status offenders as delinquents. Accordingly, such children are subject to the same dispositions and labeling processes as juveniles who have committed criminal acts. In the other states, although status offenders are treated more equitably, such children nevertheless continue to be stigmatized by official labeling that describes them as "incorrigible," "deprived," or "in need of supervision."[9] Moreover, in many states, status offenses are so ill conceived, amorphous, and vague that almost any child can be defined as a delinquent and referred for court action. Among the offenses a child can be charged with in these states are swearing and swigging, public gambling and excessive gamboling, and sex and marriage.[10]

THE LABELING PROCESS

Youthful lawbreakers, of course, did then and do now commit crimes that, if committed by adults, would result in incarceration. But labeling a child delinquent, even one who has clearly committed a serious crime, is often a pernicious process. For, although a youth may be a member of an under-class group and may therefore be labeled as a potential delinquent, he or she is not, as an individual, extremely likely to become a delinquent. A high proportion of this individual's peers will commit offenses, to be sure; but even a 70 percent risk of delinquency for this group, as Victor Eisner points out, "does not justify labeling a single member as a delinquent unless he actually becomes one."[11] Moreover, once labeled a delinquent, even justifiably, a youth is stigmatized as someone who is unreliable, dangerous, violent, and deviant. Indeed, juveniles who have been officially labeled delinquent are virtually unemployable, not because they may be members of the under class or because they are undereducated and unskilled—handicaps in themselves—but because no one will hire delinquents. Consequently, because of their unemployability, such youths often turn to or continue to engage in criminal activities.[12]

The labeling process begins with a youngster's economic, social, and ethnic origins and becomes official when the individual's behavior brings him or her into contact with the juvenile justice system. From

that point on, police officers, court standards, and community sentiment dictate who will and who will not be labeled a delinquent. In
fact, three official definitions of a delinquent now come into use. The
most sweeping and perhaps the most damning one defines a delinquent as a youth who has been "arrested or picked up informally by
the police."[13] Such a youth need never have contact with the juvenile
court for the "official delinquent" appellation to stick. If a young person
is referred to the court, however, he or she activates the second official
definition, for the child is then classified by the National Institute of
Juvenile Justice and Delinquency Prevention as a delinquent. This is
so whether or not adjudication takes place.[14] The third and most permanent official definition is invoked when an adjudication does take
place and the child is committed to a correctional institution.[15]

To understand how this process works, let us suppose that a boy
breaks the law and is arrested. When the arresting officer records the
juvenile's name, the official labeling process is under way, for the
police officer has already made three decisions: first, that a law has
been broken; second, that the offense warrants intervention; and third,
that the boy's name and offense must be recorded. In order to give
a name to the offense, the officer must choose from a long list of acts
that society has defined as delinquent behavior. Once the officer has
settled on a name, he or she fills out a form that identifies the juvenile,
provides a brief biographical sketch, and describes the offense the boy
has committed.[16]

The police department, at this point, has an official record of a
"contact" made with the youth. If the child is then warned and released, which is one option, a record of the contact is maintained for
future reference. Should the youth find himself in trouble again, the
arresting officer is much more likely to identify the juvenile as a delinquent and to file a report petitioning court action (see Chapter Six).

If a youth is referred to the juvenile court, the official labeling
process continues. An intake officer is generally assigned to investigate
the charges and make a social history of the child. Based on this
investigation, the intake officer recommends either acceptance or de-
nial of the police department's petition for court action. If the petition
is denied, the youth's name is nevertheless recorded and placed in
an "unofficial file" for future reference. Thus, as the police department
did with the initial arrest, the court now has recorded "delinquent

behavior" for the youth; should subsequent petitions be filed, this unofficial record helps intake officers identify the juvenile as a "delinquent."

If the intake department of the juvenile court accepts the police petition, the youth's case goes into an "official file." The court must then decide whether the youth will be held in custody, made a ward of the court, placed on probation, or released. Whatever is decided, however, the official labeling process continues; as the youth becomes increasingly entwined in the juvenile justice system, his identity as a delinquent becomes increasingly fixed (see Chapter Seven).

The recording of juvenile offenses by the police department and the juvenile court is, of course, essential to their operations. We are not suggesting that such records be ignored or destroyed. They do, however, contribute to the official labeling process, and they frequently stigmatize as delinquent many youths who either have not been found guilty of an offense or who did not even commit one.

Community sentiment, perhaps, plays the most important role in the official labeling process. Indeed, a delinquent activity is often defined and incorporated into law as "behavior which the people of a state and their leaders believe to be a threat to public safety or a hindrance to the best development of the child."[17] It is not really all of "the people," however, who make the final decisions, for laws defining a delinquent, like all laws, reflect the values, attitudes, desires, and prejudices of those who wield the most political power. In this country that power base has often eluded poor people, members of ethnic minorities, and others outside the mainstream of white middle-class American society. Accordingly, American justice systems, as we have seen, are inherently biased against the interests of the poor.

White-collar criminals, for example, are rarely arrested, and even when trials are held, the punishments are usually much less severe than those meted out to lower-class prostitutes, vagrants, drunks, thieves, and burglars. Society as a whole is much more likely to lose money to people or companies who charge for work not done, steal office supplies, fudge on their income taxes, illegally manipulate the stock market, or lie about the safety of their products. Yet we are usually less morally outraged by such activities than by those committed by burglars, muggers, or sneak thieves.[18] Moreover, when affluent adults or their children do appear in court, they have the distinct advantage of first-rate counsel. As a consequence, their chances of acquittal are far higher than those of the poor, who must depend on a public defender or a children's legal aid lawyer—either of whom is likely to be overworked.[19]

Clearly, then, when a youth is officially labeled a delinquent, a number of factors are taken into consideration in addition to the offense itself. Social class, past record (if any), police policies, court procedures, and whether or not the youth shows remorse—otherwise known as "playing the game" among offenders themselves—are all important factors. In the end, however, it is the concerns of the power wielders in the community that dictate who will and who will not be labeled a delinquent.

Delinquent and Deviant Labels

The concerns of those within the community's power structure also dictate whether or not a delinquent is unofficially labeled a deviant. Unfortunately, in most cases the two terms are interchangeable; that is, deviance defines delinquency, and the delinquent is also viewed as a deviant. But sound scholarly evidence indicates that even the most hardened criminal activity is not necessarily deviant behavior.[20] Juvenile offenders, after all, often are normal members of deviant groups rather than deviants from normal groups. Because our society caters to and reflects the needs, aspirations, and beliefs of its power wielders, certain groups of under-class youths are frequently forced into delinquency. Once involved, they must face institutional barriers and labeling processes that effectively reinforce not only their own identity as outsiders, but also society's view of them as deviants.*

One of the best arguments against equating delinquents with deviants is that youths labeled delinquent do not have a monopoly on lawbreaking. Indeed, an absolute 100 percent pure delinquent simply doesn't exist. As Daniel Katkin has observed, "Even most hardnosed offenders behave like 'normal' people most of the time."[21] Moreover, evidence abounds to suggest that most children in contemporary American society have committed or will commit an act that is labeled delinquent by society. In fact, given the laws that exist—especially status offenses—it is difficult for the vast majority of youths to avoid breaking the law, whether they are aware of doing so or not. Thus, to assume that anyone who breaks the law is a delinquent and that all delinquents are deviants is ludicrous.

*For more on the causes of delinquency, see Chapter Five.

Defining Delinquency and the Delinquent

Most Americans, however, are inclined to believe this misrepresentation in spite of evidence to the contrary. In fact, as Katkin points out, all the research done by those who have believed "in the existence of significant biological or psychological or sociological differences between delinquents and nondelinquents [has] failed to yield any important information on what the nature of such differences might be."[22] If there is a difference between "normal" members of society and those deemed "deviant," that difference is determined, in the words of Kai Erikson, "by the way a community filters out and codes the many details of behavior which come to its attention."[23]

The Labeling Theorists

Deviance, then, like delinquency, is any behavior the power holders in society so label. Indeed, according to certain critics of the juvenile justice system (known as "labeling theorists"), deviance is "not a property 'inherent' in any particular kind of behavior." It is, instead, "a property 'conferred upon' that behavior by the people who come into direct or indirect contact with it." Nothing can be learned about deviant behavior unless we know "something about the standards of the audience which responds to it."[24] Thus, to truly understand the nature of deviance, it is necessary to study the values and attitudes of the middle and upper-middle classes—the groups most responsible for writing laws governing the behavior of juveniles.

Chapter One and Chapter Two provide an historical analysis of how the values and attitudes of these classes affected the "invention of delinquency." From the evidence presented therein, it seems fair to conclude that what a youth does is only peripherally related to that youth's identification as a delinquent or deviant. Far more important are the child's ethnic origins, class, wealth or lack thereof, and ability to conform to dominant standards and attitudes of society. Moreover, according to the labeling theorists, societies need deviance as a means to identify and define the boundaries of socially acceptable behavior. People acting within these boundaries are accepted as useful and contributing members of the group, whereas those who do not conform are excluded, deemed inferior, and used as models to avoid. In short, society in general and smaller groups in particular create rules that members must learn.[25]

Labeling theorists maintain that whenever a society defines someone as deviant, "it is declaring how much variability and diversity can be tolerated within the group before it begins to lose its distinct shape, its unique identity."[26] To preserve the special identity, not only of the group but also of the deviants within it, the offenders are confronted with criminal trials, excommunication hearings, conferences with the principal, job transfers or firings, and other such punitive control devices. Of primary importance, labeling theorists insist, is the preservation of boundaries between "behavior that belongs in the special universe of the group and behavior that does not."[27]

Does any given society create its own deviants, then? Labeling theorists would probably answer yes. They agree, for example, that prisons and training schools or reformatories segregate people who will have one thing in common—their separation and alienation from society. Because these "misfits" are thrown together in often unbearably oppressive, crowded, and abusive surroundings, their alienation is heightened and intensified. Moreover, they tend to reinforce one another's identity as deviants by frequently sharing criminal knowledge, skills, and techniques. Sexual abuse must also be confronted and accommodated, and this, too, reinforces the inmates' sense of alienation from normal society. Consequently, the process of labeling, separating, and confining may ultimately be a self-fulfilling prophecy.

David Matza, a well-known pioneer labeling theorist, asserts that the differences between a deviant and a normal member of society, or between a delinquent and a nondelinquent, don't begin to exist until the official labeling process has begun.[28] He maintains that most children "drift" around illegal activity at one time or another and that a good deal of experimentation takes place. Those who are caught by parents, schools, or other entities outside the juvenile justice system are likely to stop experimenting. Those, however, who are caught and conducted through the various steps of the labeling process, as described above, are much more likely to develop deviant identities. They are also, as a result, more likely to repeat the behavior that provided them with their identities and to commit further offenses.[29]

Labeling theorists have made valid criticisms of the ways in which children are stigmatized by the official labeling process. They have also added immeasurably to our understanding of delinquency and deviance. There are some problems with this approach, however. For example, labeling theory largely ignores the delinquency of middle- and upper-class youths who occasionally become entangled in the juvenile justice system. Also overlooked for the most part are those juveniles who break the law but who never get caught and thus do not suffer the official labeling process. Moreover, labeling theory does not explain the behavior of children who are caught and labeled as delinquent, but who somehow manage to turn their lives around and become useful and productive members of society.

Labeling theory also suffers from a dearth of empirical evidence to support its theoretical assumptions. The reason for this is the enormous complexity involved in creating and implementing practical labeling theory experiments.[30] Accordingly, the theory is often scorned by empirically minded sociologists and psychologists who have pet theories of their own to explain delinquency (see Chapter Five). On the other hand, no irrefutable evidence exists to indicate that the labeling theorists are incorrect. The best way to approach and utilize the theory, therefore, is not as a comprehensive explanation of delinquency, but as a powerful criticism of all those definitions and interpretations of delinquency and deviance that rely exclusively upon traditional middle-class assumptions and "knowledge" concerning poverty, class, and ethnicity.[31]

Labeling theory suggests that a greater understanding of delinquency and the delinquent can be gained by focusing on the juvenile justice system, rather than on why delinquents behave as they do. Causes of delinquency are also important, however, and Chapter Five is devoted to them. Nevertheless, there is merit in the "process approach." Thus, for the most part, this book emphasizes the individual within the juvenile justice system, as well as the process itself, for it seems fruitless to examine one without examining the other. This is especially true when trying to define "official delinquency"—delinquency as determined by juvenile laws, codes, and courts—which the remainder of this chapter attempts to do.

OFFICIAL DEFINITIONS OF DELINQUENCY

We have seen in Chapters One and Two that the founders of early juvenile institutions and the first juvenile courts accepted the proposition that poverty equals delinquency. Thus, most of them believed that their primary purpose was to locate delinquents, to remove them from society for everyone's protection, and to inculcate into them the values of conformity and ideal childhood. In order to reshape and save "disadvantaged misfits," the managers of America's juvenile justice system hoped to provide delinquents with familial, educational, and social needs, and thus to erase their criminal tendencies. In the process, however, the system also provided the indelible label of delinquent to the children it encountered. As a consequence, the original purpose of the court—to protect troubled children from the punitive nature and stigmatizing effects of adult sanctions and from a criminal identity—became unavoidably perverted.[32]

As we have seen, children processed through the juvenile justice system today unfortunately continue to receive the delinquent label whether they are murderers or status offenders. This is also true for children who are merely neglected or dependent.[33] Neglected or dependent children, for the most part, have never committed any offense, save that of being born to parents unable or unwilling to provide for them. Dependent children, according to most official definitions, are youths with parents or guardians who are physically or mentally incapacitated, who "with good cause" wish to give up responsibility for their children, or who are dead or missing.[34] A neglected child is one "whose environment is injurious to his welfare," whose parent fails or refuses to provide "care necessary for his health, guidance or well being," or who suffers or is likely to suffer serious harm from the improper guardianship of his parents.[35]

Neglected and dependent children are not defined as delinquent under any of this country's juvenile codes. Nonetheless, their presence in the juvenile justice system, with mandatory appearances in juvenile courts, possible placement in foster or institutional homes, and the assignment of probation officer-caseworkers frequently stigmatizes such youths as delinquent, thus further clouding the meaning of the word. This ambiguity is heightened when a child commits an offense and is also found to be unsupervised or abused at home. How does a juvenile court define a youth who has been caught stealing cars, but who also has been kicked out of his home by his prostitute mother and her drug-dealing boyfriend and procurer? And what about the youth from the same kind of family who is a frequent runaway and school truant? Are these youths delinquents, persons in need of supervision (PINS), or neglected children? Or do they fit all three categories?

When the family situation is analyzed in a delinquency case, grounds often exist for charging the parents with neglect in addition to, or instead of, charging the youth with delinquency. No right or wrong way exists to deal with such problems, and each court system in this country does it differently. Given this diversity, one way that inconsistencies, discrepencies, and confusions in the definition can be dealt with effectively is to take each case on an individual basis and make decisions accordingly. This method may not be scientific and may not lend itself to empirical reinforcement, but it does avoid the problem of definitional imprisonment.[36] The best way to avoid these difficulties, however, is to develop and implement a new, uniform, nationally accepted definition of delinquency.

The official definitions of delinquency that exist now are simply too vague, ill defined, and confusing. All of the states, as well as the District of Columbia, Puerto Rico, and the federal government, have laws defining delinquency. Thus there are fifty-three assorted legal definitions, but all of them are based on the principle of protection for the child and the community. Many of these states have omnibus laws, which—like the first juvenile delinquency laws passed by the State of Illinois in 1899—state that delinquency is "the violation of any law of this State or any City or Village ordinance."[37] Following this statement there is usually a long list of specific delinquencies in addition to the offenses covered by criminal laws.

Omnibus laws impose severe restrictions upon the activities of juveniles, and most of the restrictions are not applicable to adults. Moreover, such legal definitions are usually so broadly based that most children could be charged with some offense and found delinquent, if the laws were applied equitably. Accordingly, a number of states have recently passed more general laws that list fewer specific offenses. These laws are more adaptable to local idiosyncrasies and to changes in what society deems "permissible behavior." As Ruth Shonle Cavan has observed, "The more specific the law, the more rapidly it becomes irrelevant."[38]

Since 1971 the Office of Youth Development of the United States Department of Health, Education and Welfare, following the trend of the states, has defined official delinquency as "the violation of a state law or municipal ordinance by children or youth of juvenile court age, or . . . conduct so seriously antisocial as to interfere with the rights of others or to menace the welfare of the delinquent himself, or of the community."[39] Although this broad definition of delinquency is clearly superior to the earlier more specific ones, it nevertheless includes the status offense—conduct that violates the law only when committed by children—and is therefore too inclusive. Indeed, this definition continues to stigmatize the juvenile delinquent, regardless of the nature of his or her offense, as "a person who has been adjudicated as such by a court of proper jurisdiction."[40]

Legal definitions of delinquency, including those used by government agencies, do not describe the quality or the causes of a child's behavior. They tell only that a youth has broken some law and because of this offense has been brought into the juvenile justice system. Scholarly work over the past three decades, however, indicates that delinquency should not be conceived of as merely the illegal acts of children, but as an evolving social phenomenon in which a child's behavior, the rules governing that behavior, and society's traditionally structured reaction to it are the most important factors.[41]

If adult criminal codes were formulated in the same way that state codes define juvenile delinquency, they would be constitutionally unacceptable. In fact, traditional criminal jurisprudence forbids vague and overly broad penal statutes. As a consequence of this inequity and because of growing pressure to alter the official definition of delinquency, the National Advisory Committee on Criminal Justice Standards and Goals recommended in 1976 the elimination of "the injustice of allowing criminal sanction for behavior violating nonspecific codes of conduct." [42]This committee pointed out that, although the behavior of status offenders is not inconsequential, such behavior has never been the target of traditional criminal law. Yet in many jurisdictions in this country the dispositional alternatives are the same. Indeed, in only nineteen states, according to the committee's report, "do the State codes place restrictions on dispositional alternatives for status offenders."[43]

Many of the states that continue to define status offenses as delinquency also define that offensive behavior in such generalized terms as "unruly behavior," "incorrigibility," and "immoral conduct." Consequently, the definitions of delinquency in some states not only transcend the boundries of adult criminal behavior but also are hopelessly muddled. The National Advisory Committee recommends that all of the states should clarify and simplify the concept of delinquency by defining it as only those "acts that would be a violations of Federal or State criminal law or of local ordinance if committed by adults."[44]

TOWARD A MORE EQUITABLE DEFINITION

Clearly, the juvenile justice system in general and juvenile offenders in particular would benefit from such a simple, straightforward, more equitable national definition of delinquency. Everyone would also benefit if the states made, in the words of the National Advisory Committee, "distinctions between misdemeanors and felonies, between crimes punishable by prison sentences and crimes punishable by fines or forfeitures." Moreover, distinctions "between violators of the criminal code and violators of regulatory statutes to which criminal penalties are attached" would also be useful. Few states currently make such distinctions, and as a result "serious criminal behavior and minor infractions may both be labeled delinquency." Accordingly, the National Advisory Committee recommends the adoption of all of these distinctions so that "a juvenile does not receive the label delinquent for a minor law infraction or a violation of a statute intended to regulate."[45]

Should the states make all of the distinctions described above, a few definitional problems would nevertheless remain. For example, only children can be delinquent, but ambiguity exists concerning the age at which an individual ceases to be a child. In some states the maximum age is eighteen; in others it is fifteen.[46] The National Advisory Committee on Criminal Justice Goals and Standards recommends that the states set the maximum age of a juvenile at eighteen. The committee argues that this is the age at which young people usually finish their secondary education and begin to separate themselves from their family unit. Most states also recognize the age of eighteen as the age of majority for other purposes. Thus, a certain symmetry would be obtained.[47]

Ambiguity also continues to exist concerning the age at which a child can begin delinquency. Many states do not specify a minimum age below which a child is incapable of discerning right from wrong. Some states have mandated the age of seven as the "age of responsibility" for a child. Any child who commits an offense before reaching that age, no matter what the offense is, cannot be held responsible.

Parents of such a child, however, may be charged with neglect or failure to provide proper supervision.[48]

The National Advisory Committee would like to see the minimum age raised to ten. To authorize jurisdiction over juveniles who are too young and immature to understand the full meaning and consequences of their behavior, it is argued, serves neither society nor the child. Because no established age exists at which children are sufficiently mature to warrant juvenile court jurisdiction, the selection of a minimum age is essentially an arbitrary decision. Nevertheless, according to the committee, "available statistics do indicate that there is a marked decline in the arrest rate of juveniles younger than age ten." Because of this and because most of the states with an established minimum age for delinquency have selected ten as that age, so too does the committee.[49]

UNOFFICIAL DELINQUENCY

In addition to the official definitions of delinquency and the delinquent, as described above, other unofficial definitions exist. These definitions are used to analyze the development and prevention of delinquency, as well as the rehabilitation of youths with behavior problems. Thus, an unofficial delinquent might be defined as one "who deviates from normal behavior so as to endanger himself, his social career, or the community."[50] But who decides what is normal or when a youth is endangering himself and the community? Parents, teachers, ministers, youth leaders, and many others, including the juveniles themselves, make these decisions. And, for the most part, their decisions are more astute than similar decisions made by representatives of the juvenile justice system.

Youths and the people within their immediate community are frequently in a much better position to determine what is and what is not acceptable behavior, for unofficial delinquency is, in fact, part of a spectrum of behavior that contains absolute conformity on one end and violent criminal activity on the other. How close a youth's behavior approaches one end or the other of the spectrum determines whether or not he or she elicits condemnation, mild disapproval, or overt acceptance. This formulation, according to Ruth Shonle Cavan and Theodore N. Ferdinand, "has now largely replaced the older idea that good and bad, delinquency and conformity are sharply defined dichotomies."[51]

When a community rejects a youth, this is evidence that he or she has been identified as a confirmed delinquent, even though the juvenile may never have been caught by the police or exposed to the juvenile justice system. Such a youth usually reciprocates the community's rejection and drops out of those groups and associations that expect his or her behavior to be somewhat less antisocial. Accordingly, schools, churches, community centers, and recreational areas all become off limits to this youngster. When he or she does interact with such institutions, it is usually as a violent adversary in a state of destructive combat.[52]

Others who have been identified as hostile and antipathetic to the immediate community, however, offer a form of refuge and camaraderie to the "confirmed delinquent." Together they construct their own social world with its own values, roles, hierarchies, and often unspoken rules and regulations. What the community at large does or thinks thus becomes irrelevant to the confirmed delinquents, except insofar as it provides them with their reason for being.[53]

The Misbehaving Nondelinquent

Another type of "unofficial delinquent," as described by Cavan and Ferdinand, is the "misbehaving nondelinquent." This youth's behavior is different from that of the confirmed delinquent who for a variety of reasons, ranging from self-protection and fear to self-hatred and ignorance, usually adapts or conforms to the common needs of an underworld "delinquent subculture or contraculture." The unofficial delinquent usually identifies with and accepts the values, morality, and authority structure of his or her social class or ethnic group. This child's "occasional delinquency," or behavior contrary to the culture's values, is generally tolerated and even expected, within limits. The confirmed delinquent, in contrast, has adapted to norms that are not only different from those of society in general, but that are also in conflict with, opposite to, and destructive of the general culture.[54]

The misbehaving nondelinquent and his or her intimate friends usually accept the authority of those institutions, such as schools, churches, and community centers, that reflect and promote societal values and norms. The confirmed delinquent, on the other hand, rejects such institutions, seeks out other anti-authoritarian individuals, and values membership in delinquent groups more than in conforming ones. Indeed, by being truant from home and school and by consistently engaging in illegal behavior, the confirmed delinquent becomes increasingly alien to and divorced from conforming institutions and authority structures. Police, teachers, parents, and court officers—in fact, all representatives of normal cultural values—are thus perceived as enemies. Moreover, the true delinquent normally considers illegal behavior as a demonstration of toughness and cunning, and he or she justifies such conduct as the only way to survive in a malevolent world.[55]

Most children who commit delinquent acts, however, do not consider themselves as delinquent, nor do most juvenile lawbreakers identify illegal activities as integral to their values, norms, and behavior. Clearly, stages of delinquency exist during which a wide variety of cultural, social, and psychological factors merge to form a delinquent personality.

DEFINITION AND PREVENTION

Delinquency cannot be prevented unless we understand what it is, who becomes delinquent, and why. Before a prevention effort can be successful governments, courts, and police, as well the public in general, must clarify their thinking about their values and about the delinquency problem. We must ask ourselves why a particular type of delinquent behavior causes community alarm and what values are threatened by different kinds of delinquent behavior. If all the participants in the delinquency problem—and they include almost everyone—examine their own implicit assumptions about delinquency, as well as their assumptions about others' views, we will all have a better chance of resolving difficult conflicts. As the National Advisory Committee on Criminal Justice Standards and Goals has observed, determination of delinquency-prevention goals "should be attempted only after participants in the planning process have a clear understanding of their assumptions about prevention. A self-assessment survey should be utilized for this purpose."[56]

Such a self-assessment, to be effective, must take into consideration that delinquency, as we have seen, includes a profoundly complex set of evolving variables, a set that comprises assumptions concerning the nature of childhood, rules and laws created to legitimize the most prevalent attitudes about childhood, the various stages of illegal behavior that victimize both society and the youths who break the law, scientific theories with their empirical and quantifiable evidence about antisocial behavior, and the "welfare-oriented system of justice that is applied only to children."[57] The remainder of this book will attempt to provide more insights into these often conflicting and confusing variables.

NOTES
CHAPTER THREE

1. See George Rosen, *Madness in Society: Chapters in the Historical Sociology of Mental Illness* (New York, 1969), p. 164.

2. See Robert M. Mennel, *Thorns and Thistles: Juvenile Delinquents in the United States 1825–1940* (Hanover, N. H., 1973), p. 198.

3. LaMar T. Empey, *American Delinquency: Its Meaning and Construction* (Homewood, Ill., 1978), p. 7.

4. See United States Commissioner of Education, *Report, 1880* (Washington, D. C., 1882) pp. clxxxi–ii.

5. See Empey, *American Delinquency*, pp. 21–24. Also see Phillipe Aries, *Centuries of Childhood* (New York, 1962), and Lloyd de Mause, *The History of Childhood* (New York, 1974).

6. Empey, *American Delinquency*, pp. 48–68.

7. Anthony M. Platt, *The Child Savers: The Invention of Delinquency*, pp. 3–4, 177.

8. For example, in 1967 the President's Commission on Law Enforcement and Administration of Justice declared, "Delinquents tend to come from backgrounds of social and economic deprivation. Their families tend to have lower than average incomes and social status. . . . It is inescapable that juvenile delinquency is directly related to conditions bred by poverty." See President's Commission on Law Enforcement and Administration of Justice, *The Challenge of Crime in a Free Society* (Washington, D.C., 1967), pp. 56–57.

9. Some of the terms such as "persons in need of supervision" or "children in need of supervision" receive the abbreviated titles of PINS and CHINS. See Daniel Katkin, et. al., *Juvenile Delinquency and the Juvenile Justice System* (North Scituate, Mass., 1976), p. 17.
   The states that bestow special quasidelinquent labels on status offenders are, as of 1980, Alaska, Arizona, California, Colorado, Florida, Georgia, Hawaii, Illinois, Kansas, Maryland, Massachusetts, Nebraska, New York, North Carolina, North Dakota, Ohio, Oklahoma, Pennsylvania, Rhode Island, South Dakota, Tennessee, Vermont, Washington, Wisconsin, as well as the District of Columbia.

10. Sexual activity of any kind, especially for girls, is grounds for incarceration in every state. Attempting to get married without permission is also a punishable offense. See Empey, *American Delinquency*, p. 5, and Katkin, *Juvenile Delinquency*, p. 17.

11. Victor Eisner, *The Delinquency Label: The Epidemiology of Juvenile Delinquency*, (New York, 1969), pp. 3–21.

12. Ibid.

13. See Ruth Shonle Cavan and Theodore N. Ferdinand, *Juvenile Delinquency*, 3d ed. (New York, 1975), p. 27.

14. Ibid.

15. According to Cavan and Ferdinand, "Research on delinquency has taken place on any one or more of these definitions. In order of size they are arrests (largest

number), referrals to court, informal or adjudicated cases (about equal in number), and institutionalized cases." See ibid., p. 27.

16. Eisner, *The Delinquency Label*, pp. 3–21.

17. Ruth Shonle Cavan and Theodore N. Ferdinand, *Juvenile Delinquency*, 3d ed. (New York, 1975), p. 31.

18. See Katkin et al., *Juvenile Delinquency and the Juvenile Justice System*, p. 59.

19. Eisner, *The Delinquency Label*, pp. 3–21.

20. Katkin et al., *Juvenile Delinquency and the Juvenile Justice System*, pp. 57–66.

21. Ibid.

22. Ibid.

23. Kai Erikson, *Wayward Puritans: A Study in the Sociology of Deviance* (New York, 1966) p. 7.

24. Ibid., p. 6.

25. Katkin et al., *Juvenile Delinquency and the Juvenile Justice System*, pp. 62–63.

26. Erikson, *Wayward Puritans*, pp. 10–11.

27. Ibid.

28. David Matza, *Delinquency and Drift* (New York, 1964). Also see Graham Sykes, *The Society of Captives* (Princeton, N. J., 1958), and Erving Goffman, *Asylums* (New York, 1962).

29. Matza, *Delinquency and Drift*.

30. Katkin et al., *Juvenile Delinquency and the Juvenile Justice System*, p. 65.

31. Labeling theory's greatest asset is its challenge to the positivists. Positivism is a system of philosophy originated by Auguste Compte that bases knowledge solely on data of sense experience or on observable scientific facts and their relations to each other, and it rejects speculation about a search for origins. Labeling theorists look for those origins because they believe that what is observable may be only a distortion of the whole. See David Matza, *Becoming Deviant*, (Englewood Cliffs, N. J., 1969).

32. See Eisner, *The Delinquency Label*, pp. 15–17.

33. "Throughout the United States and in many countries throughout the world the legal codes now specify that a child can be brought under the jurisdiction of court authorities for one of three major kinds of problems: (1) for cases in which the child has been neglected, exploited, or cruelly treated by adults; (2) for the type of criminal offenses for which adults can be punished, such as robbery, assault, or car theft; or (3) for juvenile 'status' offenses that apply only to children because of their age." See Empey, *American Delinquency* , pp. 4–5.

34. See Katkin et al., *Juvenile Delinquency and the Juvenile Justice System*, pp. 18–19.

35. Ibid. Also see Wayne County Probate Court Juvenile Division, *Annual Report*, (Detroit, 1975), pp. 2–4.

36. See Sanford J. Fox, *The Law of Juvenile Courts in a Nutshell* (St. Paul, Minn., 1971) pp. 59–70.

37. Robert H. Bremmer et al., eds., *Children and Youth in America: A Documentary History*, 2 vols. (Cambridge, 1970) Vol. 2, pp. 506–11.

38. Cavan and Ferdinand, *Juvenile Delinquency*, p. 25. Cavan and Ferdinand point out that "opinions change as to what is undesirable behavior." Indeed, they assert, "such behavior itself may change; for instance the original Illinois law forbade certain behavior on or around railroad trains, but nothing was said about autos, which were few at the time the law was passed." They conclude by arguing that "what is regarded as undesirable in one region, one social class, or one ethnic group may be regarded as normal or even desirable in some other group." Also see Irving J. Sloan, *Youth and the Law: Rights, Privileges and Obligations* (New York, 1970) pp. 55–61 and George A. and Achilles G. Theodorson, *A Modern Dictionary of Sociology* (New York, 1969), p. 106.

39. Office of Youth Development, Department of Health, Education and Welfare, *Juvenile Court Statistics* (Washington, D. C., 1971–1979).

40. See Paul Tappan, *Juvenile Delinquency* (New York, 1949) p. 30. Also see Tappan's "Who is the Criminal?" *American Sociological Review* 12 (1947): 96–102.

41. See Empey, *American Delinquency*, p. vii. Also see Edwin M. Lemert, "Juvenile Justice—Quest and Reality," *Trans-action* 4 (July, 1967); 30–40; Irving Goffman, *Asylums* (New York, 1961); Howard S. Becker, *Outsiders: Studies in the Sociology of Deviance* (New York, 1966); John I. Kituse and Aaron V. Cicourel, "A Note on the Uses of Official Statistics," *Social Problems* II (1963): 131–39.

42. National Advisory Committee on Criminal Justice Standards and Goals, *Juvenile Justice and Delinquency Prevention: Report of the Task Force on Juvenile Justice and Delinquency Prevention* (Washington, D. C., 1976), p. 295.

43. Ibid., p. 295.

44. Ibid., p. 295.

45. See ibid., p. 296.

46. See Mark M. Levin and Rosemary C. Sarri, *Juvenile Delinquency: A Comparative Analysis of Legal Codes in the United States* (Ann Arbor, Mich., 1974), p. 13.

47. National Advisory Committee on Criminal Justice Standards and Goals, *Juvenile Justice and Delinquency Prevention*, p. 299. Also see Cavan and Ferdinand, *Juvenile Delinquency*, pp. 25–26.

48. For the most current information on the minimum age for delinquency in the various states, see the latest edition of the U.S. Department of Health, Education and Welfare's, *Juvenile Court Statistics* (Washington, D.C.).

49. National Advisory Committee on Criminal Justice Standards and Goals, *Juvenile Justice and Delinquency Prevention*, p. 297.

50. See Cavan and Ferdinand, *Juvenile Delinquency*, pp. 28–34.

51. Ibid.

52. Ibid.

53. Ibid., p. 31.

54. Ibid., p. 33.

55. Ibid., p. 34. As Cavan and Ferdinand point out, "a relatively small proportion of delinquents falls outside this formulation" of misbehaving nondelinquents and confirmed delinquents. They are "the emotionally disturbed whose delinquency is a response to uncontrollable inner pressures. Such youths may be found, according to Cavan and Ferdinand, "within either the normal culture or the delinquent contraculture." If found in the latter group, however, they often fail "to achieve high status" because of "erratic and unreliable behavior."

56. National Advisory Committee on Criminal Justice Standards and Goals, *Juvenile Justice and Delinquency Prevention*, p. 41.

57. Empey, *American Delinquency*, p. viii.

4
MEASURING OFFICIAL AND UNOFFICIAL DELINQUENCY

M ost criminal justice systems do not and cannot measure delinquency adequately. Yet the majority of current attitudes and concepts concerning delinquency and delinquency prevention are gained from statistical analyses. Indeed, statistical evidence, even when misunderstood or improperly evaluated, is widely accepted as gospel in this country. It is therefore imperative that we examine the flaws inherent in official statistics. Those flaws, the differences between measuring official and unofficial delinquency, and the best ways to utilize delinquency statistics are the subjects of this chapter.

PROBLEMS IN MEASURING
UNOFFICIAL DELINQUENCY

Official delinquency statistics, of course, do not measure unofficial delinquency. Rarely, however, do laymen—or even journalists and media commentators—make this distinction. Ignored or forgotten, as a consequence, is the fact that official delinquency statistics, as gathered and published by the Federal Bureau of Investigation and the National Institute of Juvenile Justice and Delinquency Prevention, describe only those youths who have been arrested or who have been processed through the juvenile justice system.[1] Yet, every year thousands of crimes are committed by youths who are never caught or who are informally handled and diverted away from the juvenile justice system.[2] Because these illegal activities are never recorded, any official measurement of delinquency can only suggest the magnitude and nature of the problem.

Unreported Delinquency

Youths who commit offenses but are never arrested are part of the "iceberg effect" of juvenile crime. Their activities remain outside the framework of official delinquency statistics because their actions are either unobserved, unreported, or handled informally by the community or the police. Most instances of drinking, gambling, fighting, and truancy, for example, are kept secret by the lawbreaking juveniles and their friends. Moreover, more serious FBI crime index offenses, such as forcible rape, robbery, burglary, larceny, and car theft, frequently are not reported to the police because the victims are afraid, embarrassed, lazy, ignorant, or mistrustful of the police and the courts.[3]

These conditions are particularly common in communities dominated by an ethnic group that has little or no representation on the police force or in the city's political power structure. In such neighborhoods the police are often perceived as the enemy, or even as an army of occupation, and the basic information needed to locate and apprehend criminals and delinquents is therefore rarely communicated to them.

Inhabitants who have adequate political power and representation on the police force, however, usually receive appropriate protection from and response to crime problems. Indeed, when youthful misbehavior spills out of underclass neighborhoods into more middle-class areas and threatens the inhabitants' sense of well-being, the power structure usually springs into action. An example of this phenomenon occurred during the 1960s and 1970s when drug abuse—a long-ignored fact of inner city life—burst into the consciousness of mainstream America as middle-class youths began to experiment openly with drugs. As a result, the number of drug possession and trafficking arrests rose dramatically for all classes.[4]

Rape is another crime that was once viewed as being largely endemic to underclass communities, Recently, however, because of the feminist movement and other factors, women of all classes have begun to report sexual assaults to the police. Accordingly, statistics for this crime have shown a sharp increase. Nevertheless, both rape and drug arrest totals have been augmented as much by the increasing demands of the public for a concerted attack against these problems as by actual increases in the number of offenses.[5]

Because of built-in assumptions, prejudices, and inertia, moreover, the justice system tends to concentrate its efforts in under-class areas. What appears to be and usually is reported as a new wave of delinquency in the slums, therefore, is often merely an increase in arrests and record keeping of behavior previously ignored. Indeed, it would appear that as more publicity is given to a certain problem, the greater the problem becomes.[6]

This mirage effect—a spontaneous generation of delinquency statistics where none existed before—can also be seen in every community where police begin to crack down on status offenders. Delinquency statistics seem to materialize out of thin air whenever youths are arrested for offenses that in former years would have been casually handled by the cop on the beat or informally dismissed after "a good bawling out" at the police station. Because the police recorded the arrests of status offenders during the 1960s and 1970s more often than they had in previous years, the official delinquency rates in those years showed a significant rise.[7] How much an actual increase in status offenses contributed to the statistical bubble is difficult to ascertain. An argument could be made, however, that this mirage effect, although a statistical distortion, does cancel some of the countervailing distortions produced by the iceberg effect.[8]

Resolution by Diversion

Clearly, however, unrecorded delinquency is an enormous problem. Most lawbreaking youths, as we have seen, never come to the attention of the police or the courts because their delinquent behavior goes undetected. Still others avoid becoming part of official delinquency statistics because of a diversion process.[9] Diversion, which is the resolution of cases outside the juvenile justice system or during early stages of the juvenile justice process, is widely practiced in this country. It begins informally in the community, where almost 90 percent of all juveniles have performed at least one delinquent act.[10]

Many youths whose offenses are observed by family, friends, neighbors, teachers, or social workers are informally diverted from the juvenile justice system because of the changing cultural norms and evolving social expectations of the community. Fornication, adultery, prostitution, homosexuality, sodomy, and oral sex, for example, have been against the law in almost every state for generations. Enforcement of these laws, however, has grown increasingly lax in recent years as society's views on sexual behavior have become more permissive. Although illegal sexual activity has not diminished during the past few years, available statistical evidence indicates a decline. This statistical drop is a product of alterations in community tolerance, rather than of behavioral or legal changes.[11]

Juvenile delinquency statistics based on arrest records or court records are also distorted by formal diversion processes on the local level. For example, mistrust, incompetence, and vested interests prevent the sharing of information collected by various community agencies, the police, and the courts. Indeed, community agencies have frequently been accused of sending to the FBI whatever "they damn well please."[12] If a community is seeking federal funds, for example, it may report an exaggerated number of crimes to create the illusion that it is in the middle of a crime wave. Likewise, if a community sends accurate figures to Washington after years of neglecting to do so, a similar illusion may be created. In both cases the actual extent of crime may have varied minimally, but the reported statistics will indicate a sharp increase.

The police engage in formal diversion practices in other ways as well. For a variety of reasons, ranging from ineptitude to hostility toward the courts, the police are likely to divert known juvenile offenders as frequently as they detain them.[13] This kind of formal police diversion occurs more often in white middle-class neighborhoods. Take the case of a fourteen-year-old from a white working-class suburb of Detroit who is caught stealing bicycles. The boy is known to the police and so are the parents, who are called to the station house. Without filling out an official arrest form and without filing a petition for court action, the police officers warn the boy and release him to his parents. He is thereby diverted from the juvenile justice system, and his offense is never included in official delinquency statistics.

On the other hand, a black boy is picked up for shoplifting in a large department store in downtown Detroit. He is arrested by the police and immediately taken to the juvenile court's youth home. The intake officer is unable to reach the boy's mother, who is the sole parent, and as a consequence he is admitted to the detention facility. The boy's previous contacts with the police are no worse and no more numerous than the white suburbanite's. Yet, the inner city youth's offense is recorded at the police station and at the juvenile court. Thus, his delinquency becomes part of the official statistics that help reinforce the layman's assumption that black inner city youths are more often delinquent than white suburban youths are.

Inconsistent Local Reporting

In addition to problems of underreporting, overreporting, and diversion, statistics based upon police arrests and court records are unreliable for other reasons. For example, police departments report arrest records to the FBI on a voluntary basis, and not all departments participate. Those that do cooperate do not constitute a carefully chosen or scientifically valid sample of the population, for large urban areas tend to be more responsive and accurate than small towns and rural areas. The FBI Uniform Crime Reports are also flawed in that they do not indicate the number of individuals or repeat offenders involved.

Consequently, when juvenile crime statistics increase, we cannot ascertain whether this increase is caused by rampant delinquency or by recidivism. Moreover, about half of the juveniles arrested are never referred to juvenile court. Among those who are referred to court, a significant proportion are never adjudicated. Of those who are detained and adjudicated on delinquency charges, most are status offenders.[14]

It must be remembered that most local communities—especially suburbs, small towns, and rural areas—are more committed to their own area's interests than to the accuracy of the federal government's reports. Moreover, laws almost everywhere are selectively enforced. Thus, in order to interpret the meaning of official statistics properly, some knowledge of them is required. Without such knowledge, delinquency statistics may be badly misread, and prevention programs designed around the available evidence will be subsequently misdirected and almost certain to fail.[15]

METHODS OF MEASURING UNOFFICIAL DELINQUENCY

Valid information on the amounts and trends of delinquent behavior is difficult to extrapolate from official statistics; for, as we have seen, most offenses are not measured by official arrest and court records. Indeed, the figures represent only the offenses of those youths upon whom the juvenile justice system has focused its attention and been lucky enough to snare in its extremely leaky net. The official record, therefore, reflects the actions and concerns of officials within the system as clearly as it reflects juvenile crime. Because they are aware of these flaws and because they recognize the need to measure the delinquency problem more accurately, social scientists have developed the alternative techniques known as self-reporting and victim accounts.

Self-reporting Accounts

Self-reporting accounts are derived from young people themselves and utilize anonymous questionnaires, interviewing techniques, and simple observation. They therefore differ considerably from official delinquency records, for they measure "law-violating behavior" rather than how the juvenile justice system operates and who is being processed by it. Self-report studies also determine how many children violate the law and why they do it, rather than determining simply the number of arrests or court cases for any given year.[16] As a consequence of self-reporting studies, social scientists have seriously eroded the long-standing assumption that "the inclination to violate the law is more deeply ingrained in the lower-class youngster."[17]

This assumption, as well as others concerning the extent, nature, and social location of delinquency, was and often still is based on ideological and institutional biases that have been fixtures of the juvenile justice system since its inception. Self-report studies have demonstrated that such personal ideological biases as racism, bigotry, intolerance, discrimination, and class consciousness on the part of officials within the juvenile justice system have unfairly stigmatized lower-class, black, and Hispanic-American children. Self-report studies have further revealed that our laws and legal institutions have reinforced these ideological assumptions. Lamar Empey points out that even "well-meaning efforts to remedy the economic, educational, and other problems of the poor and black children" have led to their being "recorded as official delinquents." Thus, "higher official delinquency rates for minority groups and the poor" have been "inevitable."[18]

Self-report findings have done more than point out the built-in inequities of the juvenile justice system. They have also clearly revealed that official delinquency statistics grossly underestimate the extent of lawbreaking activity. Indeed, according to the findings, 90 percent of all offenses are unseen, ignored, or unrecorded.[19] Moreover, self-report studies have concluded that the odds are in favor of lawbreakers getting away with their offenses; that although black youths are more likely to commit serious crimes, delinquent acts occur with considerable frequency among members of all races and classes; that although boys break the law more often, girls are breaking the law at a faster pace, have committed a variety of so-called boys' crimes such as murder, robbery, car theft, burglary, arson, and vandalism, and have even participated in the gang rape of other girls; that although most children commit delinquent acts, most serious delinquency is the product of a small group of recidivists; and although the official juvenile justice system unfairly stigmatizes certain youths, it also tends to apprehend and prosecute the most serious offenders.[20]

Finally self-report studies have thrown new light on those official statistics that demonstrated an ever increasing rate of delinquency in

America during the past two decades. Female delinquency, both self-report and official accounts agree, has indeed risen rapidly. Nevertheless, according to self-reports, the rate of male delinquency—with the exception of alcohol and drug abuse—during these years remained relatively constant. The apparent answer to this discrepancy is improvement in official record keeping and greater police proficiency in the detection of delinquency that previously went undetected or was ignored.[21]

In spite of the invaluable investigative tool they provide for social scientists, self-report studies do have certain limitations. For example, most of the studies have been limited demographically, and so great care must be exercised when generalizing to all youths. Because of the technical difficulties in gathering self-report information, annual reports are almost impossible. Thus, it is difficult to measure or predict trends in delinquent behavior. It is also difficult, if not impossible, to determine the veracity and accuracy of the youths upon whom self-report studies rely. The interview and questionnaire method lends itself to memory distortions, flights of fantasy, misreading of questions, and outright lying. Moreover, the various studies that have been carried out have not contained standardized lists of delinquent acts. Accordingly, comparability suffers somewhat. These limitations, however, are no greater than those of any other method of research into human behavior, and most of the studies support and reinforce one another's findings. Some caution is nevertheless advised when evaluating their significance.[22]

Victim Accounts

Victim accounts of delinquent behavior offer another valuable alternative to official delinquency statistics. In 1965 President Lyndon Johnson created the Commission on Law Enforcement and Administration of Justice; one of its primary tasks was to determine the frequency and extent of crime. Consequently, the commission conducted a survey of 10,000 representative American households in order to obtain a victim account of crime. The participants were asked whether or not they had been victimized and if so, whether the police had been called. They were also asked if their lives had been altered in any significant way as a result of their victimization. The results of these initial victim accounts reinforced self-report studies and demonstrated conclusively that official statistics measured only a fraction of the nation's crime and delinquency. The findings also painted an astonishing picture of a nation gripped with fear and anxiety over personal safety and the quality of American life.[23]

The results of this survey encouraged the accumulation of further victim study accounts. Accordingly, after several years of bureaucratic paralysis and bickering, the United States Bureau of the Census in conjunction with the National Criminal Justice Information and Statistics Service (a new creation of the Law Enforcement Assistance Administration) conducted the first National Crime Survey in 1973. Eventually, this survey gathered information from 125,000 people in 60,000 households and 150,000 businesses across the nation. The specific crimes surveyed were roughly the same as the index crimes measured by the FBI Uniform Crime Reports. But in order to facilitate a better understanding of the nature of criminal victimization, the crimes were divided into three categories: 1) crimes against persons, 2) crimes against households, 3) crimes against commercial establishments.[24]

The results of this exhaustive investigation reinforced the findings of the earlier victim and self-report studies and provided a few surprises as well. For example, the number of victim-reported crimes exceeded police records eight to one. This was expected, but household victimizations were also surprisingly high, equaling or surpassing the instances of a personal attack. The victimization rate for commercial establishments, which was twice as high as that for burglary against households, was even more astonishing.[25]

Some of the other surprises this victim survey revealed, however, were somewhat more reassuring. The chances of the average person becoming a victim in any given year, for instance, proved to be remote. If victimized, this same average person would be more likely to lose money or property than to suffer an assault or robbery of some kind. Thus the survey damaged the long-held assumption that "most crimes are characterized by direct, violent contact between victim and criminal."[26]

The victim survey also shed new light on the relationship between vulnerability and crime. The results demonstrated, for example, that children are more vulnerable than adults and that young adults are more vulnerable than those over the age of thirty. Indeed, the chances of victimization steadily decrease with age. Ironically, our society is designed to protect, prolong, and preserve the blessings of a childhood that in spite of, or perhaps because of, this special treatment is the most vulnerable of all age groups to crime.[27]

It is also ironic that when crimes of violence are tabulated, they show that the vulnerability of males, blacks, poor people, and city dwellers is much higher than it is for females, whites, affluent people, and country dwellers. The most economically depressed and culturally underprivileged members of our society are thus the ones who suffer most from violent crimes. In fact, the survey demonstrated that the most likely victim, especially of a violent crime, is a young black male living in an urban ghetto. This revelation shattered the long-standing white middle-class myth that the lower classes prey upon the people, property, and prosperity of the classes above them.[28]

In addition to dispelling harmful myths, victim surveys provide several other benefits. They furnish better information on victimization numbers than do police records. They also show who is the most likely victim of crime, where most crimes are committed, and the nature of these offenses. In short, victim findings provide greater objectivity in crime reporting, but they also have some serious limitations.

One of the most important limitations of victim surveys is that they do not measure the extent of juvenile involvement in lawbreaking. Victims frequently do not know who burgled their houses or stole their cars, and even when an offender is seen, victims are often unable to judge the culprit's age. Furthermore, juvenile status offenses and cases of neglect and abuse are not measured in victim accounts. Information concerning murder and manslaughter is also not gathered, because interviewable victims do not exist. Nor are drug abuse, gambling, prostitution, and drunkenness measured because in those crimes the perpetrator and the victim are usually the same individuals, and perpetrators rarely turn themselves in. And finally, employee theft, shoplifting, blackmail, and other offenses difficult to document from the victims' standpoint are excluded from victim accounts.[29]

Another important limitation of victim studies is their omission of white-collar crimes, such as embezzlement, bribery, fraud, price fixing, securities swindles, profit gouging, and political corruption. Crimes of the lower clases and of juveniles—robbery, burglary, car theft, and rape, for example—are of course easier to document. By emphasizing such offenses and the people who commit them, however, victim studies tend to reinforce traditional middle-class fears of the under class while ignoring the extent and nature of the more subtle, but no less costly, crimes of the middle and upper classes.

Another limitation of victim studies is the potential for misunderstanding or misinterpreting the language in the information provided by the participants. Discerning truth from fantasy or fear is also a problem. In spite of these and the other shortcomings discussed, however, victim surveys can and will improve our understanding of crime and delinquency. They avoid the screening process that goes into the collection of official statistics, and they provide information and insights that have not been previously available. Accordingly, if used with caution, they can continue to be a valuable tool for the investigation of the nature and extent of delinquency and crime.[30]

METHODS OF MEASURING OFFICIAL DELINQUENCY

Official delinquency is a product of the lawbreaking activities of youths combined with the reaction of the juvenile justice system to those activities. In short, official delinquency does not exist until illegal activity has been detected and recorded.

Cohort Studies

As we have seen, there are several limitations in this method of measuring delinquency. One of the methods currently used by scientists to improve the reliability of delinquency statistics, however, is the cohort study. This is a continuous examination of a group, or cohort, of young people throughout their childhood in order to measure the frequency of delinquency within the group. Consequently, unlike arrest and court records, a cohort study can measure recidivism, as well as the number of delinquent acts for each group.

One of the most famous and important cohort studies was completed in 1972 by three sociologists in Philadelphia.[31] They selected a cohort of close to 10,000 ten-year-old boys and followed the boys' activities until they were eighteen. Then the investigators compared their own records of the cohort's illegal behavior to the officially recorded rates for the same period. The results were enlightening.

Approximately one-third of the boys in the cohort became officially delinquent during the eight years of the study. If we generalize these findings, we may conclude that for every 10,000 boys, at least one-third will be arrested or processed by the juvenile justice system.[32] Of the two-thirds in the cohort study who never had official contacts with the police, most broke the law at one time or another, but simply avoided detection. Thus, the study confirmed what unofficial delinquency measurements have also found, namely that much more illegal activity takes place than is officially recorded.[33]

The study also pointed out, however, that among those who never got caught committing an offense, most were one-time offenders or experimenters who stopped after a few excursions into delinquency. Accordingly, these findings strongly suggested that truly serious offenders, the hard-core recidivists, contributed most heavily to the delinquency rate, but formed a distinct minority in the cohort. Indeed, recidivists committed six times as many crimes as occasional delinquents and nine times as many of the seven serious FBI crime index offenses. They were also responsible for most of the arrests, whether the offenses were status offenses, misdemeanors, or felonies. Yet the recidivists constituted less than 20 percent of the boys in the study.[34]

The significance of recidivism became even clearer when the most chronic of all the offenders were examined. The results revealed that only 6 percent of the total cohort had committed five or more officially recorded delinquent acts. Yet this small group of qualified chronic offenders had been responsible for over 50 percent of all recorded offenses.[35]

Such results would seem to suggest that the juvenile justice system might serve society better by concentrating its attention on chronic offenders. Indeed, it could be argued that by attacking the particular problems of a small minority of American youths, crime in general would be suppressed. The difficulty with this approach, however, is that most chronic recidivists are poor and uneducated youths, blacks, Hispanic Americans, or other members of the under class. We have seen that official delinquency is a result of the actions of juveniles and the ways in which society and the juvenile justice system respond to those actions. Thus we must be extremely careful when analyzing the cohort study results. For, if a society creates a justice system based upon the notion that minority groups and poverty equal crime, we ought not to be surprised to discover that most of the youths drawn into the web of juvenile justice not only violate the law but are also part of the under class.

If the justice system concentrated on a small segment of the juvenile population in order to suppress crime, other problems would also be created. For example, even though recidivists account for half of all the offenses committed, someone is committing the other half. Should we ignore that someone? Should we write off the offenses of the occasional or one-time offender as inconsequential? Clearly a balance must be struck between combating and understanding recidivism among a small minority of young people and dealing with the illegal behavior of other juveniles. Cohort studies demonstrate that status offenses contribute a disproportionate share to the overall delinquency figures. Consequently, the removal of delinquent sanctions for status offenses would undoubtedly aid in achieving the necessary balance. It would also eliminate from the juvenile justice system those who are often unfairly stigmatized and as a consequence drawn into illegal activities that would otherwise be easily avoided.

Official Delinquency Statistics

Official delinquency statistics are seriously flawed, but they are not valueless. They can and do measure the ebb and flow of juvenile crime in general and of specific types of offenses in particular. Accordingly, the remainder of this chapter is devoted to an analysis of the latest figures. See Appendix.

Among the conclusions that can be drawn from the latest FBI Uniform Crime Reports are the following: during a ten-year period ending in 1978 boys committed more serious crimes* than girls did, but the rate of increase for girls was three times that for boys; cities and suburbs contained a much higher percentage of youths charged with serious crimes than did rural areas; and sixteen-year-olds were more likely to become officially delinquent than children of any other age.[36]

The findings also revealed that, among the most serious crimes committed during this ten-year period, instances of aggravated assault had increased most sharply. Among the lesser offenses, drunk driving, stolen property violations, prostitution, and drug abuse sustained respectively the greatest increases in arrests. These results and the others listed above reinforce the findings of self-report studies and victim accounts. They also reflect the broad changes in values and perspectives that occurred among young people during the 1970s.

* The FBI crime index list consists of criminal homicide, forcible rape, robbery, aggravated assault, burglary, and auto theft.

None of this is very surprising. Indeed it tends to confirm the worst fears and predictions of those who at the beginning of that decade warned that the moral fiber of American society was in danger of unraveling. A closer look at the official delinquency statistics, however, reveals some rather encouraging surprises. For example, during the 1970s car thefts, sex offenses (except forcible rape and prostitution), and drunkenness declined significantly. So too did most status offenses.[37]

The most surprising declines, however, occurred between 1974 and 1978. During that four-year period serious crime, as measured by the FBI crime index, declined 6.9 percent for those under the age of eighteen. This is especially significant when compared to the serious crime rate of those eighteen and over, which during the same period rose 7.7 percent. Of the seven major crimes listed in the FBI's index, all declined except aggravated assault, which increased only 1.8 percent.[38] Moreover, when broken down according to sex, the findings show that although the number of boys' arrest records fell faster than that of girls, the girls' rates were also declining significantly.[39]

Serious crime for girls increased in the areas of forcible rape, burglary, and car theft, which indicates that girls continued to explore illegal activity traditionally associated with boys. Nevertheless, the overall violent crime rate for girls declined 6.9 percent, and the property crime* rate declined 4 percent from 1974 to 1978.[40] These findings are reinforced by the Youth Home Admissions statistics gathered by the Wayne County Juvenile Court in Detroit. According to these figures admissions for both sexes declined 18.8 percent between 1976 and 1979, with girls' admissions dropping 28.5 percent and boys' 16.5 percent. Moreover, the number of girls and boys placed on probation that year decreased by 15.5 percent.[41]

In spite of the warnings of the nay-sayers, then, it would appear that there is reason to hope for a continuing decline in official delinquency rates during the 1980s. One of the most hopeful signs is that during the period from 1974 to 1978 arrests for drug violations fell 27.2 percent, which is one of the largest decreases for any of the non–status offense categories.[42] Also encouraging are figures showing that the juvenile share of crime in general fell. Only 23 percent of all persons arrested between 1974 and 1978 were under eighteen,

* Violent crimes are offenses of murder, forcible rape, robbery, and aggravated assault. Property crimes are offenses of burglary, larceny–theft, and motor vehicle theft.

whereas in 1969 the figure was 25 percent. Moreover, in 1978 youths under the age of eighteen constituted 41.9 percent of everyone arrested for serious crimes; in 1969 the figure had been 47.6 percent.[43]

Another surprise in the latest findings—one that is encouraging to city dwellers but discouraging to suburbanites—is that 24.7 percent of all those arrested in cities were juveniles, while in the suburbs the figure was 27.7 percent. The percentages of violent and property crime arrests for youths were also higher in the suburbs than in the cities. Furthermore, although juvenile crime in general was decreasing significantly in cities during the late 1970s, it was rising in the suburbs.[44] The reasons for this turnabout range from more sophisticated and accurate recording methods in the suburbs to the diversion of status offenders in the biggest cities. The most important reason, however, is simple demographics. That is, there are now more young people living in suburbs than in cities. Indeed, demographics help explain some of the other results listed above as well. Juvenile crime rates are declining simply because youths under the age of eighteen now constitute a smaller proportion of the total population than they did throughout most of the 1970s.[45]

Whatever the cause, the decline in official delinquency rates is a welcome trend. This is not to say, of course, that the present levels of juvenile crime are acceptable. Violence remains an integral part of the lives of far too many young Americans. Moreover, there are ominous clouds lurking on the horizon. As the 1980s begin, our country is beset by double-digit inflation, unemployment, rising energy costs, an unfavorable balance of trade, a troubled automobile industry, and an increasing imbalance between the purchasing power of the under class and that of the rest of America. These economic woes, should they continue or worsen, will undoubtedly affect the behavior of juveniles, especially those who have traditionally been the target of the juvenile justice system.

Statistics gathered by the Wayne County Juvenile Court in Detroit, although largely reinforcing the optimistic findings of the FBI Uniform Crime Reports, contain some disturbing figures which suggest that this causal relationship has already begun to develop. For example, the total number of delinquency petitions filed in Wayne County for 1979 increased by 36.7 percent over 1978, and those that alleged robbery, burglary, larceny, or receiving and concealing stolen property increased the most.[46] Because property crimes tend to rise most sharply during times of economic turmoil and because recessions and other economic downturns tend to hit Detroit first and then spread throughout the country, this sudden increase in the number of property crime petitions may be a forecast of a similar increase in delinquency across the nation.

The Wayne County statistics also demonstrate that malicious destruction of property is on the upswing.[47] Since vandalism is often the result of economic frustration and hard times, this may be another portentous sign for delinquency in the 1980s. The Detroit findings, of course, may be only a minor aberration of time and location, but we would be foolish to ignore the nation's economic condition when predicting the future of delinquency.

It would also be foolish not to develop a more comprehensive system for obtaining accurate data. Because of the flaws in the various information-gathering systems currently in use, the methods should be continually evaluated and updated. And, most important, new sources of data should be sought. Otherwise we will continue to lack a complete understanding of the delinquency problem, and delinquency prevention planning will continue to suffer.

The National Advisory Committee on Criminal Justice Standards and Goals recommends that in order to build a proper base of information and statistics "a data collection component should be established in an Office of Delinquency Prevention Planning." Such a data-gathering effort, according to the committee, "would not replace the data collection of the police or the courts, but would augment and coordinate all information sources for prevention."[48] Indeed, the police, the courts, and every other unit, resource, or institution responsible for and able to contribute to the collection of information must develop more descriptive and accurate pictures of the delinquency problems in their communities. With this data, the Office of Delinquency Prevention would be able to reanalyze official delinquency statistics "to determine which children are being served and which children are not being served by current programs."[49]

Obviously the task of obtaining a clear and accurate understanding of the nature of delinquency in any given community is extraordinarily difficult. Not only is delinquency a complex behavioral phenomenon, but it is also inextricably intertwined with attitudes and prejudices that in turn reflect and are reflected by economic, social, and political concerns. As a consequence, before delinquency can be adequately measured and understood we must begin to define delinquent offenses in a way that provides a clearer picture of the nature of delinquent behavior. Thus, the removal of all status offenses from the definition would be extremely useful. We must also be cognizant of the "diversity in community characteristics such as population density, economic levels, ethnic diversity, levels of community organization, and levels of public resources that are available for prevention."[50] And finally, little progress will be made unless we understand more fully the variety of social and personality types among delinquent youths. The following chapter on the cause of delinquency provides a few clues for understanding this problem. Nevertheless, most of the problems and difficulties described above remain unsolved. Consequently, the measurement of delinquency remains inadequate, and our understanding of the problems continues to be murky.

NOTES
CHAPTER FOUR

1. In 1940 the Children's Bureau of the Department of Health, Education and Welfare (HEW) began to publish estimates of the number of delinquency, neglect, and dependency cases being processed in American juvenile courts. In the 1960s the National Institute of Juvenile Justice and Delinquency Prevention, which is part of the Law Enforcement Assistance Administration, assumed the burden of collecting this information. The most publicized statistics, however, are those produced by the FBI, which reports the number of arrests made during a given year in its *Uniform Crime Reports*. See Lamar T. Empey, *American Delinquency: Its Meaning and Construction* (Homewood, Il., 1978), p. 117, and Ruth Shonle Cavan and Theodore N. Ferdinand, *Juvenile Delinquency*, 3d ed. (New York, 1975), p. 37.

2. National Advisory Committee of Criminal Justice Standards and Goals, *Juvenile Justice and Delinquency Prevention: Report of the Task Force on Juvenile Justice and Delinquency Prevention* (Washington, D. C., 1976), p. 27.

3. The complete FBI crime index list is as follows: *criminal homicide*—willful murder and manslaughter by negligence, *forcible rape*—rape or attempted rape by force, *robbery*—stealing or attempted stealing by force, *aggravated assault*—assault with intent to kill or do severe bodily injury, *burglary*—breaking and entering to commit a felony or theft, *larceny-theft*—any theft involving force and violence except auto theft, forgery, etc., *motor vehicle theft*—any theft or attempted theft of a motor vehicle. See United States Department of Justice *FBI Uniform Crime Reports for the United States, 1978* (Washington, D. C., 1979).

4. For the statistics on drug-related arrests for the past two decades, see the appropriate years in the United States Department of Justice, *FBI Uniform Crime Reports for the United States* (Washington, D. C.).

5. See ibid. Also see Empey, *American Delinquency*, pp. 143–44.

6. Ibid.

7. See *FBI Uniform Crime Reports* for the appropriate years' statistics on status offenses.

8. Ibid. (1978), p. 38.

9. The informal resolution of cases at early stages of the juvenile justice system's operations has had a long history in this country. Until the mid-1960s, for example, most of the juvenile courts existed in communities with populations more than 100,000. In the smaller more rural communities youths were seldom arrested and prosecuted for minor offenses because only adult jails and courts were available. Consequently, the police frequently handled juvenile cases informally, thereby diverting youthful lawbreakers away from the juvenile justice system and official delinquency statistics. See Donovan, *Wild Kids*, p. 281. Also see Daniel Katkin, et al, *Juvenile Delinquency and the Juvenile Justice System* (North Scituate, MA., 1976), pp. 132–37.

10. Ibid., p. 133. Also see National Council on Crime and Delinquency, Survey Services, *A Feasibility Study of Regional Juvenile Detention* (Hackensack, N. J., 1971) for the suggestion that almost every child under eighteen years of age in the region studied could be apprehended and placed in detention, since most of them had probably committed at least one delinquent act.

11. Empey, *American Delinquency*, pp. 142–43.

12. Ibid.

13. See Katkin et al., *Delinquency and the Juvenile Justice System* p. 135. Also see James Q. Wilson, *Varieties of Police Behavior* (Cambridge, Mass., 1968); Norman C. Weiner and Charles V. Willie, "Decisions of Juvenile Officers," *American Journal of Sociology* 77 (September, 1971): 199–21; and Jesse R. James and George H. Shepard, "Police Work with Children," *Municipal Police Administration*, George D. Eastman and Esther M. Eastman, eds. (Washington, D. C., 1971), pp. 148–57.

14. Empey, *American Delinquency*, pp. 143–44 and Donovan, *Wild Kids*, p. 281.

15. See Maynard L. Ericson and LaMar T. Empey, "Court Records, Undetected Delinquency, and Decisionmaking," *The Journal of Criminal Law, Criminology, and Police Science* 54 (December, 1963): 456–69; Martin Gold, *Delinquent Behavior in an American City* (Belmont, Calif., 1970); National Commission on the Causes and Prevention of Violence, "American Criminal Statistics: An Explanation and Appraisal," *Crimes of Violence*, Vol. 2 (Washington, D. C., 1969); and Jay R. Williams and Martin Gold, "From Delinquent Behavior to Official Delinquency," *Social Problems* 20 (Fall, 1972): 209–29.

16. See the citations in Note 15 above. Also see Illinois Institute for Juvenile Research, *Juvenile Delinquency in Illinois* (Chicago, 1972); Fred J. Murphy et. al., "The Incidence of Hidden Delinquency," *American Journal of Orthopsychiatry* (October, 1946), pp. 686–96; Nels Christie et al., "A Study of Self Reported Crime," *Scandinavian Studies in Criminology*, II (London, 1965); and R. Elmhorn, "A Study in Self Reported Delinquency among School Children in Stockholm," *Scandinavian Studies in Criminology*, II (London, 1965). Also see Empey, *American Delinquency*, pp. 141–64 and Martin Gold and Donald J. Reimer, "Changing Patterns of Delinquent Behavior among Americans 13–16 Years Old: 1967–1972," *National Survey of Youth, Report No. 1* (Ann Arbor, 1974).

17. See Albert K. Cohen, *Delinquent Boys: The Culture of the Gang* (New York, 1955) and Richard A. Cloward and Lloyd E. Ohlin, *Delinquency and Opportunity: A Theory of Delinquent Gangs* (New York, 1960). Also see Empey, *American Delinquency*, pp. 146–63.

18. Ibid., p. 162.

19. Ericson and Empey, "Court Records, Undetected Delinquency and Decision-making," *Journal of Criminal Law* 54 (December, 1963): 465; Williams and Gold, "From Delinquent Behavior to Official Delinquency," *Social Problems* 20 (Fall, 1972): 221–22.

20. The odds remain, nevertheless, on the side of the offender; see the citations for Note 16.

21. Gold and Reimer, "Changing Patterns of Delinquent Behavior among Americans 13–16 Years Old: 1967–1972," *National Survey of Youth, Report No. 1* (Ann Arbor, Mich., 1974), pp. 13–29. Also see Empey, *American Delinquency*, pp. 163–64; Gary Jensen and Raymond Eve, "Sex Differences in Delinquency," *Criminology* 13 (Feb 1976): 427–48.

22. Empey, *American Delinquency*, pp. 161–62.

23. See the President's Commission on Law Enforcement and Administration of Justice, *The Challenge of Crime in a Free Society* (Washington, D. C., 1967), and the President's Commission on Law Enforcement and Administration of Justice, *Task Force Report: Crime and Its Impact—An Assessment* (Washington, D. C., 1967). Also see Phillip H. Ennis, *Criminal Victimization in the United States: A Report of a National Survey* (University of Chicago, National Opinion Research Center, 1967), p. 9.

24. National Criminal Justice Information and Statistics Service, *Criminal Victimization in the Untied States, 1973* (Washington, D. C., Law Enforcement Assistance Administration, 1975).

25. Ibid., pp. 1–23. Also see the United States Department of Justice, *FBI Uniform Crime Reports for the United States, 1973* (Washington, D. C., 1974).

26. See Empey, *American Delinquency*, p. 178, and the National Criminal Justice Information and Statistics Service, *Criminal Victimization in the U.S., 1973*, pp. 1–23.

27. *Criminal Victimization*, p. 15.

28. For the victimization rates of crimes against persons, see ibid., pp. 14–16. For more information on, and the results of, victim surveys, see National Criminal Justice Information and Statistics Service (NCJISS), "Typical Crime Victim Is Young, Poor, and Black," *LEAA Newsletter* (Dec. 4, 1974), pp.1, 5; NCJISS, *Crimes and Victims: A Report on the Dayton–San Jose Pilot Survey of Victimization* (Washington, 1974); NCJISS, *Criminal Victimization Surveys in the Nation's Five Largest Cities* (Washington, 1975); and NCJISS, *Criminal Victimization in the United States: A Comparison of 1973 and 1974 Findings* (Washington, D. C. Law Enforcement Assistance Administration, 1976).

29. Empey, *American Delinquency*, p. 170.

30. Ibid., pp. 120–72. Also see National Advisory Commission on Criminal Justice Standards and Goals, "Victimization Surveying: Its History, Uses, and Limitations," *Report on the Criminal Justice System* (Washington, D. C., 1973).

31. Marvin E. Wolfgang, Robert Figlio, and Thorsten Sellin, *Delinquency in a Birth Cohort* (Chicago, 1972).

32. Ibid., p. 54.

33. Ibid., pp. 112–18.

34. Ibid., pp. 65–71.

35. Ibid. For another cohort study that supports these findings in small-town America, see Center for Studies of Crime and Delinquency, *Teenage Delinquency in Small Town America: NIMH Research Report, 5* (Washington, D. C., 1974).

36. United States Department of Justice, *FBI Uniform Crime Reports for the United States, 1978* (Washington, D. C., 1979), pp. 184–228. Pages 186–196 are reproduced in the Appendix.

37. By the percentage rates of 23.7, 21.8, and 32.9 respectively. See ibid., p. 188.

38. Ibid., p. 190.

39. There was a 7.5 percent decline for boys and a 4.1 percent decline for girls. See ibid., p. 191.

40. Ibid.

41. Statistics furnished by Peter Fournier, Data Control Department, Wayne County Juvenile Court, 1025 E. Forest, Detroit, Mich. 48207.

42. *FBI Uniform Crime Reports, 1978*, p. 190.

43. Ibid., p. 188.

44. Ibid., pp. 202, 211. Rural juvenile arrests were fewer in number than city or suburban arrests for almost all offenses.

45. Ibid., p. 185.

46. "Charges on Delinquency Petitions Filed During 1977, 1978, & 1979," Data Control Department, Wayne County Juvenile Court, Detroit, Mich.

47. Malicious destruction of property petitions increased 85.3 percent between 1978 and 1979. Ibid.

48. National Advisory Committee on Criminal Justice Standards and Goals, *Juvenile Justice and Delinquency Prevention; Report of the Task Force on Juvenile Justice and Delinquency Prevention* (Washington, D. C., 1976), p. 37.

49. Ibid., p. 39.

50. Ibid., p. 40.

5
CAUSES OF DELINQUENCY

O ver the past two hundred years everything from chemical imbalances in the brain to imbalances in societal organization has been blamed for delinquent behavior. Biogeneticists, sociologists, psychologists, Marxists, and a host of social scientists and commentators have developed delinquency theories based on a wide variety of assumptions concerning the nature of human beings and their environment. Unfortunately, most of these theorists have failed to provide the means by which their concepts could be realistically tested. Those who have developed methods of testing either have not followed up on the results thoroughly enough to dispel all doubts or have produced results that deny the original theoretical assumptions. Most of them have also isolated one single dominant factor as the most significant cause of delinquency. They have therefore often ignored the overwhelming evidence that, because of the complexity and varied nature of causative factors, no single theory can explain all crime and delinquency, nor indeed can a single cause of delinquency be said to apply in all cases. Still, theories of causation are useful and necessary, for they provide insights into the nature of delinquency as well as the ways society has viewed the problem over time. Accordingly, this chapter is devoted to an examination of the strengths and weaknesses of the most important theories of delinquency.

CLASSICAL AND BIOGENETIC THEORIES

Cesare Beccaria (1735–1794), among other eighteenth century criminologists, helped formulate the classical school of thought concerning the origins of crime. This eighteenth century school postulated that human beings have free will, possess reason, and are capable of choice. As a consequence of these innate capacities, the classicists argued, criminals are basically no different from "normal" members of society. Indeed, crimes are committed not because of unusual forces or circumstances, but because of the offenders' own free will. Accordingly, Beccaria and the others believed that punishments should include not only incarceration but also contemplation so that offenders could "unwill" the commission of future crimes. Moreover, they believed that punishment should be the same regardless of an offender's circumstances or mental condition. Such concepts were widely accepted at the time, and, as a result, fixed sentences were often adopted, utilized, and supported.[1]

Lombrosian Theory

The classical school began to lose favor in the nineteenth century, however, as biogenetic theories emerged. These new theories promoted the idea that criminal children inherited the anatomical or genetic weaknesses of their parents. The first and best known of the biogenetic theorists was Cesare Lombroso (1835–1909). Borrowing liberally from contemporary Darwinian ideas, Lombroso asserted that approximately one-third of all criminals, both juvenile and adult, were unevolved atavistic beings who behaved more like primitive ape-like creatures than fully evolved modern men. The essence of his theory can be summed up as follows:

1. Law violators are a distinct physical type at birth.
2. Law violators can be recognized by certain stigmata such as a long lower jaw, an abnormal nose, bulbous lips, ape-like arms, wrinkles, and peculiar sex organs, which are characteristic of a primitive form of evolutionary development.
3. Such stigmata or physical distortions do not cause crime but enable identification of criminal types.
4. Born criminals can be controlled only through severe social intervention.[2]

Lombroso developed his ideas after observing and examining inmates in Italian prisons, but he never tested his theories empirically by comparing criminals to noncriminals. Nevertheless, his concepts dominated European and American criminology during the second half of the nineteenth century. Indeed, Lombrosian ideas continued to dominate until 1913 when Charles Goring, an English prison doctor, used the evidence gathered from 3,000 case histories to demonstrate that Lombroso's "criminal man" simply did not appear often enough.[3] A decade later, another Englishman, Cyril Burt, determined that physical differences did in fact exist between delinquents and the general population, but that these differences were attributable to socioeconomic factors such as diet, hygiene, and poverty.[4]

Lombroso's theories were also refuted by identical-twin research carried out in Denmark between 1890 and 1910. These studies revealed that if one twin became delinquent, the chances were one in three that the other one would as well. Two-thirds of the twins studied, however, did not become criminal when or after their identical siblings did, so Lombroso's biogenetic theories suffered. For, according to Lombrosian concepts, if one identical twin was criminal the other one also had to be criminal. Nevertheless, the twin studies did demonstrate that heredity, if not the dominant factor, clearly played a role in certain kinds of criminal behavior. Otherwise the high correlation among identical twins would not have been almost three times as great as it was for fraternal twins.[5]

The Chromosomalists

In spite of research done in England, Denmark, and elsewhere that refuted Lombrosian ideas, biological and genetic theories did not disappear entirely. They resurfaced in the work of Ernest Hooten, William H. Sheldon, and the "chromosomalists." Hooten, for example, after "anthropometrically" comparing thousands of prisoners with a smaller group of civilians, declared that criminal behavior was, in fact, induced by biological inferiority. Certain types of physically defective persons committed particular crimes, and members of different races and ethnic groups committed characteristic offenses. Moreover, Hooten concluded, environment's role in criminality was negligible when compared to biologically inherited character flaws and physical defects.[6]

Although Hooten's findings, as well as his research methods, were ridiculed and largely rejected,[7] William H. Sheldon continued the biological quest. Combining the findings of Lombroso, Hooten, and others, Sheldon developed the body classifications of endomorph, mesomorph, and ectomorph to explain tendencies toward criminal behavior. He claimed that people with rotund, or endomorph, bodies tend to be jovial and gregarious; those who have muscular, or mesomorph, bodies are usually aggressive, competitive and energetic; and small and skinny, or ectomorph, people are often shy, introverted loners. Sheldon argued that delinquents and criminals demonstrated mesomorph characteristics more than they did the other two and that offenders in general are more openly aggressive, competitive, and driven than nonoffenders.[8]

Sheldon's findings, like previous biogenetic studies, did not find favor among most social scientists. Contradictions, superficialities, gross generalizations, and outright error were found in Sheldon's work, and his theories, as a consequence, were largely dismissed.[9] Nonetheless, biogenetics revived and received considerable publicity recently when a few studies revealed that offenders and nonoffenders often have differing chromosomal structures.[10]

Chromosomes are the structural carriers of our hereditary characteristics. They appear microscopically as a linear arrangement of genes, the factors that determine the inherited characteristics of all living organisms. Sexuality, among other traits, is determined at the moment of conception by the arrangement and combination of genes in the fertilized egg. These genes, which are carried in every living cell, clearly resemble the letters X and Y. Every female has two X chromosomes, whereas every male has one X chromosome and one Y chromosome. If a sperm cell contains the X chromosome at the moment of fertilization, an XX combination will form, and the baby will be a girl. If the sperm carries a Y chromosome, an XY combination will form, and the baby will be a boy.[11]

Beginning in the early 1940s scientists began to detect abnormal combinations of chromosomes that produced deformed, retarded, or mongoloid children. Then in 1961 scientists discovered the XYY combination in a man who had been producing malformed offspring.[12] This discovery stimulated further study, and by the late 1960s researchers were claiming that those few men who had the extra Y chromosome were much more likely to become criminally insane than normal males were.[13]

Research has continued on the "chromosomal man," but it remains sketchy and inconclusive. What is certain is that the XYY syndrome does not explain criminality.[14] Nevertheless, it cannot be dismissed outright, for even if the extra Y chromosome theory has only marginal value, it still helps us to understand the behavior of a few delinquents and criminals. Indeed, even though all of the biogenetic theories have fallen short as explanations of crime, they remain important, if only because they have stimulated research that has been productive and enlightening.

The Positivists

One of the greatest contributions made to the study of crime by the biogeneticists has been the founding of the "positive school" of criminology. Lombroso and others who followed him used criminals rather than criminal law as their basic frame of reference. They concentrated, in short, on the behavioral and environmental elements of offenders' lives rather than on the criminal justice system. Positivists rejected the classicists' view of free will and instead emphasized personal and environmental determinism. They also viewed delinquents and criminals as decidedly different from normal members of society. Indeed, positivists considered offenders to be sick, to have fallen victim to forces and situations within their personalities, families, and society over which they had no control. According to the positivists, if delinquents and criminals could somehow be made to understand their psychological and sociological disorders, they could be successfully treated. Most modern theories of delinquency and crime continue to subscribe to this basic positivist assumption.[15]

The positive school is also responsible in large measure for the heavy emphasis modern social scientists place on empirical evidence and on the collection of sensory data. Positivists looked disapprovingly upon "knowledge" based on faith, intuition, or pure reason, as do modern social scientific researchers regardless of their discipline. Thus, although Lombroso's theories were incorrect, he and the other positivists were responsible for the application of scientific methodology to the study of human behavior, and this contribution of the positive school must be acknowledged.

SOCIOLOGICAL THEORIES

Sociology is the behavioral science that examines groups, communities, and societies. Sociologists consider themselves scientific positivists, and they share with the earlier positivists described above the assumption that delinquents are different from nondelinquents. According to sociological theory, the deciding factor in determining who becomes an offender and who does not, however, is environmental influence on the individual and not, as the earlier positive school believed, genetic inheritance. Thus, sociologists focus their attention on evolving attitudes and values and attempt to determine how these characteristics are modified by current experiences.[16]

The branch of sociology best suited to the study of delinquent and criminal behavior is social psychology, for sociologists working in this field consider both social and psychological factors in relation to crime and its causes. They have been diligently searching for solutions to the problem for the past half-century, and they have developed a diversity of explanations which, although contributing greatly to our understanding of delinquency, have sometimes contradicted one another. One reason for this has been the tendency to set up each major theoretical orientation against the others to determine which is the true explanation. The competing perspectives have been described in dozens of ways, but essentially the major theories can be broken down into three categories: strain theory, subculture theory, and control theory.

Strain Theory

Strain theory postulates that youths become delinquent because of the frustration of experiencing or anticipating failure. For such juveniles, discrepancies exist between the aspirations and goals society promotes and their own realistic expectations. Their learned goals and needs cannot be met legitimately, for normal avenues of social mobility and economic success are closed to them. This condition produces the frustration, anxiety, and anger that cause the "strained" youths not only to obtain illegally the material possessions society has taught them are essential, but also to strike out against the source of their anguish.[17]

The original strain theorists, such as Robert K. Merton, assumed that delinquent children were usually the products of lower-class environments. In 1938 Merton made the following observations concerning juvenile offenders:

1. Aspirations are approximately the same in all social classes.
2. Expectations are reduced among lower-class adolescents because of their disadvantages in the competition for educational, occupational, and economic success.
3. The pressure toward delinquency is proportional to the discrepancy between aspirations and expectations.
4. Delinquent behavior is therefore primarily a lower-class phenomenon.[18]

Richard A. Cloward and Lloyd E. Ohlin, writing in 1960, reinforced this assumption of greater lower-class deviance. They also pointed out that children from deprived socioeconomic environments face a constant struggle to avoid the opportunities, temptations, and peer group pressures to engage in antisocial behavior. Cloward and Ohlin often cited Albert Cohen's research, which had been published a few years earlier and which attempted to explain the higher percentage of lower-class lawbreakers by promoting the concept of "status deprivation"—in other words, they said that lower-class youths have the deck stacked against them from the start because of deficient socialization, middle-class educational biases, and constant exposure to the "American dream of success." Cloward, Ohlin, and Cohen therefore agreed that, as a result of these conditions, attitudes, and deprivations, lower-class youths experience status frustration, or strain, which often is converted into delinquent behavior.[19]

Subculture Theory

The emphasis that strain theorists place on lower-class delinquency is shared by subculture theorists; in fact, Cohen, Cloward, and Ohlin promoted both theories. A number of other social scientists, such as Edwin Sutherland and Walter Miller, have also contributed to subculture theory. And, although their jargon and emphases differ, they all seem to agree that "affiliation" is the determining factor in delinquency. Indeed, according to subculture theory, juveniles are lured into delinquency by the glittering expectations of greater peer acceptance. Thus, deviance is viewed as conformity to the antisocial norms, expectations, and attitudes of one's peer group, or subculture.[20]

Cohen, for example, argues that a youth gang often creates norms that prescribe delinquent behavior. Gangs, therefore, become subcultures characterized by negativistic, malicious, and nonutilitarian behavior. Middle-class norms, values, and expectations are consciously flouted and ridiculed, and the members of the gang form ever stronger bonds of camaraderie as they move further away from socially acceptable behavior.[21] Miller agrees with Cohen and adds that lower-class culture in general is distinctly different from middle-class culture. According to Miller, the two classes "are to an important degree different worlds, with different emphases, different values, different bases of concern, and different definitions of reality."[22]

Edwin Sutherland, perhaps the most systematic and comprehensive of the subculture theorists, also considers delinquency to be a direct result of affiliation. He promotes the concept of "differential association," which states the following:

1. Criminal behavior is learned.
2. Criminal behavior is learned in interaction with other persons in the process of communication.

Causes of Delinquency

3. The learning of criminal behavior occurs principally within intimate personal groups.

4. Learned criminal behavior includes not only techniques for committing often complicated crimes, but also a convoluted value system that provides motivation, rationalization, and legitimacy.

5. This value system is learned from perceptions of legal codes as favorable or unfavorable. In American society the perceptions are often mixed, creating cultural conflict with legal codes.

6. A youth becomes delinquent because of an excess of perceptions favorable to violation of law.

7. Differential association may vary in frequency, duration, priority, and intensity.

8. The process of learning criminal behavior by association of criminal patterns involves all of the mechanisms that are involved in any other learning.[23]

This theory of differential association is rooted in the assumption that delinquency is learned later in life rather than induced in infancy. It is only when normal and mentally healthy children interact with "significant others" in their environment that criminal behavior surfaces. Most youths at one time or another bend society's rules to please or impress people they like, admire, or respect. The degree to which they are willing to do this, however, and the concomitant satisfaction, pleasure, or status that is differentially associated with their actions determines the extent of their ultimate criminal or antisocial behavior. Children who grow up in slums and who are forced to attend inferior schools, for example, are much more likely to interact with, and desire the friendship of, delinquent peer groups or older antisocial individuals who have some status in the predominant subculture. In short, emerging delinquents strive for money, status, and happiness just like everyone else, but the values, aspirations, and attitudes that have been inculcated in them as a result of their strongest personal relationships have taught them illegal rather than legal methods of satisfying their needs and reaching their goals.[24]

One of the weaknesses of strain and subculture theories in general and of Sutherland's concept in particular is that they do not offer satisfactory explanations of middle- and upper-class delinquency. Nor do these theories explain why most lower-class youths, who are apparently vulnerable to the same deprivations, forces, temptations, and pressures as those who become delinquent, manage to avoid lives of crime. Moreover, the few studies that have examined middle-class delinquents generally depict such youths as "disturbed" and lower-class delinquents as "normal."[25] Thus, the common implication of strain and subculture theories is not only that there is more delinquency within the under class, but that "qualitatively different processes lead to delinquent behavior, depending on social class position."[26]

Official statistics, police records, and court records support the claim that delinquency is predominantly a lower-class phenomenon. But, as we have seen, such records tell us more about society's reaction to delinquent acts than they do about the nature of those acts. Moreover, as Travis Hirschi observed in 1969, "Careful quantitative research shows again and again that the relation between socioeconomic status and the commission of delinquent acts is small or nonexistent.[27] Hirschi's views have been supported by the most recent investigations, which have tested communities of various sizes, both boys and girls, numerous types of offenses, and diverse locations.[28]

These recent studies also revealed that the vast majority of American juveniles commit at least one chargeable offense. Yet most youths do not become delinquents, and fewer still become involved in repetitive offending patterns.[29] Evidence of extensive but episodic delinquent behavior seriously damages the strain and subculture theorists' assumptions that deprived and oppressed children are driven or drawn into careers of crime. To be sure, some recent findings have suggested that the types of offenses committed by youths vary systematically according to socioeconomic status and area of residence,[30] and this evidence does complicate the problem somewhat. Nevertheless, it is clear that social class by itself is not the principal cause of delinquency. Indeed, the most that can be said, strain and subculture theories to the contrary notwithstanding, is that the class of a neighborhood, especially in the case of the large urban lower-class slum area, probably does generate a certain type of gang delinquency.[31] But no conclusive evidence exists to support the theory that frustrations derived from anticipated career failures or pressures from peer group associations drive adolescents to delinquent behavior.[32]

Control Theory
Control theory, the third major sociological orientation of delinquency causation, does not focus on social class or peer groups, for it is not concerned with motivational theories. Both strain and subculture the-

ories are constructed on the assumption that the disposition to deviate "(a) derives from certain interpersonal or social conditions, (b) is essentially a permanent aspect of the personality or value framework of the individual, and (c) propels the person into illegal behavior."[33] Control theory, however, assumes that all children are at birth impulsive, self-centered, unable to control themselves, and devoid of any sense of social responsibility. It also assumes that the tendency to be delinquent is inherited. As a consequence, control theorists are less concerned with knowing why children become delinquent than with discovering why it is that some refrain from becoming delinquent.[34]

According to the most prominent control theorists, all juveniles attempt to form social bonds with conventional society, and in the process they develop varying degress of conformity to the rules, regulations, values, attitudes, and laws of that society. The potential for delinquency diminishes as youths are controlled by their attachment to and desire for parental love and approval, educational success and advancement, extracurricular and career-advancing activities, and the values and norms of conventional society. Thus, control theorists consider delinquency to be the result of declining or nonexistent social restraints. In short, once society's natural controls are relinquished or modified, once adolescents are freed from constraints, deviant behavior inevitably follows.[35]

Unlike strain and subculture theories, control theory examines irrational and situational rather than environmental aspects of deviant acts. That is, control theorists focus their attention on the dynamics of what Clarence Schrag describes as "the interactional processes by which people move toward and beyond the brink of deviant behavior."[36] According to Schrag and other control theorists, it is an uncommon occurrence when a juvenile decides to commit a crime and then sets forth on a committed course of action to implement that decision. Indeed, delinquency is not activated because the pull of delinquent associates or social class influences demands it, but because internal control, or conscience, or belief in the moral validity of social norms becomes inoperative.[37]

Given these assumptions, it is not surprising that control theory views official apprehension and the perceived risk of apprehension as major deterrents for youths considering illegal behavior. Subculture theory, on the other hand, assumes that peer group approval will supersede and take precedence over fears of official sanctions. And strain theory presumes that because of the frustration and anxiety created by blocked opportunities, the risk of official apprehension becomes only incidental in the decision-making process. Control theory, however, considers a youth's "image" and future goals an even more powerful, though less obvious deterrent than the fear of official sanctions. In fact, control theory turns strain and subculture theories inside out by arguing that most juveniles refrain from delinquency "because of the likelihood of its visibility to close associates who would disapprove and because of the negative implications of categorization as delinquent for institutional ties and future success chances."[38]

Control theories tend to be more amenable to testing than the other theories. They also pay more attention to the role of childhood and the status of children in American culture. Moreover, control theorists have gathered more empirical evidence to support their claims than have the other two groups of theorists. Nevertheless, the assumptions that control theorists make about human nature and the social order—that all people are disposed to violence and misbehavior and that only society's structure and cohesion prevent people's baser instincts from dominating—are not fully supported by the available evidence and thus are not fully persuasive. Furthermore, as LaMar Empey observes, "The assumptions that 'control theories' make about human nature and social order are open to other interpretations; many questions remain unanswered about the role of subcultural and peer group influences outside the family and school; and the overall effects of social change require consideration."[39] And finally, control theories, like the others discussed so far, have failed to develop a practical and workable plan of delinquency prevention and control. This would seem to indicate that all these sociological theories remain just that—theories.

PSYCHOLOGICAL AND PSYCHOANALYTIC THEORIES

Psychologists have not devoted as much time and energy to the study of delinquency as have sociologists. In fact, delinquency and criminality did not emerge as a unique field of study for psychologists until recently. And even now, when psychologists examine the problems of juvenile offenders, they do so because they perceive delinquency to be a manifestation of the more critical dilemma of "mental illness." Nevertheless, psychologists have published a considerable body of literature on delinquency, and their theories are worth exploring.

Psychologists and psychologically oriented criminologists consider delinquency and criminality to be the result of serious imbalances or conflicts in the personalities of individuals. Accordingly, they see offending behavior as a symptom that offenders are different from, at odds with, or opposed to the values and mores of their groups. According to most psychologists, offenders are not only violators of the law but deviants from the moral sensibilities of those who are closest to them. In short, psychologists view delinquents as individuals with twisted personalities that act as catalysts for deviant behavior and alienate such youths from their immediate social environment.[40]

Like sociologists, psychologists do not, as a group, emphasize the same areas of investigation, and wide differences of opinion can be found within their ranks. Indeed, some psychologists are more sociologically oriented than sociologists, and vice versa. Nevertheless, the psychologists who have contributed the most to our understanding of delinquency causation have been those who are grouped loosely in the psychoanalytic school.

Sexual Repression

Psychoanalytic theory, which is based upon Freudian principles, posits that emotional conflicts lead to delinquency and that these conflicts can be diagnosed and treated. According to those psychologists who support psychoanalytic theory, children exhibit three general personality patterns that signal emotional conflict and that lead to delinquency unless altered.[41] The first of these patterns is associated with repressed sexuality. For example, children who are severely punished for demonstrating any signs of sexual curiosity or experimentation often repress their desires to such an extent that their sexual feelings become sublimated; that is, their sexual needs become unconscious but are nevertheless expressed in other forms of behavior. When such children become adolescents, their sexual longings surface even more vigorously, but their abhorrence and fear of such feelings do not diminish. As a result, the sublimations of these extremely disturbing sensations often take the form of aggression, hostility, antisocial behavior, and ultimately delinquency.[42]

Psychologists point out that although the personalities of such sexually repressed juveniles may be perfectly well adjusted in other areas, the intensity of their unconscious sexual needs is so powerful that it often causes impulsive behavior and thus interferes with normal adaptive processes. Depending on the repression and level of sublimation, psychologists assert, this impulsive behavior usually manifests itself in a wide range of behaviors from exhibitionism to window-peeping. These manifestations of delinquent aberrations are annoying and somewhat disturbing, but their intent is generally not destructive or malicious, and the youths involved are frequently sorry and embarrassed. According to psychoanalytic theory, however, until these youths understand and relate to their sexual sublimations, their bizarre behavior will continue.[43]

Unsocialized Aggression and Overindulgence

The second pattern of behavior that leads to delinquency, according to many psychoanalytic theorists, can be traced to a youth's conscious motives. For example, many youngsters have difficulty expressing what is on their minds, because of their exposure to extremely intense hostility emanating either from their parents, siblings, peers, or from all these sources. As a consequence, such children develop highly aggressive behavioral patterns. Then, as they become adolescents, they not only become unmanageable and antisocial, but also extremely volatile and thus dangerous. Such "malevolent transformations" produce only hatred and maliciousness; as these youths mature physically, their potential destructiveness increases accordingly. Indeed, their behavior increasingly consists of unprovoked, impulsive assaults on others. Thus, they are described by psychoanalytic psychologists as "unsocialized aggressive children."[44]

Overindulged children, ironically, may exhibit similar patterns of behavior. According to psychoanaltyic theorists, when children become extremely attached to one parent at the expense of the other, they often do not acquire the inner discipline necessary for the acceptance of criticism or opposition. Consequently, when they are confronted by frustrating social experiences or when their perception of their special condition in life is not confirmed outside their parental relationship, they often become enraged. As long as such youths are admired, or liked, their behavior remains normally docile. When they meet resistance or rejection, however, their inner turmoil rushes to the surface and explodes in violence directed at their "tormentors." The theorists point out that such youths are natural exploiters of others. Thus they often encounter resistance and soured relationships, and this increases their hostility and alienation and produces walking time bombs.[45]

Clearly, not all overindulged youths become violent or delinquent, and psychologists do not suggest this. What they do say, however, is that, although the delinquency of such youths does mirror the disorganization of their homes, their behavior often extends far beyond the patterns established in the family. The family patterns trigger a tendency or predilection within the personalities of these juveniles. Some respond and adjust in socially acceptable ways. Others turn to violence and delinquency. Thus, "from the standpoint of psychoanalytic theory the 'structure' of the personality is every bit as important as the environment in fixing personality development, and it is an oversimplification to suggest that an individual's attitudes and motives will inevitably reflect the values and norms of his social groups—especially when delinquents are the focus."[46]

Impaired Ego Function

The third recognizable pattern of behavior that can develop into delinquency is associated with the ego functions of juveniles. Youths afflicted with low self-esteem or an "inferiority complex," for example, often confront the extremely difficult adolescent years with a sense of social impotence. Moreover, psychoanalytic psychologists point out that such juveniles, even if gifted, doubt their abilities and strengths and are attracted to and seduced by the whims and trends of their peers. In short, they tend to drift, and this drifting creates an even greater sense of emptiness and incompetence; then their identities, weak to begin with, become ever more amorphous.[47]

According to psychoanalytic theorists, children with impaired ego functions typically emerge from families that, although intact, are often stressful and discordant. Contradictory standards and mixed signals concerning appropriate behavior frequently create a constant sense of tension, and such familial inconsistencies also tend to diminish or retard a strong sense of self among the children. As a result, they are often antagonistic toward all adults, resentful of their more self-assured peers, and thus isolated, alienated, and often extremely hostile. Unable to express their hostility toward their parents overtly because of their overwhelming feelings of inadequacy, they strike out in more subtle but nevertheless attention-provoking actions such as maliciousness, theft, sexual promiscuity, or worse. Their goal is to inflict psychological wounds upon their parents, to embarrass them, and to punish them in a sense for their improper parenting.[48]

In the long run, this kind of behavior complicates the lives of the offending adolescents more than it serves their interests, for it prevents them from forming normal social bonds with nondelinquent peer groups. Psychoanalytic psychologists reason that the delinquency of these youths is not only "an expression of inner confusion brought on by a contradictory and defeating social environment,"[49] but also behavior that precludes acceptance into "normal" society. Erik Erikson, for example, points out that, because "ego diffusion" results whenever youths, for whatever reasons, fail to develop self-confidence and a well-defined purpose, the formation of bonds with their immediate peers and the acquisition of a legitimate self-concept is at first inhibited and then prevented. Accordingly, youths are unable to relate positively to their social environment and thus are also unable to adopt their peer groups' values.[50]

Unable to find direction within the family, and excluded from normal peer group relationships and values, these ego-diffused juveniles often turn to delinquent groups for identity and purpose. When a delinquent identity is formed, some of the problems of ego impairment are solved, just as normal teenagers find consolation and a stronger sense of self within their peer groups. But there are significant problems created as well. For example, although delinquent youths may be thoroughly accepted by other delinquents, society as a whole scorns them. As a consequence, the bonding within a delinquent group is often much stronger and frequently more permanent than in normal groups. This is so because the members need one another's strength, approval, and reinforcement in order to prevail against society's condemnation. They therefore resist giving up this support and identity, even after they are no longer adolescents. Indeed, their delinquent bonds are often merely exchanged for the bonds of the criminal subculture.[51]

All of the psychoanalytic theories discussed above are relevant to the study of the causes of delinquency. Social scientists from a variety of disciplines have described delinquent types that fit squarely into the molds fashioned by psychoanalytic theorists. Clearly, then, the personality patterns revealed by psychologists do exist and do play a role in generating delinquency by some adolescents at some times. These patterns appear to be very useful when describing and explaining primitive, unself-conscious patterns of behavior or the behavior of those individuals who have undergone extensive testing, observation, and analysis. Psychoanalytic theories are also especially helpful in understanding two types of delinquents: (1) those who commit unusual crimes and (2) those offenders who behave in a persistent and especially troublesome manner.[52]

Psychoanalytic theories have serious shortcomings as general explanations of delinquency, however. Their major flaw is the same one affecting sociological theories—a paucity of scientific evidence. Some social scientists go so far as to reject psychoanalytic claims and notions about psychopathy as untestable. They argue that "the mass of studies which have searched for these severe emotional disturbances have failed to find them." Indeed, it would appear that "delinquents are no more or less ridden with personality pathology than are nonoffenders."[53] Moreover, as Ruth Shonle Cavan notes, the more complex forms of behavior, "particularly those which depend upon shared values, reciprocal responsibilities or self-conscious deliberations" are beyond the scope of psychoanalytic theories.[54]

Another significant problem with psychological theories is that they tend to be imprecise when differentiating between the patterns of emotional conflict and the specific traits of delinquents. As a consequence, it becomes difficult to distinguish delinquents from the mentally ill. To be sure, many delinquents are emotionally disturbed, but many more are not. Conversely, most emotionally disturbed or mentally ill children do not become delinquents. Furthermore, not all behavior is determined by childhood experiences. Environment can and does play a role, but many psychoanalytic theorists fail to take this into consideration, thereby ignoring a vast body of relevant data and variables.[55]

CONTAINMENT THEORY

A few social scientists have successfully attempted to blend together the salient features of psychological and sociological theories. Walter

C. Reckless, for example, has developed a "containment theory" to explain both conforming and deviant behavior. According to this theory, most juveniles manage to contain their passions and emotions through processes of both inner and outer control. When such control systems are balanced properly, conformity results. When the equilibrium is disturbed, deviance is usually the result. Reckless assumes that "strong inner and reinforcing out containment constitutes an isolation against . . . violation of the socio-legal conduct norms."[56]

Reckless points out that a youth's inner containment is aided by self-control, a good self-image, high frustration tolerance, and a well-developed sense of right and wrong. Outer containment is the product of the institutional reinforcement of an individual's norms, goals, and expectations. Social control factors such as supervision, discipline, and limits are also important. If one of these aspects of control becomes weak, the other must assume the burden. Reckless believes, however, that effective control of behavior is impossible unless the conscience and environment are working together actively and successfully. For, more often than not, delinquency results when either the inner or the outer containment system breaks down.[57]

LABELING THEORY

All of the theories of delinquency causation we have examined so far have had one thing in common: the identification of those factors that distinguish offenders from nonoffenders. The basic characteristics of individuals, the organization of communities, and the groups or peers with whom delinquents form bonds have all been identified as the principal causes of delinquency. Labeling theory—a relatively recent supposition—is, on the other hand, more concerned with the stigmatizing effects of arrest and trial on juveniles than with the biological, social, or psychological forces that produced the delinquency in the first place.

Labeling theorists, as we have seen in Chapter Three, assume that delinquents are, for the most part, normal people. Thus, whenever youths persistently break the law and become recidivists, they do so not because they are inherently wicked but because of the negative effects of police, courts, and correctional institutions upon them. Labeling theorists also assume that these arms of the juvenile justice system reflect the power, influence, and interests of society's dominant classes. Accordingly, the less powerful groups are consistently identified as delinquent or criminal by society's power wielders, who express their dominance by legislating and legitimizing their own brand of morality. In short, "children become delinquent, not because of their behavior or because they are predisposed to do so, but because they are labeled by someone in a position of power."[58]

The earliest advocates of labeling theory argued that youths turn to delinquency because their primary acts of deviance are unduly emphasized. By continually stressing the deviant actions of certain children and by drawing attention to their "character flaws," the juvenile justice system creates a delinquent identity for them. As a consequence, many such youths continue their misbehavior and become recidivists.

More recent labeling theorists, on the other hand, have depicted typical delinquents as basically helpless youths who have been transformed from innocents to quasi-criminals by society's legal apparatus. Do-gooders create unnecessary and arbitrary rules that are selectively and arbitrarily enforced. And those who are singled out as transgressors of these artificially imposed and prejudicially enforced restrictions are stigmatized as delinquent, deviant, or criminal. Once identified as such, these "social misfits" are used as yardsticks to measure social conformity and stability.[59]

The implications of labeling theory—whether of the earlier or more recent variety—are that the juvenile justice system is a fraud, that it ought to be used only as a last resort, and that under ideal circumstances it would not exist at all. Recently, society has, in fact, been moving away from the old *parens patriae* notions, mentioned in Chapter One and Chapter Two, and has initiated such labeling theory reforms as decriminalization, diversion, and due process.

Decriminalization is the process of limiting the jurisdiction of the court, eliminating status offenses, and concentrating on criminal actions. Diversion is the process of deflecting youths away from the juvenile justice system and utilizing community resources as alternatives. Due process is the legal definition of the movement to professionalize court procedure so that alleged delinquents are provided with the same constitutional rights, guarantees, and protections as adults.[60]

Labeling theorists have performed a valuable service by initiating these reforms. They should also be commended for demonstrating that official delinquency involves rule making and the prejudices and reactions of society's power wielders, as well as the behavior of children. Labeling theory does have its limitations, however. For example, little proof exists to support the contention that community resources are less likely than the juvenile court to stigmatize diverted children. Moreover, it is extremely difficult to support the assumption that because some juveniles are unjustly labeled delinquents, the juvenile justice system must therefore be the major cause of delinquency. Indeed, a large number of adolescents commit offenses against their families, friends, and neighbors without ever becoming ensnared in the web of juvenile justice. In such cases, when the police and courts do become involved, they do so in response to complaints from those who know the juveniles best. Accordingly, the identification, or label, of delinquent is often affixed to many youths long before the juvenile justice system knows of their existence.[61]

Labeling theory also ignores the fact that elite power wielders are not responsible for all of society's accepted standards and values. All of society, for example, from the lowest classes to the highest, determines that such actions as murder, rape, and robbery are criminal. Labeling theory, moreover, frequently seems unconcerned with victimology—the study and awareness of the victims of crime. As a consequence, official delinquents are the only youths with whom labeling theorists seem to be concerned. Those who are never labeled, but who continue to victimize society, are largely ignored (see Chapter Three). And finally, labeling theory tends to overlook the fact that the labeling process does act as a deterrent to certain youths who might otherwise continue their deviant behavior.

Because of these limitations, labeling theory studies should not replace studies of delinquents. Indeed, as often as not, offending youths contribute to their label as much as the system does. Moreover, although the biological, sociological, and psychological theories all have serious flaws, we cannot rely exclusively on the social reaction approach of labeling theorists either. Instead, as LaMar Empey points out, "all the actors in the drama of creating delinquency must be studied: rule maker, rule breakers, and rule enforcers."[62]

RADICAL THEORY

Radical theory is the result of an increasingly popular belief among certain scientists that delinquent tendencies are not inherent in children. The source of delinquency, according to radical theorists, is really in the political and economic organization of society. A never-ending class struggle is taking place wherein the ruling classes of capitalist society "(1) define what delinquent behavior is, based on their particular self-interest, (2) create the social conditions which make delinquents out of the children of working-class people, and, then (3) devise legal machinery by which to maintain control over these children." Accordingly, "the inequities and injustices of a capitalist social order" produce the conditions for, as well as the perpetrators of, delinquency.[63]

Radical theorists assume that human nature is benign and that mankind's basic inclination is toward an enlightened and liberated civilization. A perpetual class struggle based upon an insidious and malevolent capitalism, however, has prevented these natural inclinations from reaching fulfillment. Moreover, the masses are oppressed and exploited by society's power wielders today just as they were in the past. Indeed, modern societies, especially capitalistic ones, such as America, are controlled and organized to serve vested interests. Delinquency, therefore, according to radical theorists, is any behavior that threatens society's organization and control, and thus those special interests.[64]

Radical theory posits that delinquency cannot be eliminated, or even controlled, unless our capitalist society and its juvenile justice system are eliminated first. Attempts at reform are doomed to failure, for our society has not reached the proper stage of class consciousness yet. Once this stage is reached through the process of political, economic, and social turmoil, however, capitalism will be overthrown and a socialist society established. According to radical theorists, once pure socialism has been accomplished, crime and delinquency will wither away with the state that created and needed such "deviance."[65]

Radical theory has provided us with many important insights into the nature and origins of delinquency. For example, like labeling theory, it has directed our attention to the sources and effects of existing law. It has shown that delinquency was legally invented in the nineteenth century and that delinquency is not a "universal concept, timeless and unchanging throughout the ages."[66] Radical theory has also demonstrated that laws are often written in order to control the lower classes and to ensure the dominant position of the power wielders. Moreover, evidence exists to support the contention of radical theorists that affluent and influential people are much less likely to be convicted of crimes, even if caught, because of their ability to afford superior legal assistance and simply because of their social position. And finally, radical theorists have focused our attention on the persistence of racism, sexism, and exploitation in America and in other modern societies.[67]

On the other hand, radical theory contains numerous flaws and contradictions. For example, its argument is circuitous and thus unverifiable; that is, it is impossible to prove or disprove. It views all societies, past and present, as being in conflict, with certain classes oppressed and others the oppressors. Thus, radical theory cannot describe the perfect social order wherein law would not be abused by some special interest group. As a consequence, when radical theorists prescribe a socialist society as the answer to all social problems, they are prescribing a fantasy without precedent, a mystical hope more than a concrete, obtainable reality.

By emphasizing that delinquency is solely the result of political and economic pressures, moreover, radical theorists deny the existence of personal determinism or motivation. They also tend to ignore the existence of personality disorders or, indeed, the existence of delinquents and criminals who are indigenous to the ruling classes. To be sure, radical theory depicts capitalists and other socio-politico-economic exploiters as criminals. But this presents another problem. If crime is to disappear in a liberated socialist society, how will the former enemies of socialism—"the capitalist criminals"—be treated? Are they to be reeducated, imprisoned, or perhaps executed? How *will* the new utopian society deal with those who are "misfits"?

Clearly, radical theory suffers in its insistence that only political and economic forces created our modern concept of childhood and thus invented delinquency. By concentrating obsessively upon class conflict, radical theorists have ignored the verifiable fact that, regardless of the political economic nature of the society, "age is usually more closely related to the commission of delinquent acts than is the class structure."[68] Indeed, radical theorists ignore a great deal that does not fit into their preconceived notions, and they often do not weigh the merits of other arguments as much as they use research data to justify their preconceptions.

The other theorists we have discussed are also often guilty of this same approach.

EVALUATING THE THEORIES

For the past hundred years, our understanding and definition of delinquency has reflected our evolving attitudes and beliefs as much as it has reflected the weight of confirmed scientific evidence. We have seen that all theories concerning the causes of delinquency suffer from a paucity of empirical verification. Like radical theory, they are often stronger in doctrine than in evidence. Accordingly, no single theory stands out as the most persuasive. All have their merits and demerits. All are worth understanding for what they reveal, as well as for what they conceal. Ultimately our comprehension of the origins of delinquency is served best if we selectively accept those bits of theory that can be supported by evidence and reject or hold in abeyance those that are unverifiable.

Our understanding of delinquency causation will also be served if we recognize that all delinquency theories are derived from the study of those offenders who are identified. If identified offenders represent a cross-section of the delinquent population, then the theories have some validity. If they do not, then the theories about criminal and delinquent behavior are not theories at all. Rather, they are conjectures based on a limited and distorted population sampling.

We have already seen that identified offenders represent only a fraction of all delinquents. Indeed, self-report and victim studies reveal that the police are cognizant of less than half of the serious felony offenses. And the majority of offenses the police do become aware of are seldom resolved; that is, the police know an offense has been committed but they do not know who committed it. Moreover, the police are persuaded to arrest or not to arrest by such subjective variables as their perception of the "offender's" socioeconomic status, race, and ethnic origins. As a consequence, under-class children are more likely to be arrested than white middle-class children. Accordingly, it is a mistake to assume—as all of the theories discussed in this chapter do—that the social and behavioral characteristics of those who are caught represent the juvenile offender population as a whole. Without dismissing the major contributions of these theories, we believe that any theory concerning delinquency causation must be based on the unidentified as well as the identified juvenile offender population. To date no such theory has surfaced.

NOTES
CHAPTER FIVE

1. See Martin R. Haskell and Lewis Yoblonsky, *Crime and Delinquency* (Chicago, 1970), p. 344; Robert C. Trojanowicz, *Juvenile Delinquency: Concepts and Control* (Englewood Cliffs, N. J., 1973), pp. 25–28; Cesare Beccaria, *On Crimes and Punishments* (Indianapolis, 1963).

2. Edwin H. Sutherland and Donald R. Cressey, *Criminology* (Philadelphia, 1974), p. 53. Also see Marvin Wolfgang, "Cesare Lombroso," in *Pioneers in Criminology*, 2nd ed., H. Mannheim, ed., (Montclair, N.J., 1972), p. 257; and Cesare Lombroso, *Criminal Man According to the Classification of Cesare Lombroso* (New York, 1911).

3. Charles Goring, *The English Convict* (London, 1913). Also see J. Michael and M. Adler, *Crime, Law and Social Science* (Montclair, N. J., 1971), pp. 150–152.

4. Ibid., pp. 155–57.

5. See J. McCary, *Human Sexuality*, 2nd ed. (New York, 1973), pp. 137–39; Nigel Walker, *Crime and Punishment in Britain*, 2nd ed. (Edinburgh, 1968), pp. 49–50; M. G. Ashley Montague, "The Biologist Looks at Crime," *Readings in Criminology and Penology*, 2nd ed., D. Dressler, ed. (New York, 1972), pp. 250–67; and Daniel Katkin et al., *Juvenile Delinquency and the Juvenile Justice System* (North Scituate, Mass., 1976), pp. 35–36.

6. Ernest A. Hooten, *Crime and the Man* (Cambridge, 1939), p. 130.

7. See George B. Vold, *Theoretical Criminology* (New York, 1958) and Sutherland and Cressey, *Criminology*, p. 119.

8. William H. Sheldon, *Varieties of Delinquent Youth*, (New York, 1949). Also see Marshall B. Clinard, *Sociology of Deviant Behavior* (New York, 1936), p. 120; Sheldon Glueck and Eleanor T. Glueck, "Early Detection of Future Delinquents," *Journal of Criminal Law, Criminology, and Police Science* 47 (1956): 169–81; and J. B. Cortes and F. N. Gatti, *Delinquency and Crime: A Biopsychosocial Approach* (New York, 1972).

9. See the comments of S. L. Washburn in "Reviews of W. H. Sheldon, Varieties of Delinquent Behavior," *American Anthropologist* 53 (December, 1951): 561–63.

10. See "Born Bad?" *Newsweek* (May 6, 1968):87.

11. J. McCary, *Human Sexuality*, 2nd ed. (New York, 1973), pp. 137–39, 38, 71–73.

12. See *The Lancet* (August 26, 1961).

13. W. W. Price et al., *The Lancet* (March 12, 1966):565–66.

14. See Richard G. Fox, "The XYY Offender: A Modern Myth?" *The Journal of Criminal Law, Criminology, and Police Science*, 52:1 (March, 1971): 62.

15. See Trojanowicz, *Juvenile Delinquency*, p. 25.

16. See M. Sherif and C. Sherif, *Social Psychology* (New York, 1969), p. 8.

17. See Robert K. Merton, "Social Structure and Anomie," *American Sociological Review* 3 (October, 1938): 672–82; Albert K. Cohen, *Delinquent Boys* (Glencoe, Ill., 1955); and Richard A. Cloward and Lloyd E. Ohlin, *Delinquency and Opportunity* (New York, 1960).

18. See Richard E. Johnson, *Juvenile Delinquency and Its Origins* (Cambridge, 1979), p. 3.

19. Cloward and Ohlin, *Delinquency and Opportunity*, pp. 86–105. Cohen, *Delinquent Boys* pp. 26–42.

20. In addition to Cloward and Ohlin and Cohen, cited above, see Walter B. Miller, "Lower Class Culture as a Generating Milieu of Gang Delinquency," *Journal of Social Issues* 14 (No. 3, 1958): 5–19; Sutherland and Cressey, *Criminology*; Ronald L. Akers, "Socio-economic Status and Delinquent Behavior: A Retest," *Journal of Research in Crime and Delinquency* 1 (January, 1964): 38–46; and David Matza, *Delinquency and Drift* (New York, 1964).

21. Cohen, *Delinquent Boys*, pp. 119–30.

22. See William C. Kvaraceus and Walter B. Miller, *Delinquent Behavior: Culture and the Individual* (Washington, D. C., 1959), p. 59. Also see Ralph Segalman, "The Conflict of Cultures between Social Work and the Underclass," *Rocky Mountain Social Science Journal*, 2 (October, 1965): 161–73.

23. Edwin Sutherland, *The Sutherland Papers*, Albert K. Cohen et al., eds. (Bloomington, Ind., 1956), pp. 8–10.

24. D. J. West, *The Young Offender* (Baltimore, 1967), pp. 84–85.

25. See Jerome G. Miller, "Research and Theory in Middle-Class Delinquency," *British Journal of Criminology* 10, (January, 1970): 33–51; Cohen, *Delinquent Boys*, pp. 162–69; Talcott Parsons, "Certain Primary Sources and Patterns of Aggression in the Social Structure of the Western World," *Psychiatry* 10 (May 1947): 167–81; and Edmund W. Vaz, "Self-reported Delinquency and Socio-economic Status," *Canadian Journal of Corrections* 8 (1966): 203–7.

26. Johnson, *Juvenile Delinquency and Its Origins*, p. 5.

27. Travis Hirschi, *Causes of Delinquency* (Berkeley, 1969). p. 66.

28. See Alan S. Berger and William Simon, "Black Families and the Moynihan Report: A Research Evaluation," *Social Problems* 22 (December, 1974): 145–61; Jay R. Williams and Martin Gold, "From Delinquent Behavior to Official Delinquency," *Social Problems* 20 (Fall, 1972): 209–29; Delos H. Kelly and William T. Pink, "School Commitment, Youth Rebellion, and Delinquency," *Criminology* 10 (February, 1973): 473–85; Kelly and Pink, "Status Origins, Youth Rebellion, and Delinquency: A Reexamination of the 'Class Issue'," *Journal of Youth and Adolescence* 4 (December, 1975): 339–47; Dean Frease, "Delinquency, Social Class and the Schools," *Sociology and Social Research* 57 (July, 1973): 443–59; Joseph G. Weis, "Delinquency among the Well to Do," unpublished doctoral dissertation, University of California, Berkeley, 1973; Ivan F. Nye, James F. Short, Jr., and Virgil J. Olson, "Socioeconomic Status and Delinquent Behavior," *American Journal of Sociology* 63 (January, 1958): 381–89; Robert A. Dentler and Lawrence J. Monroe, "Social Correlates of Early Adolescent Theft," *American Sociological Review* 26 (October, 1961): 733–45; John P. Clark and Eugene P. Wenninger, "Socioeconomic Class and Area as Correlates of Illegal Behavior among Juveniles, *American Sociological Review* 27 (December, 1962): 826–34; Walter L. Slocum and Carol L. Stone, "Family Culture Patterns and Delinquent-type Behavior," *Journal of Marriage and Family Living* 25 (May, 1963): 202–28; Ronald L. Akers, "Socioeconomic Status and Delinquent Behavior: A Retest," *Journal of Research in Crime and Delinquency* 1 (January, 1964): 38–46; Ivan F. Nye, *Family Relationships and Delinquent Behavior* (New York, 1958); Gerald Pine, "Social Class, Social Mobility, and Delin-

quent Behavior," *Personnel and Guidance Journal* 43 (April, 1965): 770–74; T. C. N. Gibbens and R. H. Ahrenfeldt, *Cultural Factors in Delinquency* (Philadelphia, 1966); Arthur L. Stinchcombe, *Rebellion in the High School* (Chicago, 1964); Harwin L. Voss, "Socioeconomic Status and Reported Delinquent Behavior," *Social Problems* 13 (Winter, 1966): 314–24; and Richard Jessor et al., *Society, Personality, and Deviant Behavior: A Study of a Tri-Ethnic Community* (New York, 1968).

29. See Williams and Gold, "From Delinquent Behavior to Official Delinquency," *Social Problems* 20 (Fall, 1972): 209–29; Wolfgang et al., *Delinquency in a Birth Cohort* (Chicago, 1972), pp. 244–55; and Roger Hood and Richard Sparks, *Key Issues in Criminology* (New York, 1970).

30. See Harwin Voss, *Society, Delinquency and Delinquent Behavior*, 2nd ed. (Englewood Cliffs, N. J., 1976), p. 38.

31. Ibid., p. 115.

32. Johnson, *Juvenile Delinquency and Its Origins*, pp. 138–142.

33. Ibid., p. 2. Also see Scott Briar and Irving Piliavin, "Delinquency, Situational Inducements, and Commitment to Conformity," *Social Problems* 12 (Summer, 1965): 35–45.

34. LaMar T. Empey, *American Delinquency: Its Meaning and Construction*, (Homewood, Ill., 1978), p. 239.

35. See Ivan F. Nye, *Family Relationships and Delinquent Behavior* (New York, 1958); Travis Hirschi, *Causes of Delinquency* (Berkeley, 1969); John P. Hewitt, *Social Stratification and Deviant Behavior* (New York, 1970); Jackson Toby, "Social Disorganization and Stake in Conformity: Complementary Factors in the Predatory Behavior of Hoodlums," *Journal of Criminal Law, Criminology, and Police Science* 48 (May–June. 1957): 12–17; Larry Karacki and Jackson Toby, "The Uncommitted Adolescent: Candidate for Gang Socialization," *Sociological Inquiry* 22 (Spring, 1962): 203–15; Kenneth Polk and D. Halferty, "Adolescence, Commitment, and Delinquency," *Journal of Research in Crime and Delinquency* 4 (July, 1966): 82–96.

36. Clarence Schrag, *Crime and Justice: American Style* (Washington, D. C., 1971), p. 109.

37. Johnson, *Juvenile Delinquency and Its Origins*, p. 8.

38. Ibid., p. 9.

39. Empey, *American Delinquency, p. 241*.

40. Ruth Shonle Cavan and Theodore N. Ferdinand, *Juvenile Delinquency*, 3rd ed. (Philadelphia, 1974), p. 73.

41. Theodore N. Ferdinand, *Typologies of Delinquency* (New York, 1966), pp. 116–201.

42. Ibid.

43. See Ernest Simmel, "Incendiarism," in *Searchlights on Delinquency*, K. R. Eissler, ed. (New York, 1949) pp. 90–101; and Otto Fenechel, *The Psychoanalytical Theory of Neurosis* (New York, 1945) pp. 341–49; 370–72. Also see Cavan and Ferdinand, *Juvenile Delinquency*, pp. 14–75.

44. Ibid., p. 75. Also see Lester E. Hewitt and Richard L. Jenkins, *Fundamental Patterns of Maladjustment* (Springfield, Ill., 1947), pp. 34–42.

45. See Margaret S. Mahler, "Les Enfants Terribles," in *Searchlight on Delinquency*, K. R. Eissler, ed., (New York, 1949), pp. 77–89.

46. Cavan and Ferdinand, *Juvenile Delinquency*, p. 77.

47. See Fritz Redl and David Wineman, *The Aggressive Child* (Glencoe, Ill., 1957), pp. 74–140.

48. Cavan and Ferdinand, *Juvenile Delinquency*, p. 77. Also see Sheldon and Eleanor Glueck, *Physique and Delinquency* (New York, 1956), Chapters VIII and IX.

49. Ibid.

50. See Erik H. Erikson, "Identity and the Life Cycle," *Psychological Issues* (New York, 1959): Chapter 3.

51. Ibid.

52. Katkin et al., *Delinquency and the Juvenile Justice System*, p. 45.

53. See Don C. Gibbons, *Delinquent Behavior*, 2nd ed. (Englewood Cliffs, N. J., 1976), p. 87. Also see Hans Eysenck, *Crime and Personality* (Boston, 1964), p. 142.

54. Cavan and Ferdinand, *Juvenile Delinquency*, p. 80.

55. Trojanowicz, *Juvenile Delinquency*, p. 56.

56. Walter C. Reckless, "A New Theory of Delinquency and Crime," in *Juvenile Delinquency: A Book of Readings*, Rose Giallombardo, ed. (New York, 1966) p. 223.

57. Ibid., p. 229. Also see Trojanowicz, *Juvenile Delinquency*, p. 56.

58. Empey, *American Delinquency*, p.342

59. See Jack P. Gibbs, "Conceptions of Deviant Behavior: The Old and the New," *Pacific Sociological Review* 9 (Spring, 1966): 9–14; Erick Goode, "On Behalf of Labeling Theory," *Social Problems* 22 (June, 1975): 570–83; Clarence Schrag, "Theoretical Foundations for a Social Science of Corrections," *Handbook in Criminology*, Daniel Glaser, ed. (Chicago, 1974), pp. 705–43; Edwin M. Schur, *Labeling Delinquent Behavior* (New York, 1971); Howard S. Becker, "Labelling Theory Reconsidered," *The Aldine Crime and Justice Annual*, Sheldon Messinger et al., eds. (Chicago, 1974), pp. 3–32; Edwin M. Lemert, *Human Deviance, Social Problems and Social Control*, 2nd ed. (Englewood Cliffs, N. J., 1972).

60. See Empey, *American Delinquency*, pp. 364–65.

61. Ibid. Also see Cavan and Ferdinand, *Juvenile Delinquency*, pp. 81–85.

62. Empey, *American Delinquency*, p. 365. Also see Katkin et al., *Delinquency and the Juvenile Justice System*, pp. 57–66.

63. See Empey, *American Delinquency*, pp. 369–99.

64. For the best known works of the radical theorists see Roscoe Pound, *Social Control through Law* (New Haven, Conn., 1942); Richard Quinney, *Criminal Justice in America* (Boston, 1974); William J. Chambliss, *Functional and Conflict Theories of Crime* (New York, 1973); William J. Chambliss and Milton Mankoff, eds., *Whose Law? What Order?* (New York, 1976); Rolf Dahrendorf, "Out of Utopia: Toward a Reorientation of Sociological Analysis," *American Journal of Sociology* 67 (September, 1958): 115–27; Austin T. Turk, *Criminality and the Legal Order* (Chicago, 1969); Ian Taylor et al., *The New Criminology* (New York, 1973); Herman and Julia Schwendinger, "Defenders of Order or Guardians of Human Rights?" in Ian

Taylor et al., eds, *Critical Criminology* (Boston, 1975), pp. 113–38; and Anthony Platt, *The Child Savers* (Chicago, 1969).

65. Empey, *American Delinquency*, p. 396.

66. Ibid.

67. Ibid., pp. 386–87, 396.

68. Ibid., pp. 397.

6
THE POLICE AND
DELINQUENCY PREVENTION

T he relationship of the police to delinquency prevention is often confusing and shrouded in misinformation. Are the police too heavy-handed? Or are they too lenient? What policies and procedures do the police follow when they arrest a juvenile? Under what circumstances do they release youths or refer them to the juvenile court? What is the role of the police in delinquency prevention? These are the questions that this chapter attempts to answer.

APPREHENSION AND PROCESSING

When youths are arrested, the role of the police in the juvenile justice process begins. The processing may include counseling, informal supervision, and/or referral to the juvenile court. Recently a Police Foundation analysis of police juvenile units demonstrated that such units usually engage in three functions:

1. Investigation of criminal allegations against a child.

2. Case screening designed to reach an appropriate disposition concerning diverting a child from, or referring that child to, the juvenile court.

3. Programs to prevent delinquency or to rehabilitate a delinquent child.[1]

Most large police departments have a juvenile unit, or at least one or more juvenile officers. When a crime is committed that is typical of those committed by juveniles, or when an investigation focuses upon juveniles as suspects, the case is usually assigned to a juvenile officer. This officer is then responsible for processing the case to its conclusion, which may include, ultimately, preparing an application for petition to the juvenile court. Some police departments routinely file applications for petitions on every juvenile in custody and deliver the offenders to the county probation officer or juvenile justice center. Other police departments do not refer juveniles to county juvenile authorities until the youths have committed three or four minor offenses, or until they have committed an offense serious enough, as judged by the police, to warrant juvenile court proceedings. The police have considerable latitude within which to operate. Indeed, Stanley Vanagunas in a recent article stated:

Disposition of children who violate criminal laws is still approached from the *parens patriae* perspective which dictates that the function of juvenile justice is not to punish a child but to take such action which would best serve the children's rehabilitative interest. Because of this premise the police have wider discretion for disposing of young offenders. They can, with greater latitude than in the case of an adult offender, divert the child from court.[2]

RESPONSES TO SUSPICIOUS BEHAVIOR

Police also exercise a wide range of options in response to suspicious behavior by a juvenile. These options include the following:

1. Doing nothing.
2. Preparing a field interrogation report, contact report, or incident report.
3. Detaining the juvenile at the station pending release to the parents.
4. Detaining the juvenile at the station; requiring the parents to return to the station for a conference.
5. Placing the juvenile on informal probation (under threat of referring him or her to the probation department).
6. Referring the juvenile to a noncriminal justice agency, such as a family services or mental health unit.
7. Referring the juvenile to the county probation officer or juvenile justice center.

Let us take a look at these options one at a time.

Doing Nothing

To "do nothing" means that an officer either ignores illegal behavior or contacts the juvenile without writing a report. Nathan Goldman has provided a list of factors that enter into an individual police officer's decision to do nothing, or perhaps to do something short of referring juveniles to the court. These factors include:

- The police officer's attitudes toward the juvenile court
- The impact of special individual experiences in the court, or with different racial groups, or with the parents of offenders, on an individual police officer
- Apprehension about criticism by the court
- Publicity given to certain offenses either in the neighborhood or elsewhere that may cause the police to feel that these are "too hot to handle" unofficially and must be referred to the court
- The necessity for maintaining respect for police authority in the community
- Various practical problems of policing
- Pressure by political groups or other special interest groups
- The police officer's attitude toward specific offenses
- The police officer's impression of the family situation, the degree of family interest in and control of the offender, and the reaction of the parents to the problem of the child's offense
- The attitude and personality of the child
- The fact that a black juvenile offender is sometimes considered less tractable and in need of more authoritarian supervision than a white child
- The degree of criminal sophistication shown in the offense
- The fact that juvenile offenders apprehended in a group will generally be treated on an all-or-none basis.[3]

Some of the factors are related to the juvenile's delinquent behavior, demeanor, socioeconomic status, and color. Other factors are related to police officer's prior experiences in dealing with the juvenile court, their racial biases, and their perceptions of the possible consequences to them of particular decisions.

If the officer does contact the juvenile, it may be simply to counsel the offender not to continue the unacceptable behavior. Of course, the fact that no report is written does not necessarily mean that the behavior will go unremembered. Individual police officers are usually assigned to relatively small areas in terms of geography and/or population; and they usually get to know everyone who lives in their districts, including those juveniles who are perceived as potential or actual troublemakers. Officers usually take these perceptions into account when they decide what action to take.

There may be strong arguments to justify making a limited response to juvenile misbehavior. For example, Erving Goffman, in his discussion of the effects of institutionalization, suggests, in effect, that bringing a subject into a system increases the probability that the system will have to deal with the subject again.[4] Moreover, juveniles who have not had prior contact with the police may find this contact quite traumatic and therapeutic. Therefore, sound strategy suggests that, in many cases, limited rather than increased interaction with the juvenile may be more beneficial in reducing the probability of further unacceptable behavior. If, however, limited interaction proves to be ineffective, an escalation of response may always be initiated.

Preparing a Field Interrogation Report

The field interrogation report (FI), contact report, and incident report are basically the same; the different terms are used in different parts of the country. The purpose of such a report is to provide a written record of an interaction between a police officer and a subject, juvenile or adult. FI reports, or FI cards, are recorded in some central place, so that this information may be used in later decision-making by criminal justice personnel. In California, for example, the county sheriff maintains a Central Juvenile Index (CJI), which contains all information submitted by police departments, probation departments, courts, and other institutions that have interacted with juvenile offenders. Hence, a police officer encountering a juvenile after curfew hour in a wealthy neighborhood with burglary problems might contact CJI to determine whether this was an isolated incident or part of a pattern of suspicious behavior. The information thus obtained would aid the officer in deciding whether to simply fill out an FI card or to take the juvenile to the station for further investigation. Juvenile intake probation officers (see Chapter Seven) also utilize the CJI. After receiving application for petition, intake officers often consult the CJI before they decide whether or not to file a petition.

Detaining Pending Release to Parents

To take a minor into the police station and call his or her parents is a step up the escalator of response to unacceptable juvenile behavior.

Such a response causes some inconvenience to the parents or guardians, since the juvenile usually is not released until a parent comes to the police station to accept custody. Moreover, this action also ensures that the juvenile's parents are made aware of their child's misbehavior and that they have received notice of possible further action if the unacceptable behavior continues. By following this procedure, the police hope that the juvenile may be chastised in some way by the parents upon returning home.

Detention at the station may be particularly useful as a device to stimulate parental control over such minor offenses as continued curfew violations. If parents ignore this behavior, occasional phone calls from the police in the middle of the night to request that they pick up their child may result in sufficient irritation to make the parents try harder to control the child's late-night wanderings. If parents are able to control the behavior of their children, however, it should not be necessary for police, schools, or probation officers to intervene. Therefore, parents should be given every encouragement to exercise such control.

Detaining and Requiring Parents to Return

The next step in the escalation is to require the parent or parents of the juvenile offender to return to the police station at a later time for a counseling session. The parents are usually required to bring the child in at a later time as a condition of release. This later meeting is designed both to emphasize the seriousness of the juvenile's behavior and to further inconvenience both the juvenile and the parents. Suggestions may be made to the parents that they seek help for the child from public or private agencies. Both the parents and the child may be warned of the consequences of future misconduct by the child.

Placing the Juvenile on Informal Probation

This step is not a particularly common one and would occur only in those police departments that have juvenile divisions, as well as the time and resources to devote to supervising juveniles. Neither children nor adults can be put on probation against their will. Therefore, children may refuse informal probation, but, if they do, they may be referred to the county probation officer and face court action. Most juveniles, given the option, will take the police probation.

The Police and Delinquency Prevention

Police probation is not significantly different from probation imposed by the juvenile court. An agreement is made between the child and a police juvenile officer. This agreement imposes restrictions and requirements on the child for some limited period of time, usually less than a year. If the child behaves during that period, he will be released from his probation. If he does not, he may be referred to the county probation officer for formal court action.

In most states police cannot take fingerprints or photographs of juveniles. This creates some problems in obtaining identifications of juvenile offenders. However, some police departments resolve this problem by obtaining yearbooks from local junior and senior high schools. Regrettably, elementary schools do not usually publish yearbooks.

Referring to a Noncriminal Justice Agency

There are various agencies that may permit diversion of the juvenile from the criminal justice system. These include public and quasi-public agencies, such as mental health agencies, family services, and youth service bureaus. Also available, if the juvenile's parents can afford them, are private practitioners, such as psychiatrists, psychologists, and other therapists.

In most jurisdictions, there are not sufficient public funds available to meet the needs of children in trouble. As a result, most children from lower socioeconomic classes are unable to avail themselves of such alternative services. Children of more affluent parents, however, are often referred to private agencies, thereby avoiding the stigma of the juvenile court.

The Youth Services Bureau is one of the alternative referrals that police and other social agencies make, instead of referring children to the juvenile court.[5] As such it is an effort at pre-adjudication diversion (see Chapter Seven). The Youth Services Bureau may be established by a variety of agencies, "by state or local government, a health and welfare planning council, a committee of the state legislature, a delinquency prevention commission, a state youth service bureau, a university, private foundation, or a 'red feather' council."[6]

Referral to a Youth Services Bureau requires the voluntary cooperation of the children and their parents. Of course, this "voluntary cooperation" may be induced by threatening to refer the child to the court if cooperation is not forthcoming.

The Youth Services Bureau functions as a social agency, attempting to determine the causes of delinquent behavior and treat them in the same way as does the juvenile court, but without the stigma and penalties attached to court processing. It is quite possible, however, that a stigma may also attach itself to children processed by a Youth Services Bureau.

Referring to the County Probation Officer

In most areas, the county juvenile authority is the probation department of the juvenile court, although other names may be used. Referring children to the probation department is the last and strongest step that a police department can take. Taking such a step means giving up on children at the local level and turning them over to another, higher jurisdiction. This step is usually not taken until the police have gone through one or more of the steps described above.

There are some exceptions. Some police departments, because of managerial philosophy or because of limited resources, routinely refer all juveniles to the probation department, regardless of the seriousness of the offense. In effect, such departments reject the view that they have any responsibility for juveniles, except to arrest and apprehend them.

Another factor that often leads to immediate police referral of a juvenile to the probation department is the nature of the offense. The escalation of responses discussed above assumes that the misbehavior of the juvenile is not perceived as serious. The offense might be classified as a felony, a misdemeanor, or a status offense and still not result in immediate referral, if no violence or bizarre behavior was involved. Homicide, robbery, or rape, however, would probably result in immediate referral to probation by all police departments. Examples of bizarre behavior that might lead to immediate referral include sex offenses other than rape, unprovoked violence, or other actions inconsistent with the surrounding circumstances.

The view that some criminal behavior is bizarre and that some is not bizarre might be difficult to comprehend for those who view all criminal behavior as irrational or bizarre. Some examples might clarify. An armed robber enters a liquor store, points a gun at the clerk, and demands the contents of the cash register. The clerk cooperates in every way, gives the money to the robber, who then leaves. This is routine behavior for an armed robber. However, if the robber, as he is backing out of the door, gratuitously shoots the clerk in the head, this would be bizarre behavior, because it was unnecessary and inconsistent with the surrounding circumstances.

Consider another example. A ten-year-old boy uses an air rifle to shoot a hole through a neighbor's picture window. This behavior hardly calls for probation-department or even police-department intervention if the child's parents accept financial responsibility for the boy's actions. However, if the child takes his air rifle to his school on a Sunday morning and shoots out every window in the building, reference of the matter to the probation department would seem to be appropriate. Such malicious destruction of property suggests that the child has some emotional problems that need to be resolved.

Once the police have decided to refer a juvenile to the juvenile court, they must file an application for petition, which is the juvenile equivalent of an adult criminal complaint. Probation officers (or other court officers fulfilling the juvenile intake function) have a choice of filing or not filing the petition, depending on the situation. This is discussed in Chapter Seven.

THE POLICE AND DELINQUENCY PREVENTION PROGRAMS

Delinquency prevention is a term whose meaning seems obvious, but is in fact ambiguous. Typically, one thinks in terms of preventing delinquent acts, of keeping children who are not yet delinquents from becoming delinquents. However, delinquency prevention may properly be defined to include all of the actions taken by the various elements of the juvenile justice system. The purpose of these actions is to cause offenders to desist from further delinquency. If the actions of the juvenile justice system do not reduce or prevent delinquency, then they are meaningless.

What is the role of police in the prevention of delinquency? All of the actions discussed above in this chapter fit the broader definition of delinquency prevention. But there are other actions police may take that are proactive rather than reactive to unacceptable juvenile behavior. Included among these proactive actions are steps designed to improve relations and communications between police and juveniles.

The Officer Friendly Program

One such effort is the Officer Friendly Program in Kansas City, Missouri. Officers are selected for their demonstrated ability, as shown by their records, to get along with young people. They make scheduled visits to area elementary schools and give lectures to students in kindergarten through third grade. They respond to questions, but attempt at all times to avoid saying anything that will place them in an adversary relationship with the children. The primary goal of the Officer Friendly Program is to encourage young children to perceive police officers as friends, rather than as enemies.[7]

Many teenagers take a hostile view of police officers. Teenagers are often rebellious toward authority, and police are symbols of authority, regardless of the race or ethnicity of either the officers or the teenagers. This hostility is exacerbated by parents who threaten to turn children over to police if they misbehave. The police officer is held up to be a bogey man, an object of fear to children. It becomes difficult, then, for police officers to develop good relationships with children. And only by developing good relationships with children can police hope to have significant success in encouraging children to refrain from engaging in delinquent behavior.

The problem is substantially greater in ghetto areas in which the population is predominantly black and/or Hispanic. Teenagers in these communities often perceive, sometimes quite correctly, that police officers are members of an army of occupation, operating in behalf of the white power structure. When this kind of attitude exists, programs like Officer Friendly or the Police Athletic League can have little impact.

Liaison Officer Programs

Another program that has been undertaken as a measure to prevent delinquency is the school liaison officer, or school resource officer.[8] In this type of program, a police officer, usually not in uniform, is assigned to a position equivalent to membership on the school staff. The officer has some counseling duties and is secondarily concerned with preventing crime and delinquency, particularly offenses occurring in the school.

The role of a school liaison officer is different from that of a police officer assigned a beat within a school that has severe crime problems (see Chapter Ten). In some schools, an armed police officer in uniform is needed to deter rape, assault, and theft. The officer is concerned primarily with preventing overt criminal behavior within the school setting, not with improving relations between police and teenagers.

Limitations of Prevention Programs

There are practical arguments to be made against a school liaison officer program. Most police departments do not have the financial resources to permit the assignment of officers to such a function.[9] Delinquency prevention programs must compete with other police programs for limited funds, and delinquency prevention is usually not a high-priority program.

Further, the presence of an assigned officer at a school, regardless of the officer's function, might stigmatize the school and its students and staff. Such stigmatizing, or labeling, should be done only as a last resort.

The strongest limitation upon police programs with predelinquents or nondelinquents is the constitutional one. The Fifth and Fourteenth Amendments to the Constitution require due process of law. The police and other members of the criminal justice system are not permitted to interfere in a person's life unless that person is alleged to have committed a delinquent or criminal act. To define a person as a predelinquent, or as having a "predilection to commit a delinquent act," does not give police the jurisdiction to interfere in that person's life. Only the actual commission of a delinquent act permits interference by police.

Thus, programs designed to deal with predelinquents cannot provide the officer with jurisdiction to act with authority and cannot require mandatory participation by juveniles or their parents. Under such conditions, many police agencies take the position that their limited resources should be expended on dealing with people who have committed crimes, rather than with people who might commit crimes.

NOTES
CHAPTER SIX

1. See Stanley Vanagunas, "Police Diversion of Juvenile Offenders: An Ambiguous State of the Art," *Federal Probation* 43 (September 1979): 50.

2. Ibid., p. 49.

3. Nathan Goldman, "The Differential Selection of Juvenile Offenders for Court Appearance," *The Ambivalent Force*, Arthur Niederhoffer and Abraham S. Blumberg, eds. (Hinsdale, Ill., 1976), pp. 185–86.

4. Erving Goffman, *Asylums* (Garden City, N. Y., 1961).

5. Thomas A. Johnson, *Introduction to the Juvenile Justice System*, (St. Paul, Minn., 1975), pp. 249–67.

6. Ibid., p. 254. Also see U. S. Department of Health, Education and Welfare, *The Challenge of Youth Service Bureaus* (Washington, D. C., 1973) and Elaine Duxbury, *Evaluation of Youth Service Bureaus*, (Sacramento, Calif., Department of the Youth Authority), November 1973.

7. Personal communication from Captain Richard K. Burnett, Kansas City (Missouri) Police Department.

8. Paul H. Hahn, *The Juvenile Offender and the Law*, (Cincinnati, Ohio, 1971), pp. 205–09.

9. Ibid., p. 205.

7
THE JUVENILE COURT PROCESS

In most states, youths are not brought before the juvenile court until two official documents have been filed. The first is an application for petition, or affidavit, which may be filed by any adult and which alleges that a youth has committed a delinquent or status offense. The second document, the petition, is filed after receipt of an application for petition by a juvenile probation officer who has determined that grounds exist for court action. In some states, this responsibility is shared or taken over by the prosecutor. In California, for example, probation officers process status offenses,[1] including the filing of petitions. However, they screen out applications for petitions for delinquent offenses[2] and then refer the remaining applications to the prosecutor, who evaluates them and decides whether or not to file petitions.

THE COURT PROCESS IN THE PAST

The full participation of prosecutors in the juvenile court process is a new phenomenon. Prior to the mid-1960s, prosecutors and defense attorneys rarely became involved. Most cases in those days were handled rather informally because illegal behavior was perceived as an opening through which the probation department could step to obtain jurisdiction. Once delinquent children were made wards of the court, they could be helped, and their problems could be overcome. Thus, prosecutors and defense attorneys were not necessary.

Because of the *parens patriae* doctrine, moreover, procedural safeguards typically found in adult criminal courts were also unnecessary. For instance, minors had no right to a jury trial or release on bail, and they still do not. Juvenile court trials often permitted illegally obtained and hearsay evidence, which would have been inadmissible in any adult court. After informal questioning, most juveniles admitted to the allegations of the petitions, resulting in a high number of uncontested hearings. Even when a youth did not confess, however, and a contested hearing followed, defense counsel usually did not appear. Instead, the probation officer, who had up to this time been the juvenile's counselor, now acted as prosecutor and presented evidence and witnesses.

The concept of due process suffered because the system was predicated on the assumption that hearings were held in the interests of

troubled youth. Many probation officers believed that legal techni-
calities and lawyers only stood in the way of the court and probation
staffs doing their duty. Attorneys were also suspect because many of
them were, and still are, woefully ignorant about juvenile law and the
juvenile court process. This condition has changed somewhat over
the past ten to fifteen years, as many private attorneys, prosecutors,
and public defenders now specialize in juvenile justice. Indeed, some
of the most vocal critics of juvenile injustice are lawyers who have
worked exclusively with children.

RECENT CHANGES IN THE
PROCESS

The most significant changes in the juvenile justice system, however,
occurred in the late 1960s and early 1970s, primarily as a result of
Supreme Court decisions. The most important of these decisions were
Kent,[3] *Gault*,[4] and *Winship*.[5] The *Kent* decision, as is discussed below,
stipulated that juveniles were entitled to hearings with some semblance
of due process before they could be waived to adult criminal court
jurisdiction. The *Gault* decision required the extension of due process
to all juvenile court proceedings. The process did not have to duplicate
that in the adult courts, but substantial improvement over what had
existed quickly became evident. Moreover, the *Gault* decision, more
than any other, brought attorneys into the juvenile court.

Prior to the *Winship* decision, a juvenile court could "sustain the
allegation of the petition" (find the child guilty) based solely upon a
"preponderance of the evidence." This represented a substantially
lower requirement than the "beyond a reasonable doubt" requirement
of the adult criminal court. The *Winship* decision did not require the
use of the adult standard in the juvenile court, but it did considerably
increase the evidentiary requirement necessary to sustain the allegations. In addition, it raised standards concerning admissibility of evidence in the juvenile court.

These Supreme Court decisions may have had less impact upon
juvenile court proceedings than one might assume, for they primarily
affect contested hearings. However, as is the case in adult criminal
court, only a small percentage of juvenile court hearings are contested.

In adult criminal court, about 90 percent of convictions result from negotiated pleas of guilty, usually to reduced charges or in exchange for a commitment by the prosecutor to a reduced sentence or probation. The majority of allegations in juvenile courts are also not contested, often because the petitions have been amended to reflect reduced charges, also as a result of the plea-bargaining process. The following example should clarify this process.

David was a sixteen-year-old boy who lived in a black ghetto area of Baltimore. One day David and a close friend got into a strong argument. David took a .25-caliber handgun from his pocket and shot the other boy in the abdomen. An ambulance was called, and David disposed of the handgun before the ambulance and police arrived. The police took David into custody and later delivered him to the juvenile justice center.

David was initially charged with aggravated assault. He denied the allegation, and the victim refused to testify. Ultimately a plea bargain was arranged, and David admitted to the allegation that he had discharged a firearm within the city limits of Baltimore. The court adjudged David delinquent and committed him to a juvenile institution for an indefinite term. He served nine months before being released on parole.

David had not been aware that, in Maryland as in most states, there were few limits to the court's sentencing powers over an adjudged delinquent. In fact, according to Ted Rubin, only three states limit juvenile courts from imposing sentences upon youths greater than those imposed upon adults adjudged guilty of the same offenses.[6] Had David been sentenced as an adult, it is unlikely that he would have been given more than ninety days in jail.

THE JUVENILE INTAKE PROCESS

The probation officer who screens applications for petitions and decides whether or not to file petitions is usually referred to as an intake officer.[7] The decision to begin the intake procedure takes place whether or not the juvenile is in custody. If the intake officer decides not to file a petition, the matter is usually closed. If the juvenile is in custody, he or she is released. The intake officer, shortly thereafter, usually notifies the person or persons who filed the application for petition and explains why the petition was not filed. In some states, the petition applicants have the right to appeal the decision or submit supplemental information for a refiling, but such appeals are rare.

When an intake officer decides to file a petition, it is filled out and filed with the clerk of the court. For juveniles not in custody— that is, not in the court's youth home, shelter, or detention center— this decision-making process may be a leisurely one. For example, some states allow thirty days. For children in custody, however, the decision must be prompt or they must be released and their cases processed as noncustody. California, which is fairly typical, requires the filing of petitions within two court days after the child is taken into custody; Saturdays, Sundays, and holidays do not count in the calculations. Once a petition is filed, a court hearing must be held within one court day to determine whether or not the child will continue to be detained until the formal court hearing.

The decision, by the intake officer or the juvenile court judge or referee, to detain the child cannot be arbitrary. Most jurisdictions have laws defining the conditions that must be met in order to retain a juvenile in custody. If one or more of the conditions are not met, the juvenile must be released. The pertinent California conditions are contained in Section 628 of the Juvenile Court Law, which states, in part:

> Upon delivery to the probation officer of a minor who has been taken into temporary custody under the provisions of this article, the probation officer shall immediately investigate the circumstances of the minor and the facts surrounding his being taken into custody and shall immediately release such minor to the custody of his parent, guardian, or responsible relative unless one or more of the following conditions exist:
>
> (1) The minor is in need of proper and effective parental care or control and has no parent, guardian, or responsible relative; or has no parent, guardian, or responsible relative willing to exercise or capable of exercising such care or control; or has no

parent, guardian, or responsible relative actually exercising such care or control.

(2) The minor is destitute or is not provided with the necessities of life or is not provided with a home or suitable place of abode.

(3) The minor is provided with a home which is an unfit place for him by reason of neglect, cruelty, depravity or physical abuse of either of his parents, or of his guardian or other person in whose custody or care he is.

(4) Continued detention of the minor is a matter of immediate and urgent necessity for the protection of the minor or reasonable necessity for the protection of the person or property of another.

(5) The minor is likely to flee the jurisdiction of the court.

(6) The minor has violated an order of the juvenile court.

(7) The minor is physically dangerous to the public because of a mental or physical deficiency, disorder or abnormality.

The first three conditions and the seventh condition are most likely to apply to dependent (neglected, deprived, or abused) children as defined by Section 300 of the Juvenile Court Law of California, and of similar statutes in other jurisdictions. Section 300 states:

Persons within jurisdiction of court. Any person under the age of 18 years who comes within any of the following descriptions is within the jurisdiction of the juvenile court which may adjudge such person to be a dependent child of the court:

(a) Who is in need of proper and effective parental care or control and has no parent or guardian willing to exercise or capable of exercising such care or control, or has no parent or guardian actually exercising such care or control. No parent shall be found to be incapable of exercising proper and effective parental care or control solely because of a physical disability, including, but not limited to, a defect in the visual or auditory functions of his or her body, unless the court finds that the disability prevents the parent from exercising such care or control.

(b) Who is destitute, or who is not provided with the necessities of life, or who is not provided with a home or suitable place of abode.

(c) Who is physically dangerous to the public because of a mental or physical deficiency, disorder or abnormality.

The Juvenile Court Process

(d) Whose home is an unfit place for him by reason of neglect, cruelty, depravity, or physical abuse of either of his parents, or of his guardian, or other person in whose custody or care he is.

The fifth and sixth conditions of Section 628 refer primarily to delinquent offenders and status offenders—PINS, JINS, YINS, CHINS, and incorrigibles.[8]

Incorrigibles are defined by Section 601 of the Juvenile Court Law of California, which states, in part:

Any person under the age of 18 years who persistently or habitually refuses to obey the reasonable and proper orders or directions of his parents, guardian, or custodian, or who is beyond the control of such person, or who is under the age of 18 years when he violated any ordinance of any city or county of this state establishing a curfew based solely on age is within the jurisdiction of the juvenile court which may adjudge such person to be a ward of the court.

Section 601 also defines school misbehavior and school truancy as incorrigible acts, or status offenses, as they are more commonly called.

Delinquents are defined by Section 602 of the Juvenile Court Law of California, which states:

Any person who is under the age of 18 years when he violates any law of this state or the United States or any ordinance of any city or county of this state defining crime other than an ordinance establishing a curfew based solely on age, is within the jurisdiction of the juvenile court, which may adjudge such person to be a ward of the court.

In some other states, truancy and curfew violations are regarded as delinquent acts, rather than as status offenses (see Chapter Three). In California, juveniles cannot be detained for truancy or runaway violations.

The fifth condition of Section 628 refers to children who have a prior history of failure to appear in court. The sixth condition would normally refer only to children who are already on probation. When an intake officer encounters a child who is already on probation, the child is normally referred to his supervising probation officer, who, having greater knowledge of the child's background and circumstances, is in a better position to make decisions concerning the filing of new petitions and/or continuing detention.

A grant of probation is made by court order. Therefore, any violation of the terms and conditions of probation constitutes a violation of a court order. Under laws in California and various other states, violation of a juvenile court order is a delinquent act, because it is also a violation of state law. Thus, children who are on probation for status offenses and who subsequently violate the conditions of their probation may be returned to court and adjudged delinquent, rather than incorrigible. The difference is not insignificant, since courts typically have a wider range of disposition (sentencing) options available for delinquents than for status offenders (incorrigibles).

The fourth condition of Section 628 might refer to dependent children, incorrigibles, or delinquents, depending on the nature of the offense for which they were referred to the court. Most juvenile courts would rather release than detain these children, as well as those who fall into other categories. Juvenile court philosophy posits that children are better off in the home than in any other place and should be left there unless circumstances exist that preclude such a disposition. When children are removed from their homes, juvenile court philosophy and many state laws require that they be placed in settings that are as homelike as possible.

Intake officers do not normally leave all decisions concerning detention to the juvenile court judge. Instead, they usually release those children who, in their view, do not meet the statutory conditions for continued detention and detain those who do for detention hearings. At those hearings, a juvenile court judge or referee releases or detains the children and sets a date for jurisdictional hearings. For detained children, these subsequent hearings must usually be held within a short period. California allows fifteen court days. For children not detained, prompt hearings are usually not necessary. In such cases, the intake officer files the petitions with the clerk or other officer of the court, who sets the dates for the jurisdictional hearings. This usually completes the action of the intake officer. Further work on the cases is performed by juvenile investigators.

In a small probation department, one probation officer may carry out more than one of the various juvenile functions, or may carry out all of them. However, in a large department, there is substantial functional specialization and division of labor into such categories as intake—custody or non-custody; investigation; supervision—male or female; supervision—foster homes; supervision—institutions, and so forth.

Regardless of the size of the probation department, however, another option available to the intake officer is to divert the child away from official processing and into some form of informal processing. The decision as to whether or not to divert usually depends upon such factors as the child's behavior, prior record, family background, and so on. Subject to the voluntary cooperation of the child and the parents or guardians, a probation officer may agree not to file a petition for some limited period, such as six months. The child agrees, under this diversion option, to behave in a prescribed manner, which may include informally reporting to a supervising probation officer. If the child fails to conform during this informal probation period, the probation officer may then file the petition.

THE JUVENILE INVESTIGATION PROCESS

Juvenile investigators attempt to determine the circumstances that led to a juvenile's court appearance. They also write reports to the court, which serve as guides for judicial decision-making. Moreover, in the absence of a prosecutor, juvenile investigators may also present cases to the court, call witnesses, and perform a variety of other services. And, finally, if the court sustains the allegations of a petition (finds the juvenile guilty), the investigator may also make recommendations for disposition of the offender.

Juvenile investigators are probation officers who specialize in juvenile investigating and report writing. When cases are received through channels from the intake section, the juvenile investigators begin to study the cases as thoroughly as possible. Frequently their investigations are hampered by problems of time limits, uncooperative sources, and the use of form letters. Ideally, however, the investigators gather information from all sources familiar with the juveniles or with the offense, or both. They request information from the police, school authorities, relatives and friends of the juvenile, the victim, the victim's relatives and friends, witnesses, and anyone else who might be able to contribute information that is relevant and pertinent to the case.

Some of the information is gathered by submitting mailed questionnaires, some by telephone, and some by face-to-face interviews. These interviews are conducted with the juvenile offenders, unless they are contesting the allegations of the petition (pleading not guilty). Most cases are not contested, however, and the process of preparing for a contested hearing is dealt with later in this chapter.

It is interesting to observe that when reports from school authorities are returned to the investigating probation officers, they almost universally contain negative information. Juveniles who present problems at home or in the community almost invariably also present problems in school. These problems may relate to academic performance, general behavior, truancy, or a combination of all three. This is not to suggest that most children who have problems in school also have problems in the community, but the opposite does seem to be true.

Many authorites have speculated about the relationship between schools and the problems of juvenile misbehavior. Some see schools as making a significant contribution toward solving the problem, but others regard schools as a significant part of the problem. This subject is discussed at length in Chapter Ten.

When the process of data collection is completed by the investigators, the juvenile court reports are prepared. They normally include such sections as the following:

The present problem (the offense)

The juvenile's statement

The parent's statement

The victim's statement

Reports of interested parties

The juvenile's prior record

The juvenile's social history

School report

Evaluation (by the investigator)

Recommendation

The present problem is normally derived from the police report. It is a statement of the nature of the offense, the circumstances that brought the matter to the attention of the police, and the action taken by the police. If the application for petition was made by parents, school authorities, or others, this section will say so.

The juvenile's statement is derived by interviewing the juvenile. The juvenile is given the opportunity to review the police reports and to comment upon them. This section includes a statement to the effect that the juvenile admits to the allegations of the petition. Also included here is the opinion of the juvenile about how the court should dispose of the case.

The parent's statement includes the parent's opinions about the present problem and how it came about, the child's adjustment in the home, and what should be done by the juvenile court judge. Some probation officers regard parents' statements as often being defensive in nature as a result of parents seeking to resolve their own feelings of guilt or complicity.[9]

The victim's statement gives the victim an opportunity to have a "day in court." This section should reflect the victim's views concerning the defendant, the accuracy of the police report, and the manner in which the case should be resolved in court. This section may be omitted, if there is no tangible or live victim.

Reports of interested parties might include reports of witnesses, references supplied by the juvenile, or reports by anyone else who has a contribution to make.

The juvenile's prior record contains information gathered from local police agencies and from the files of the probation department, if there has been prior contact with the juvenile. If the juvenile has lived in another geographical area, the investigators often seek information from police and probation authorities in that area.

The juvenile's social history is the life story of the juvenile, omitting information that appears elsewhere in the report. Included here is a discussion of the child's relationship with parents and siblings; information about where the child has lived and gone to school, any physical or mental problems, work experiences if any; and any other information that is relevant to the case.

The school report presents a summary of the information contained in the questionnaires that (the investigators hope) have been filled out and returned by school authorities. Cooperation between probation departments and schools in large cities, however, is sometimes lacking.

The evaluation summarizes the prior areas of the report. Also included here are the investigator's opinions about the case and a statement of what the investigator would regard as an appropriate disposition. Juvenile court judges should be able to understand the cases before them if they read only this summary, and, in fact, because of constraints of time and workloads, judges often do rely exclusively on this section.

Investigators are expected to be as objective as possible. Obviously they cannot report information based on their personal eye witness observations. Nevertheless, they are expected to report factually and to summarize the information supplied. The evaluation is expected to reflect the personal opinion of the investigator, however, and should lead logically to the formal recommendation that is the final section of the report.

The recommendation, in effect, often puts words into the judge's mouth. Here is an example of a formal recommendation:

> It is respectfully recommended that the court sustain the allegations of the petition; that the juvenile be declared a ward of the court; that the juvenile be subject to the supervision of the probation officer; that the juvenile be ordered to obey the normal rules and regulations of the probation department.

At times, overworked judges merely second whatever the reports recommend. Ideally, however, all of the evidence presented at the hearings is weighed and considered before judgments are rendered.

The juvenile court report outlined above should be regarded only as an example. Reports vary in context from one jurisdiction to another. Some sections are added and others deleted. Some judges want only the factual parts of the report and do not want the evaluation or recommendation included in the report.

In cases involving dependent children (victims), under statutes such as Section 300 of the Juvenile Court Law of California, the procedure is identical to that followed for incorrigible or delinquent children. In California, processing is done by the county welfare agency rather than by the probation department. Dependent children are more likely to be detained than the others, however, because their classification suggests a need for protection. As further protection, California and many other states do not detain or hold dependent children in the same facility with alleged or adjudged incorrigibles and delinquents.

When the juvenile court report is completed, a copy is forwarded to the juvenile court judge, usually at least one or two court days before the hearing. In most jurisdictions, a copy is also made available to the defense attorney, if one is involved. The report may also be used as a tool for supervising probation officers, if the child is put on probation.

THE CONTESTED HEARING

Contested hearings are scheduled whenever children deny the allegations made in petitions. For such cases, juvenile investigators consider only the issue of jurisdiction. In other words, the only question they consider is "Should the court sustain the allegations of the petition?" or "Is the juvenile guilty of the offense?"

The court reports are also different for contested hearings, which are similar to criminal court trials. Indeed, in some jurisdictions, no court report is prepared. Where court reports are prepared, they are typically brief and include only names of witnesses and what each witness is expected to say. No personal opinions are expressed concerning the guilt or innocence of the juvenile.

In some jurisdictions, prosecutors are responsible for preparing and presenting all contested cases. In other jurisdictions, that responsibility belongs to juvenile investigators, who subpoena witnesses as necessary, call and question these witnesses, and thus for all practical purposes prosecute the cases. When juveniles are represented by counsel, however, prosecutors representing the state are usually present.

At the conclusion of the contested hearings, the juvenile court judges either sustain or fail to sustain the allegations of the petitions. If the allegations are not sustained, the cases are dismissed, and the juveniles are released from further jeopardy.

If the allegations are sustained, the judges normally continue the proceedings for a limited period (usually seven to fourteen calendar days) in order to permit the juvenile investigators to prepare dispositional reports upon which the judges can base their decisions. In some jurisdictions, investigators prepare dispositional reports prior to the contested hearings. These reports are not read by the judges before the hearings, but if the juveniles are found guilty, the judges can read them before rendering dispositional decisions.

THE UNCONTESTED HEARING

At formal court hearings, which are usually uncontested, the court decides both the jurisdictional and dispositional phases of cases. "Jurisdictional hearings," in this context, means determining whether or not the court can continue to exercise jurisdiction over children found to be dependent, incorrigible, or delinquent. Once this is determined, the judges can find the children to be "dependent children of the court" or "wards of the court." Only after such findings can judges make rulings on dispositions.

The Jurisdictional Hearing

The purpose of a jurisdictional hearing is to determine whether or not the allegations of the petitions are correct. In uncontested hearings, no doubt exists, since the youths have already admitted to the allegations. In such cases, the judge (or referee, in some jurisdictions), after reading the court report, asks the juveniles if they wish to admit to the allegations in court and to make whatever other comments they so desire. When defense counsel are present, they speak for the juveniles. Parents or guardians are also offered a chance to speak. Subsequently, the judges render their decisions. Normally the allegations are sustained, since the cases are uncontested. On occasion, however, judges may dismiss uncontested cases, on the grounds that the offenses are too minor to merit further court proceedings. Once the petitions are sustained, the dispositional phase of the hearings begin.

The Dispositional Hearing

The last step in formal court hearings is the disposition of the juveniles. In order to retain jurisdiction in most states, judges must declare youths to be wards or dependent children of the court. In so doing, juvenile court judges take legal custody of children from parents or guardians and vest it in the court. This does not necessarily mean physical custody, for juveniles may be made wards of the court and still continue to reside at home under supervision of probation officers.

The wide variety of disposition options for court wards that are available to judges will be discussed in Chapter Eight. These options include:

Money fine

Community work project

Probation for a specific term

Probation for an indeterminate term

Probation, plus a specific commitment to a county juvenile facility

Probation, plus an indeterminate commitment to a county juvenile facility

Probation, plus removal from the home for placement in a
    Foster home
    Relative's home
    Group home
    Mental institution

Commitment to a state youth authority

When juveniles are placed on probation, they are normally supervised by probation officers and are subject to the normal rules and regulations of the probation department. If conditions demand it, judges may also impose any additional conditions they deem appropriate.

Whenever juveniles are declared dependent children of the court, the dispositions available are somewhat more limited, because such youths are victims needing protection, not guidance or punishment. Included in these disposition options are:

Supervision by a probation officer or welfare worker for a specific term

Supervision by a probation officer or welfare worker for an indeterminate term

Supervision by a probation officer or welfare worker, plus removal from the home for placement in a

    County facility for dependent children
    Foster home
    Relative's home
    Group home

The treatment of dependent children is discussed further in Chapter Eight.

DIVERSION

We have already seen that police use informal strategies and efforts to divert juveniles from the court process and that pre-adjudication diversion options are available to juvenile intake officers. Juvenile court judges also employ strategies of pre-adjudication and post-adjudication diversion. Indeed, whenever it is feasible, most police officers, juvenile investigators, and judges attempt to avoid the stigmatization of juveniles that is frequently associated with being wards of the court. Such attempts may be carried out in a variety of ways, all of which require the voluntary cooperation of the juveniles and their parents or guardians. This cooperation, or at least the promise of cooperation, is usually forthcoming, however, because the alternatives are generally perceived as undesirable.

Many juvenile court judges practice a form of diversion by issuing continuances, which postpone jurisdictional hearings and judicial decision-making for a specific period of time, pending the good behavior of the youths involved. If a juvenile misbehaves during this period, the case is returned to court sooner than the "continued" date, and the adjudication process is completed. When this occurs the original allegations are usually sustained, and a disposition is made. If the youth stays out of trouble, however, the original charges are usually dismissed at the continued hearing.

When a case has been continued for purposes of diversion, a probation officer is often assigned to monitor the youth's behavior. Just as often, however, because of undermanned or overworked juvenile staffs, this cannot be done. As a consequence, informal probation is not utilized as a diversion option as frequently as the circumstances and conditions of many juvenile court cases would warrant. On the other hand, it could be argued that by assigning probation officers to juveniles whose cases have been continued, the juvenile justice system defeats the purpose of diversion, because the presence of a probation officer in a youth's life increases the chances of stigmatization.

Another pre-adjudication diversion situation may arise when the parents or guardians of a juvenile on trial propose a satisfactory alternative disposition at their own expense. For example, they might agree to place their child in a military school or in some private treatment facility, preferably in another county. Such a placement would probably be as good as, or better than, any alternatives a probation officer might suggest. It would have the additional advantage of relieving the county of a possible financial burden. This solution, however, is notable for its infrequent invocation.

A more common form of diversion initiated by parents is to send a child to relatives in another geographical location, preferably at some distance. This is a tempting solution and is often adopted, because it costs the county nothing and removes the child from the court's jurisdiction. Occasionally, if the child is not sent back within the first few months, the new environment may lead to improved behavior. But, more frequently, the child's problems are merely transferred to another jurisdiction. Accordingly, although the court's problems are resolved, the child's problems are not.

Post-adjudication diversion takes place after a jurisdictional hearing—in other words, after the court has sustained the allegations of a petition, but before the juvenile is declared to be a ward of the court. When a judge chooses this form of diversion, he or she usually continues the hearing for a specific period, such as six or twelve months, and places the youth under the supervision of a probation officer. If the child violates the terms and conditions imposed by the judge, the probation officer returns the boy or girl to the court for a dispositional hearing. If the juvenile conforms to the terms and conditions, however, he or she is not made a ward, and the probation is terminated.

At first glance, because it spares youths the stigmatization of court wardship, pre-adjudication diversion appears to be more desirable than post-adjudication diversion. Whether or not youths are on formal probation or have been made wards of the court, however, they are subject to a certain loss of liberty whenever their behavior is controlled or limited by police or probation officers. Consequently, even though an overtaxed formal juvenile justice system might opt for a greater use of pre-adjudication diversion, it is worth noting that this could result in the widespread use of an informal system that is lacking in due process.

WAIVER OF JURISDICTION

At the time of, or at any time prior to, a formal hearing, the court may, with appropriate legal notice, hold a hearing to determine whether or not a minor is unfit to be tried as a juvenile and should instead be tried as an adult. If the court so determines, it can waive jurisdiction of the youth to the adult criminal court. Such a waiver (or remand) cannot take place unless the minor has reached a specific age, which in the majority of states is sixteen and in many other states is fourteen.

A waiver hearing must be held, consistent with the due process requirements spelled out in the Kent decision. Examples of the criteria to be considered in a waiver hearing are found in Section 707 of the Juvenile Court Law of California, which says, in part:

> The juvenile court may find that the minor is not a fit and proper subject to be dealt with under the juvenile court law if it concludes that the minor would not be amenable to the care, treatment and training program available through the facilities of the juvenile court, based upon an evaluation of the following criteria:
>
> **(1)** The degree of criminal sophistication exhibited by the minor.
>
> **(2)** Whether the minor can be rehabilitated prior to the expiration of the juvenile court's jurisdiction.
>
> **(3)** The minor's previous delinquent history.
>
> **(4)** Success of previous attempts by the juvenile court to rehabilitate the minor.
>
> **(5)** The circumstances and gravity of the offense alleged to have been committed by the minor.
>
> A determination that the minor is not a fit and proper subject to be dealt with under the juvenile court law may be based on any one or a combination of the factors set forth above, which shall be recited in the order of unfitness.

If the court makes such a determination, jurisdiction is waived, the juvenile is remanded to the appropriate adult court, and the criminal court process is initiated.

Waiver of jurisdiction for juveniles may initially appear to be extremely harsh treatment. To be sure, it does mean moving youths out of a system ostensibly oriented toward treatment and rehabilitation and into a system that is ostensibly oriented toward punishment. And some juveniles' lives are ruined as a result. But, for others, the punishment received is often less severe than that meted out in the juvenile court. To clarify, consider the three true cases presented below. In the first case, George would have been an ideal candidate for waiver, except that he was thirteen years old, and thus two years under the minimum age necessary for waiver in his state. In the cases of Louis and Steve, jurisdiction was waived with mixed results.

George was a thirteen-year-old boy who lived in Detroit. One night he and a twelve-year-old friend waited outside a neighborhood bar for the purpose of "ripping off" patrons as they emerged. When a middle-aged man came out, George put a gun to his head and demanded his money. The man protested that he had spent all his money, so George put a bullet in his brain, killing him instantly. The boys then dragged the body into a parking lot, in order to search it. After they found that the man had been telling the truth, George and his friend returned to the bar entrance to await another victim. They had been observed dragging the first man's body, however, and police arrived shortly thereafter and took them into custody.

When George was interviewed by police and probation officers, he stated, "The sucker had no green so I blew him away. It was no big thing." Throughout the interview, George indicated no remorse, admitted that he had killed before, and expressed the view that he would probably kill again.

Both the police and probation officers felt that George would in fact kill again if he could. They also felt that he should be confined for a very long period, not for rehabilitation purposes, but to protect society. George was only thirteen, however, and the juvenile court judge could not waive jurisdiction and certify George to the adult court. Accordingly, George was adjudged a juvenile delinquent and committed to a boy's training school for an indeterminate period, not to go beyond his seventeenth birthday.

It is regrettable that the Michigan law did not permit a waiver in this case, since clearly an extended period of confinement was indicated in order to protect society. But, because George was tried as a juvenile, he was freed a few years later and was thus at liberty to kill again.

Louis, a sixteen-year-old boy, and some friends started a small fire on an upper floor of a Tucson hotel. They intended to yell "Fire!" and, after the occupants had fled in panic, steal everything that they could from the vacated rooms. Unfortunately the fire, which was only supposed to produce a little smoke, got out of hand, and twenty-eight people died. Louis was taken into custody the next day and celebrated his seventeenth birthday at the county juvenile justice center. If he had been processed as a juvenile, the maximum confinement would have been in a state industrial school until he had attained his twenty-first birthday. Louis was waived to adult court, where he was arraigned on twenty-eight counts of capital murder and one count of felony arson. (A charge of capital murder may arise when a person is killed by someone who is committing a felony. Since Louis was guilty of felony arson, he was guilty of capital murder for the twenty-eight deaths that resulted from his crime.) Shortly thereafter, a jury found Louis guilty on all counts, and he received twenty-eight life sentences.

One might possibly argue that Louis should have been tried as a juvenile, because the deaths were unintentional and because Louis's previous juvenile record was minor. However, when twenty-eight people die, intentionally or otherwise, society rightfully expects that the perpetrator will be confined for more than the four years possible under juvenile court provisions.

Steve and two of his friends, all aged seventeen, offered a ride to a thirteen-year-old girl who was running away from home. Soon they all engaged in sexual intercourse with her. Then, they broke into an unoccupied beach house and kept her there against her will, while forcing her to engage in sexual acts with other young boys. Steve threatened to kill her if she attempted to escape. The girl later reported that she had engaged in a variety of sex acts with eighty-three male partners over a period of five days.

The three boys were arrested and confined in the county juvenile hall pending their formal court hearings. The girl was placed in a county facility for dependent children. The charges against Steve and his friends included burglary, contributing to the delinquency of a *minor, statutory rape, seduction for purposes of prostitution, sex perversion, and kidnapping. Given the severity of the offenses, the probable disposition would have been a commitment to the state youth authority. Indeed, they probably would have been confined in a state institution for at least one year before being considered for release on parole.*

At the formal court hearing, however, the juvenile court judge determined that the three boys were unfit to be processed as juveniles, ordered them transferred in custody to the county jail, and ordered the county district attorney to file criminal charges. Within one day the boys, who had been locked up in the juvenile hall for more than three weeks, were arraigned in an adult court. Upon request of their attorneys, they were released from custody on nominal bail. Within a few weeks, through the usual plea-bargaining process, the boys were allowed to plead guilty to a reduced charge of misdemeanor child molestation and sentenced to six months each in the county jail.

Clearly this waiver of jurisdiction from the juvenile court to the adult criminal court benefited the juveniles substantially. They were released from custody on bail and were confined for less than half the time that they would have served had they been processed as juveniles.

Thus, waivers are not the solution to serious juvenile crime that some reformers would have us believe. And yet, the process is necessary. Indeed, for some juveniles, like George, the minimum age for waivers should be lowered. Once again, we are confronted with conflicting and confusing evidence in our examination of the juvenile justice system. What is the answer? More clearly defining the problem is a start (see Chapter Three), but it is only a start.

PRIVACY

Most states have laws that limit access to the juvenile court and that forbid the release of information about juveniles arrested and/or brought into the juvenile court. For example, the California Juvenile Court rule 1311e states:

Unless requested by the minor and any parent, guardian or adult relative present, the public shall not be admitted to a juvenile court hearing. The court may nevertheless admit any person it deems to have a direct and legitimate interest in the particular case or the work of the court, subject to the condition that neither the name of the minor, parent, or guardian nor any means of ascertaining their names be disclosed by that person.

The view that juvenile proceedings should be secret is shared by many of the professionals who are invovled in the juvenile justice process.

In some states, such as Kansas, juvenile court judges may release names to the press. Even in those states, however, most judges do not do so. Those judges who do release names take the position that this will act as a deterrent to juveniles. They believe that youths who know that their names will be made public will not commit delinquent acts for fear that they will be held up to shame and ignominy. No evidence exists, however, to support the view that stigmatizing or publicly labeling a juvenile delinquent will improve that juvenile's ability to function as a law-abiding member of society. Instead, most of the evidence supports the opposite view (see Chapter Three and Chapter Five).

A substantial percentage of children arrested and brought into court, moreover, come from lower socioeconomic groups and/or minority subcultures. To many of these young people, appearances in court and, perhaps, institutional commitments are regarded not as symbols of shame but as badges of honor. Indeed, in some subcultures in southern California, youths committed to local juvenile institutions tattoo a small cross on the right hand, between thumb and forefinger. A star is added for each additional local commitment and a crescent moon for a commitment to the California Youth Authority. It is unlikely that these juveniles would be deterred from delinquent behavior by the threat of publicity. Instead, they might well decide to engage in delinquent behavior to obtain publicity and thus to enhance their status with their peers.

There is yet another factor to be considered regarding the question of privacy in the juvenile court process. Participants in the juvenile justice system may use the issue of privacy to cover up their own questionable behavior—behavior that might not stand exposure by news media. For example, the *Kansas City Times* reported the case of a fifteen-year-old rural Missouri girl who was arrested for slapping her sister's husband during a family dispute:

> She was confined to a jail cell for twenty-one days... was not informed of her rights, was not allowed visitors for at least 12 days, was not given a hearing before a judge for 16 days, and was not allowed to phone her mother when first imprisoned. The court never appointed a lawyer for her because, she says, the judge and juvenile officer told her she had waived her right to one.
>
> It was ten days before she got a change of clothes, she says. It was 18 days before she was given something to read—a Bible.[10]

If the newspaper report is accurate, it points out a problem that is not uncommon within segments of the juvenile justice system. The juvenile court procedure is civil, not criminal. Technically, the court is acting in the interests of, and for the benefit of, the child. In spite of the *Gault* decision, there are many juvenile court judges and probation officers who view due process rights of children as interfering with their efforts to rehabilitate delinquents.

Certainly, sometimes juvenile justice personnel help children. However, it is easy for judges or probation officers to delude themselves into believing that they are helping children when, in fact, they are only inflicting revenge. A man may be convicted of a criminal act and sent to an institution "for punishment." A boy may be declared a ward of the juvenile court and sent to the very same institution, subjected to the same institutional treatment "in his own best interests." It is hard to see how such a situation can be defended.

NOTES
CHAPTER SEVEN

1. Section 601, California Juvenile Court Law.

2. Section 602, California Juvenile Court Law.

3. *Kent* v. *United States,* 383 U.S. 541 (1966).

4. *In re Gault,* 387 U.S. 1, (1967).

5. *In re Winship,* 397 U.S. 358 (1970).

6. H. Ted Rubin, "Retain the Juvenile Court? Legislative Developments, Reform Directions, and the Call for Abolition," *Crime and Delinquency* 25 (July 1979): 281–98.

7. The juvenile court process varies from state to state, and no single description can be valid for all states. This description follows the California model. For other jurisdictions, the reader should consult state statutes.

8. *Persons In Need of Supervision, Juveniles In Need of Supervision, Youth In Need of Supervision, Children In Need of Supervision, Children In Need of Services.*

9. Personal communication from James Paul Burns, Orange County (California) Probation Department.

10. *Kansas City Times,* Kansas City, Mo., (May 27, 1980): 1.

8
JUVENILE PROBATION AND THE PROBATION DEPARTMENT

P robation is a function of the local juvenile court and serves as an alternative to incarceration, under the control of the juvenile court judge. When juveniles are granted probation, including or not including a commitment to a local juvenile facility, they remain under the jurisdiction of the juvenile court judge. Supervision of the probation is the responsibility of the probation department. However, when children violate its terms, the probation cannot be revoked, nor can children be incarcerated by decisions made within the probation department. Instead, children must be returned to the juvenile court, where the judge makes the appropriate decision.

Parole differs from probation, in that parole involves release from incarceration, usually from a state facility, prior to completion of the maximum determinate sentence, or at any time after commitment for an indeterminate sentence. When juvenile court judges commit juveniles to state youth authorities, or to state juvenile facilities, jurisdiction of the juvenile is usually transferred to the state, which decides when children are to be released on parole. The state is also responsible for parole supervision.

There is no predominant pattern of operation and control of probation departments. Some counties have separate juvenile and adult probation departments, and some have unitary departments combining juvenile and adult services. In some states, probation departments are operated and controlled by the counties, and in some states probation departments are operated by the state without regard for county borders. Some states that operate probation departments combine the probation and parole functions, whereas in other states the functions are separated. In some rural counties, the entire probation department consists of one probation officer, with or without clerical assistance. On the opposite end is the Los Angeles County Probation Department, which has more than two thousand probation officers, plus clerical and other support personnel. No matter how the probation agencies are controlled, however, the juvenile court judge generally retains jurisdiction over probationers, but not over parolees.

Because this book is concerned essentially with juveniles, the adult functions of the probation department will be generally disregarded throughout this chapter. The discussion will also be based primarily on the large urban juvenile probation department.

In Chapter Seven we considered the juvenile court process. The probation department plays an integral role in this process, for it carries out the intake and investigation functions for the court and supervises or detains juveniles prior to their court hearings. The probation department also usually prepares and presents court cases and makes dispositional recommendations to the juvenile court judge.

In addition, a number of other functions are performed by the probation department. It supervises the behavior of wards who have been released to the community on probation, it watches over dependent children released to the community or to foster parents, and it is usually responsible for the detention and delivery of youths committed to a state institution, although in some areas this function is performed by police, particularly if there is no local facility for confining juveniles.

The probation department often operates confinement facilities for juveniles, as well as juvenile schools, ranches, farms, and forestry camps. Indeed, probation departments in heavily populated counties usually have available a wide variety of alternative resources, which offer several treatment options. As a consequence, individual differences in juveniles can be considered in the decision-making process. These departmental functions and resources are the subject matter of this chapter.

Before that discussion commences, however, it is appropriate to consider some of the general characteristics of agencies involved with changing people's behavior, as well as the problem of measuring and evaluating the performance of such agencies. Therefore, the first part of this chapter is devoted to a discussion of performance evaluation in a probation department. Following this, we will review the juvenile court dispositions discussed in the previous chapter, as a basis for analyzing the remaining roles and functions of the juvenile probation department.

EVALUATING THE PERFORMANCE OF A PROBATION DEPARTMENT

Every public (government) agency—whether local, state, or federal—is faced with the necessity of demonstrating that it is performing some necessary service so that it will continue to receive funds from the legislature. The agency can do this by convincing the legislature that it has a useful social purpose and that it is continuing to serve that purpose. If the agency can develop a political constituency among the public or some portion of it, this will also enhance its ability to attract or increase its share of legislative appropriations.

Police agencies find it relatively easy to develop political constituencies, particularly among the middle and upper classes and within the business community, for the police protect lives and property and arrest and confine lawbreakers. Because these classes have a need to be protected and also considerable political power, police budget requests usually receive sympathetic consideration from legislatures.

Probation departments and other correctional agencies are not as well situated to develop political constituencies. They do not usually arrest and jail lawbreakers or protect lives and property. Their clients come mainly from lower socioeconomic classes and ethnic minorities, groups that have relatively little political power. Further, these clients would hardly be prepared to lend whatever political support they might have to a probation agency. Probationers do not usually feel a positive identification with probation officers. Few people want to be on probation, except when it is an alternative to something more unpleasant.

Typical probationers perceive the probation officer as someone who butts into their lives and interferes with their pleasures. This is not always the case, however, and there are occasional exceptions. For example, consider the case of Billy:

Billy was a sixteen-year-old boy who lived in a suburban area near Los Angeles. He did not like to go to school and had been truant for extended periods on three separate occasions in one semester. At the request of the boys' vice-principal of a local high school, Mr. Brown, a probation officer working in juvenile male supervision, filled out an application for petition and submitted it to the noncustody intake section of the probation department. Billy was interviewed by an intake officer; a petition was filed and ultimately was referred to a juvenile investigator.

When interviewed by the investigator, Billy stated that he was no longer truant and that he had been back in school for more than two weeks. The investigator asked why, and Billy said that he had tried for two months to get a job. He had been unsuccessful, however, because every prospective employer had demanded to see his high school diploma as a precondition of employment. Billy had given up trying to find a job and reluctantly decided to return to school and stay there until graduation.

Upon hearing this, the investigator stated that, after verification, he would arrange to have the petition dismissed. After all, the boy had rehabilitated himself; there was no purpose to be served by stigmatizing him or wasting the time of the court and the probation department any further.

At this point, Billy became hostile. He stated, "All of my friends have Mr. Brown for a P.O. If I don't get him for my P.O., I will quit going to school." Billy was adamant in his position, so the investigator wrote a juvenile court report, and later the juvenile court judge reluctantly put Billy on probation.

It was clear that Billy felt deprived because he didn't have his own probation officer. He regarded a P.O. more as a status symbol and big brother than as a watchdog who limited and controlled his behavior.

Because the probation agency has little capacity to build a political constituency, it must convince the legislature that it is worth funding because it is performing useful functions. But, in any agency that deals primarily in the delivery of intangible services, it is very difficult to measure performance as it relates to meeting the goals of the organization. The primary external goals of the probation department are to protect the community and to cause the offenders (delinquents) to change their behavior, to stop doing whatever it was that caused them to be brought to the attention of the criminal justice system. In addition, like all organizations, the probation department has additional goals, including organizational survival and providing satisfactions to its members.[1]

An organization that does not survive cannot attain any of the external goals for which it was created, nor can it provide satisfactions to its members. Employees cannot receive income, pursue work careers, or accomplish personal goals unless the organization survives. Therefore, in decision-making, the organization must always consider how any decision or policy may affect its ability to survive, both in the short run and in the long run. As Thomas Johnson has correctly pointed out, "Decision-making in the juvenile justice system is based on what is good for the system, and not necessarily the system's client."[2]

The probation department cannot, in fact, demonstrate that it is effective either in protecting the community or in rehabilitating the juvenile offender. The typical juvenile probationer may see the probation officer not even once a month or as many as three times a month. Even at the higher figure, the time the probation officer spends each month with the probationer is only a small fraction of the probationer's waking hours, and it would be difficult to demonstrate the impact, for good or ill, of these probationer–probation officer interactions.

This one-to-one interaction between probation officer and probationer, however, is the primary rehabilitative technique of the juvenile probation department,[3] in spite of the fact that the department cannot demonstrate any relationship between means and end—the means being the one-to-one interaction (personal contact), and the end being rehabilitation of the offender. But, in order to survive, the probation department assumes the validity of the means–end relationship. In a classic example of goal displacement,[4] it then ignores those ends that cannot be measured and instead measures those that can be measured, although they are trivial. It reports to the legislature not how many offenders were rehabilitated, but how many one-to-one interactions occurred, how many juvenile court reports were written, how many children were supervised, and how many children were committed to county, state, and private institutions. The agency may not be able to demonstrate that it is accomplishing something useful, but it can certainly demonstrate that it is keeping busy.

Employee performance also is measured not in terms of offender rehabilitation, but in terms of making the appropriate number of personal contacts, writing the appropriate number of court reports, and doing other paper work. For example, probation officers and others are required to fill out self-report forms to demonstrate that their performance is appropriate. This leads to what V. F. Ridgway refers to as the "dysfunctional consequences of performance measurement." According to Ridgway,

Even where performance measurements are instituted purely for purposes of information, they are probably interpreted as definitions of the important aspects of that job or activity and hence have important implications for the motivation of behavior.[5]

Consider the example of a probation department in California. At the behest of the county legislature, the probation department hired a consulting firm to analyze the work effectiveness of probation officers. Among other results, the consultants concluded that a typical probation officer in juvenile supervision should average 5.4 personal contacts per day, or about 120 per month, based on 22 working days per month.

Department management made it clear that the probation officer who made substantially fewer than 120 calls was probably wasting time, and the probation officer who made substantially more was probably not having "meaningful interactions." Therefore, the primary goal of a probation officer working in juvenile supervision was not to change the behavior of the client, but to average 120 calls per month.

In juvenile supervision in that county, clients were assigned on the basis of geography and sex. Thus, for example, male probation officers would supervise male juvenile probationers within limited geographical areas. It was a relatively simple matter to do most of the month's work in a few days. There was a close working relationship between juvenile officers and school authorities. Accordingly, probation officers could drop in on a junior or senior high school vice-principal and arrange for their probationers to be called out of classes one at a time for short stereotyped interviews. They could easily have fifteen to twenty-five personal contacts apiece per day this way, thus completing most of their required monthly work in the first week of the month. The probation officers could then spend the rest of the month doing what they (correctly or not) thought was useful. During the last week of the month, they could rush around again seeing any clients they might have missed earlier. This strategy served the additional purpose of allowing the probation officers to ascertain whether or not the juveniles were having school problems.

Comparable strategies were employed in other divisions of the probation department, in addition to juvenile supervision. It was clear that the majority of probation officers in the department worked less than four hours out of an eight-hour day. Further, it was relatively easy to give supervisors the figures they wanted to see on the monthly reports, and it was foolish not to do so.

The majority of probation officers in that department had other interests, in addition to their work for the agency. A number of them were attending graduate school, usually seeking degrees in the social sciences, management, or law. It was relatively easy, by proper management of time, to study or do homework for three or four hours every working day. Some probation officers who were not going to school were doing other work or were in business for themselves.

The department placed a high value on conforming behavior by its employees, and innovative behavior was often perceived by superiors as disloyalty to the organization, since innovative ideas on the part of employees implied that they lacked respect for their superiors.[6] Therefore, there was a high turnover among innovators and nonconformists, who were perceived as troublemakers.

Given this kind of a setting, it is easy to understand how the needs of the client come into conflict with the needs of the probation officer to survive and advance within the probation department bureaucracy. It is difficult or impossible to measure the probation officer's success in changing the behavior of the juvenile client, but it is quite easy to measure whether or not the probation officer is conforming to the department's expectations concerning the number of personal contacts per month, the number of court reports completed, and other busywork. Thus, the client's interests are shunted aside.

Another conflict arises in small departments in which a probation officer may be engaged in both juvenile supervision and juvenile investigation. This may also occur in large departments, if officers engaged in juvenile supervision are required to write court reports on their probationers who get into trouble. Court reports have deadlines that must be met, but juvenile supervision does not have such time demarcations. If for some reason a probation officer is short of time, he or she must put supervision aside in order to write court reports. In studies conducted by McEachern and Taylor, it was found that almost 25 percent of juveniles put on probation were not seen by their supervising probation officers for a full year after they were placed on probation.[7] McEachern and Taylor also reported that those juveniles who had committed the largest number of reported offenses in the year prior to their court appearances were least likely to be seen by their supervising probation officers. Those with the worst delinquent records prior to their court hearings were least likely to be given probation supervision, *but improved the most* and committed the fewest offenses in the year following their court hearings. Those juveniles who had been charged with the fewest delinquent offenses prior to their court hearings were most likely to be given probation supervision, *but improved the least* and committed the most offenses.[8]

McEachern and Taylor's study would seem to suggest that, by design or otherwise, the probation officers gave the most delinquent minors the best opportunity for rehabilitation; in other words, they ignored them. A cynic might suggest that probation officers could conceivably aid more juveniles by adopting a policy of "benign neglect."

A further area of conflict for probation officers lies in the bulit-in role conflict of their position.[9] They have two goals: to protect the community and to rehabilitate the offender. The first goal requires probation officers to play the role of police officer, watching juveniles and returning them to court for further disposition (punishment) if they violate the terms of their probation. The second goal requires probation officers to develop counseling relationships—relationships in which juveniles can discuss their problems freely and openly. However, it is difficult or impossible to develop such a relationship if children believe or know that honesty on their part will lead their probation officers to arrest them. Carl Klockars reports that some probation officers resolve this role conflict by emphasizing the police role, but that most probation officers emphasize the counselor role and largely ignore the police role of protecting the community.[10]

DISPOSITION OPTIONS

As we saw in Chapter Seven, the dispositional options that can be used by a judge for children who have been declared wards of the court include:

Money fine

Community work project

Probation for a specific term

Probation for an indeterminate term

Probation, plus a specific commitment to a county juvenile facility

Probation, plus an indeterminate commitment to a county juvenile facility

Probation, plus removal from the home, for placement in a
> Foster home
> Relative's home
> Privately operated juvenile facility
> Mental institution

Commitment to a state youth authority

Money Fine

A money fine is normally used for minor matters, such as routine traffic offenses. This disposition is meant as a deterrent against infractions not regarded as criminal or delinquent in character.

In most jurisdictions, declaring children wards of the court is tantamount to putting them on probation and would hardly be appropriate for minor traffic offenders, who probably do not need probation supervision. In such cases, therefore, the court usually either requires immediate payment and terminates the proceedings, or continues the case for a limited period so that the minors can have some time to pay. The main idea, of course, is to avoid the necessity of court wardship.

Before imposing a money fine, however, the court would do well to ascertain that a particular juvenile has the money or the capacity to earn money, for, if the fine is paid by the child's parents or guardian, the desired deterrent effect may be lost.

Community Work Project

Like a money fine, this may also be an alternative to wardship and probation, or it may be one of the conditions of probation imposed by the court. This disposition may be appropriate as an alternative to a money fine, if the juvenile has no source of income. It also may be regarded as poetic justice, if the juvenile's misbehavior involves malicious mischief or willful destruction of property.

Assignment to a community work project requires the juvenile to perform work, usually for a local government agency or perhaps a charitable agency. The work is supervised or observed, and failure to perform may result in the return of the juvenile to the court for further action. The work normally involves simple tasks such as cleaning streets, sidewalks, and parks. In cases involving destruction of private property, the court may assign the juvenile to work for the victim for some specific period, as a form of reimbursement.

Both a money fine and assignment to a community work project may appropriately be perceived as punishment. The latter disposition assures that it is the juvenile who is being punished, and not the juvenile's parents. Such assignments are usually scheduled after school and on weekends, so as not to interfere with schoolwork.

Probation for a Specific Term

Probation for a specific term is not very commonly employed as a disposition. It is more commonly used in adult criminal courts where probation is typically the equivalent of a suspended sentence. A comparable strategy in the juvenile court would be the use of a continuance.

Probation for an Indeterminate Term

This is probably the most common disposition made by the juvenile court, particularly with minor and first-time offenders. It provides the probation department with jurisdiction over the minor for an indefinite period, or until the age at which the juvenile court loses jurisdiction over the child. This age varies from state to state, but in most states jurisdiction ends with the minor's twenty-first birthday.

Only rarely is a minor on probation that long, however. When a child is placed on probation, the probation officer typically develops, over a period of time, some expectations about improvements in the child's behavior. If these expectations are met, the probation officer usually returns to the juvenile court with a request that the judge release the minor from probation.

Even if the juvenile's behavior does not meet expectations, the probation officer will usually request termination of probation when the child is old enough to be dealt with in an adult court. In California, for example, the juvenile court retains jurisdiction of minors until their twenty-first birthdays. However, the adult courts have jurisdiction over criminal offenses committed by persons who are eighteen years of age or older. Therefore, California probation officers usually ask for probation termination when a client's eighteenth birthday approaches. Further illegal behavior is the concern of the adult court.

Juveniles who are placed on probation and continue to misbehave may be returned to the court for further disposition. On occasion, some juveniles assume that a grant of probation without any confinement means that they have gotten away with something, and they will continue to misbehave. Sometimes informal strategies may be employed in such situations. Consider the case of Joseph:

Joseph was a thirteen-year-old boy, small in stature, who was arrested for petty theft—stealing food and candy bars from a delivery truck. A number of other, larger boys participated in the theft, but only Joseph was caught. He had no prior arrest record, but police records reflected three field interrogations, all indicating that Joseph walked the streets in better-class neighborhoods in the middle of the night. Joseph was released to his mother, and the police mailed an application for petition to the probation department. In due time, Joseph appeared in juvenile court, where he was declared a ward of the court and placed on probation. Joseph had not been locked up by the police or by the court.

Joseph's probation officer felt concern about what he perceived as Joseph's flippant attitude. The officer suspected that Joseph thought he had gotten away with something by being placed on probation without being locked up. The probation officer, as required by departmental rules, went over the terms and conditions of probation with Joseph. The officer also asked Joseph to sign a statement indicating that he had read and understood the terms and conditions of probation, which included stipulations that he violate no laws, attend school regularly, and not be out of the house after the 10 P.M. curfew.

A few weeks later, the probation officer checked with school authorities and police. He learned that Joseph had been absent from school an average of two days a week, and that the police had observed him walking in an upper-class neighborhood one morning at about 2 A.M. The probation officer called Joseph at home early one Friday morning and ordered Joseph to visit him at the probation department that afternoon after school.

When Joseph appeared that afternoon, he was castigated by the probation officer, who told Joseph that he did not deserve the con-

sideration he had been given. Joseph was told that the probation officer intended to file a petition that would force Joseph to be returned to court where the judge would "put him away forever." Joseph was then handcuffed, taken to a waiting police car, and whisked away to Juvenile Hall. Upon his arrival, Joseph was taken to a holding cell and locked up.

Most of the children confined in Juvenile Hall were kept in dormitory units, which were segregated by age and sex. The units were quite pleasant, the food was good, and there was a library and a television set. The holding cells were supposed to be used for children who were "acting out," or for other children who, for various reasons, required isolated quarters. The holding cells were sparsely decorated and had solid steel doors with small observation windows. At the bottom of each door there was an opening that permitted a tray of food to be slipped into the cell three times a day.

From Friday afternoon to Sunday afternoon, Joseph was held incommunicado. His mother, who had been notified of his arrest on Friday, was asked to meet the probation officer at Juvenile Hall on Sunday afternoon. The probation officer had not been required to file an application for petition, since Saturday and Sunday were not court days. During the meeting at Juvenile Hall, the probation officer indicated to Joseph's mother that he was prepared to reconsider his decision to take Joseph back to court, if Joseph showed appropriate remorse and a willingness to cooperate. Joseph was then brought from his cell, and the situation was explained to him. Joseph had undergone what appeared to be a total personality change. He promised to never again cause any problems. He was, accordingly, released to his mother, and he kept his promise. About a year later his probation was terminated.

One might regard the treatment of Joseph as cruel and callous. However, the job description of a probation officer does not include the need to be loved. Within the limits of the law and of conscience, a probation officer may use whatever strategies are most likely to be effective and that require the least expenditure of resources.

The use of a "shock therapy" technique, such as that used on Joseph, may be very unpleasant for a limited period, but may eliminate the necessity for extended periods of supervision or confinement. If so, it may be a highly desirable alternative. Of course, if it is to be effective at all, such a shock therapy strategy must be used early with first-time offenders, and certainly not with juveniles who have been previously detained. At the Juvenile Hall in which this incident occurred, most of the children came from low socioeconomic backgrounds. Indeed, many of the children confined in the dormitory units considered this Juvenile Hall a substantial improvement over their living conditions at home.

Some additional factors must also be considered. First, the probation officer must be prepared to carry out the threat that is the core of the shock therapy. If Joseph had not shown remorse, the probation officer would have had no alternative but to return him to court with a recommendation that he spend some time in confinement. Not to have done so would have led to a substantial loss of the probation officer's credibility with Joseph and with most of the other juvenile offenders in the county. The delinquent subculture in an area usually has an excellent grapevine, and the news of a failure to carry out a threat would have spread very quickly.

Second, the threat must be appropriate to the misbehavior. As the saying goes, one should not "swat flies with a sledgehammer." If a probation officer threatens to send a probationer to the state youth authority for a minor matter such as a curfew violation, for example, that officer is left with no credible threat to use in case of a more serious violation. In addition, if the level of threat is too high for the level of misbehavior, the juvenile will probably not perceive it as credible to begin with. Further, juvenile court judges usually will not accept a probation officer's recommendation for punishment, if it is too great for the level of misbehavior.

Another form of shock therapy has been presented in a movie called *Scared Straight,* which was shown on television in the late 1970s. This movie reported on a program developed by inmates at the State Prison in Rahway, New Jersey. Juveniles with serious delinquent records were brought to the prison to spend a few hours with long-term prisoners, who, in succinct street language, warned the delinquents about what would happen to them if they continued their unacceptable behavior and ended up in prison. To date, no data are available to indicate whether or not this form of shock therapy has had any long-term effect.

Still another form of shock therapy called "shock probation" is being employed on a small scale with adult offenders.[11] When this form of therapy is used, an offender is granted probation with the condition that a nominal period, such as thirty to sixty days, is to be spent in a state prison. Thus, the probationer will become aware of the consequences of a future violation.

Probation plus a Specific Commitment

Probation plus a specific commitment to a county juvenile facility is a disposition that might be employed for juvenile offenders with histories of delinquent behavior. It would not usually be used for children who appear in juvenile court for the first time. The custom of the juvenile justice system is to escalate the severity of the response with successive misbehavior by juveniles. Thus, unless first offenses are unusually serious, dispositions including confinement are usually not made. In most circumstances, first-timers are put on probation without confinement, with the understanding that subsequent probation violation might well result in confinement.

Probation plus an Indeterminate Commitment

The imposition of an indeterminate commitment to a county facility as an adjunct to probation would normally be an escalation for a juvenile who has previously been confined one or more times for limited periods. Such a disposition would be unusual for a first-timer, unless the child's behavior problems are quite severe. Often, an indeterminate commitment to a county facility is the last alternative prior to a commitment to the state youth authority.

Counties vary in the number and kinds of confinement resources available to them. Some large urban counties have juvenile halls, schools, ranches, forestry camps, and possibly other open or closed facilities. However, some rural counties, and even some urban counties, have no juvenile confinement facilities whatsoever. Whenever children are detained prior to court hearings in such areas, they are confined at the local jail. If decisions are made at juvenile court hearings for confinement, the dispositional alternatives may be private juvenile facilities, state youth authorities, or the department of youth services. If the choice is confinement in a private juvenile facility, it will normally be at the expense of the county, although some states partially reimburse counties for the cost of confinement in a private facility. Although the cost of some private facilities is as little as thirty to forty dollars a day per resident, in many such facilities, the cost exceeds one hundred dollars a day. As Jerome Miller has pointed out, "I could send the child and a parent on an around-the-world cruise for less than the cost of locking him up for a year."[12]

If a child receives an indeterminate commitment to a youth facility, the length of stay and date of release will depend upon how the child behaves while institutionalized. Regrettably, there are no data to demonstrate that good behavior within the institution is necessarily followed by good behavior after discharge.

Probation plus Removal from the Home

When the judge declares a child to be a ward or dependent of the court, the court takes legal custody of the child. It can, if it chooses, transfer physical custody of an individual child from one parent to another, from a parent to an institution, or from a parent to a foster parent or to another relative. In most states, a juvenile court order supersedes the orders of other courts. Therefore, for example, if the order of a divorce court action gave legal custody of a child to the mother, a juvenile court order could transfer custody to the father, if he is willing to accept it. Such a transfer of custody, however, can extend only through the period of time during which the minor remains a ward or dependent child of the court.

Custody may also be transferred, in the case of a dependent child, if the parent or guardian is found to be abusing or neglecting the child and if the situation does not appear to be immediately correctable. The transfer would be for the protection of the child, not for rehabilitation. Another candidate for such a transfer is the ward who refuses "to obey the reasonable and proper orders or directions of his parents, guardian, or custodian."[13] This definition fits children who cannot get along with their parents. Often, the child is a girl who cannot get along with her mother. A foster home might also be appropriate for a delinquent offender, if it seems that the child has little chance of improvement unless removed from the home environment. This might occur when there is a high level of hostility in the home or when one or both of the parents are role models for the child's illegal behavior.

If the nature of the problem does not require that the child be confined in a secure setting, placement with a parent or other relative is usually the most desirable solution. It causes the least emotional dislocation for the child and probably requires the least utilization of public funds. Normally, the county does not pay a parent to care for a child who has been placed by the court, although sometimes payment is appropriate. Other relatives of the child may also be willing to accept placement without reimbursement.

If placement is made in a foster home with persons unrelated to the child, then reimbursement is mandatory in all but the most unusual cases. Although foster parents are often very caring, it is unusual to find a foster parent who can provide the child with the love and affection of a parent or close relative.

There are also privately operated facilities to which the court may send a juvenile. Some are proprietary institutions operated for profit, some are privately owned and not operated for profit, and many are church-related. Various religious denominations have historically had a deep interest in the care and treatment of children. This interest is often manifested in the establishment of facilities for troubled or dependent children. Church-related facilities have tax advantages not normally enjoyed by other facilities and are perceived as having a legitimacy that may improve their capacity to seek and obtain grants from government and from foundations.

Many of the privately operated facilities may be characterized as "theme" institutions; that is, they adhere to one particular therapeutic concept or another. Thus, some specialize in individual psychotherapy, or milieu therapy, or confrontation therapy, or intensive group interaction, or challenge, or religion. These strategies are the subject of the next chapter.

Commitment to a mental institution is probably the least used institutional option available to the court, because it requires clear evidence that the child is suffering from some mental illness. Such evidence is usually lacking in cases that come before the juvenile court. Occasionally an offender commits an act so gross that most people assume the perpetrator is insane. If the grossness of crimes defined insanity, more offenders would be diverted into mental institutions rather than into jails, prisons, and juvenile institutions.

Commitment to a State Youth Authority

A decision to commit a juvenile to the state is a recognition that there are no local alternatives left to the court. Many regard it as an admission of failure. In a state that has few local resources available, it might be necessary to make such a commitment, since the local court may have no other confinement option available. Some counties are reluctant to pay the costs of commitment to a privately operated facility and prefer that the juvenile court judge commit the child to the state. Some states charge back to the counties a nominal monthly or annual fee for wards committed to the state, and some states charge nothing. Either way, from a financial point of view, commitment to the state is, for the county, the most economical option.

As we have indicated in this and the previous two chapters, the best strategy in dealing with juveniles is to do as little as possible to involve them in the criminal justice process. Whenever possible, the police attempt to deal with juveniles informally, as do the juvenile authorities and the courts. If a youth continues to misbehave, however, an escalation of response by the criminal justice system occurs, which follows a pattern from informal to formal processing, from local to county and ultimately, from county to state. Since commitment to the state is the last resort, it is a step that is not lightly taken.

Commitment to the state often has the effect of removing children from the immediate geographical area, which may or may not be regarded as an advantage. It also has the effect, usually, of removing children from the jurisdiction of the court and thus of the county probation department. In most states, the state youth authorities have the option of accepting or rejecting children committed to it. However, once the state has accepted jurisdiction and delivery, the local juvenile court has no further jurisdiction. When children are processed through a state youth reception or diagnostic center, they are almost always transferred to a state youth institution. Instead of confinement, however, some states choose to release children on parole to parents or to foster homes in the same community.

OTHER PROBATION
DEPARTMENT FUNCTIONS

In this and the previous chapter, we have analyzed several functions of the juvenile probation department or juvenile justice center. These functions have included custody intake, noncustody intake, investigation and processing of juveniles through the court, as well as supervision of wards and dependent children in their homes, in foster homes, and in public and private facilities. The balance of this chapter will be devoted to a consideration of some of the other functions of the juvenile probation department.

Although operations vary from state to state, it may be said that the probation department does whatever state law requires it to do, plus whatever the county legislature wants it to do, if it is financed by the county, plus whatever the juvenile court judge wants it to do.

Thus, in a state like California, probation officers perform many duties that would appear to be only tangentially related to the care and processing of children in trouble. For example, under certain circumstances, in divorce or dissolution of marriage cases in which custody of the children is contested, probation officers investigate the children and parents and make reports and recommendations to the court. Similar investigations are undertaken in the case of underaged persons who require the permission of a juvenile court judge to get married.

In some states, including California, parents are legally responsible for the financial support of their children. For example, if the confinement results from an order of the court, California law permits the county to seek and obtain reimbursement from the parents for the costs of confinement of the child at county expense. Therefore, if a child is detained by order of the court prior to an adjudication hearing or is committed to confinement at a dispositional hearing, the parents are financially liable. This financial liability extends to natural and adoptive parents, but not to step-parents. The county cannot accept reimbursement if a child is being supported by Aid to Families with Dependent Children (AFDC).

The threat to demand reimbursement from parents is sometimes a useful technique. It is not at all uncommon for a parent to bring an unruly child to the juvenile center and demand that the child be locked up. Apparently, many parents believe that, if they get tired of parenting, they can simply turn the child over to a probation officer, thus absolving themselves of any further responsibility for the child's care and support.

One can, of course, be very sympathetic toward parents who are having trouble supporting or controlling their children. However, probation officers cannot accept the responsibility of replacing all of the parents who wish to abandon their children. But, if parents bring in a child and want to file an application for petition alleging incorrigibility, they have the right to do so in most states. However, it is appropriate to advise parents when they are filing that they will have to pay for the child's confinement and future placement at a daily or monthly rate substantially higher than the cost of supporting the child at home. It is truly inspiring to observe parents have a change of heart, upon hearing this news, and decide that they really love their children after all and want to take them home.

The probation officer must be very careful in the employment of this financial weapon against parents, for it is very easy to fall into the trap of allowing the costs to the county or state to become the primary factor in deciding what to do about children. Intake officers must carefully analyze the nature of the parent-child relationship. If they feel that detention of the child is necessary, it should be done. However, if approrpiate, the intake officer may also choose to file petitions alleging that the children involved are dependent, rather than incorrigible.

NOTES
CHAPTER EIGHT

1. James G. March and Herbert Simon, *Organizations* (New York, 1958).

2. Thomas A. Johnson, *Introduction to the Juvenile Justice System* (St. Paul, Minn., 1975), p. 307.

3. National Advisory Commission on Criminal Justice Standards and Goals. *Corrections* (Washington, D. C., 1973), p. 320.

4. David Duffee, Frederick Hussey, and John Kramer, *Criminal Justice: Organization, Structure and Analysis* (Englewood Cliffs, N. J., 1978), p. 444.

5. V. F. Ridgway, "Dysfunctional Consequences of Performance Measurement," *Some Theories of Organization,* Albert H. Rubenstein and Chadwick J. Haberstroh, eds. (Homewood, Ill., 1960), p. 377.

6. See Robert Presthus, *The Organizational Society,* 2d ed. (New York, 1978).

7. Alexander McEachern and Edward Taylor. *SIMBAD Simulation as a Basis for Social Agent's Decisions,* Rev. (Los Angeles, 1967).

8. Ibid.

9. Louis Tomaino, "The Five Faces of Probation," *Federal Probation* 39 (December 1975): 42.

10. Carl B. Klockars, Jr., "A Theory of Probation Supervision," *Corrections in the Community,* George G. Killinger and Paul F. Cromwell, Jr., eds. (St. Paul, Minn., 1974), pp. 194–210.

11. National Advisory Commission on Criminal Justice Standards and Goals, *Corrections* (Washington, D. C., 1973), p. 321.

12. Personal communication from Jerome Miller.

13. Section 601, California Juvenile Court Law.

9
JUVENILE INSTITUTIONS AND TREATMENT

As was stated in the previous chapter, commitment to a juvenile facility is usually regarded as a last resort, after other disposition options have been tried and found to be unsuccessful. Sometimes, juvenile offenders are committed to an institution on the occasion of their first appearance in court, even on the occasion of their first contact with the criminal justice system.

In some cases, the court may conclude that institutional confinement is necessary in order to protect the public. This situation might arise if a child's appearance before the court results from the commission of an offense or offenses involving violence, or attempted or threatened violence. Such offenses include, among others, murder, aggravated assault, rape, and armed robbery.

In other cases, the court may conclude that confinement is necessary for the protection of the minor, particularly if the minor has demonstrated a tendency toward self-injury or suicide. Also possibly in this category are minors who have a pattern of dangerous-drug usage that might lead to bizarre and life-threatening behavior. Such drugs include amphetamines, barbiturates, PCP, and LSD, among others.

In still other instances, a case may have received so much publicity that the public demands confinement, particularly if some heinous offense has been committed. This category includes offenses in which the victims are small children, since such offenses usually receive substantial publicity.

Generally speaking, it is difficult to be optimistic about the probability of rehabilitation of any individual committed to an institution for either juveniles or adults.[1] The theory of differential association[2] does not lend support to the belief that the unsatisfactory behavior of a juvenile delinquent can be improved by confinement in an institution with a large number of other juvenile delinquents. People tend to emulate the behavior of those with whom they associate. Putting a delinquent in a facility with a few hundred or a few thousand other delinquents is therefore likely to result in less satisfactory, rather than more satisfactory, behavior.

Even putting the matter of differential association aside, institutional confinement does not appear to be a good strategy for preparing people to function well outside the institution.[3] In order to control an institution, particularly if it has a large population, the staff must require conforming behavior by the inmates. The inmates tend to be stripped of individuality and to think of themselves as objects or numbers, rather than as individuals, since it is easier for the staff to control and manage objects than people.

Particularly in large institutions, inmates are told when to get up in the morning, when to eat, what work to do, and when to go to bed. They are discouraged from thinking for themselves and accepting responsibility for their actions. The inmates learn a pattern of acceptable institutional behavior, which keeps them out of trouble. However, all of this does not prepare them to function well when they return to the outside world. Often, this experience can result in inmates who function less adequately after they get out of the institution than they did before they went in.

In most institutions, there is a conflict between the goals of control and the goals of treatment. Custodial staff members are primarily concerned with controlling the behavior of the inmates while they are in the institution, whereas treatment staff members are concerned with changing and improving the behavior of the residents after their release from the institution. In this conflict between custodial and treatment personnel, the custodial personnel often prevail. Treatment personnel cannot improve the behavior of an inmate unless custodial personnel can secure the continued presence of the resident in the institution. The whole character of institutional life in a correctional facility is such that custodial considerations usually have priority over treatment considerations.

The relationship of custodial to treatment considerations varies with the nature of the facility. In a detention center, custody is the primary consideration. It is usually a short-term facility whose purpose is to hold the juvenile pending some sort of action, often by the juvenile court. It is often a period of high anxiety for the inmate, who may seriously consider an attempt to escape. A show of security may well serve to reduce the inmate's anxiety.

At the other end of the custody continuum is the group home, or halfway house, which often has no custodial personnel. The inmates are expected to exercise self-discipline by choosing not to walk away from the facility, even though no one prevents them from doing so. Between these ends of the continuum are several other kinds of juvenile facilities in which the relationship between custodial and treatment staff varies from situations in which they are equals to those in which one side dominates the other, as in a facility that features individual or group psychotherapy, in which treatment personnel usually exercise control over custodial staff.[4]

Because of the widespread view throughout the juvenile justice system that institutionalization makes little or no demonstrable contribution to rehabilitation, there has been great interest in recent years in developing programs to reduce confinement of minors. These programs generally are referred to as either *diversion* or *deinstitutionalization*. The definitions of these two terms overlap. *Diversion* usually refers to programs or efforts, at any point in the system, to reduce or eliminate the interaction between the offender and the criminal justice system. *Deinstitutionalization* may refer to programs or efforts to reduce the use of confinement as a disposition for either status offenders or delinquent offenders. It also refers to efforts or programs designed to remove from institutions those who have already been confined. Particularly well known in this context has been the work of Dr. Jerome Miller in Massachusetts in the early 1970s. That work will be discussed later in this chapter.

Efforts toward deinstitutionalization have been especially concerned with the reduction of confinement of status offenders. The reduced institutionalization of status offenders was one of the goals of the Juvenile Justice and Delinquency Prevention Act of 1974.[5] This act made funds available for a limited number of demonstration projects in "jurisdictions which would remove status offenders from detention and correctional institutions within two years."[6] The emphasis on programs for status offenders may result from the belief that it is not fair to lock up a child for an act for which an adult could not even be arrested. Further, in many jurisdictions, studies have reported that status offenders who are institutionalized are often confined for longer periods of time than delinquent offenders.[7]

Such findings should not be surprising. Juvenile court judges and probation officers operate on the assumption that they intervene in children's lives in order to help them. The delinquent offender, particularly one with an extensive record, may be unworthy of receiving the "beneficial" services available from the court and the probation officer. The status offender, however, is not really a bad kid, and would probably benefit more from these services. It is easy to rationalize, therefore, that institutionalization should be denied or limited for undeserving delinquent offenders, so that its benefits can be provided for more deserving status offenders.

A recent report, *Children in Custody*,[8] divides juvenile facilities into two groups:

Short-term facilities
  Detention centers
  Shelters
  Reception and diagnostic centers
Long-term facilities
  Training schools
  Ranches, forestry camps, or farms
  Halfway houses or group homes

The report also notes that facilities are either public or private. These classifications are used here. Like all broad classification systems, this one tends to blur differences between various subtypes of facilities. For example, some jurisdictions use detention centers only for detaining children prior to their court hearings. Other jurisdictions also use detention centers to confine children who have been sentenced by the juvenile court. For example, a county facility in California is called the Juvenile Hall *and* the Juvenile Home. When children are detained pending their court hearings, they are ordered to be held in the Juvenile Hall. When children are sentenced at their dispositional hearings, they are ordered confined in the Juvenile Home.

Some counties have no detention centers or other juvenile facilities. If children are arrested or detained, they will probably be locked up in a city or county jail pending juvenile court action. If the dispositional hearing results in an order for commitment, they may again be confined in a jail, transferred to a privately operated juvenile facility, or transferred to a state youth authority for further processing.

Training schools vary in their program offerings. Some concentrate on academic instruction, some concentrate on vocational training, and some offer a mixture of both.

A substantial majority of the children confined in juvenile facilities are male. As of mid-1975, there were 46,980 juveniles held in public detention and correctional facilities. This included 37,926 males and 9,054 females. There were 27,290 juveniles held in private facilities, including 19,152 males and 8,138 females. Thus, males represented 80.7 percent of juveniles in public institutions and 70.2 percent of

TABLE 9.1
Juvenile Facilities and Populations, Mid-1975
(from *Children in Custody*, 1979, 15–17)

Type of facility	Public and private	Midyear population	Public	Midyear population	Private	Midyear population
All facilities	2,151	74,270	874	46,980	1,277	27,290
Short-term	453	13,555	387	12,725	66	830
Detention centers	350	11,089 +	347	11,089	3	n.a.*
Shelters	81	869	23	200	58	669
Reception or diagnostic centers	22	1,436 +	17	1,436	5	n.a.*
Long-term	1,698	60,715	487	34,255	1,211	26,460
Training schools	254	30,408	189	26,748	65	3,660
Ranches, forestry camps, and farms	398	18,479	103	5,385	295	13,094
Halfway houses and group homes	1,046	11,828	195	2,122	851	9,706

*Not available

Juvenile Institutions and Treatment

TABLE 9.2
Juvenile Facility Population by Detention Status, Mid-1975
(from *Children in Custody*, 1979, 16–17)

	Public facilities	
	Individuals	Percentage
Detention status		
Total	46,980	100.0
Male	37,926	80.7
Female	9,054	19.3
Dependent-neglected	451	1.0
Male	236	0.5
Female	215	0.5
Status offenders	4,494	9.6
Male	2,539	5.4
Female	1,955	4.2
Delinquent offenders	34,107	72.6
Male	29,229	62.2
Female	4,878	10.4
Others	7,928	16.9
Male	5,922	12.6
Female	2,006	4.3
Pending court disposition or transfer to another jurisdiction	7,403	15.8
Male	5,536	11.8
Female	1,867	4.0
Voluntary	516	1.1
Male	379	0.8
Female	137	0.3
Emotionally disturbed or mentally retarded, awaiting transfer	9	*
Male	7	*
Female	2	*

*Less than 0.1 percent

Private facilities	
Individuals	Percentage
27,290	100.0
19,152	70.2
8,138	29.8
4,844	17.8
3,185	11.7
1,659	6.1
4,316	15.8
2,614	9.6
1,702	6.2
9,809	35.9
7,641	28.0
2,168	7.9
8,321	30.5
5,712	20.9
2,609	9.6
529	1.9
351	1.3
178	0.7
5,879	21.5
4,053	14.9
1,826	6.7
1,913	7.0
1,308	4.8
605	2.2

juveniles in private facilities. Females represented 19.3 percent of juveniles in public facilities and 29.8 percent of juveniles in private facilities.[9]

There were 874 public juvenile detention and correctional facilities in 1975, and 1,277 such private facilities. Broken down by categories, they were as shown in Table 9.1.

Of the 874 public facilities, 423 were administered by the state and 451 were locally administered. Of these institutions, 326 were for males only, 92 were for females only, and 456 were coeducational. Population capacity ranged from fewer than five residents to more than five hundred residents. Of the public facilities 79.2 percent were designed for fewer than one hundred residents each, and 20.8 percent were designed for one hundred residents or more.[10]

Of the 1,277 private facilities, 637 were for males only, 304 were for females only, and 336 were coeducational. A large majority—97.1 percent—of the facilities were designed for fewer than one hundred residents each, and 2.9 percent were designed for one hundred or more residents.[11] A breakdown of population by detention status appears in Table 9.2.

An analysis of Table 9.2 shows some similarities and some significant differences between the populations of public and private juvenile detention and correctional facilities: the majority of the populations of both public and private facilities are male; most of the neglected and dependent children who are institutionalized reside in private facilities; the focus of public facilities is primarily on offenders, either status or delinquent; there are few voluntary residents in public facilities since, in most jurisdictions, admission to a public juvenile facility is made only by an order of the court. (The term "voluntary," as used here, means that commitment was not made by court order.)

A significant percentage of the population of private facilities resulted from voluntary admissions. Such admissions might have resulted from commitment by parents or guardians, by welfare departments, and by other social agencies. Few, if any, public juvenile facilities will accept "disturbed" children. If residents are later diagnosed as emotionally disturbed or mentally retarded, they will be transferred, by court order, to other specialized public or private facilities. Clearly, on the basis of the data shown in Table 9.2, most private juvenile facilities accept a substantial number of residents who are later diagnosed as "disturbed." Most of these residents were probably admitted on a voluntary basis, since most court commitments are preceded by some sort of diagnostic process that screens out disturbed children.

SHORT-TERM FACILITIES

Short-term facilities include detention centers, shelters, and reception or diagnostic centers. Detention centers and shelters are normally regarded as terminal facilities; that is, the child will often be released from such facilities directly to the community. However, sometimes children may be detained at one of these centers pending transfer to a long-term facility. The status or delinquent offender may be held at a detention center, whereas the neglected or abused child might stay at a shelter. Most children in reception or diagnostic centers are there pending evaluation and transfer to a long-term care facility. However, some of them also may be released back to the community, usually on parole.

Detention Centers

The juvenile detention center may be compared in function to a county jail. It is usually a secure facility, with high fences, locked doors, and custodial personnel to discourage escape attempts. Juveniles are detained there pending their jurisdictional or dispositional hearings. If, at the dispositional hearing, the child is committed to another institution, he or she may be kept at the detention center until transfer can be effected. The detention center may also serve to confine juveniles who at the dispositional hearing have been ordered confined for some relatively short period.

Detention centers usually have little that could be regarded as rehabilitative services, because most children will be there only for a few days or weeks. In dual-purpose centers, which are used for confinement both before and after the hearings, some rehabilitative resources may be available. These might include counselors, access to psychiatric or psychological staff, and access to school, so that detainees can keep up with their schoolwork. Some large detention centers have complete elementary and secondary schools within their facilities.

Where psychiatric or psychological personnel are maintained in a juvenile detention center, their priority is usually to provide diagnostic services for children who are awaiting court appearances. These services may be available both to children who are being detained and to children who are not. These staff members may provide therapy to inmates, if they have any time available. However, the preparation of diagnostic reports on children awaiting court appearances has absolute priority.

Shelters

As detention centers are used for status and delinquent offenders, so shelters are used for dependent and neglected children. Unlike detention centers, they are usually not secure, since the residents would not ordinarily be regarded as escape risks.

Shelters usually have a small number of residents, often only one or two, or at most, ten to fifteen. Publicly operated facilities usually contain only children committed or detained by order of the court or temporarily confined by the probation department or by some other public welfare agency. Privately operated shelters may also accept referrals from the court or from public and private social agencies, as well as voluntary self-commitments, or walk-ins. These walk-ins may include children who regard their home lives as unsatisfactory or runaways who may be passing through a community in their travels. Juveniles may now travel around the country, stopping for food and shelter at publicly or privately operated shelters or in other amenable environments, such as college campuses.

Because shelters are short-term facilities, they usually have no rehabilitative services available. School-aged residents who are in the shelter for more than a few days are encouraged or required to attend nearby public or private schools.

Reception and Diagnostic Centers

Reception and diagnostic centers are facilities, usually publicly operated, which may be regarded as way stations for children moving from other short-term facilities into long-term facilities. These reception centers have the responsibility of receiving children committed to them, diagnosing their problems, and, based on the diagnoses, assigning them to appropriate programs or facilities. Reception centers may go under other names, such as diagnostic centers or guidance centers. Regardless of what they are called, their functions are the same.

Reception centers are often part of multifacility, state-operated juvenile systems. In many states, juvenile court judges cannot order that a child be committed to a particular state institution. Instead, the child is delivered to a reception center. Following a diagnostic study, the child is transferred to whatever facility seems most appropriate. In some states, the reception center also has the option of releasing the child back to the community on parole. Even in states with only one statewide juvenile facility, or one male and one female institution, some part of each institution is set aside as a reception center in which to segregate new arrivals until they have been evaluated.

The reception center serves the additional function of "cooling" new inmates, that is, of reducing tension during what for most people is a traumatic period. The inmates are provided with some time to become adjusted to their new status and to learn what is expected of them—in other words, to learn to play the inmate role. This should contribute to a reduction of the behavior problems that might occur in the facilities that receive inmates from the reception center.

The diagnostic studies done at reception centers are similar in structure and methodology to the juvenile court reports prepared earlier in the process by juvenile investigators, and their preparation may be regarded as duplication of effort. The diagnostic studies, however, contain two features that may not be present in the juvenile court report: the evaluation of the child in confinement and a psychological evaluation. These features may exist in the juvenile court report, but only if the child was detained and the probation officer felt that a psychological evaluation was pertinent.

LONG-TERM FACILITIES

All long-term facilities, as well as the short-term reception and diagnostic centers, may be referred to as "people-changing organizations."[12] That is to say, the primary function of juvenile facilities is to cause a change in the behavior of people, so that they will stop doing whatever they did that caused them to come to the attention of the criminal justice system. As part of this attempt to change the behavior of juveniles after they leave the institution, the staff of the facility will certainly attempt to control their institutional behavior, and they may well attempt to change the inmates' attitudes, values, beliefs, and life goals. But, ultimately, it is the children's post-institutional behavior that is the criterion against which the success or failure of the institution must be measured.

Consider the hypothetical example of a boy who is committed to a long-term facility because he raped a young girl. After a year in the facility, during which the boy exhibits model behavior, he is paroled to the community. Shortly thereafter, he rapes another young girl. The staff of the facility can hardly argue that it successfully changed the boy's post-institutional behavior. At best, it can make the modest claim that, for the year that the boy spent in the facility, he was restrained from raping other young girls. Such a modest claim might be acceptable to some people, who could argue that, at least for the time that the boy was in the institution, the outside community was marginally safer.

Training Schools

Training schools are often located in rural areas, although some may be found in urban areas. Some juvenile and adult correctional facilities were built many years ago in rural areas, but have since been absorbed into expanding urban and suburban areas. Street, Vinter, and Perrow have defined the primary goals of the training school as reeducation and development.[13] They say, "Inmates are to be changed through *training*. Changes in attitudes and values, acquisition of skills, the development of personal resources, and new social behaviors are sought."[14] An additional goal of the training school and other juvenile facilities may be to instill obedience and conformity.[15] According to Street, Vinter, and Perrow,

> Habits, respect for authority, and training in conformity are emphasized. The technique is *conditioning*. Obedience/conformity maintains undifferentiated views of its inmates, emphasizes immediate accommodation to external controls, and utilizes high levels of staff domination with many negative sanctions. It is the most custodial type of juvenile institution presently found in the United States.[16]

Training schools are usually secure facilities with large custodial staffs to help the residents learn obedience and conformity.

Some training schools emphasize vocational training, some emphasize academic training, and some provide a mixture of both. Unless they have a demonstrated record of acceptable academic performance, most older residents of training schools participate primarily in vocational training. Residents under a certain age, which may vary from one facility to another, are likely to participate primarily in academic training. Other factors that may affect placement of a child into the vocational or academic area may include the socioeconomic status of the child's family and the ethnic background of the child. The juvenile justice system does not act as an instrument for upward mobility. Members of ethnic subcultures and/or low socioeconomic groups are not encouraged to attempt to improve their social status.[17]

Because most residents of training schools have received indeterminate sentences, paroles are usually granted only after residents have completed some sort of training program. Thus, children may be retained in the training school until they finish a particular vocational course or a particular school grade, or until they receive a high school diploma or its equivalent.

Ranches, Forestry Camps, and Farms

Facilities in this category are, of course, located in rural areas. Ranches and farms produce agricultural goods. Forestry camps, which are usually concerned with maintenance and fire protection in wooded areas, typically have few or no academic or vocational training programs, except on-the-job training. Ranches and farms may have some training programs. In all these facilities, however, work and a healthful environment are considered to be the major therapeutic tools.

An assumption widely held in the United States is that urban areas are essentially evil and rural areas are essentially good. If we accept this assumption, then it is logical to assume further that one way to improve the behavior of urban children is to put them into a rural area, give them fresh air, sunshine, hard work, and exposure to traditional American values. The validity of this assumption is supported by the "fact" that delinquency is less common in rural areas than in urban areas.

This "fact" is not necessarily a fact, however. As was stated earlier, the processing of offenders is usually more formal in urban areas than in rural areas. Thus crimes and delinquent acts are more likely to be reported to authorities and to be recorded officially in urban areas than in rural areas. As the bureaucratization of rural criminal justice agencies proceeds, an increase in officially reported delinquency and crime has been noted. As this process continues, we may find little or no significant difference in the crime rates of rural and urban areas.

Even if placing children in rural facilities improves their behavior, it does not necessarily mean that this improvement will continue when they return to the urban environment. Ultimately, children must function adequately in the home, in the school, and in the community in which they resided before confinement and to which they will inevitably return after confinement. If we assume that environmental factors have some negative effect on juvenile behavior, then we must also assume that these environmental factors may again have their negative effect after the children return.

Most juvenile facilities do not adequately deal with the problem of preparing the offender to function adequately in the community, nor do they attempt to change the community so as to make it more amenable to the offender. This may explain why many researchers in crime and delinquency conclude that few, if any, institutional programs may be regarded as successful.[18]

Economy is another reason for the utilization of ranches, forestry camps, and farms. Unlike residents of most training schools, residents of forestry camps do useful work, and residents of farms and ranches produce agricultural goods, thus reducing the facilities' operational costs. For example, the 1975 costs, although obviously outdated by inflation, are still useful for purposes of comparison. In that year, the per capita annual expenditures for public training schools was $11,398. For ranches, forestry camps, and farms it was $9,313, and for halfway houses and group farms it was $8,588. The comparable figures for private facilities were $10,943, $10,101, and $8,058, respectively.[19]

Group Homes

Group homes are usually located in urban areas. They are relatively small facilities, often old houses, and most have a capacity of fewer than fifteen residents.[20] They are usually not secure facilities, having few, if any, custodial personnel. The residents normally leave the facility to go to school or to jobs in the community. Although the goal of the group home may be treatment, there are few professional treatment personnel. The focus of treatment is usually on the group process, on learning to get along with peers and to cooperate with other residents and staff members in maintaining the facility. The director of a small group home is often a college graduate with a degree in the social sciences and some counseling skills. Sometimes the facility is managed by a husband and wife, who serve as surrogate parents to the residents. The use of community volunteers contributes to the range of treatment resources available in the facility and helps to reduce operating costs.

Depending on the skills of the director and staff, any one of a variety of group therapies is employed. Johnson refers to four group therapy methods. They are group psychotherapy, social group work, guided group interaction, and group counseling.[21] Each of these techniques employs some method of group interaction among the residents, with or without staff. Intensive group interaction exercises are not uncommon.[22] Often, some sort of residents' council will be formed to make decisions about the operation of the facility.

Halfway Houses

Many halfway houses are similar to group homes. Residents may be sent there as a halfway-in measure, as an alternative to confinement in a more secure facility. Conversely, residents may be halfway out; that is, they may have come from a training school or a rural facility to be prepared for release to the community. Because discipline is minimal in a halfway house, such residents can make the transition from the total control to which they were subjected in a facility stressing obedience and conformity, to the self-control necessary to function adequately in the community.

The halfway house also serves as a place of residence for those who may have no satisfactory alternative living arrangement in the community. It provides opportunities for access to the community for residents returning from facilities in rural areas.

The halfway house may have a variety of programs comparable to those in a group home, or it may simply function as a residence and a place for inmates to live while they make or renew community contacts. Often, in both group homes and halfway houses, members of the families of residents are invited to participate in group interactions.

Facilities Stressing Psychotherapy

According to Street, Vinter, and Perrow,

> The treatment institution focuses on the psychological *reconstitution* of the individual. It seeks more thoroughgoing personality change than other types. To this end it emphasizes gratifications and varied activities, with punishments relatively few and seldom severe. In the individual treatment-variant considerable stress is placed on self-insight and two-person psychotherapeutic practices.[23]

Facilities such as that described above are often privately operated, serving relatively small populations. They may accept voluntary commitments by parents or guardians, as well as referrals by the court and by social agencies. They are often supported in part by grants from charitable organizations and purchase-of-services agreements with public agencies.

These facilities have very little impact on the juvenile justice system. Even assuming that they are completely successful in improving the behavior of their residents, they can service only a small number of offenders. The use of skilled clinicians—psychiatrists and clinical psychologists—in personal interaction with clients places severe constraints upon the number of clients who can be treated. In addition, the criminal justice system cannot compete with the private sector in paying the salaries that these professionals command. Without arguing the relative merits of individual and group therapy, it seems clear that group techniques must be undertaken, because of the costs of individual therapy and because of the length of time usually involved in individual psychotherapy.

Some treatment facilities also make extensive use of medication as part of their treatment programs. Jerry Bailey did a study of eight group home–residential treatment centers in and near Kansas City, Missouri. Of eight homes studied, six made use of various medications, including tranquilizers, antidepressants, cerebral stimulants, anticonvulsants, and antiparkinsonism medications. In the six facilities using medication, the number of residents medicated ranged from 17 percent to 94 percent.[24]

CORRECTIONAL PROGRAMS

There is a substantial body of literature evaluating the effectiveness of correctional programs and the reliability of the evaluations. The consensus of this literature, to quote Scioli and Cook, is that, "with regard to offender rehabilitation, we simply do not know what works or what doesn't work.[25] A comparable position has been taken by Lipton, Martinson, and Wilks,[26] in what must be the most massive study of evaluation yet undertaken in the field of corrections. Martinson has summed up this study, by stating,

> The *addition* of isolated treatment elements to a system (probation, imprisonment, parole) in which a given flow of offenders has generated a gross rate of recidivism has very little effect (and, in most cases, no effect) in making this rate of recidivism better or worse.[27]

Martinson goes on to suggest that future research should not focus on the effect of a particular treatment program upon the recidivism rate. Instead, it should focus on the effect of various program alternatives upon the crime rate, however that is to be defined.

Others who have analyzed the methodology of correctional research include Bailey[28] and Logan.[29] Both have concluded that treatment programs were either ineffective or that their effectiveness had not been demonstrated. A comparable position has been taken by Cressey, who stated in part,

> We do not *know* that imprisoning men deters others, reinforces anticriminal values, corrects criminals, or in some other way promotes social solidarity. Neither do we *know* that inflicting other kinds of pain corrects criminals or, generally, integrates society. Moreover, we do not *know* that inflicting pain by imprisonment or some other means is an *inefficient* system for achieving the desired ends.[30]

There are many researchers who have reported negative, inconclusive, or mildly positive results. Adamson and Dunham reported on a program of individual psychotherapy for young male probationers. There was no significant difference in the recidivism rates of experimentals and controls.[31]

Daniel Glaser summed up extensive research, in *The Effectiveness of a Prison and Parole System,* when he stated,

> Our data suggest that prison does deter men from crime, and in this sense it is a punishment. Our data also indicate that the men released from prison generally have had little reward for behavior that is an alternative to crime. Consequently, from the learning theory frame of reference . . . one would not expect criminal response patterns to be extinguished unless some gratification in legitimate occupational and social pursuits is experienced in the post-release world.[32]

Glaser also reported that the results of research on the effect of prison education tend to be inconclusive.[33]

Kassebaum, Ward, and Wilner reported on the effectiveness of group counseling programs conducted at the California Men's Colony–East in the 1960s.[34] Subjects were randomly distributed into five groups: voluntary small-group counseling, mandatory small- and large-group counseling, and voluntary and mandatory controls. The concept of "parole success" was used, and it was concluded that there was no significant difference in parole success among subjects in the five groups and that group counseling in the prison did not significantly affect parole outcomes. They further reported that, based on this research, the California Assembly Office of Research had concluded that "there is no evidence to support claims that one correctional program has more rehabilitative effectiveness than another."[35]

Another report prepared by the California State Assembly Office of Research measured the impact of the criminal justice system upon the California crime problem. This was done by comparing "felony crimes reported" with such variables as "adult arrests," "adults convicted," and "committed to state prison." In 1966, there were 56,942 felony crimes of personal violence reported to the police, and 2,017 persons were committed to the Department of Corrections or to the

Youth Authority from adult courts. A total of 362,025 property felonies was reported to the police, and 2,995 persons were committed to the Department of Corrections or to the Youth Authority. The report goes on to state, "With the exception of crimes of personal violence, the present criminal justice system has little quantitative impact upon the mass of offenders and offenses."[36] This comment is not dissimilar to that of Martinson, cited above.[37]

Some penologists have taken a more optimistic position. One of these is Herbert Quay. With respect to approaches to behavioral change, he stated, "The best judgment that can currently be made about their effectiveness is that the majority of these approaches are effective for some people at some point in time under some conditions."[38] Thus, it becomes important to improve the skills of correctional diagnostic staff, as well as their ability to classify offenders.

A similar approach was taken by Palmer, in a critique of Martinson. Martinson had stated that, "with few and isolated exceptions, the rehabilitative efforts that have been reported so far have had no appreciable effect on recidivism."[39]

Palmer was less pessimistic than Martinson. He felt, however, that instead of viewing offenders in the mass, it was necessary to improve the classification process. The question to be asked, according to Palmer, was "Which methods work best for *which* types of offenders, and under *what* conditions or in what type of setting?"[40]

To sum up, there is a large body of opinion that holds that correctional treatment is generally ineffective or that its effectiveness cannot presently be demonstrated. However, there is also a body of opinion that holds that certain treatment methods may be effective with certain kinds of offenders. It is important, therefore, to classify offenders carefully, so as to match offenders to the appropriate programs.

More recently, Dennis Romig has made a substantial contribution to the literature on the effectiveness of juvenile delinquent rehabilitation programs.[41] He reviewed the research carried out on a variety of treatment programs for juveniles and concluded that many of them are of little value. Among the program interventions he evaluated were casework, behavior modification, academic education, vocational and work programs, group counseling, individual psychotherapy, family therapy, and therapeutic camping.[42] A review of Romig's findings follows. Although Romig reviewed a wide range of programs with an assortment of goals, generally the effectiveness of the programs was measured by rates of recidivism of clients, and by studying police records, court referrals, reconviction rates, and so forth.

Casework

According to Romig, "Casework basically involves three ingredients: diagnosis, recommendations, and direct services."[43] The first two ingredients may be found in the typical juvenile court report, and the third ingredient is provided in the relationship between the probation officer and the juvenile probationer.

After a review of the studies, in which "casework was utilized with almost 3,000 youths," Romig concluded that "casework was *not effective* in the rehabilitation of delinquent youth."[44] Further, he recommended that "casework should be discontinued as a program for delinquency prevention or for the rehabilitation of delinquent youth."[45]

Behavior Modification

Behavior modification employs a reward, or positive reinforcement, system to encourage good behavior. Rewards may be intangible—verbal praise, for example—or tangible—cigarettes, candy bars, and cash bonuses.[46] Rewards may also be in the form of special institutional privileges or relief from institutional tasks. Some institutions use a token system, in which good behavior is rewarded with credits that residents may use to make purchases in the commissary, to advance up the institutional privilege ladder, or, in some cases, to obtain release from the institution. Bad behavior may be either punished or ignored.

In general, Romig's conclusions were negative. He stated, "Behavior modification will work only when the behavior to be changed is specific and behaviorally simple. . . . Behavior modification should not be offered as a treatment modality for juvenile delinquency reduction."[47] Put another way, behavior modification may be effective if the goals are limited and specific. The reduction of delinquency is too broad and vague a goal to be effectively treated by behavior modification. However, variants of behavior modification continue to be used, because of their apparent success as devices for controlling institutional behavior, although they have limited effect on post-institutional behavior.

Academic Education

Romig examined sixteen studies evaluating academic education as a rehabilitative technique. The number of experimental subjects in the various studies ranged from as few as four, to as many as 632.[48] Ten of the studies did not follow up to ascertain whether or not their programs reduced recidivism. Two studies reported reduced recidivism, and four reported no reduction in recidivism.

Romig concluded that academic programs with specific objectives, such as providing minors with the General Equivalency Diploma (equivalent to a high school diploma), seemed to contribute to rehabilitation. However, he went on to state, "Rehabilitation programs that focus only upon the teaching of academic skills will fail to reduce recidivism."[49]

Vocational and Work Programs

Twelve studies were evaluated, with the number of experimental subjects ranging from as few as ten to as many as 970. Two studies did not provide follow-up results concerning rehabilitation, seven studies reported no reduction in recidivism, and three reported some success in reducing recidivism. One of Romig's conclusions was that "vocational training, work programs, and job placement are not effective in and of themselves to rehabilitate juvenile delinquents."[50] However, he added, "Any rehabilitation program that holds out concrete hope for improvement to the client and has a relatively detailed plan for delivering on that hope has a greater likelihood of success than programs that neglect these two areas."[51] In addition, Romig suggested that vocational programs for delinquents should include the following program components:

Educational programs that support career goals

Systematic career decision-making

Job advancement skills

Career advancement plans

Follow-up help after job placement[52]

It is clear from a review of the literature that simply providing delinquent offenders with some sort of generalized academic or vocational programming does not contribute to their rehabilitation. The programs must offer skills that are useful to the delinquents and that they perceive as contributing to their immediate and long-term goals.

Group Counseling

Romig reported on twenty-eight studies of group counseling, group therapy, and group discussions.[53] Thirteen studies did not provde follow-up results. Seven studies reported no reduction in recidivism, three reported some reduction, one reported an increase in recidivism, and the balance showed mixed results.[54] Romig concluded:

> The results of the majority of studies were that group counseling did not result in significant behavioral changes. At best, group counseling allowed for the verbal ventilation of negative feelings of institutionalized delinquents. Such emotional catharses did at times positively affect the youths' immediate institutional adjustments. However, institutional behavior changes did not transfer outside the institution.[55]

Most programs that employ group counseling do not seem to be effective in reducing recidivism or rehabilitating either adult or juvenile offenders. However, they will surely continue to be used within institutions. As was pointed out earlier, they simplify control problems within institutions, even if they do not usually improve post-institutional behavior. In addition, they can be operated economically, because they do not require the continuing participation of professional clinical staff. Most of the members of the institutional staff can, with a modicum of training, function as group leaders. In addition, volunteer group leaders can be recruited from the community and often from colleges in the vicinity of the institution.

Individual Psychotherapy

Romig reported on ten studies employing individual counseling and individual psychotherapy.[56] Most of the studies reported no reduction in recidivism, some reported an increase in recidivism, and some reported mixed results, including some improvements. A study of unusual interest was reported by Adams.[57] Four hundred youths were classified by diagnostic staff as "amenable" or "not amenable" to individual psychotherapy.

As Romig reported:

After the determination of the youths' amenableness to the individual interview therapy, they were randomly assigned to either the control group or the treatment group. Altogether there were four groups with 100 youths per group:

1. Treatment amenables
2. Treatment nonamenables
3. Control amenables
4. Control nonamenables

The boys in the study were approximately 20 years of age, and the length of treatment averaged nine months.[58]

As to the results of Adams's research, Romig reported:

The individual therapy was found to result in a significant difference in parole performance in favor of the amenable youths who received the individual therapy. The nonamenable . . . youths did worse on parole, but the difference was not significantly greater than the comparable control group. The conclusion is that some youths who are diagnosed by a clinical staff to be open to individual psychotherapy can use the therapy to make a better adjustment while on parole.[59]

Romig concluded:

The utilization of individual psychotherapy or counseling as treatment for juvenile delinquency will be unsuccessful. . . . Individual counseling and psychotherapy, as it is now practiced and relied upon, should be discontinued.[60]

We concur with Romig's opinion that individual psychotherapy and counseling are not useful techniques for treating juvenile delinquents. As was pointed out earlier, even if individual therapy were demonstrated to be effective, it would still not be economically practical, particularly in publicly operated juvenile facilities. However, it might be appropriate in some privately operated facilities with adequate financing and competent diagnostic personnel.

Family Therapy

Romig pointed out that family therapy is of recent origin and that "the dominant ingredient in . . . programs [is] some type of involvement of the youth's family."[61]

Romig evaluated twelve studies in family therapy. Some results were unfavorable, and some studies reported no significant differences.[62] The conclusions were summarized as follows:

1. Family counseling does not always work.
2. Teaching improved-communication behavior does work.
3. Crisis intervention works when it is used to teach systematic problem-solving.
4. Parent education works when it teaches parents disciplining and decision-making skills.[63]

Romig went on to suggest, "All treatment programs involving delinquent youths and their families should provide the family and the youth [with] training in communication, problem-solving, and disciplining skills."[64]

Therapeutic Camping

According to Romig, "*Therapeutic camping,* or wilderness camping, attempts to change the delinquent youth's behavior by improving his self-concept through successfully coping with the challenges of the wilderness."[65] Because this is a relatively new approach, only two studies were reviewed. In neither case did the research support the conclusion that therapeutic camping makes a significant difference in the recidivism rates of delinquent offenders.

Therapeutic, or wilderness, camping is popular now. A number of such programs have been publicized in the media, particularly on television. Like many other fields of human endeavor, offender rehabilitation is subject to faddism. Whether or not such fads contribute ultimately to lower recidivism rates is not necessarily important. What is important is that the juvenile justice system keep trying new methods and new variations of old methods—because success rates to this point have been quite low. As to therapeutic camping, Romig concluded, "If therapeutic camping is the primary treatment utilized to rehabilitate juvenile offenders, it will fail."[66]

Reality Therapy

Reality therapy is an approach developed by Dr. William Glasser; it was used extensively by him at the Ventura School for Girls, a facility operated by the California Youth Authority.[67]

Traditional psychoanalysis involves a process of long-term interaction between therapist and clients, in which the therapist assists the clients in searching for the root causes of their behavior—roots that are usually put down in early childhood. Therefore, traditional therapy is a costly and time-consuming process.

Reality therapy, on the other hand, does not deal with the past, but with the here and now. Clients are helped to understand that they are responsible for their own present and future behavior, that what happens to them is determined by how they behave, and that they cannot justify their behavior on the basis of "unconscious motivations."[68]

Reality therapy is less impractical than other forms of individual psychotherapy, in that it requires less time and participation by the clinician. As Tom Johnson stated:

> In the institutional setting, treatment depends on simulation methods. The institutional environment is intentionally arranged to provide for both immediate punishment for irresponsible behavior and immediate rewards for responsible behavior.[69]

DIVERSION

The arguments for and against diversion and deinstitutionalization have been presented in a number of places throughout this book and need not be repeated in detail here. In summary, many criminal justice practitioners and scholars take the position that intervention of the juvenile justice system into the child's life is likely to be ineffective. Further, the more extensive the intervention is, the greater is the likelihood that the results will be ineffective. In addition, because intervention is costly, it should be carried out only in order to protect the community or when it appears that intervention will improve the child's performance. Also, when intervention is necessary, less intervention is better than more intervention.

Many criminal justice agencies have formally adopted the policy outlined above. In addition, many agencies that have no such formal policy do, in fact, informally operate within such guidelines. Police officers exercise a great deal of discretion. They are not required to arrest every adult and juvenile they see committing an offense. They may ignore behavior; they may admonish the offenders at the scene; they may take the offenders to the station house and release them, and so on. The probation officer may or may not choose to file a petition to bring a child into court, and may simply dismiss the application for petition or propose informal handling of the matter. If a prosecutor is involved in the decision process, he or she also may choose to go on with the matter or to dismiss it. If the case does go to the juvenile court, the judge has almost unlimited discretion in adjudication and disposition. After disposition, substantial discretion is exercised by supervising probation officers and institutional authorities.

The juvenile justice system may be perceived as a series of decision points. At each of the points, some decision-maker determines whether the juvenile is to proceed further into the system or whether the intervention shall cease. One negative decision ends the intervention. Thus, for a delinquent offender to be institutionalized in, let us say, California, positive decisions must first have been made by a police officer, an intake officer, a prosecutor, a juvenile investigator, and a juvenile court judge. And, usually, each of these participants in the decision-making process prefers, when possible, to make a negative decision rather than a positive one.

Every action that reduces the degree of intervention may appropriately be regarded as diversion. This would certainly include:

Informal processing by police

Informal processing by an intake officer

Pre-trial release

Grant of a continuance, or informal probation, by a juvenile court judge

Probation instead of institutionalization

Early release on parole from an institution

DEINSTITUTIONALIZATION

Deinstitutionalization refers to programs or efforts to reduce the use of confinement as a disposition, for either status offenders or delinquent offenders. It also refers to efforts or programs designed to remove from institutions those who have already been confined.

One can certainly argue that some persons must be confined, because they represent a danger to themselves or to the community. However, most juvenile offenders do not fall into this category, and most juveniles who appear before the court were not detained prior to their court hearings or confined after the hearings. Furthermore, most juveniles who were detained prior to their court hearings were released before or at the time of their court hearings.

A review of the 1975 figures on public and private juvenile facilities will serve to clarify this point. There were 641,189 admissions to public juvenile detention and correctional facilities in 1975, and there were 632,983 departures. The number of juveniles actually in custody in such facilities in mid-1975 was 46,980.[70] Admissions to private facilities stood at 56,708 and departures at 50,986. Juveniles in custody in mid-1975 numbered 27,290.[71] Most of the admissions and departures can be accounted for by short-term detention of juveniles in detention centers.

Many of the variables that enter into the decision to detain or confine an offender have been discussed above. The single most important variable, however, has not. That variable is bed space. Whether we are discussing confinement of juveniles or adults, the decision to imprison or to grant probation, the decision to release or not to release on parole, the matter of bed space is almost always a consideration. If a facility is full and more people are to be admitted, then somebody must be released.

Public correctional institutions typically have little or no control over admissions. If inmates have received indeterminate sentences, however, institutional management may have substantial discretion about releasing them on parole. Thus, inmates may be released earlier if the facility is full, or they may be released later if the facility is not full.

For those who are interested in deinstitutionalization, one strategy is to discourage the building of new facilities and to close facilities that currently exist. In effect, judges cannot confine juveniles in institutions that do not exist. Instead, judges may be forced to use community-based alternatives. This is not to suggest that all or most judges are eager to commit juveniles to institutions; many judges favor deinstitutionalization.

The forces supporting deinstitutionalization include an assortment of people with differing motivations. Many conservatives may support it because they oppose spending the money to build and maintain correctional facilities. Many liberals may support it because they regard institutionalizing children as inhumane. Many practitioners and academicians, who regard themselves as pragmatists, support it because they regard present programs of institutionalization as unproductive. At this time, however, there is no consensus for deinstitutionalization.

Deinstitutionalization in Massachusetts

The most widely publicized effort toward deinstitutionalization is the Massachusetts Deinstitutionalization Project, which may be said to have begun in early 1972, with the closing of all but one of the juvenile institutions operated by the Department of Youth Services.[72] The action was taken under the direction of Dr. Jerome Miller, who became head of the Department of Youth Services (DYS) of Massachusetts in 1969.[73] The appointment of Miller occurred during a period of widespread political support for change in the operation of the DYS. However, after the closings, the political support weakened substantially, and Miller resigned in January, 1973.[74]

When the secure state facilities were shut down, with considerable fanfare, most of the inmates were transferred to open community-based facilities, mostly privately operated. According to Michael S. Serrill:

> Throughout the tumultuous period when Dr. Jerome Miller was closing the public training schools in Massachusetts, he and his supporters hammered home one point: that the training schools were not only ineffective at reforming juvenile lawbreakers, but that they were profoundly destructive, and that those children who went through them were more likely

to commit new crimes when they left than when they were admitted.[75]

However, the project did not demonstrate that community-based programs were more effective than the institutional programs that had been operated by the DYS. According to Romig:

Increases in runaway rates, deaths of youths, higher recidivism rates with girls, increases in the institution of criminal proceedings, and the high recidivism rate of Boston youths have all been reported.[76]

The "increases in the institution of criminal proceeding" refers to the certification of juveniles to adult courts. Judges who were dissatisfied with deinstitutionalization increasingly certified juvenile offenders to the adult criminal courts to increase the likelihood that these offenders would be institutionalized.

The apparent failure of the Massachusetts Deinstitutionalization Project cannot necessarily be generalized. Because of political considerations, the training schools were closed abruptly, without adequate alternatives having been developed. There were changes in economic conditions in the Boston area that may have contributed to the high recidivism rate of Boston youths in the community programs. However, one must also acknowledge that there are many delinquent offenders who should not be placed in open facilities or in community programs, because they are incapable of controlling their behavior. It is unfortunately true that many people, when free, will kill, assault, rape, rob, start fires, and commit other acts that make them a physical threat to others. As long as people like this exist, society will insist on secure institutions in which to keep them.

The Outlook for Deinstitutionalization

For those offenders who are not a physical threat to others or to themselves, one can argue that deinstitutionalization may be a sound strategy. Even if the recidivism rate were the same or a little higher, it would appear to be more humane and is less costly to operate than other programs. Analysis of research into the effectiveness of correctional treatment programs leads to the conclusion that most programs are not particularly effective and that one program is as good as another.[77] Further, the study *Crime and Penalties in California* concludes that the California criminal justice system made no significant reduction in the crime rate.[78] If this is correct, then it can be argued that appropriate factors to consider in sentencing should include humaneness and economy, if the offender is not violent.

Acknowledging the ineffectiveness of most juvenile correctional programs should not be regarded as being pessimistic. Most programs have some successes and some failures. Most programs seem to make some people better, make some people worse, and have no effect on the rest. The appropriate areas for research at this time would seem to lie in the areas of diagnosis and classification. If we can successfully predict which offenders will be improved by which treatment programs, we can substantially increase success rates of those treatment programs. Regrettably, the development of methods of accurate diagnosis and classification is not an easy task.

Romig has taken a negative view of deinstitutionalization at the juvenile level, arguing that the goal should be deinstitutionalization at the adult level. He says, "The goal of the juvenile justice system is to intervene so successfully with the offenders as juveniles that when they become adults, they will be productive citizens rather than chronic offenders."[79] This position presents a number of problems. First of all, it seems to imply that perhaps the best way to accomplish this goal is not to intervene at all. Second, the record of programs that intervene in the life of the juvenile offender is rather poor. Third, such a position ignores the possible contribution of society in the behavior of the offender. Even if an institutional treatment program is demonstrably successful in improving the behavior of offenders, these offenders must eventually function in the community. If that community is socioeconomically deprived, the offender is likely to get into trouble again. The juvenile justice system must address itself to changing society, in order to make it more amenable to the offender.

NOTES
CHAPTER NINE

1. See Gene Kassebaum, David Ward, and Daniel Wilner, *Prison Treatment and Parole Survival* (New York, 1971); Douglas Lipton, Robert Martinson, and Judith Wilks, *The Effectiveness of Correctional Treatment* (New York, 1975); and Dennis A. Romig, *Justice for Our Children* (Lexington, Mass., 1978).

2. Edward H. Sutherland and Donald R. Cressey, *Criminology*, 9th ed. (Philadelphia, 1974).

3. Erving Goffman, *Asylums* (Garden City, N. Y., 1961). Also see Donald Clemmer, *The Prison Community* (Indianapolis, 1971).

4. Romig, *Justice for Our Children.*

5. National Institute for Juvenile Justice and Delinquency Prevention, *National Evaluation Design for the Deinstitutionalization of Status Offender Program* (Washington, D. C., 1977), p. 1.

6. Ibid.

7. Gerald R. Wheeler. *Counter-Deterrence: A Report on Juvenile Sentencing and Effects of Prisonization* (Chicago, 1978).

8. National Criminal Justice Information and Statistics Service, *Children in Custody: A Report on the Juvenile Detention and Correctional Facility Census of 1975* (Washington, D. C., December, 1979), p. 5.

9. Ibid., p. 49.

10. Ibid., p. 15.

11. Ibid., p. 17.

12. David Street, Robert D. Vinter, and Charles Perrow, *Organization for Treatment* (New York, 1966), p. 3.

13. Ibid., p. 21.

14. Ibid.

15. Ibid.

16. Ibid.

17. Aaron V. Cicourel and John I. Kitsuke, *The Educational Decision-Makers* (Indianapolis, 1963).

18. See Kassebaum et al., *Prison Treatment and Parole Survival;* and Lipton et al., *Effectiveness of Correctional Treatment.* Also see Romig, *Justice for Our Children.*

19. *Children in Custody,* p. 11.

20. Ibid., pp. 15–17.

21. Thomas A. Johnson, *Introduction to the Juvenile Justice System* (St. Paul, Minn., 1975), pp. 286–90.

22. Carl Rogers, *Carl Rogers on Encounter Groups* (New York, 1970).

23. Street et al., *Organization for Treatment,* p. 21.

24. Jerry Bailey, *Juvenile Group Homes and Medication,* unpublished, Avila College, Kansas City, Mo., 1980.

25. Frank P. Scioli, Jr., and Thomas J. Cook, "How Effective are Volunteers—Public Participation in the Criminal Justice System," *Crime and Delinquency* 22 (April 1976): 192–200.

26. Lipton, et al., *The Effectiveness of Correctional Treatment.*

27. Robert Martinson, "California Research at the Crossroads," *Crime and Delinquency* 22 (April 1976): 180–91.

28. Walter C. Bailey, "Correctional Outcome: An Evaluation of 100 Reports," *Journal of Criminal Law, Criminology and Police Science* 57 (June 1966): 153–60.

29. Charles H. Logan. "Evaluation Research in Crime and Delinquency," *Journal of Criminal Law, Criminology and Police Science* 63 (September 1972): 378–87.

30. Donald R. Cressey. "The Nature and Effectiveness of Correctional Techniques," *Law and Contemporary Problems* 2 (1958): 754–71.

31. LaMay Adamson and H. Warren Dunham, "Clinical Treatment of Male Delinquents: A Case Study in Effort and Result," *American Sociological Review* 21 (1956): 312–20.

32. Daniel Glaser, *The Effectiveness of a Prison and Parole System* (Indianapolis, 1964), pp. 487–87.

33. Daniel Glaser, "The Effectiveness of Correctional Education," *American Journal of Correction* 28: 4–9.

34. Kassebaum et al., *Prison Treatment and Parole Survival.*

35. Ibid., p. 323.

36. California State Assembly Office of Research. *Crime and Penalties in California* (Sacramento, 1968), pp. 31–32.

37. Martinson, "California Research at the Crossroads."

38. Herbert C. Quay, "What Corrections Can Correct and How," *Federal Probation* 37 (June, 1973): 3–5.

39. Robert Martinson, "What Works—Questions and Answers about Prison Reform," *The Public Interest* (Spring 1974): 22–54.

40. Ted Palmer, "Martinson Revisited," *Journal of Research in Crime and Delinquency* 12 (July, 1975): 133–52.

41. Romig, *Justice for Our Children.*

42. Ibid., pp. vii–ix.

43. Ibid., p. 7.

44. Ibid.

45. Ibid.

46. Ibid., p. 12.

47. Ibid., p. 21.

48. Ibid., p. 25.

49. Ibid., p. 37.

50. Ibid., p. 52.

51. Ibid., p. 53.

52. Ibid.

53. Ibid., p. 57.

54. Ibid., pp. 69–72.

55. Ibid., p. 68.

56. Ibid., p. 81.

57. S. Adams, *Effectiveness of Interview Therapy with Older Youth Authority Wards: An Interim Evaluation of the PICO Project.* Research Report No. 20. California Youth Authority, 1961.

58. Romig, *Justice for Our Children,* 78.

59. Ibid.

60. Ibid., p. 81.

61. Ibid., p. 87.

62. Ibid., pp. 89–90.

63. Ibid., p. 93.

64. Ibid.

65. Ibid., p. 97.

66. Ibid., p. 99.

67. William Glasser, *Reality Therapy: A New Approach to Psychiatry* (New York, 1965).

68. Robert J. Wicks, *Correctional Psychology* (San Francisco, 1974), p. 16.

69. Tom Johnson, op. cit., p. 285.

70. *Children in Custody,* pp. 28–30.

71. Ibid., pp. 38–39.

72. Romig, *Justice for Our Children,* p. 174.

73. Lloyd E. Ohlin, Robert B. Coates, and Alden E. Miller, eds. "Radical Correctional Reform: A Case Study of the Massachusetts Youth Correctional System," *Juvenile Correctional Reform in Massachusetts* (Washington, D. C., 1976), p. 4.

74. Romig, *Justice for Our Children,* pp. 173–174.

75. Michael S. Serrill, "Harvard Recidivism Study," *Corrections Magazine* II (November/December 1975): 21.

76. Romig, *Justice for Our Children,* 180.

77. See Lipton et al., *The Effectiveness of Correctional Treatment.* Also see Kassebaum et al., *Prison Treatment and Parole Survival.*

78. *Crime and Penalties in California.*

79. Romig, *Justice for Our Children,* p. 182.

10
DELINQUENCY PREVENTION AND THE SCHOOLS

A goal of the socialization process is to prepare the young to become useful citizens. Primary instruments of socialization include the family and the school. When these instruments do not accomplish this goal, the juvenile justice system may enter into the process.

To a large extent, both the home and the school do a good job of preparing children to be good citizens. Only about 20 percent of children can be expected to appear in juvenile court at one time or another, prior to reaching the age of legal adulthood. For many of those who come to the attention of the court, the appearance will be for a relatively minor matter, and it will be their one and only appearance.

For the other 80 percent of the children, their misbehavior does not result in the intervention of the juvenile justice system. Undoubtedly, many of these children have committed delinquent offenses for which they were not apprehended.[1] However, the juvenile justice system is not able to concern itself with undiscovered delinquents. Its resources barely permit it to deal with the children who are brought to its attention.

The role of the family in fostering or preventing delinquency is dealt with elsewhere in this book . Suffice it to repeat here that, by and large, the family is a successful instrument of socialization. Most parents, within the limits of their knowledge, background, and capabilities, try to raise their children properly. Few parents deliberately encourage their children to become delinquent. Some parents, however, simply lack adequate skills and resources.

The school, also, can be said to be moderately successful as an instrument of socialization. The majority of children complete high school without getting into trouble. The percentage is higher for children who are white and who come from middle-class backgrounds, and lower for children from lower socioeconomic classes. Among black students, the percentage of children who complete high school is substantially lower than among white students, and a lower percentage of students of Hispanic background receive high school diplomas.[2]

Thus, the schools tend to perpetuate the inequities that exist in society. This should not be surprising , since the school is an instrument of society. It is usually not an instrument of social mobility. Rather, in many schools, both the teachers[3] and the counselors[4] act to discourage social mobility.

ACADEMIC TRACKING AND ITS EFFECTS

One of the authors of this book was a faculty member of a state college in Appalachia. Many students told of their difficulties in being permitted to take high school courses that would prepare them for college admission. Area high schools had three academic "tracks": college preparatory, general, and agricultural–vocational. Students on the college preparatory track would automatically complete all college entrance requirements; students on the general track could, by careful selection of courses, complete minimum requirements for college entrance; students on the agricultural–vocational track could not complete college entrance requirements.

Apparently, when children in the area entered high school, counselors assigned them to tracks, not on the basis of their prior scholastic performance, but on the basis of their socioeconomic status. Children could change tracks, but only if they were prepared to challenge counselors. Many who did were advised that their ambitions were unrealistic and were told, "You should know your place." One student, who was graduated from college magna cum laude and went on to complete law school, reported that he had spent two years in high school on an agricultural–vocational track, because his father had a farm. At the beginning of his junior year of high school, he reported, he convinced a counselor to change him to a general track only by threatening to use physical force.

Black students, as well as white, may be discriminated against on the basis of socioeconomic class. Ray C. Rist reported on a study in an urban ghetto school in which most of the faculty and administration and all of the students were black. Students were classified as fast learners or slow learners on the basis of socioeconomic criteria. Among the criteria were parents' income, parents' education, number of children in the family, number of parents in the home, and whether the child wore new clothes or hand-me-downs to school. On the basis of such criteria, children were classified and assigned by their eighth day of kindergarten, and these assignments continued from one year to the next.

Children who were classified as fast learners received more attention and classroom instruction from the teachers than did slow learners. The students performed on the basis of teachers' expectations, because they did not have the option of doing otherwise. According to Rist, "This is, in a sense, another manifestation of the self-fulfilling prophecy in that a 'slow learner' has no option but to continue to be a slow learner, regardless of performance or potential."[5]

Children of lower-class black parents are likely to receive a poorer education than children of middle-class blacks, thus reducing their chances for upward mobility. But upward mobility increases access to the legitimate opportunity structure and reduces the necessity to turn to crime in order to acquire material resources.[6] Therefore, schools that discourage or prevent upward mobility are actually encouraging delinquency and crime, rather than contributing to the prevention of delinquency.

TEACHER EXPECTATION AND STUDENT PERFORMANCE

Rist's findings are consistent with the views of Kenneth Clark. Clark discounts the theories that attempt to explain academic retardation in ghetto schools in terms of "general environmental disabilities." He argues that blacks often do poorly in school, not because they are culturally deprived, but because the schools do a poor job of teaching. Part of this teaching failure may be caused by the lack of ability of some ghetto teachers. Clark suggests that ghetto children "do not learn because they are not being taught effectively and they are not being taught because those who are charged with the responsibility of teaching them do not believe that they can learn, do not expect that they can learn, and do not act toward them in ways which help them to learn."[7]

Richard Johnson has suggested that students become aware of a teacher's lack of expectations about their performance and become less likely to put forth the effort required in order to succeed.[8]

Walter Schafer and Kenneth Polk take essentially the same position as does Clark. They state:

> The first necessary condition of effective instruction is the belief by school personnel in the intellectual potential and the educability of the students being taught. . . . On the other hand, if one begins with the opposite assumption, that students have limited capabilities and are essentially ineducable, it becomes fruitless to attempt to accomplish very much in the classroom.[9]

Schafer and Polk go on to point out that as children enter the school system, they are labeled as slow learners (basic track) or fast learners (regular track), based on IQ tests, or other tests of questionable validity. Slow learners are then segregated into classes that receive less instruction because they have been labeled as less capable of learning. Because of the quality of instruction, then, they learn little, thus fulfilling the prophecy that they were less capable of learning.[10]

Paul Hahn concurs in the position taken by Schafer and Polk. He argues that the focus of many schools upon middle-class values and concomitant "testing and classifying based upon verbal skills and cultural enrichment" have caused the schools to be perceived as trivial and irrelevant to students from lower-class backgrounds.[11]

An additional problem for inner city schools results from changes in patterns of urban development, which have led to suburbs that are predominantly white and middle class, while the central cities have become increasingly made up of lower-class whites and members of ethnic minorities, mostly blacks and Hispanics.[12] Many of the more affluent whites still residing in central city school districts have moved their children from public schools to private schools.

Not only do these actions reduce the tax base available to public schools, but they also reduce the willingness of local legislatures to provide adequate financial support to public schools. This has led to poorer quality public education in the central cities than in the white suburban school districts.

Gene Kassebaum has presented a model that may explain how school failure leads to delinquent behavior:

1. Failure of a child to succeed in schoolwork decreases rewards for that child while in school; it may also lead to attempts to withdraw or rebel.

2. Misconduct according to school regulations also decreases rewards and increases penalties for staying in school.

3. The experience of irrelevance of curriculum content and indifference or incompetence of teachers increases felt need to leave school.

4. Lower competence, poorer resources, and decreased amenities of lower-class area schools decrease rewards of school attendance for children who attend these schools.

5. Truancy, school misbehavior, and school-related (or school-referred) offenses may directly lead to a delinquency record.[13]

DELINQUENCY AS A RESULT OF LACK OF ATTAINMENT

Schafer and Polk suggest that delinquency may be a result of lack of attainment.[14] In other words, the students, for whatever reasons, fail to fulfill their own expectations and the expectations of others. They receive failing grades; they are perceived negatively by teachers, by other students, and by their parents. They are denied access to certain curricular and extracurricular activities. This leads to a pattern of continuing failure, to a negative self-image, and perhaps to dropping out or developing peer relationships with other students who have the same problems.[15]

The reasons for the students' failures may be beyond the control of the school. They may result from factors in the students' homes or in other areas outside the school. As presented by Schafer and Polk, the argument for this position is as follows:

> Because of broken homes, crowded and inadequate housing, anti-intellectualism, and lack of effective discipline, it is contended that these children come to school with educational handicaps such as the following: lack of "elaboration" of communication styles; poor auditory and visual discrimination; inability to think conceptually; inability to use "adults as sources of information, correction and reality testing, and as instruments for satisfying curiosity"; unfamiliarity with books

and writing material; inability to sustain attention; lack of development of internal controls over personal behavior; and inexperience in formal situations like the classroom.[16]

To the extent, if any, that this position is valid, the schools have the responsibility to devise strategies to overcome such limitations.

CAUSES OF FAILURE IN SCHOOL

However, students' failures may also result from the behavior of teachers, counselors, and other school personnel.[17] Among the possible contributory factors that may result in increased school failures and possibly increased delinquency are:

1. Discriminatory treatment of ethnic minorities and lower-class children.
2. Lack of shared perceptions between teachers and students.
3. Inflexibility of curriculum and teachers.
4. Inadequate preparation and selection of teachers.

These topics have been discussed above and are treated at greater length below.

"Delinquent behavior is seldom the product of the school alone"—a quotation from an essay by John Eichorn[18]—fairly represents the literature on the contribution of the school to juvenile delinquency. The common theme of this literature is that although elementary and secondary schools try to function so as to reduce delinquency, they are not particularly successful. Indeed, much of the literature is quite critical of schools, teachers, and counselors. Schafer and Polk have expressed this view:

> Juvenile delinquency has its roots in the fundamental failure of the school to adapt to outside changes and that so long as that failure persists, delinquency, as well as other school related problems, will persist.[19]

Eichorn has commented, "To some [boys and girls] the school is an intolerable place where they have encountered many unpleasant tasks and unsympathetic adults."[20]

And Paul Hahn stated, "It is quite apparent that in all too many cases, not only have the schools been unable to prevent delinquent conduct, but they have shared in contributing to its development."[21]

For many teachers, as for many children, schools are not pleasant places. Teachers are confronted by students who are rebellious and hostile. They are often the victims of physical assaults or other criminal conduct. For example, one study reported that "approximately 70,000 teachers are attacked by students every year."[22] It is suspected that the actual incidence of assaults on teachers is much greater, because the vast majority of such offenses go unreported.[23] In recent victimization studies of twenty-six major American cities in 1974 and 1975, some 270,296 victimizations were reported to have occurred in schools.[24]

Offenses include rape, robbery, simple or aggravated assault, and larceny with or without contact. Most of the victimizations were larceny without contact (theft). Of the victims, 78 percent were students, 8 percent were teachers, and the balance included nonteaching personnel and visitors.[25]

Discriminatory Treatment

This topic has been discussed at length above, but a summary might be appropriate. Society as a whole discriminates against minorities and the poor. The schools are a subsystem of society, and societal discrimination pervades them.[26] There is segregation in living patterns, based on race and income, and this segregation is then reflected in the neighborhood schools.

Public schools in ghetto areas or in central city school districts tend to be of inferior quality. They are usually underfinanced, as compared to schools in suburban areas or in white middle-class urban areas. Teachers in the central city schools are often inferior, sometimes having been assigned to those schools because of their inferiority, or as punishment.[27] Sometimes they have emotional problems that infect their behavior toward students.[28]

Most teachers are white and middle class and they lack shared perceptions with the central city students.[29] They often assume that the students have limited learning capabilities and teach them little, thus creating a self-fulfilling prophecy.[30]

An additional problem, based often on racial discrimination, is the inability of minority youth to find employment, even if they successfully complete high school. As Schafer and Polk pointed out:

> The result is that many youth find themselves unable to get work even after successful completion of an educaton built on the promise of work after high school. It is only reasonable to expect that this message will be communicated back to students still in school and will lessen their commitment to school and its promises.[31]

One may properly argue that many of the central city high school graduates remain unemployed, not because of racial discrimination, but because they lack marketable skills. Even if that is the case, it is no less an indictment of the central city schools, which should send graduates out with marketable skills.

Lack of Shared Perceptions

As was stated above, many teachers in central city school districts are white and middle class and had little or no exposure to ethnic minorities or to lower-class children before assuming their teaching positions. Because of this lack of exposure, "few teachers are able to project themselves into the lives of lower class children."[32] They are often unsympathetic to the feelings and interests of their students. As Eichorn has stated, "Teachers have been found to favor upper class status children and to handle lower class children with more directness and less regard for their feelings or their educational welfare."[33]

This teacher insensitivity, together with the problems of large classes and working in what is often a hostile environment, may result in the abandonment of any efforts to improve the skills of problem students. The teachers, appropriately, may become concerned with their own physical survival. They may decide, often incorrectly, that some students are ineducable and devote their efforts to those students whom they perceive to be educable.

Inflexibility of Curricula and Teachers

According to Eichorn, "Schools which attempt to have every child fit a single prescribed curriculum foster behavioral problems."[34] The problems related to inflexibility of curriculum are critical. Teachers start the school year with a curriculum, or teaching plan, which they follow on a day-to-day basis, more or less. The average students should perform adequately. The above-average students will probably do well, although boredom may affect their behavior. The below-average students will fall behind, unless they receive some assistance. But we have already commented on the likelihood that the students who are not doing well, or are perceived as not capable of doing well, are likely to receive less attention from teachers, rather than more attention.

Thus it becomes probable that students who fall behind are likely to stay behind. This does not necessarily mean that they will not be moved to the next grade at the beginning of the next academic year. In many schools today, students are promoted on the basis of their age, rather than their school performance. It is not unusual, then, for example, to find some sixth grade students reading at the second or third grade level, if they are reading at all.

Reading failure has been found to be significantly related to delinquency. Eichorn states, "One study revealed 84 percent of the cases at the treatment center of a New York children's court had reading disabilities."[35]

Eichorn reports a finding by M. Roman, who stated, "In retracing the development of an individual's delinquent behavior, it is not unusual to find the triad: reading retardation—truancy—delinquency."[36]

Both of the authors, in their work with juveniles, encountered children whose behavior fit the triad. Every year they fell further behind in school. They were objects of derision by other students and by teachers. They were harassed by parents to improve their school performance. They started skipping school irregularly, and then their truant behavior became routine. Ultimately they were referred to juvenile probation for truancy or for delinquent acts committed while they were truant from school.

The schools must find a way to increase flexibility, to assist students to learn at their own pace, rather than to put them into curricular straitjackets. This would probably require smaller class sizes, so that teachers would be able to give more individual attention to students. It would also require changes in teacher education, to cause teachers to want to help *all* of their students to learn.

Teacher Inadequacy

Most of what has already been written in this chapter relates to the inadequacy of teachers. This inadequacy is evident in both suburban and central city schools, although it is more widespread in the central city. Much, but not all, of the problem stems from the inadequate preparation of teachers in colleges that offer programs in teacher education. Some of the problem also results from the biases that students in teacher-education programs bring with them to college.

Although many graduates of teacher-education programs will teach in central city schools, they are not educated to cope with the kinds of students that they will encounter. As Schafer and Polk pointed out:

> A major reason for the inappropriateness of teaching methods in lower income schools is that teacher training institutions persist in training all teachers as though they were going to be fed into suburban middle class schools. . . . The use of inappropriate teaching methods, largely resulting from inadequate and unimaginative preparation of teachers, is one of the factors contributing to educational failure, progressive loss of interest, alienation, and subsequent delinquency, among many lower income and non-white pupils, especially in the cities.[37]

Teacher-education programs often do not require that their students be exposed to courses dealing with juvenile delinquency, juvenile justice, criminology, or minority relations, although they may be tangentially exposed to these areas in some introductory courses in psychology or sociology. Many teacher-education programs require a great many courses in methodology and relatively few courses that deal with social problems, unless they are preparing the students for careers in teaching social studies. It is not surprising, then, that such teachers are at a loss when they encounter the kinds of situations that occur in schools, particularly central city schools. Further, many of them have lived relatively sheltered lives in white middle-class suburbs. This isolation from urban reality only increases their inability to cope with classroom problems.

REDUCING DELINQUENCY

To reduce delinquency, the schools must stop doing those things they are now doing that increase delinquency. Regrettably, this is easier said than done. Such a change would require a commitment by society to change patterns of discrimination. In many instances, it would require desegregation of schools and increased allocation of resources to central city schools.

It would also require a complete revision of teacher-education programs in many, if not most, colleges and universities in the United States. Such programs would have to teach education majors about urban problems. A significant change for the better might require the selection of increased numbers of minority students to enter teacher-education programs. This might not be effective, because many qualified, competent teachers of minority backgrounds also prefer to teach in white suburbs rather than in the central city.

IDENTIFYING THE PRE-DELINQUENT

In Chapter Six, we discussed the problems police face in dealing with the pre-delinquent. The same kinds of problems, and others, exist when we consider the role of the schools in attempting to identify and treat pre-delinquents.

An effort to predict which children are likely to become delinquents would result in classifying children into four categories:

1. Children correctly classified as pre-delinquent
2. Children incorrectly classified as pre-delinquent
3. Children correctly classified as not pre-delinquent
4. Children incorrectly classified as not pre-delinquent

Such an effort at classification would be useless unless followed by some treatment program for those children classified as pre-delinquent (categories 1 and 2). As Peter F. Briggs and Robert D. Wirt have pointed out, this would involve certain costs for errors. Children incorrectly classified as pre-delinquent (category 2) would be treated unnecessarily. Children incorrectly classified as not pre-delinquent (category 4) would not receive needed treatment.[38]

One instrument to assist teachers in identifying pre-delinquents was developed by William Kvaraceus. His "Delinquency Proneness Checklist"[39] is duplicated in Table 10.1.

TABLE 10.1
Kvaraceus Delinquency Proneness Checklist

Yes	No	Not Sure		
___	___	___	1.	Shows marked dislike for school.
___	___	___	2.	Resents school routine and restriction.
___	___	___	3.	Uninterested in school program.
___	___	___	4.	Is failing in a number of subjects.
___	___	___	5.	Has repeated one or more grades.
___	___	___	6.	Attends special class for retarded pupils.
___	___	___	7.	Has attended many different schools.
___	___	___	8.	Intends to leave school as soon as the law allows.
___	___	___	9.	Has only vague academic or vocational plans.
___	___	___	10.	Has limited academic ability.
___	___	___	11.	Seriously or persistently misbehaves.
___	___	___	12.	Destroys school materials or property.
___	___	___	13.	Is cruel and bullying on the playground.
___	___	___	14.	Has temper tantrums in the classroom.
___	___	___	15.	Wants to stop schooling at once.
___	___	___	16.	Is truant from school.
___	___	___	17.	Does not participate in organized extracurricular programs.
___	___	___	18.	Feels he does not "belong" in the classroom.

According to Kvaraceus:

> Since these 18 factors have been shown to be significantly characteristic of delinquents when contrasted with nondelinquents, it is suggested that classroom teachers keep a weather eye open for those pupils in their classes who show a *saturation of these characteristics*. We should give them a second look and a helping hand.[40]

One of the authors of this book filled out the Delinquency Proneness Checklist as he perceived it would have been filled out by his classroom teachers when he was in school. He scored thirteen Yes, four No, and one Not Sure. This would suggest that either this checklist has dubious validity or this author should have been in a delinquency-prevention program.

It should be added that nothing in this chapter to this point would demonstrate that the typical classroom teacher is qualified to exercise competent judgment about which students are or are not pre-delinquent. One would suspect that students would likely be classified as pre-delinquent on the basis of the same criteria that have been used to classify students as fast learners and slow learners.[41] The criteria would probably include those factors that distinguish inner city children from white middle-class suburban children.

Even if pre-delinquents could be accurately identified, the problem of how to treat them would still exist, in view of the lack of success reported for most programs to treat delinquents (see Chapter Nine). Another problem would be the cost. Kassebaum cited proposals discussed by Thomas S. Szasz to diagnose all school children and treat "about 7.5 to 12 percent of grade school children . . . sufficiently emotionally disturbed to require treatment."[42] As Kassebaum pointed out, "The scope of such a program, *were* it ever to be implemented, is to be counted in the millions of children."[43] Such a program, if it were implemented, would also cost many billions of dollars per year. It would probably be greater in scope than the entire present juvenile justice system.

An even greater problem, however, is lack of jurisdiction. As was mentioned earlier, the constitutional requirement for due process would not appear to be satisfied by a psychiatric finding that a child is pre-delinquent. Any program to enforce treatment of children who have committed no offenses would assuredly suffer defeat in the courts.

NOTES
CHAPTER TEN

1. William C. Kvaraceus, *Juvenile Delinquency* (Washington, D.C., 1958), p. 6.

2. Gilbert A. Pompa, "Hispanic Tide Can't Be Ignored" *Kansas City Times* (July 7, 1980): 9.

3. Ray C. Rist, "Student Social Class and Teacher Expectations: The Self-fulfilling Prophecy in Ghetto Education" in *Human Services Organizations*, Yeheskel Hasenfeld and Richard A. English, eds. (Ann Arbor, Mich. 1974), pp. 517–39.

4. Aaron V. Cicourel and John I. Kitsuse, *The Educational Decision-makers* (Indianapolis, 1963), p. 6.

5. Rist, "Student Social Class," pp. 518–19.

6. Richard A. Cloward and Lloyd E. Ohlin, *Delinquency and Opportunity* (New York, 1960), pp. 144–60.

7. Kenneth B. Clark, *Dark Ghetto* (New York, 1965), pp. 130–31.

8. Richard E. Johnson, *Juvenile Delinquency and Its Origins* (Cambridge, 1979), p. 142.

9. Walter Schafer and Kenneth Polk, "Delinquency and the Schools," *Task Force Report: Juvenile Delinquency and Youth Crime*. The President's Commission on Law Enforcement and Administration of Justice. (Washington, D. C., 1967), p. 236.

10. Ibid., pp. 240–42.

11. Paul H. Hahn, *The Juvenile Offender and the Law* (Cincinnati, 1971), p. 202.

12. Schafer and Polk, "Delinquency and the Schools," p. 226.

13. Gene Kassebaum, *Delinquency and Social Policy* (Englewood Cliffs, N. J., 1974), p. 157.

14. Schafer and Polk, "Delinquency and the Schools," p. 226.

15. Ibid., p. 230.

16. Ibid., pp. 234–35. Also see John R. Eichorn, "Delinquency and the Educational System" in *Juvenile Delinquency*, Herbert C. Quay, ed. (Princeton, N. J., 1965), p. 314.

17. Schafer and Polk, "Delinquency and the Schools," p. 235.

18. Eichorn, "Delinquency and the Educational System," p. 301. Also see George W. Noblit and Thomas W. Collins, "Order and Disruption in a Desegregated High School," *Crime and Delinquency* 24 (July, 1978): 277.

19. Schafer and Polk, "Delinquency and the Schools," p. 277.

20. Eichorn, "Delinquency and the Educational System," p. 313.

21. Hahn, *The Juvenile Offender and the Law*, p. 202.

22. John R. Ban and Lewis M. Ciminillo, *Violence and Vandalism in Public Education* (Danville, Ill., 1977), p. 107.

23. Ibid., p. 108.

24. M. Joan McDermott, *Criminal Victimization in Urban Schools* (Washington D.C., 1979), p. 16.

25. Ibid., p. 21.

26. Schafer and Polk, "Delinquency and the Schools," p. 244.

27. Ibid., pp. 243–44. Also, see Eichorn, p. 318, and Ban and Ciminillo, *Violence and Vandalism*, p. 104.

28. Eichorn, "Delinquency and the Educational System," p. 317.

29. Ibid., p. 314.

30. Hahn, *The Juvenile Offender and the Law*, p. 202.

31. Schafer and Polk, "Delinquency and the Schools," p. 247. Also see Alexander Liazos, "School, Alienation, and Delinquency" in *Crime and Delinquency* 24 (July, 1978): 355–70.

32. Eichorn, "Delinquency and the Educational System," p. 314.

33. Ibid., p. 315.

34. Ibid., p. 314.

35. Ibid., p. 312.

36. M. Roman, *Reaching Delinquents through Reading* (Springfield, Ill., 1957), cited in Eichorn, "Delinquency and the Educational System," p. 312.

37. Schafer and Polk, "Delinquency and the Schools," p. 239.

38. Peter F. Briggs and Robert D. Wirt, "Prediction," in *Juvenile Delinquency*, Herbert C. Quay, ed. (Princeton, N. J., 1965), p. 182.

39. Kvaraceus, *Juvenile Delinquency*, p. 17.

40. Ibid., p. 16.

41. Rist, "Student Social Class," p. 537.

42. Thomas S. Szasz, *Ideological Insanity: Essays on the Psychiatric Dehumanization of Man* (New York, 1970), p. 145, cited in Kassebaum, *Delinquency and Social Policy*, p. 160.

43. Kassebaum, *Delinquency and Social Policy*, p. 160.

11
REVOLUTION AND COUNTERREVOLUTION

U ntil the nineteenth century American society attempted to control crime and delinquency through the policy of retribution. The often cruel punishments inflicted upon offenders were rationalized on the ground that the suffering befitted the offenses and that justice was therefore balanced. Redemption for criminals or delinquents was not considered.

As the nineteenth century began to unfold, however, society invoked the policy of restraint much more frequently than that of retribution. Criminals and delinquents were incarcerated in prisons and reformatories for as long as the seriousness of their offenses warranted. Reformers believed that the inmates would experience remorse, would see the error of their ways, and would thus ultimately alter their behavior patterns and become useful members of society.

During these years Americans also became extremely sensitive to the role that children would play in the future and destiny of their nation. As a consequence, the concept of childhood changed considerably. Indeed, childhood came to be seen as a vulnerable time and was extended into adolescence; adolescence, in turn, was extended into adulthood. This was done to protect, educate, and control America's "most valuable natural resource," its youth.

By the end of the nineteenth century, this new concept of childhood had helped produce the new correctional philosophy of "rehabilitation." According to the rehabilitative approach, the needs of the individual offender had to be attended to through the implementation of complicated programs of diagnosis and treatment. If this could be done, reformers believed, not only would delinquents be rehabilitated, but crime among dependent and unruly children would also be prevented.[1]

This is the approach that continues to dominate today. It is important to understand, however, that neither retribution nor restraint has been entirely rejected. They continue to exist in less obvious forms. For example, although punishments are considerably milder now than they were in earlier times, punishment for the sake of punishment is still, regrettably, a major element of our contemporary juvenile justice system. Even the most vociferous proponents of rehabilitation have not been averse to the use of reformatories and training schools as "correctional utopias." Thus, all three of the major American correctional philosophies continue to exert an influence upon the juvenile justice system and probably will do so for some time to come.

The rehabilitation philosophy of juvenile justice, nevertheless, is the one that guided and shaped the separate system of justice for children during most of the twentieth century. Therefore, the first section of this chapter briefly reexamines the origin and evolution, or devolution, of this philosophy and of the juvenile court system. The next section analyzes the current revolution against that philosophy and system, a revolution that has significantly altered the treatment of "delinquent" children. This is followed by an examination of the counterrevolution against this alteration, a movement demanding that society be provided with the security necessary to defend itself against juvenile crime.

THE FIRST REVOLUTION

A revolutionary separate system of justice for children, as we have seen, originated in the late nineteenth century and reflected the moral concerns, attitudes, and prejudices of white middle-class reformers (see Chapter One and Chapter Two). These child savers perceived that the moral and spiritual climate necessary for the proper development of American children was being threatened by the overwhelming immigration of the poor and destitute to this country. They equated this flood of immigrants to American cities with the horrors of industrialization, economic instability, massive poverty, and the loss of traditional agrarian values.

The child savers believed that deviance, crime, and delinquency were also directly related to contemporary urban conditions. Thus they focused their attention on crowded and corrupt American cities filled with "depraved and degenerate" foreigners. Moreover, they believed in a new concept of childhood that mandated an extended and protected adolescence. Only by providing this protection, or by removing endangered children from the "urban cesspools" that bred delinquency, however, could America's destiny be fulfilled. As a consequence of these beliefs and conditions, the child savers worked to establish the juvenile court, a revolutionary new juvenile justice system that not only would serve the needs of America's underprivileged urban waifs, but also would preserve the greater glory of America itself.

Many of these reformers were women and mothers, and what they created was a juvenile court that, in effect, became a substitute parent and protector for delinquent and dependent children. They wanted to locate, treat, and control troubled urban youths and inculcate into them traditional American agrarian values and morals. The goals of care and reformation superseded any considerations of individual liberty. Indeed, due process protections were viewed as obstacles and thus were minimized or abandoned. Legal procedures, lawyers, and constitutional protections were not needed, according to the reformers, because children appearing before the new court would not be viewed as criminals. Instead they were defined as youths in need of care, treatment, discipline, and supervision. They were *respondents* rather than *defendants*. No *sentences* were handed out after adjudication. *Dispositions* "in the best interest of the child" were made instead. Moreover, if found guilty, the youths were not *imprisoned* in penal institutions. Rather, they were *remanded* to *reformatories* or *training schools* for *rehabilitation* and *supervision*.[2]

The child savers considered youths who broke the law to be victims of the same socioeconomic forces that produced neglected, abandoned, or abused children. Indeed, they believed that dependent juveniles inevitably became delinquent. Thus, they used the *parens patriae* doctrine to blur the formal distinctions between potential and actual delinquents. As a consequence, the concept of delinquency expanded to include all of the status offenses with which we are familiar today.

The first juvenile court networks created at the turn of the century (Illinois in 1899, Wisconsin and New York in 1901, Ohio and Maryland in 1902, and Colorado in 1903) incorporated this new rehabilitative philosophy, as well as the child savers' concepts of delinquency and childhood. Accordingly, the new juvenile justice system dispensed the treatment, care, and supervision that only parents or community authorities had previously provided. Moreover, the children brought before the juvenile courts were not involved in adversary proceedings. Because the courts were viewed as protectors and rehabilitators of America's wayward youth, they were authorized to investigate and ultimately to modify every social, psychological, and moral element of children's lives. Indeed, the courts often intervened and exercised their power in cases where children had not broken any laws, but had merely caused problems for adults.

Juvenile court judges were viewed as the instruments of protection and rehabilitation, and they were given an extremely wide range of powers over the lives of the children brought before them. They often functioned as doctors, psychologists, and family therapists rather than as lawyer fact-finders. As a consequence, medical and psychological rhetoric often dominated the proceedings. One early judge even suggested that the juvenile court should be a "laboratory of human behavior" and its judges trained as "specialists in the art of human relations." Another corrections "expert" claimed that it was the judge's task to "get the whole truth about a child" in the same way that a "physician searches for every detail that bears on the condition of a patient."[3]

In spite of, or perhaps because of, this new rehabilitative philosophy of juvenile justice, the juvenile court movement increased rather than decreased the number of children placed in state-run institutions. This increase occurred in part because the child savers had altered the concepts of childhood and delinquency and in the process ignored, or were blind to, the negative effects of institutionalization. To be sure, training schools did replace jails, but reformatories, which were often glorified prisons, continued to be used. Thus, the institutions and vocabulary of the "rehabilitative" juvenile court merely camouflaged the reality of incarcerated children.

The number of institutionalized children also increased because the reformers believed that the only way to change delinquent behavior was to remove children from those environments that bred crime. The child savers argued that delinquency was not a result of conscious choice. Children were drawn into lives of crime by social and economic forces beyond their control. Once separated from those forces, however, youths could be treated and ultimately cured of their criminal propensities. In short, the American juvenile justice system was viewed as a better source of education, discipline, and supervision than the "depraved" urban slums and the foreign influences that lurked therein.[4]

As the juvenile court evolved, it therefore received an ever increasing amount of discretionary power. Without this power, it was argued, the care, treatment, supervision, and control necessary to rehabilitate delinquents could not be provided. As a consequence, the detention and institutionalization of delinquents and potential delinquents increased in proportion to the court's discretionary power.

By the 1960s, however, the reliance upon detention and institutionalization as a rehabilitative response to deviant behavior came to be increasingly criticized as unjustifiable, and the second revolution in American juvenile justice began.

THE SECOND REVOLUTION

During the 1960s and 1970s the American juvenile justice system did, in fact, experience a second revolution. It was triggered by the belief that the system had failed to provide protective care or effective treatment to children, and by revelations concerning incarcerated children. Critics asserted that thousands of children were being needlessly brutalized and stigmatized, even though delinquency had been neither controlled nor abolished. Moreover, reformers argued that socially responsible theory promoting the institutionalization of antisocial or delinquent children in order to correct behavior problems simply did not exist.[5]

Critics acknowledged that the community is protected when serious offenders are removed from the streets, but they also claimed that such offenders are rarely rehabilitated or deterred from committing similar acts after they are released and that recidivism is, in fact, directly related to a child's interaction with the juvenile system. In short, any youth who is arrested, appears before the court, and is subsequently incarcerated is more likely to become a recidivist than is a youth who commits the same offense but is never caught.[6]

The most damning evidence against the incarceration of children, however, concerned the "treatment" received in various institutions. For example, investigators revealed that in order to control, discipline, and punish inmates, many state children's prisons or training schools practiced the following:

1. Indiscriminate use of tear gas and chemical control devices

2. Regularly scheduled beatings

3. Uncontrolled use of mind-altering drugs

4. Torture and physical abuse of children by other children

5. Invoking bizarre rituals and codes of conduct with children, many of whom were less than thirteen years old

6. Brutally punishing youths for expressing disrespect for corrections officers or teachers

7. Allowing extortion, assault, rape, and violence among children

8. Selecting certain inmates as "office boys" who acted as informers and enforcers

9. Falsifying injury reports to protect guards and favored office boys

10. Firing corrections personnel or teachers who complained about conditions

11. Using solitary confinement, often for several weeks, for trivial reasons

12. Ignoring basic rules of safety and sanitation

13. Binding children hand and foot with handcuffs, chains, or rope

14. Refusing to allow recreation or exercise

15. Subjecting status offenders, dependent children, and those merely awaiting trial to the shameful conditions described above[7]

According to the theories and goals of the juvenile court's original creators, the validity of the American juvenile justice system depends upon protecting and rehabilitating children, rather than punishing them. Juvenile court critics pointed out, however, that if after adjudication juveniles are incarcerated in institutions of penal servitude, the entire claim of *parens patriae* becomes worse than an illusion: it becomes a sham and a miscarriage of justice. Unfortunately, hard evidence continued to mount in support of the conclusion that, "regardless of the label, children adjudicated in juvenile court are often committed to penal institutions."[8]

As a direct result of this evidence, more and more reformers and liberal critics argued that the incarceration of children was destructive of the human spirit. They declared that the juvenile court process did not rehabilitate or treat wayward youths. Instead, the system stifled any potential for growth and adjustment. The critics also argued that reformatories and training schools were lawless and violent environments and that children should never be placed in them. Consequently, they concluded that the American juvenile justice system interfered with the lives of too many youths, that too many children had been institutionalized, and that child care and family service agencies outside the court's jurisdiction must be strengthened and utilized more fully. In short, the power of the court to incarcerate children had to be severely curtailed.[9]

In 1965 President Lyndon Johnson established the Commission on Law Enforcement and Administration of Justice (the President's

Commission) in order to investigate these complaints and charges, analyze rising crime rates, and recommend reforms. When the commission's recommendations were published in 1967, they reflected the current state of unhappiness with the juvenile system and promoted reintegrative reforms. The commission implied that poverty, discrimination, and the lack of opportunity had been major causes of delinquency, and that if America's destiny and mission were to be preserved and our children saved, these causes had to be eliminated. Hence, the war on poverty. According to the commission, however, one of the greatest perpetuators of juvenile delinquency was the juvenile justice system itself.[10]

The commission arrived at this conclusion for two reasons. First, the juvenile court system had clearly not lived up to its expectations. Indeed, a growing body of evidence indicated that correctional programs, even under the best of circumstances, did not make a difference. The second and more important reason, however, was the commission's acceptance of labeling theory.[11]

According to labeling theory, as we have seen, poverty and lack of opportunity do not create or cause serious delinquency. Rather, society's reaction to offenders is the key element. The commission adopted this view of youthful lawbreaking and declared that the juvenile court had failed because it had identified, labeled, and stigmatized children who would have been better off had they never entered the bizarre labyrinth of juvenile justice. In fact, the commission suggested that, instead of "leaving children alone, thus keeping them on the conventional path that leads from childhood to adulthood, the court had only made them more delinquent."[12]

The President's Commission was convinced that the juvenile court had been a major contributor to, if not the principal cause of, the perpetuation of juvenile crime. As a consequence, it recommended a series of reintegrative reforms designed to drastically limit the court's power and jurisdiction. Basically, the reforms can be broken down into four categories: decriminalization, diversion, due process, and deinstitutionalization.

Decriminalization

Decriminalization is a reform that suggests that the moral behavior of children ought to be freed from the legal controls of society, that all status offenses should be eliminated, and that juvenile delinquency must be limited solely to violations of criminal law. This is not how the recommendations of the President's Commission were implemented, however. In fact, most states merely gave status offenders a different, "less stigmatizing" name and allowed the juvenile court to exercise a continuing jurisdiction over them. Names such as 601s, CHINS, MINS, JINS, and YINS did help foster a growing public recognition that status offenders are not violators of the criminal law. But, as the 1980s unfold, only a handful of states have made status offenders subject to juvenile court jurisdiction solely as dependent or neglected children. And, although legislation is pending in a few states, not one has freed status offenders entirely from juvenile court jurisdiction.[13]

To free status offenders from juvenile court jurisdiction, of course, would not solve the problem of runaways, truants, and other unruly children who do, in fact, need some form of supervision. Changing the rules does not eliminate the problem, nor does changing the labels attached to the youths who caused the problem. The word "delinquent," after all, was invented to decriminalize, and to distinguish from adults, all misbehaving children, criminal or not. And history has shown that any name given to youths who are processed through the juvenile justice system is stigmatizing. The only solution to the problem is to avoid such stigmatization and still provide some form of remediation for troubled, but not criminal, youths. How can this be done? According to the President's Commission, and according to most liberal reformers today, we must decrease the influence of the juvenile court by increasing the use of diversion, due process, and deinstitutionalization.

Diversion

Diversion, as we saw earlier, is the process of turning aside status, first-time, or petty offenders from the juvenile justice system and using community resources to serve in the court's stead. The President's Commission on Law Enforcement and Administration of Justice recommended that the police play a larger role in the diversion process by taking care of the most innocuous offenses at the station. The biggest change recommended, however, was the creation of community youth service bureaus, which would become courts of law, coordinate all youth services, and thus perform the functions for which the juvenile court system had originally been designed.

To date, youth service bureaus are scarce. Diversion, however, has proven to be extremely popular and has been widely implemented. Few people disagree with the basic premise that the number of children being processed through the juvenile justice system must be reduced. Unfortunately, however, the methods of interpreting and implementing diversion have varied considerably, and thus its success rate has been less than spectacular. For example, labeling theorists, and others who believe juvenile courts to be utterly worthless, think of diversion as a juvenile justice alternative that would allow children, even unruly ones, to grow up in peace. They argue that delinquency is a product of labeling and age. Thus, if trouble-prone youths were not stigmatized they would eventually grow out of their rebellious stage and be useful and productive citizens.[14]

Other reformers, who are social activists, however, believe diversion means more, not fewer, programs for children. Although they favor the exclusion of legal processing, they do not consider home and school truancy, male and female prostitution, and other youthful problems to be behavior that society can afford to ignore. These activist reformers believe that diversion offers an opportunity to treat troubled children and find solutions for their problems without involving the juvenile justice system. To do nothing, they believe, would be socially irresponsible.

Still others—primarily court workers, attorneys, and judges who are overwhelmed with case loads, paperwork, obscenely crowded detention centers, and other problems caused by too many children in the system—think of diversion as a means to cut down on the overloading. Petty, first-time, and status offenders, they believe, can be better dealt with elsewhere. They would prefer to concentrate the efforts of the juvenile courts on controlling the murderers, rapists, muggers, pimps, and other assorted "punks" who are committing "real" crimes. They argue that this kind of diversion would not only serve the interests of society in general, but would also raise the morale of court workers, attorneys, and judges in particular.

Finally, there are some reformers who believe that the police allow far too many troubled children to go uncontrolled and unsupervised. They see diversion as a means to counsel and treat those children who are normally warned and released at the police station. As LaMar Empey observes, "A movement is afoot to decriminalize these kinds of troublemakers, [and] diversion is an alternative means for keeping them under control."[15]

In the years since the President's Commission made its recommendations, diversion has been used in various forms all over the country. It has not, however, kept children out of the juvenile justice system, as labeling theorists hoped it might. Indeed, juveniles in general are subject to a new and complex child-saving bureaucracy today that did not exist in 1967.[16] This bureaucracy consists of many private agencies. In spite of diversion's original purpose, however, most of these agencies' programs are either supervised by, or connected with, juvenile court personnel. Without referrals from the police or court workers most of the new child-saving agencies would not be able to exist. Accordingly, although much of the work, supervision, treatment, and control previously exercised by probation officers has been assumed by others, diversion has not meant escape from the juvenile justice system for most juvenile offenders. In large measure, diversion has simply come to mean "referral to some other agency."[17]

Other flaws in diversion have become visible over the years as well. For example, the number of juveniles either referred to court or subjected to a formal hearing has not been reduced,[18] nor are youths involved in diversion programs necessarily stigmatized less than those who are processed normally. Often their schools, peers, and potential employers find out about the programs and immediately assume that the participants are undesirable. Moreover, due process rights are flagrantly ignored when youths who are alleged but not convicted offenders are involuntarily assigned to diversion programs.

Donald R. Cressey and Robert A. McDermott have summed up what we know about diversion as follows:

1. The faddist nature of diversion has produced a proliferation of diversion units and programs without generating a close look at whether the juvenile subject to all this attention is receiving a better deal.

2. So far as we know, no one has shown that the juvenile offender and his family perceive their handling as materially different under the auspices of a diversion unit than under a more traditional justice agency. . . . For this reason, it seems that in-depth qualitative and longitudinal studies be the first order of business for subsequent diversion research.[19]

Due Process

Due process, the third major reform recommended by the President's Commission, promotes the idea that the juvenile court should serve as a court of law, rather than as a substitute parent. The *Kent* (1966) and *Gault* (1967) Supreme Court decisions reinforced this concept and gave credence to labeling theorists' contention that children involved in the American juvenile justice system received neither protection nor rehabilitative treatment (see Chapter Two). As a consequence, during the 1970s most juvenile courts began to resemble more closely the adult criminal court model. Parents were notified well in advance of any court action; defense attorneys were automatically appointed; evidence was properly presented; excessive informality, hearsay, and rumor disappeared; and adjudicatory hearings were differentiated from dispositional ones.[20]

This shift from the civil proceedings of previous years to the more formal character of criminal trials has not occurred everywhere. Many courts have part-time or incompetent judges who are either ignorant of the latest reforms or who simply cling to the past. But the trend has clearly been in the direction of providing juvenile lawbreakers with most of the rights afforded adults. Accordingly, in the majority of juvenile courts today judges no longer have the power to remove children from their families unless due process is exercised. Nevertheless, although formality is the rule now, we should not assume that absolute justice for children has been achieved.[21]

Adult criminal courts have always attempted to operate under a system of due process and formality. And yet, adult courts are also often guilty of dispensing a diluted form of justice in order to handle massive backlogs of cases. Formality and due process require more time, manpower, and expertise; as a result, cases often do not reach courts for months and sometimes years. Slow and unwieldy justice, therefore, is the rule rather than the exception in adult courts. Consequently, plea bargaining—pleading guilty to lesser charges—is used in the vast majority of criminal cases simply to avoid the extremely long wait for trial.[22]

Juvenile courts are already experiencing identical problems. Moreover, not only are the offenses, rather than the offenders, the focus of the courts' attention now, but due process has also had the unintended effect of further diminishing the chances of fair trials for under-class youths. Children whose parents can afford the services of first-rate attorneys are much more likely to be treated justly than those whose parents must rely on overworked, court-appointed, or less-than-skillful lawyers. Only a massive infusion of funds, facilities, and personnel can alter this condition.[23] But, given the mood of the country and its economic malaise as the 1980s begin, such an infusion is not likely to occur.

Deinstitutionalization

Deinstitutionalization is the reform that promotes the removal of in-carcerated children from training schools and reformatories to open community settings. The guiding principle behind this reform is that troubled youths are far more likely to benefit from the nondelinquent activities of the community than they are from the closed, suffocating, and often corrupting influences of institutions.[24] Like diversion, dein-stitutionalization is predicated upon the belief that serious crime is a product of the delinquent identities and behavior of youths who have been unnecessarily branded as "bad." Thus, according to this reform, the power and jurisdiction of the juvenile court must be restricted, status offenses decriminalized, and criminal offenders left alone when-ever possible.[25]

Those who are in favor of deinstitutionalization argue that the incarceration of children breeds adult criminals and does not reha-bilitate anyone. They also point out the need for a broader under-standing and acceptance of an integrative philosophy that stresses greater community participation in restructuring young lives. This can only be done, they claim, if society recognizes the civil rights of children and realizes the long-term benefits that will accrue to both America and its youth when the overwhelming use of custodial insti-tutions is eliminated.

Deinstitutionalization for status offenders is already in effect in a number of states. The Juvenile Justice and Delinquency Prevention Act of 1974 mandated the removal of all status offenders from places of detention and incarceration within two years in those states that received federal funds for new community programs and services. California and several other states soon passed local legislation that conformed to the federal law. Thus, instead of incarceration these states now stress "diagnostic services, short-term crisis intervention, counseling, temporary placement in shelter care homes, or long-term placement in foster or group homes.[26]

As we have seen with the other new reforms, however, deinsti-tutionalization has some serious flaws. First, although several states now refrain from locking up status offenders and have attempted to improve family relations, little or nothing has been done to modify the schools, neighborhoods, and communities that produce or reinforce the behavior of status offenders. Second, when parents, schools, and other community resources cannot live up to the task of controlling and modifying misbehaving youths, no institutional network exists as a supporting element. And finally, where incarceration is forbidden, many children are forced to remain in homes that encourage, allow, or are indifferent to sexual abuse, prostitution, drug addiction, alcoholism, school truancy, and violent or uncontrollable behavior. For these children, incarceration is frequently the lesser of two evils.[27]

As for the deinstitutionalization of criminal offenders, over the past two decades several experiments have been undertaken that provide many interesting insights. Beginning with the Provo Experiment that operated in Utah from 1960 to 1966, continuing through the Silverlake Experiment in Los Angeles from 1964 to 1968, and culminating in the closing of juvenile institutions in Massachusetts in 1972, the new reintegrative philosophy has been severely tested.[28]

The development of community programs, nevertheless, has been slow to catch on, largely because most people still believe that offenders, regardless of their age, ought to be punished. Self-serving, unreachable, and unmovable bureaucracies have also been reluctant to give up any of their powers or preserves. Reintegrative proposals are not politically popular either, for rarely is a community pleased about the placement in its midst of halfway houses or other homes for troubled youths. Moreover, it is doubtful that many people, predisposed as they are to considerations of public safety, would support deinstitutionalization, even if they were confronted with conclusive evidence of the merits of such programs.

The evidence accumulated from the experiments listed above, as well as from other programs, suggests that youths under supervision in the community are significantly less delinquent than are juveniles placed on regular probation. Community-based offenders also tend to be no more delinquent than youths incarcerated in state training schools. In addition, post-program recidivism rates for those involved in community programs are no greater than for those who have been incarcerated.[29] Most important, however, community treatment is more humane, less costly, and of shorter duration than institutional incarceration. And finally, although community programs are not overwhelmingly positive, they are not—unlike institutional placements—destructive either. In fact, serious recidivists are much more likely to be products of incarceration than of community programs. Thus, community protection, as well as the interest of offenders, would appear to be better served by reintegrative, deinstitutionalized community efforts than by the juvenile justice system.[30]

As we saw in Chapter Nine, little evidence exists to prove satisfactorily that one correctional approach is superior to another. Indeed, they are all flawed, including deinstitutionalization. For example, no matter how successful a community program may be, there will always be a few serious offenders who will not respond, and who will continue to be a menace to society.[31] If this criminal minority could be identified and weeded out before placement, the community programs would have a very impressive success record. To date, however, scientifically valid ways of doing this have not been developed.

Another flaw in deinstitutionalization is that many community-based programs have widened the power and jurisdiction of the juvenile justice system. Training school, reformatory, and youth home populations remain as high as ever. Indeed, most of the youths being treated in the community, it is argued, are those who would ordinarily be on probation or ignored. Consequently, deinstitutionalization, like diversion, has been used to legitimize control over and treatment of an ever increasing number of children, many of whom would be better off left alone.

A final problem with deinstitutionalization is that many community reintegration centers end up looking very much like the old rehabilitative institutions. Delinquents, for purposes of expediency and show, are often placed in centers that were once institutions of treatment. Whereas the previous residents were pre-delinquents or "disturbed" children, the new clientele consists of adjudicated delinquents. More often than not, however, the treatment practices remain the same. Furthermore, many community group homes, private shelters, or ranches isolate their residents from family, friends, school, and neighborhood. Accordingly, the effect is identical to institutional confinement, for these facilities "may be located in or near a community, but they are not part of it."[32]

What may we conclude, then, about decriminalization, diversion, due process, and deinstitutionalization? Has the reintegrative method recommended by the President's Commission succeeded or failed? Let us examine the data. On the positive side, the power and jurisdiction of the juvenile court have been reduced somewhat; due process and formality do preserve the rights of youths on trial for breaking the law; and many community programs have proven to be much cheaper, more humane, and less degenerative than the normal institutional operations of the juvenile justice system.

On the negative side, however, is the fact that none of these reforms has lessened the extent of the juvenile court's intervention in children's lives. Diversion, for instance, was supposed to lighten the juvenile justice system's burden, but it became instead a euphemism for referring juveniles, whom the court ordinarily would have left alone, into compulsory "unofficial" probation programs. As a result, LaMar Empey points out, "diversion has apparently contributed to the development of a new semilegal system of social control which is far from free from the influence of law enforcement and correctional, if not judicial authorities."[33]

Deinstitutionalization, despite the good intentions of its innovators, has likewise developed extensive community programs that treat children who normally would have avoided the clutches of the juvenile court system. Moreover, the number of institutionalized children has not significantly lessened, in spite of the potential and promise of community programs. Indeed, given the current trends, the new reforms will probably continue to expand the number of children who are affected by the juvenile justice system.

To date, moreover, little evidence exists to demonstrate that decriminalization, diversion, due process, and deinstitutionalization have reduced delinquency rates. Neither have these reforms effectively reintegrated delinquent youths back into society. Rather, they have become new attempts at rehabilitation. As a result, in spite of their original goal of preventing future delinquency, these reforms have not even modestly changed or modified the socializing influences of schools, neighborhoods, peer groups, or communities. Nevertheless, as LaMar Empey reminds us, "any new form, particularly in its early days, is better recognized by the ideals it proposes than by the actual practices that it disposes."[34]

COUNTERREVOLUTION

The revolutionary movement to lessen the influence and impact of the juvenile court has created a punitive counterrevolutionary movement.

Revolution and Counterrevolution

The revolutionary movement, which we have just discussed, is the gentler, more humane approach. Reforms in this direction include legislative restrictions on jurisdiction and confinement, with alternative reliance on diversion and community-based treatment programs. Little objection has been raised to the treatment of noncriminal, status offenders in this way. But the "mollycoddling" of delinquent offenders, especially those charged with felony violations, has been fiercely resisted by a group of conservative reformers who are devoted to an iron-fisted "punishment as deterrence" approach to juvenile crime.[35]

Deterrence Theory

These deterrence theorists are traditionalists who often refer to the negative consequences of the current reforms when arguing for a counterrevolution in juvenile justice. For example, they point out that if children are to have the same rights and freedoms as adults, they should also be subject to the same punishments for their crimes. Furthermore, if status offenders are to be diverted or treated by some resource outside the juvenile justice system, the youths who commit serious crimes must be punished quickly and certainly. The new juvenile court can no longer afford to be permissive and treat young criminals as it has in the past. And finally, the traditionalists contend that, since youths have been denied due process rights in the juvenile court, they should be tried in adult criminal courts where due process, as well as more suitable punishments, would be assured.[36]

In addition to these conservative back-to-the-basics reforms, deterrence theorists promote several other conservative issues. For example, they believe that the juvenile justice system is far too lenient and that the current liberal reforms are responsible for this condition. They also argue that decriminalization, diversion, due process, and deinstitutionalization have given unnecessary advantages to offenders while denying rights to victims. The whole ideology of current reforms, they maintain, reflects an excessively permissive society that has allowed respect for the authority of parents, schools, police, and courts to dissipate.[37]

The cost of crime, the traditionalists claim, has fallen on "the silent majority" of honest and industrious Americans who will continue to suffer unless the overindulgent protection of juvenile criminals is ended. Indeed, the entire fabric of American social order is in danger of unraveling. To prevent this catastrophe, these conservative critics argue that the courts must toughen up, victims' rights must be acknowledged and promoted, discipline must be resurrected everywhere, and criminals must literally begin to pay for their crimes. Concomitant with these reforms, they believe that the decline in sexual morality must be reversed, schools must return to the basics, the American family must regain its dominance, and children must at long last learn their place.[38]

For all of this to occur, for America to return to its former morality and virtue, and for the assurance of America's future greatness, the traditionalists would like to initiate the following reforms:

1. The implementation of fines and set terms of punishment in the juvenile courts to match those of the criminal courts

2. The lowering of the age of accountability for crime from eighteen to sixteen or lower, so that serious offenders may be remanded as a matter of course to regular criminal courts

3. The swift and certain punishment of offenders so that they will be incapacitated and thus unable to commit more crimes

4. The ultimate abolition of the juvenile court because "it is a diseased organ that no longer performs any useful function" (see Chapter Twelve)

5. The creation of family courts to handle status offenders and dependent children—all other offenders being disposed of in criminal courts[39]

The traditionalists point out that the juvenile court's biggest failures have been its rehabilitative philosophy and programs. They argue that as early as 1940, in the Cambridge–Somerville Youth Study, the clinical case-work approach to delinquency was shown to be unworkable.[40] Moreover, recent studies done by economists, political scientists, and sociologists have reinforced the earlier findings. These studies urge the juvenile courts to abandon their rehabilitative philosophy and implement a punitive approach. There is no grace in punishment, deterrence theorists argue, but there is justice.[41]

Deterrence theorists also argue that understanding the causes of delinquency does not control the problems, for most of the causes cannot be rectified. What is known, they point out, is that most crimes are committed by recidivists. Thus, the principal purpose of the juvenile justice system must be the swift and certain punishment of all offenders. Those who violate the law occasionally will fear this certainty and expeditiousness, and most, as a consequence, will refrain from committing offenses. For the habitual offender, incarceration and isolation from the community will prevent repeat offenses.

According to the traditionalists, moreover, indeterminate sentences and paroles should be abolished. All sentences, whether for juveniles or adults, should be of a fixed length determined by the nature of the offense and the offender's record, if any. Those delinquents with records should have their sentences doubled for a second offense, tripled for a third, and so on. Since most crimes are committed by the young, deterrence theorists reason, the purpose of increasingly tough sentences would be to expunge young recidivists from society and render them harmless until they reach the age of thirty-five.[42]

Deterrence theorists acknowledge that some 40 percent of all young offenders are not likely to commit serious crimes again and that their extended incarceration may do them more harm than good. But they also argue that society is better off in the long run if 40 percent of the delinquents in this country suffer somewhat more than they should so that the rest of society can feel safe in their homes and on the streets. The social adjustment of delinquents is not to be ignored, of course, but it must play a distinctly secondary role to "the goals of protecting victims, of deterring further crime, and of insuring that justice is uniform for all."[43]

In spite of the findings, beliefs, and goals of deterrence theorists, however, the correlation between crime rates and the severity and certainty of punishment is inconclusive. For example, seemingly irrefutable evidence exists to demonstrate that when arrest rates are high, crime rates tend to be low.[44] On the surface, this evidence would seem to support the idea that whenever deterrence is certain, delinquency and criminal activity decrease, but alternative explanations easily account for such decreases. High arrest rates, for example, remove active criminals from opportunities to commit crimes; it is this incapacitation that reduces crime, not the fear of arrest and punishment. Furthermore, although arrest rates do influence the number of offenses committed, crime rates also influence the number of arrests made. Thus, a crime wave may cause a concomitant increase in arrests, or a reduction in arrests may occur because of overburdened police resources.[45]

Deterrence theory findings are further flawed by their tendency to focus exclusively on penal sanctions or high arrest rates as determinants of crime. Consequently, traditionalists neglect the influence of unemployment, unequal opportunities, social class and cultural deficiencies, and other factors known to be related to delinquency and crime. More important, by considering only one-way causation, they ignore the possible effects that crime rates may have on the juvenile justice system's generation and administration of sanctions. That is, the traditionalists fail to understand that high crime rates can so overburden a juvenile court's operations that—as in the arrest situation described above—it is unable to provide the sanctioning capacity necessary to cope with the circumstances.[46]

Clearly, then, the simplistic model of crime and punishment that traditionalist reformers advocate does not adequately take into consideration the overloading of juvenile courts and training schools and the severe manpower and resource shortages that exist throughout the juvenile justice system.[46] Accordingly, these conservative reformers also do not grasp the fundamental fact that the increased use of diversion, deinstitutionalization, probation, plea bargaining, parole, and suspended sentences during the 1970s has been caused by an increasing delinquency rate. Indeed, the deterrence theorists argue just the opposite. They claim that the utilization of these liberal reforms has handicapped the juvenile justice system and in the process has stimulated delinquency. Only an increased use of "good old-fashioned" punishment can turn the tide.

Deterrence theorists also point out that in spite of the "new revolution," the number of children processed by the juvenile justice system has not decreased. As they see it, if a new juvenile crime wave sweeps across the country, it will be the direct result of failed reforms and the kid-glove approach to youthful criminals. As we have seen, however, deterrence theorists ignore the fact that overloaded juvenile courts stimulated these reforms in the first place. Thus, the traditionalists are also blind to the fact that further increases in the volume of delinquency must lead to further reductions in the certainty and severity of punishment. For the means to punish or incarcerate every "bad kid" in the country simply does not exist. In short, and in spite of deterrence theory, crime rates influence the certainty of punishment more strongly than the certainty of punishment influences crime rates.[48]

There is also the problem of undetected delinquency. Only about 10 percent of all delinquent acts result in arrests. Of those arrested, perhaps half—and probably fewer than half—are referred to the juvenile court. Of these, fewer than half reach the adjudication stage, because of the filtering process done at the intake level. Consequently, considerably fewer than 2.5 percent of all delinquent acts result in conviction and disposition. Of those convicted, most are from the under class for reasons described in Chapter Five. Would the swift, certain, and severe punishment of these children prevent the undetected delinquency of the middle and upper classes? Would the suppression of chronic offenders reduce delinquency if only 2 percent of all delinquent acts are ever noticed by officials? These are questions that deterrence theorists do not answer, for they cannot.

The answers are obvious, however. Unquestionably society would be safer if all recidivists were incarcerated. But crime would not disappear, and people would continue to be victimized. In order to prevent all delinquency, to control all crime, and to punish all offenders, a police state would be necessary. And even in the most totalitarian state imaginable, some crime would exist, for the human spirit—or call it man's baser passions, or original sin, or man's basic antipathy to authority—is unconquerable and will manifest itself in some way.

Unless we resurrect a mandatory capital punishment system for all felony crimes and for all ages, deterrence alone cannot solve the problem of an overburdened juvenile justice system. In fact the overburdening would be greater. Moreover, as we have seen, the punishment response in justice is simply not supported by the facts. Indeed, most of the evidence suggests that juvenile crime is deterred more by normative factors than by the punitive approach.[49] Nevertheless, deterrence theory continues to exercise a tenacious grip on our cultural and legal philosophy, for "common sense" tells us that it must work. But, as Charles H. Logan points out,

> There is little doubt in my own mind, based as much on *common sense* as on the whole range of deterrence literature,

that legal sanctions do in fact deter many people from committing criminal acts. But what I think we *cannot* do is to make estimates as to the marginal effects on crime rates that will result from given increases or decreases in some form of the criminal sanction.[50]

It would appear, therefore, that if we want to be protected from juvenile crime, we need fresh perspectives and new approaches. We need to know more about how to prevent crime, how to promote moral order, and how to make our streets and homes safer while preserving our free and democratic society. Perhaps we need to know the unknowable.

NOTES

CHAPTER ELEVEN

1. LaMar T. Empey, *American Delinquency: Its Meaning and Construction* (Hometown, Ill., 1978), p. 515.

2. Milton G. Rector and David Gilman, "How Did We Get Here and Where Are We Going—The Future of the Juvenile Court System," *Criminal Justice Review* 1 (Spring, 1976): 77–90.

3. See J. W. Mack, "The Chancery Procedure in the Juvenile Court," *The Child, The Clinic, and the Court* (New York, 1925), p. 315; Anthony M. Platt, *The Child Savers* (Chicago, 1969), pp. 142–143; and Rector and Gilman, "How Did We Get Here," pp. 80–81.

4. See Frances Barry McCarthy, "Should Juvenile Delinquency Be Abolished?" *Crime and Delinquency* 23 (April, 1977): 196–203.

5. Rector and Gilman, "How Did We Get Here," p. 83.

6. Ibid. Also see M. Gold and J. Williams, "National Study of the Aftermath of Apprehension" *Prospectus* (December, 1969): 3–12.

7. See Rector and Gilman, "How Did We Get Here," pp. 83–87.

8. Ibid., p. 87.

9. See H. Ted Rubin, "Retain the Juvenile Court?—Legislative Developments, Reform Directions, and the Call for Abolition," *Crime and Delinquency* 25 (July, 1979): 281–98; and Frank Hellum, "Juvenile Justice: The Second Revolution," *Crime and Delinquency* 25 (July, 1979): 299–317.

10. Rector and Gilman, "How Did We Get Here," p. 88.

11. Empey, *American Delinquency*, pp. 530–32.

12. Ibid., p. 531.

13. Florida, Pennsylvania, Iowa, and Washington now make status offenders subject to juvenile court jurisdiction only as dependent or neglected children. See Rubin, "Retain the Juvenile Court," p. 283. Also see the National Task Force to Develop Standards and Goals for Juvenile Justice and Delinquency Prevention, *Jurisdiction—Status Offenses* (Washington, D. C., 1977): and Empey, *American Delinquency*, p. 538.

14. See Edwin M. Schur, *Radical Nonintervention: Rethinking the Delinquency Problem* (Englewood Cliffs, N.J., 1973).

15. Empey, *American Delinquency*, p. 539.

16. See Robert M. Carter and Malcolm W. Klein, *Back on the Street: The Diversion of Juvenile Offenders* (Englewood Cliffs, N.J., 1976); and Andrew Rutherford and Robert McDermott, *Juvenile Diversion, Phase I Summary Report* (Washington, D. C., 1976). Also see Empey, *American Delinquency*, pp. 539–40.

17. See Malcolm W. Klein et al., "The Explosion in Police Diversion Programs," in Malcolm W. Klein, ed., *The Juvenile Justice System* (Beverly Hills, Calif., 1976), p. 113. Also see Malcolm W. Klein and Kathie S. Teilmann, *Pivotal Ingredients of Police Juvenile Diversion Programs*, (Washington, D. C., 1976), p. 108. For a

persuasive response to the diversion critics, see Diane L. Gottheil, "Pretrial Diversion: A Response to the Critics," *Crime and Delinquency* 25 (January, 1979): 65–75.

18. Gottheil, "Pretrial Diversion," and Empey, *American Delinquency*, p. 541. Donald R. Cressey and Robert A. McDermott, *Diversion for the Juvenile Justice System* (Ann Arbor, Mich., 1973), pp. 59–60.

19. Ibid.

20. Empey, *American Delinquency*, p. 533.

21. See H. Ted Rubin, *The Courts: Fulcrum of the Justice System* (Pacific Palisades, Calif., 1976), p. 83. Also see Michael Sosin and Rosemary Sarri, "Due Process—Reality or Myth?" in Rosemary Sarri and Yaheskel Hasenfeld, eds., *Brought to Justice? Juveniles, the Courts, and the Law* (Ann Arbor, Mich., 1976); and Jerry Franklin and Dan C. Gibbons, "New Directions for Juvenile Courts—Probation Officers' Views," *Crime and Delinquency* 19 (October, 1973): 508–18.

22. See Robert Lefcourt, ed., *Law Against the People* (New York, 1971).

23. Empey, *American Delinquency*, p. 544.

24. President's Commission on Law Enforcement and Administration of Justice, *Juvenile Delinquency and Youth Crime* (Washington, D.C., 1967), p. 28.

25. Empey, *American Delinquency*, p. 534.

26. National Institute for Juvenile Justice and Delinquency Prevention, *National Evaluation Design for the Deinstitutionalization of Status Offender Programs* (Washington, D. C., 1977). Also see Empey, *American Delinquency*, p. 548.

27. See *The Los Angeles Times* (February 12–13, 1976).

28. See LaMar T. Empey and Maynard L. Erickson, *The Provo Experiment: Evaluating Community Control of Delinquency* (Lexington, Ky., 1972); LaMar T. Empey and Steven Lubeck, *The Silverlake Experiment: Testing Delinquency Theory and Community Intervention* (Chicago, 1971); and Lloyd E. Ohlin et al., *Juvenile Correctional Reform in Massachusetts* (Washington, D. C., 1977).

29. See Ohlin, *Juvenile Correctional Reform in Massachusetts*, pp. 35–79; and Empey, *American Delinquency*, p. 553.

30. See Empey and Erickson, *The Provo Experiment*, Chapters 9 and 11. Also see Empey, *American Delinquency*, p. 554; Ohlin, *Juvenile Correctional Reform in Massachusetts*, p. 30; Vinter et al., *Juvenile Corrections in the U.S.*, p. 45; and Empey and Lubeck, *The Silverlake Experiment*, p. 309.

31. See Andrew Scull, *Community Treatment and the Deviant—A Radical View* (Englewood Cliffs, N. J., 1977), pp. 152–53. Also see Empey and Erickson, *The Provo Experiment*, p. 68; and Empey and Lubeck, *The Silverlake Experiment*, pp. 186–210.

32. Empey, *American Delinquency*, p. 556.

33. Ibid., p. 557.

34. Ibid., p. 558.

35. Hellum, "Juvenile Justice: The Second Revolution," p. 300.

36. Empey, *American Delinquency*, pp. 583–84.

37. Walter B. Miller, "Ideology and Criminal Justice Policy: Some Current Issues," in Sheldon L. Messinger et al., eds., *The Aldine Crime and Justice Annual* (Chicago, 1973), pp. 454–55.

38. Ibid.

39. See Edwin H. Sutherland and Donald R. Cressey, *Criminology*, 8th ed. (Philadelphia, 1970). Also see the *California Welfare and Institutions Code*, Assembly Bill No. 3121, Chapter 1071 (1976), pp. 1–24; Francis B. McCarthy, "Should Juvenile Delinquency Be Abolished?" *Crime and Delinquency* 23 (April, 1977): 196–203; Norval Norris, "The Future of Imprisonment: Toward a Punitive Philosophy," *Michigan Law Review* 72 (1974): 1161–80; James Q. Wilson, *Thinking about Crime* (New York, 1975); and Ernst van den Haag, *Punishing Criminals* (New York, 1975).

40. See Robert Martinson, "What Works?—Questions and Answers about Prison Reform" *Public Interest* (Spring, 1974): 22–54; Robert Martinson, "California Research at the Crossroads," *Crime and Delinquency* 22 (April, 1976): 180–91; Judith Wilks and Robert Martinson, "Is the Treatment of Criminal Offenders Really Necessary?" *Federal Probation* 40 (March, 1976): 3–8; and Edwin M. Schur, *Radical Nonintervention* (Englewood Cliffs, N. J., 1973). Martinson asserts that the juvenile courts have spent far too much time, effort, and money on rehabilitation programs that have not significantly affected recidivism. The reduction of crime rates therefore, ought to be the major focus of the juvenile justice system. In fact, Martinson argues, treatment programs should be abandoned entirely and replaced by a punitive system that would serve as a crucial deterrent to law violation.

Schur agrees with Martinson and thoroughly castigates clinical and group method rehabilitative treatment programs. He does not rely, however, on generalized assumptions concerning the benefits of punitive deterrence as does Martinson. Instead, Schur promotes a "return to the rule of law" in which the juvenile justice system would return to the more fundamental and traditional task of handling serious violators. Formality and due process would be observed, as would the other established legal procedures of adult criminal courts. Status offenses would be decriminalized, the discretionary powers of the juvenile court would be reduced significantly, and lesser offenders would be diverted. Nevertheless, those offenders who are adjudicated would not be treated with a velvet glove, and quick and certain punishments would be administered.

The Attorney General's Office of the State of Illinois conducted a study in 1979 which also demonstrated that delinquency and recidivism are reduced only when the juvenile court dispenses swift and certain punishment. For information regarding this study, write to the Attorney General's Office, State of Illinois, Springfield, Illinois.

41. See J. P. Gibbs, "Crime, Punishment, and Deterrence," *Southwestern Social Science Quarterly* 48 (1968): 515–30; C. R. Tittle, "Crime Rates and Legal Sanctions," *Social Problems* 18 (1970): 200–17; C. H. Logan, "General Deterrent Effects of Imprisonment," *Social Forces* 51 (1972): 64–73; and W. C. Bailey and R. W. Smith, "Punishment: Its Severity and Certainty," *Journal of Criminal Law, Criminology and Political Science* 63 (1972): 530–39. Also see Graeme Newman, *The Punishment Response* (New York, 1978), p. 287.

42. Empey, *American Delinquency*, p. 506. Also see Ernst van den Haag, *Punishing Criminals* (New York, 1975).

43. Empey, *American Delinquency*, p. 586.

44. Charles H. Logan, "Arrest Rates and Deterrence," *Social Science Quarterly* (December, 1973): pp. 376–89.

45. Hellum, "Juvenile Justice: The Second Revolution," p. 303. Also see Charles R.

Tittle and Charles H. Logan, "Sanctions and Deviance: Evidence and Remaining Questions," *Law and Society Review* (Spring, 1973): 371–92; and Franklin M. Zimring and Gordon J. Hawkins, *Deterrence* (Chicago, 1973).

46. Henry N. Pontell, "Deterrence: Theory Versus Practice," *Criminology* 16 (May, 1978): pp. 3–21.

47. Ibid., p. 7.

48. Ibid., pp. 8, 19.

49. See Maynard L. Erickson, Jack P. Gibbs, and Garry F. Jensen, "The Deterrence Doctrine and the Perceived Certainty of Legal Punishments," *American Sociological Review* (April, 1977): 305–17; and Maynard L. Erickson and Jack P. Gibbs, "Objective and Perceptual Properties of Legal Punishment and the Deterrence Doctrine," *Social Problems* (February, 1978): 253–64.

50. Logan, "Arrest Rates and Deterrence," p. 389. Also see Jack P. Gibbs, "Another Rush to Judgment on the Deterrence Question," *Criminology* 16 (May, 1978): 22–30; Charles R. Tittle, "Comment on 'Deterrence Theory Versus Practice'," *Criminology* 16 (May, 1978): 31–34; and Richard L. Henshel, "Considerations on the Deterrence and System Capacity Models," *Criminology* 16 (May, 1978): 35–46.

12
CHILDREN, CRIME, AND JUSTICE: THE FUTURE

The American juvenile justice system was originally designed at the turn of the century to prevent crime and to rehabilitate juvenile lawbreakers. It was also created to free all children, criminal and otherwise, from the stigmatization and obvious inequities of adult courts, jails, and sanctions. The creation of the juvenile court and the invention of delinquency, moreover, reflected the newly accepted assumption that children were qualitatively different from adults and had to be pampered and protected from the hazards of growing up in a newly industrialized and urbanized society. Unfortunately, the juvenile court system failed to achieve any of its goals. It has gone through a revolution and is now in danger of being abolished. Indeed, the future of the juvenile court is very much in question. As a consequence, we will attempt in this final chapter to analyze the problems involved, make a few recommendations, and try to bring some clarity to this confusing issue.

THE ABOLITION MOVEMENT

The juvenile court system has not controlled delinquency, nor have its goals of treatment, rehabilitation, and reintegration been achieved. Moreover, it may ultimately damage the lives of the children it processes. Because of these and other failures and problems, a growing movement has been generated to abolish the juvenile court. Indeed, many liberal and conservative critics, including social scientists, lawyers, judges, and caseworkers, advocate the court's demise.

The traditionalists were the first to suggest the abolition of the juvenile court. They were stimulated into action by the Surpreme Court's *Gault* decision of 1967, which gave juveniles the right to counsel, to confront the accuser, and to cross-examine witnesses.[1] The traditionalists were also motivated by the *Winship* decision of 1970, which mandated that when children are tried for serious criminal offenses, proof beyond a reasonable doubt is necessary for conviction.[2] Five years later the Supreme Court issued the *Breed* v. *Jones* decision, which prohibited the adjudication of children in both juvenile and criminal courts for the same offense.[3] Conservative critics responded to this decision as they had to the others, and as they had to the implementation of the liberal reforms of decriminalization, due process, diversion, and deinstitutionalization—with outrage and with new demands for the abolition of the juvenile court.[4]

These traditionalists were joined by many members of America's law enforcement community. Together they contended that if children had the same rights as adults, they should be treated as adults. The Supreme Court decisions, however, had not given juveniles the same rights as adults. In fact, the Court had rejected the right of juveniles to jury trials.[5] And, to date, children still do not have the right to bail or to public hearings.[6]

Nevertheless, the conservative call for abolition continued unabated, and during the 1970s a growing group of liberal critics joined the cause. The liberals, of course, believed that the Supreme Court decisions had not gone far enough and that the rights of children continued to be denied. Thus, they argued for the abolition of the juvenile court so that children would be guaranteed all the rights of adults. If that meant trials and dispositions in adult courts, so be it. At least the rights of children would be protected.

The conservatives, on the other hand, argued that they could not perceive any significant differences between a juvenile delinquency proceeding and an adult criminal prosecution. They asserted, in fact, that there are no differences substantial enough to warrant the separate existence of a juvenile court. Thus, why have one?[7]

The call for abolition, then, consists of both conservative and liberal assumptions. These assumptions, as listed by H. Ted Rubin, are as follows:

1. Juvenile court judges and other agents repeatedly fail to apply the statutory and constitutional protections that have been mandated.

2. Criminal courts would provide wider protection of juvenile rights than do juvenile courts.

3. The proposed rationale for criminal sanctions, which is a shift from treatment to proportionality and punishment, parallels the criminal court model more closely than it does the traditional juvenile court approach.

4. A juvenile court model based on proportionality and punishment is dysfunctional with other components of the juvenile court work load, such as the legal processing and court protective and service orders necessary for neglected and abused children.

5. The criminal justice process now accommodates the juvenile system practices of intake and diversion as well as more diversified sentencing alternatives.

6. A juvenile's criminal court defense attorney would be free to function in an adversarial role.[8]

The juvenile court abolitionists have gathered considerable support from several distinguished law professors who argue persuasively from these assumptions. Sanford J. Fox, for example, has written that serious and chronic offenders must be processed in the more legalistic criminal courts, because the juvenile court system has failed to deal adequately with such youths. Judicial child-raising with its emphasis on treatment and rehabilitation, Fox argues, is conceptually flawed, unworkable, and a threat to society. The juvenile court system is simply too cumbersome, unfocused, and antiquated to proffer the necessary remedies for hard-core delinquents.[9]

As for status offenders and lesser delinquent youths, Fox proposes that they be the concern of community agencies and informal arbitration services that can provide assistance without stigmatization or coercion. He believes that the valid humanitarian ideals that originally gave rise to the juvenile court are now more predominant in the community, and that the help bestowed upon children therein would be free of legal threats and thus less ambiguous. In short, Fox would like to see all juveniles subject to an adult justice system that utilizes a rational classification of crime and sentencing based on graded severity. Under this system, status offenses would not exist. But recidivists and serious offenders would be tried like adults in adult courts, and the type and duration of their punishments would be related to the severity of their offenses and past records, not to their age.[10]

Frances McCarthy, another law professor, agrees with Fox that the rights of juveniles are better protected in adult rather than juvenile courts. Rehabilitation considerations, McCarthy also insists, ought to be secondary to the rule of law. Furthermore, since most juvenile offenses are misdemeanors, the lower courts would handle most juvenile offenders. Indeed, in many rural areas, McCarthy points out, misdemeanor court judges already handle the cases of juveniles, and there have been few complaints.[11]

McCarthy also maintains that, because adult diversion has recently been expanded, juvenile court intake procedures are now no longer unique. In fact, the latest American Bar Association criminal justice standards have urged prosecutors to consider noncriminal dispositions before pressing criminal charges. Thus, according to McCarthy, the same individualized treatment so cherished as an ideal of the juvenile justice system is now a component of the adult system. Given this growing similarity of dispositional procedures, as well as the recognized need to sanction juvenile offenders with reference to adult penalties, McCarthy reasons that it would make sense to remove the superfluous juvenile system and incorporate whatever sanction distinctions might be necessary into adult criminal statutes. New criminal statutes, McCarthy maintains, would also provide a means of handling the problems of confidentiality and of protecting convicted juveniles from adult offenders.[12]

Stephen Wizner and Mary F. Keller, supervising attorneys in the Yale Law School Clinical Programs, are also in favor of ending juvenile court jurisdiction over criminal acts. They are cognizant of current reform proposals, but they are convinced that the results of these reforms would be "only briefer sanctions and such special defenses as immaturity or lack of criminal intent as the remaining distinctions between the systems."[13]

Wizner and Keller also contend, as McCarthy does, that the criminal courts have developed their own diversion programs, that criminal prosecutors often dismiss lesser cases, that criminal courts do consider leniency, and that many states now provide a special youthful-offender category. Moreover, "safeguards are taken for granted" in adult court processing, and defense attorneys are not pressured by paternalistic judges or antiquated traditions concerning the benevolence of the court. An attorney's primary concern in an adult court is defending the rights of the child. Consequently, Wizner and Keller conclude that the delinquency jurisdiction must be removed from the juvenile court.[14]

Martin Guggenheim, director of the Juvenile Rights Clinic, New York University School of Law, supports the contentions and proposals of Fox, McCarthy, Wizner, and Keller. He believes that the juvenile court is such a maze of contradictions and convolutions that it is incapable of reforming itself. Indeed, as it is currently operated, the juvenile court system does not adhere to the rule of law, nor does it protect the children it processes. The rights of children, Guggenheim claims, are notoriously ignored, abused, or contravened. Attorneys, more often than not, serve the interests of judges and caseworkers rather than the children. Guggenheim argues, moreover, that the system, because of its specialized structure, is oblivious to the harm it causes juveniles in the name of beneficence.[15]

Guggenheim also believes that because adult courts openly acknowledge punishment as a purpose, sentences would be harsher for serious offenders, but children in general would be much better off. Status offenders would no longer be subject to judicial interference, and lesser delinquents would be identified as such, separated from older and more serious offenders, and subject only to appropriate losses of liberty.[16]

RECENT REFORMS

The criticisms, comments, and recommendations of highly respected and authoritative legal experts and law professors are not to be ignored. But should the juvenile court be abolished completely? Or can it be reformed to accommodate the contemporary needs, problems, and concerns of American children? In order to answer these questions it is necessary to examine some reforms legislated in recent years, as well as those projected for the near future. Juvenile justice practices and strategies for dealing with juvenile law violators are undergoing continuous reform and change, and it is possible that the charges of many of the court's severest critics will be answered by these reforms and changes.

One of the most significant changes that the juvenile court system has undergone in recent years is in the area of its status-offender policies and strategies. By creating separate categories for status offenders, by using names such as 601s, PINS, CHINS, and JINS, juvenile courts across the country have drawn attention to the fact that "it is delinquent youths, not status offenders, who have violated the criminal law."[17]

Obviously, changing the names of status offenders is not enough. Several states, however, prohibit or restrict the detention and incarceration of such youths. The United States Juvenile Justice and Delinquency Prevention Act of 1974 has also aided in deinstitutionalizing status offenders. Moreover, Florida, Pennsylvania, Iowa, and Washington have passed state laws forbidding jurisdiction over status offenders unless they can also be classified as dependent or neglected children. And all across the country community resources have been assuming an ever growing responsibility for providing assistance, direction, and structure for children in need of supervision.[18]

Juvenile codes concerning serious offenders have also changed considerably during the past decade. Alarming delinquency rates and a growing fear of juvenile violence have precipitated new punitive state laws concerning serious and repeat juvenile offenders. This new emphasis on protecting the public's interest has not replaced the traditional preoccupation with the best interests of the child, but it has achieved a better balance. Indeed, because of this new punitive emphasis, legal protections for youths have been strengthened. At the same time, serious offenders are much more likely to be punished.

This balance between the interests of society and the interests of the child can be seen in other legislative changes as well. For example, previous juvenile statutes generally incorporated the following principles:

1. The child should remain in the care of his or her family, if possible.
2. The child should be removed only when necessary for his or her welfare or that of others.
3. If removed, the child should receive the care, guidance, and discipline necessary for constructive citizenship.[19]

Now, however, several states have added qualifications to these principles. Virginia's Domestic Relations enactment of 1977 is a case in point. This act specifies that in addition to securing the best interests of children, the state is obliged "to protect the community against those acts of its citizens which are harmful to others and to reduce the incidence of delinquent behavior."[20]

Another significant legislative change in which a certain balance has been struck has occurred in the transferrence of jurisdiction from the juvenile to the criminal court. The certification of juveniles has been increasing rapidly for the past decade, and many states have lowered the minimum transfer age to fourteen. They have also expanded the range of crimes for which the waiver of juvenile rights is appropriate. Moreover, some states have made the commission of certain crimes by juveniles cause for mandatory transfer hearings.[21] Other states, on the other hand, had been authorizing certification for any youngster over the age of fourteen or had not been specifying appropriate offenses. All of these states, however, revised their juvenile codes in the late 1970s to define the type of offenses necessary for certification. Thus, the requirements for transfer have become much more balanced and standardized all over the country.[22]

A balance between the rights of children and the interests of society has also been struck in the controversial area of dispositional strictures. New York and Colorado, for example, have instituted minimum institutional stays for designated offenses and offenders in order to put an end to two dispositional abuses of the juvenile court system. Some children were being incarcerated—and in many states still are—for longer periods of time than adults can be sentenced for identical offenses. Other youths were receiving probation or insignificant terms in training schools for murder, rape, and other assorted mayhem. Now, however, in New York and Colorado juveniles who are convicted of a violent offense, or who are second-felony offenders, must stay in maximum-security institutions for at least a year. Their sentences, however, may never exceed adult maximums.[23]

Proportionality is another dispositional idea that has been gaining ground since its widely publicized implementation in Washington. Basically it is a sentencing system that assigns age and offense points to a youth and then multiplies that total by points received for criminal history. The resulting point total determines institutional stay and character. Less serious, or first-time offenders, are often ineligible for institutional confinement under this system, but they are sentenced to community service and supervision or are fined, nevertheless. Thus, youths who are serious and consistent troublemakers are punished accordingly, whereas those who are not chronic offenders are saved the often stigmatizing and harmful effects of institutionalization. Thus, once again a certain balance is achieved.[24]

Several states have recently legitimized financial reimbursement and restitution of service hours for convicted juvenile offenders. Police, intake officers of the juvenile court, and some judges have been practicing unofficial restitution for decades. But because of the increasing concern for the rights of victims and the pervasive recognition that treatment and rehabilitation techniques have not been effective, Kentucky, Washington, Maine, and other states have now mandated various forms of restitution. Several other states have also increased the maximum fines that judges may levy on juveniles. On the surface these changes appear to be heavily weighted in favor of society's rights. Yet even the most liberal juvenile court critics recognize that restitution and fines are far superior to incarceration or other forms of institutionalization. Indeed, it is difficult to argue that making young offenders pay back their victims or society is inequitous.[25]

Of all the reforms recently legislated for the "new" juvenile court system, the expanded role of the juvenile court prosecutor is perhaps the most fitting example of the balance we have been discussing. The *Gault* decision, as we know, ushered in the era of juvenile defense counselors to defend the rights of children. Today, the trend is to balance the presence of defense attorneys with prosecutors who represent the interests of society. To be sure, many states continue to require the presence of prosecutors only after judicial requests are made. Other states are still debating the flow pattern of petitions; that is, should referral documents be screened by intake officers first or should they go directly to the prosecutor? Nevertheless, the power, influence, and role of the prosecutor have clearly been enhanced. Accordingly, those who have clamored for more public protection are appeased, and those who have lamented the repeated disregard for tests of legal sufficiency at the intake stage are also mollified.[26]

PROPOSED REFORMS

In addition to the reforms we have just discussed, other changes in the areas of process and prevention have been proposed. If implemented, these reforms will continue to modify and perhaps strengthen the American juvenile justice system.[27] In 1971, for example, the Institute of Judicial Administration–American Bar Association (IJA-ABA) Juvenile Justice Standards Project published twenty-three volumes of standards and commentary relating to juvenile justice. Ten general principles served as guides for their work:

1. Proportionality in sanctions
2. Determinate sentences
3. The least restrictive alternative for intervention
4. The repeal of court jurisdiction over status offenses
5. Visibility and accountability of decision-making
6. The right to counsel at all processing stages
7. The right of juveniles to decide on actions affecting their freedom

except where they are found incapable of making reasoned decisions

8. A redefinition of the parental role with particular regard to conflicts of interest between parent and child

9. Substantial restrictions on intervention before adjudication and disposition

10. Strict criteria governing waiver of juvenile court jurisdiction and transfer of juveniles to criminal court[28]

Many of these IJA-ABA principles, such as items 1, 2, and 10, have already been legislated into the juvenile court systems of several states. Many of the others are pending, and all are likely to be adopted in one form or another in the near future. Even before these changes took place, however, the IJA-ABA reaffirmed the juvenile court's responsibility and importance and urged continuing court jurisdiction over all delinquent offenses committed by youths between the ages of ten and eighteen.[29]

Nevertheless, the IJA-ABA also recommended the restructuring of the juvenile court into a family court division of the general trial court. Jurisdiction over delinquency, neglect, domestic relations, and certain other family-related matters would be combined to form a single judicial center where all family problems could be attended to without the stigmatization commonly associated with juvenile courts.[30]

The IJA-ABA also recommended the following specific reforms for the juvenile court:

1. Termination of all court-administered pretrial detention, intake, and probation services

2. Creation of an executive agency to handle these functions so that the juvenile judge and the court may be free for their primary judicial activities

3. Elimination of pretrial detention for children who have committed only minor offenses

4. Confining detention to violent felony offenders

5. Determining informal versus formal handling of all cases by the prosecutor

6. Providing youths with the unwaivable right to legal counsel at every step of the judicial process

7. Limiting information given to a judge at dispositional hearings to the legal facts: age, circumstances related to the offense, and any prior record of adjudicated delinquency and disposition

8. Orientation toward equal rather than individualized justice

9. Correlating and classifying juvenile sentences with adult sentences

10. Affording juveniles the right to refuse psychological counseling during their incapacitation[31]

In 1978 the report of the Twentieth Century Fund Task Force on Sentencing Policy Toward Young Offenders was published. This report focused primarily on sentencing policies for serious offenders and recidivists, but it also recommended reforms in the areas of processing, correctional programs, and utilization of community resources. As had the IJA-ABA publications, the Task Force report urged the continuation of the juvenile court and listed the principles upon which its youth crime policy was founded:

1. Culpability

2. Diminished responsibility resulting from immaturity

3. Providing room for reform

4. Proportionality

5. Restricting transfer and waiver to defendants past their early teens who are accused of serious criminal violence

6. Confining transfer to those who, if found guilty, would merit punishment substantially more severe than that available to the juvenile court

7. Limiting confinement authorized by the juvenile court to two and one-half years

8. Waiving cases that demand more than two and one-half years' confinement to criminal court where procedural guarantees are more readily available

9. No formal juvenile court handling of first property offenses except burglary of a dwelling

10. Formal juvenile court handling for a second serious property crime

11. Prohibition of custodial confinement beyond one year for any property offense

12. Use of restitution, including service and fines, as a noncustodial alternative[32]

ABOLITION OR PRESERVATION?

The Twentieth Century Fund Task Force did discuss the possibility of abolishing the juvenile court, but decided that the court was the best possible alternative, provided that it continue to reform itself. The IJA-ABA Commission, on the other hand, never seriously considered eliminating the court. Nevertheless, many abolitionists, including those we have already discussed, argue that the full implementation of the reforms recommended by these organizations would virtually eliminate the procedural and sentencing distinctions between juvenile and criminal courts. Thus, the juvenile court would become superfluous, if it is not already.[33]

This brings us back to the question originally posed: "Should the juvenile court be abolished?" If, in fact, most of the recommended standards and reforms are slowly being incorporated into the daily operations of juvenile courts across the country, is specialized juvenile processing warranted? Regardless of the answer to this question, another question must be answered as well: "Is the disappearance of the juvenile court likely to occur?" For, even if the answer to question number one is yes, it does not mean much unless the answer to question number two is also yes.

Let us therefore approach the second question first. Critics, commentators, reformers, and legal theorists have been exposing faults, inconsistencies, and pretensions with the juvenile justice process for two decades. Yet the juvenile court system remains intact. Moreover, although substantial changes have been implemented recently, the assessments of scholars have not had as much influence on reforming the court as have public opinion and political policy. Thus, the court remains both a helper and a punisher, and some abolitionists see this as a glaring conflict of interest. Reformers who wish only to reform and not to abolish the court, however, view this apparent inconsistency as a judicially achieved balance of interests. Indeed, they argue that the more the court accommodates itself to procedural and dispositional reforms, the more it will be balanced between the rights of children and the interests of society. After all, they point out, the rights of children are in the interest of society.[34]

These same reformers do acknowledge that the temptation remains for judges to act as superparents, counselors, and psychologists. But, they argue that since *Gault,* judges are more often lawyers who are aware of and follow strict legal procedures. Furthermore, the judges themselves are reluctant to throw in the towel. They are effective at drumming up popular support for their cause, and as H. Ted Rubin observes, "No one should underestimate their energies or political skills in preserving their courts."[35] Thus, the judges are fully prepared to fight the abolitionists and strongly support what they view as "the most rational public policy for structuring juvenile proceedings."[36]

The likelihood of the juvenile court system disappearing in this country, therefore, appears rather remote. But, for the sake of answering the original question, let us assume for the moment that, in fact, the court was abolished. Would the rights of children and the interests of society be protected any better? The answer to this, and therefore to the question concerning the abolition of the court, is no.

With or without a juvenile court most juvenile offenders would still have to face some form of pretrial detention, residential or institutional placement, specialized judges, and probation officers. Moreover, specialized statutory laws and rules of procedure would still be necessary for juvenile offenders, even if they were all tried in adult courts. Reduced sentences would not suffice.

Nor would abolishing the juvenile court solve the immense problems of the current criminal process. For example, criminal courts today are characterized by "overcriminalization, ineffective defense representation, rehabilitation rhetoric, and severe punishments"—the same problems the juvenile court is facing. Furthermore, "processing delays, an insufficient number of judges, excessive public defender caseloads, poor administration by prosecutors, inadequate use of diversion, insufficient sentencing alternatives, ineffectual probation departments, and overreliance on plea and sentence bargaining" also afflict felony courts.[37] It would be foolish to assume that these conditions would be altered for the better if criminal courts had to contend with the additional burden of juvenile offenders.

Abolitionists maintain, nevertheless, that the legal procedures of the felony courts are far superior to those of the juvenile court. But felony courts receive only 10 percent of all adult defendants, while misdemeanor and ordinance violation courts adjudicate the rest. Unfortunately these lower courts, which would also receive the largest number of juvenile cases, are hopelessly inconsistent at best and a "blight on American judicial administration" at worst.[38] People charged with misdemeanors or ordinance violations in many lower courts, for instance, are often denied their right to counsel.[39] Prosecutors are frequently guilty of not screening cases for legal sufficiency. Judicial quality is not up to the standards set in felony courts, or even in juvenile courts. And diversion, which is used in perhaps 5 percent of the lower court case flow, has not caught on as widely as it has elsewhere. Indeed, prosecutors in these courts tend to shy away from noncriminal dispositions of any kind.[40]

The problems of the adult courts, it would appear, approach, if not equal, those of the juvenile court. Unfortunately abolitionists have, for the most part, chosen to overlook such shortcomings. Thus, although the abolitionist criticisms of the juvenile justice system are useful and may lead to further reforms, they are not sufficient to warrant the elimination of the juvenile court. To be sure, a change in the rationale of the juvenile court is necessary and is occurring. But this need not, as H. Ted Rubin points out, "necessitate a change in the structure and organization of the juvenile court, which still has some spirited concern and useful affection for those brought to its door."[41]

REFORM AS AN ALTERNATIVE TO ABOLITION

When the child savers designed the juvenile court system at the turn of the century, they were largely motivated by a desire to preserve, protect, and extend the childhood of America's youth. They were also appalled by the filth, degeneracy, and punitive nature of the adult system and the irreparable damage done to juveniles who had been incarcerated with adult criminals. Today's reformers, although not as idealistic, class conscious, or paternalistic, share the fears of the earlier reformers. Added to these fears, however, is a genuine concern for the rights of children—a concern that often directly contradicts the original goals of the child savers—and for the interests of society. As a consequence, their proposals for change, which we largely support, bring a more rational and realistic response to juvenile offenders and the juvenile justice system.

Obviously the juvenile court has evolved out of its pre-*Gault*, *parens patriae* system of juvenile justice. Equally obvious is the fact that this evolutionary process is continuing unabated. But to hope, as some reformers do, that it evolves into extinction is to hope for change for the sake of change. Not much substantial or measurable good would result. Indeed, in many states such a turn of events would throw the process of relinquishing and adopting children into utter confusion. Changes would be necessary in paternity suit proceedings and in disputes over the guardianship and support of children. Moreover, juvenile traffic offenders would have to be dealt with elsewhere, as would a host of other related matters.[42]

Many non-abolitionist reformers favor the IJA-ABA proposal to restructure the juvenile court into a family court division of the general trial court. It is an attractive idea, but unless considerable analysis and planning were done, metropolitan family courts would have the same troubles and problems as the current juvenile courts. Still, the proposal does offer a reasonable organization of jurisdiction, and as H. Ted Rubin observes, "It could lessen the current fragmentation of issues related to the family by their distribution among different courts and different judges."[43] The establishment of a family court would also answer the charges of those abolitionists who argue that the elimination of status offenses would eliminate the juvenile court's reason for existence. Moreover, a family court would be able to give more time and attention to those neglected and abused children who are of only secondary importance in most juvenile court operations today.[44]

As we saw in Chapter Four, the most recent official delinquency statistics indicate that serious juvenile crime is declining. This decline is more the result of a decreasing number of youths at the most crime-prone ages than of a concerted juvenile court policy. But if the decline continues, those who have been demanding an ever stronger punitive approach will have less fuel for their fires of retribution. Clearly, an approach that balances children's rights against the interests of the community is the best approach. Neither side of this equation should be emphasized to the exclusion of the other. With this in mind, we believe that the following reforms, if implemented, would serve both the interests of children and those of the state:

1. Repeal of the juvenile court's jurisdiction over status offenses

2. Legislation prohibiting waiver of counsel at any stage of the process

3. Final prosecutor control of intake determinations

4. Requirements of accountability for the use of each more restrictive sanction

5. Restriction of judicial and correctional system discretion to comport with proportionality, determinacy, and "equal handling of equals"[45]

Some of the most ardent juvenile court abolitionists appear to have forgotten that providing assistance, comfort, and structure—as well as a degree of punishment—to children who have violated legal norms continues to be a crucial obligation of society. The retention of a juvenile court system does not necessarily mean the retention of the status quo. Major changes have occurred, are occurring, and will continue to occur in the future. As H. Ted Rubin so aptly comments, "Reform, better than re-form, can advance the constitutional fairness, legal regularity, and judicial self-control that are in our enlightened best interest."[46]

In addition to the reforms suggested above, we believe there is room for improvement in two other crucial areas of the juvenile justice system: incarceration and prevention. If the juvenile court system is to have a future unclouded by the charges, criticisms, and attacks of the past—if, in fact, it is to have a future at all—a great deal of attention must be devoted to these areas.

Incarceration

Locking up children in jails, detention centers, reformatories, or training schools has been described by reformers as "destructive of the human spirit" and a retardant of "children's potential for normal growth and adjustment."[47] These reformers believe that we must keep the number of children entering the juvenile justice system to a minimum and severely restrict the use of institutionalization. If this is not done, they argue, the juvenile court will not survive.[48]

How can this be accomplished? How can the numbers be reduced? The most obvious method would be to prohibit the incarceration of children who have not been found guilty of violent offenses. Two sets of reform assumptions would be reflected in a prohibition of this nature. First, the principles of proportionality and the least restrictive sanction would have to be implemented. Second, the old principle of rehabilitation as a goal and responsibility of the juvenile court would have to be discarded and picked up by society in general.

Traditionalist reformers and juvenile court abolitionists tend to ignore the fact that the vast majority of institutionalized or incarcerated children are not violent. To be sure, the old saying, "Out of sight, out of mind," holds true, at least for a time. But, when nonviolent youths are incarcerated, not only are they stigmatized, but they are also inevitably and deeply affected by the experience. They learn to hate society and to blame it, rather than themselves, for their wretched lives. Furthermore, they learn from other jailed youths and from the system itself that violent behavior can bring such rewards as power, prestige, status, and identity. Accordingly, the very act of incarcerating youths breeds violent behavior and when once nonviolent but otherwise "delinquent" juveniles are released from training schools, reformatories, detention centers, or other jails, many of them are more likely to commit violent acts than they were prior to their incarceration.[49]

The obvious solution to this problem is the development and utilization of community-based alternatives. Until commitment to secure facilities is legislatively prohibited, however, this is not likely to happen. Nor will it have any chance of success—legislative mandates aside—without full community acknowledgment and the community's acceptance of its responsibility to expand and develop noninstitutional correctional and rehabilitative programs.

We must, as a society, attempt to rid ourselves of our antiquated, counterproductive, and ultimately debilitating ideas about institutionalization. Such notions are based on the assumption that unwanted matter, difficulties, complexities, and obstacles will disappear if they are removed from our immediate field of vision. We have a tendency to throw the aged, psychotic, and delinquent into institutional toilets, where we hope they will be flushed away and never seen again. But we can no longer afford to approach the problem of delinquency, or any other social problems, by decreasing their visibility. We can no longer afford to remove the underlying problems of youthful lawbreakers farther and farther from our daily experience and consciousness. If we continue to do so, the knowledge, skill, resources, and motivation necessary to deal with such problems will atrophy.[50]

It has been estimated that, should the juvenile justice system incarcerate only violent offenders, the juvenile institutional population would be reduced by almost 90 percent.[51] The enormous cost of housing, feeding, clothing, teaching, counseling, and supervising these youths would also be reduced. Moreover, the cost and technical problems involved in constantly constructing new facilities would be removed as well. Much of this saved public money might then be channeled into community-based programs.

How do we decide which juveniles to incarcerate and which to deal with in noninstitutional ways? How can the juvenile court determine which youths must be removed from society in order to protect the community? Given everything that has been discussed in this book, and given our own peculiar prejudices, we recommend an incarceration standard similar to the one developed by Milton G. Rector and David Gillman. Our standard would read as follows:

> The juvenile to be incarcerated has been adjudicated for an act that would be a felony if he or she were an adult and that inflicted serious bodily harm or seriously endangered the life or physical safety of another, or the juvenile has a prior record of one or more adjudications involving similar acts of violence.

If this standard were put into effect, equal rather than individualized justice would be the result. The court would focus solely on the defendant's acts of physical violence. A child's individual idiosyncrasies, socioeconomic status, and family background would be of secondary interest. Past convictions, however, would be of primary importance. The judge would therefore be forced to make dispositional decisions based on the nature and severity of the offense, and on past offenses, if any. If the juvenile should desire the admission of clinical or social materials to demonstrate mitigating or aggravating circumstances, however, such information would be allowed. Nevertheless, the emphasis of the adjudication hearing would remain on known or acknowledged patterns of violence in the past and present, not on psychiatric predictions of future behavior, which are notoriously inaccurate.[53]

If a youth's offense did not involve serious physical violence, or if no prior pattern of violence existed, then that juvenile would not be incarcerated, If, however, a child's first offense were so heinous and shocking that incarceration would obviously be appropriate, then the judge would clearly have that option. Nevertheless, the judge would not have the option to apply severe sanctions to those youths who have not demonstrated a history of, or an affinity for, violent behavior.[54]

To sum up, the juvenile court will continue to harm more children than it helps as long as its power to incarcerate children is not restricted. Violent offenders, of course, must be kept off the streets to protect society, but less serious offenders, who constitute the vast majority of delinquents, are better served through community-resource programs. If the overwhelming number of children in institutions is to be reduced, however, it will take more than the willingness of the juvenile court to reform itself. The power to institutionalize must be regulated by statute, and society in general must remove its collective head from the sand and recognize its responsibilities and obligations. In short, it is up to society to protect, preserve, and control its youth, even the unruly, rebellious, and incorrigible. And it should be up to the juvenile court to see that the rights of those youths are protected. At the same time, the court must incarcerate children who are dangerously violent so that society, other children, and even the violent youths themselves are protected.

Prevention

The balancing effect of the newly legislated and proposed reforms described above has diminished, if not eliminated, the juvenile court's original rehabilitative ideal. It has also greatly reduced the court's attachment to preventive intervention. At the same time, however, it has opened the doors to an objective examination of past prevention programs and their failures. These examinations are very instructive, for they not only demonstrate why prevention efforts failed in the past, but they also provide clues to what might be done by the courts and, even more important, by society and social scientists to improve such efforts in the future.

In general, three types of prevention efforts have been used by the juvenile justice system: punitive, corrective, and mechanical.[55] Punitive prevention, as we have seen, assumes that the threat of swift and certain punishment deters delinquency and crime. Corrective prevention assumes that delinquency has causes that can be identified and that therefore can be controlled and corrected, or eliminated. Mechanical prevention attempts to obstruct the commission of offenses by such devices as sophisticated alarm systems, increased police surveillance, or better neighborhood lighting. Unfortunately, these projects have not successfully prevented delinquent behavior, and the juvenile court has received most of the blame.[56]

The reasons for failure are complex and varied. All of the prevention techniques have been notoriously imprecise and need to be sharpened or improved.[57] Often the gap between theoreticians and practitioners has been too great, and better working relationships need to be established. Furthermore, too few experimental programs have been launched, and those that do exist have been either overly criticized or overly relied upon.[58]

More significantly, however, prevention programs have failed because social scientists and other reformers have consistently lacked the descriptive data necessary to fight delinquency effectively. Not enough studies contain scientifically valid facts about the lives of delinquents. In fact, court and police records rather than direct observation have furnished most of the evidence gathered over the years. As a consequence, social scientists have focused on such factors as neighborhood, family relations, personality, and ethnic origins rather than "what a juvenile delinquent does in his daily round of activity and what he thinks about himself, society, and his activities."[59]

Because of insufficient data, as well as too many inflexible prejudices and assumptions, we do not really know what causes delinquency. As we saw in Chapter Five, the causation theories that do exist are at best imprecise and, at worst, contradictory. Some sort of synthesis is obviously needed, but given the vested interests and personal status of many of the researchers, an interdisciplinary approach is not likely to emerge soon. Unless new approaches are developed, however, our juvenile justice system, if it continues to exist, will continue to be severely handicapped. As R. J. Lundman has noted, "If we do not know what causes delinquency it is extremely difficult to prevent it."[60]

Even if adequate data become available, however, enormous obstacles remain that have little to do with court reforms. Funding, for example, is always a vexing issue and, given the nation's economic difficulties, it probably will remain so. Community sensitivities, prejudices, and fears also inhibit the translation of theory into practice. For example, deinstitutionalization, diversion, and other community-resource programs have never been fully tested. As a result, all intervention techniques have suffered, and so has the reputation of the juvenile court, even though this has clearly been a community failure.[61]

There is also the problem of due process and constitutional safeguards. As we have seen, a number of experiments and reforms designed to prevent delinquency involve intervention *prior* to the commission of an offense. But to intervene before an offense has been committed creates a host of legal difficulties concerning the rights of children. Hence, the legality of intervention needs to be clarified, either through legislation or by the Supreme Court. Until that happens, however, all pre-offense prevention programs will be operating in a legal and constitutional fog, and their impact on delinquency and the operation of the court will be affected accordingly.

To sum up, a number of problems need to be solved and reforms implemented before prevention programs—whether punitive, corrective, or mechanical—will have any chance of success. Adequate data, accurate or more complete theories, community cooperation, and uncompromised intervention strategies would help enormously. Thus, the solutions must include direct field observation of delinquents, construction of integration theories that reflect these field data, and an elimination, or at least a lessening of the community constraints that currently inhibit prevention efforts.[62]

When particular projects fail, moreover, we rarely learn why. All too often researchers are embarrassed because of their failure, and they are reluctant to disclose all of the results. But even failures provide useful information. Thus, if more social scientists made all of their results public, we would learn much more about prevention strategies and delinquency prevention in particular, and the juvenile court in general would be aided considerably.

Researchers would also be furthering the cause of delinquency prevention, and thus aiding the juvenile court, by broadening their attack. That is, in the future they should examine juveniles who are demographically different from the stereotyped under-class youths who have been "measured to death" in the past. In short, more studies on females and middle- and upper-class youths should be undertaken.[63]

No matter what type of prevention programs are developed and implemented, however, the rights of children must be protected. More often than not, the subjects of prevention are youths who have not been found guilty of anything. Indeed, they are usually selected because they possess certain characteristics or exhibit certain behaviors that a few social scientists have deemed to be indicative of future delinquency. Pre-delinquent or delinquency-prone children, however, are entitled to the same rights as other children. Thus future delinquency programs, as R. J. Lundman and F. R. Scarpitti insist, "must be sensitive to and protect the rights of the juvenile subjects involved."[64]

If all of these suggestions for improving delinquency prevention were followed by social scientists and if society in general cooperated more fully, the juvenile court's chances for survival would be greatly enhanced. But is this the primary purpose of prevention? What about the youth of this country? Would they be better off? Unquestionably they would. But the primary goals of prevention ought not to be to preserve and improve the operations of the juvenile court, although we believe those are worthy goals. The primary goals of prevention ought to be "the development of a legitimate identity among young people and a belief in an importance of conforming to social rules."[65]

The elimination of overinstitutionalization and excessive legal processing and the extended use of diversion and community-resource programs are, to be sure, valuable prevention techniques. On the other hand, such methods are used after the fact of delinquency and therefore can be considered negative programs. The more difficult task, and the one the juvenile court must be left out of, is the prevention of delinquency before it occurs.

Many social action programs, including urban renewal, the poverty program, and remedial job training, have been introduced to prevent rising crime rates. To date, none of them has had much success. To give up and to conclude that throwing money at social problems is mindless and wasteful, however, will not make the essential problems of delinquency vanish. Investing money in social, educational, and welfare programs never is very popular, but the alternative—doing nothing—is not popular either. What can be done? Where should our money be going?

FUNDING SOCIAL PROGRAMS

Basically there are four areas that desperately need funds: child care, schooling, school and work programs, and job creation. The remainder of this concluding chapter will attempt to demonstrate how we might make the most out of funding these areas and thus help prevent delinquency before it gestates.

Child Care

Evolving ideas concerning the nature of marriage and the role of women in society, as well as changing economic conditions that make it necessary for mothers to work, have affected the ways in which children are raised. Child abuse, neglect, and abandonment have increased astonishingly during the past two decades, and there is a direct link between this surge and delinquency. Consequently, a pressing need has been created for day care and communal child-rearing arrangements. Such needs must be met for any parents who are unable for whatever reason to provide a conventional, safe, two-parent home. Obviously, not all delinquent children are products of inept parents or non-families, but just as obviously we need to find reasonable substitute families for children whose futures are endangered.[66]

Schooling

As we saw in Chapter Ten, our schools have failed miserably to provide uniform socialization, equal opportunity, and resolutions for class, ethnic, racial, and religious differences. Indeed, our schools often intensify these differences and are notoriously prejudicial. The administration and policies of our schools, especially in urban centers, are largely in the hands of people whose world views, attitudes, life-styles, and perceptions are certainly very different from, if not opposite to, those of the children and parents being "served." The result of this condition is noncommunication, anxiety, frustration, and ultimately violence and delinquency.

In order to break this vicious circle and to provide children with a greater wish to become productive and integral members of American society our schools must alter their fundamental philosophies and programs considerably. They must become aware of and sensitive to the peculiar characteristics of the neighborhoods in which they are located. After gaining an understanding of the character of the communities they are serving, they then must alter their curricula, organizations, and activities accordingly.

The schools must also foster associations and connections with other legitimate institutions in the community. Teachers and parents must work together more closely to establish standards of achievement, and they must agree on methods to enforce those standards. Few parents want their children to be ignorant or delinquent. Given the proper motivation and stimulation by active and concerned schools, most parents will stretch a little for their children. The biggest obstacle in such cooperative enterprises, however, is lack of communication. Communication must begin with the schools. They must reach out to the parents as well as the children. When children, parents, and schools begin to work together, not only is the educational process improved, but networks of social controls are established that have nothing to do with the police or the juvenile court system. And it is precisely for that reason that such controls are desperately needed.

LaMar Empey has suggested several other innovative educational reforms that might help to prevent delinquency. For example, the creation of teacher–parent councils to analyze the tracking, stratification, and discipline systems of the schools in order to promote involvement and concern, rather than alienation, would be beneficial. Tutorial programs in which the best students would aid those who can barely read and write would also be extremely useful. Schools might establish more drug education programs and encourage students to educate adults as well as the reverse. Moreover, schools could represent their students when policy decisions are made by community groups and agencies. And finally, schools could create and sponsor constructive community programs such as "cleaning the environment, registering voters, participating in crisis-intervention and delinquency prevention programs."[67]

These reforms are not likely to be implemented in the immediate future because of resource, philosophy, and mandate problems. Most people simply do not perceive any connection between delinquency prevention and schools or perceive only a negative connection. Thus, they often lay the blame on a specific school system. If that is the case, many parents either move out of the area or enroll their children in private schools. Most schools do not properly perceive the potential they possess for delinquency prevention either. The schools and the public obviously need to be reeducated to understand that prevention means more than merely controlling deviance. It also means enhancing legitimacy, channeling youthful energies into productive efforts, and creating healthy self-concepts. If schools and parents understood this, the educational reforms discussed above would be justified, a mandate would form, and resources would be found.

School and Work Programs

It is a sad fact that, for the most part, a child's educational experience in this country is totally separated from the world of work. Recently, however, various communities have used the Comprehensive Employment and Training Act of 1973, a federally funded program, to place students in subsidized positions within public and private agencies. By providing youths with such economic incentives, as well as general, remedial, and occupational education, these communities have discouraged school dropout rates considerably. Most important, however, the juveniles involved in the CETA programs are now much more deeply committed to conventional pursuits, have raised their self-concept levels, and have enhanced their socialization process as a result.[68] Other such programs are needed.

Job Creation

As the 1980s begin, unemployment in general is a blight on the economy, but teenage unemployment, especially among members of the under class, is a disgrace. Even in the best of times, however, not enough attention is paid to the shortage of jobs available to adolescents. Clearly, juveniles who work, even if only for a few hours per week, are less likely to commit delinquent acts than are those who do not work. But where are the jobs to come from? Should government be the employer of last resort? Many critics of government interference in our lives argue that government job creation is not only inflationary, but also deleterious to the interests of private enterprise.

Nevertheless, the government and the private sector have in some cases pooled their resources and created a few encouraging projects. For example, the Maverick Corporation of Hartford, Connecticut, has provided both work experience and income for ghetto dwellers between the ages of seventeen and twenty. The experiment has also given the youths involved a greater sense of self-esteem and a feeling of commitment to their community. The program, in fact, established a network of social controls that defined appropriate behavior and bestowed rewards upon those who conformed to that definition. Young workers who did not conform were not rewarded. Thus the emphasis was obviously on rewards rather than punishment, and it worked.[69]

When jobs are unavailable or when adolescents are turned down for work because of their age, lack of experience, or in many cases because of a delinquency record, the social, emotional, and economic costs are enormous. For example, the present cost of incarcerating or institutionalizing one juvenile for one year can be as high as $30,000.[70] More often than not these costs are ignored when the public thinks about the cost of delinquency. This is extremely unfortunate, because the cost of educating and boarding children at the best schools in the country does not approach the cost of incarceration. Furthermore, most youths would jump at the chance to earn what it costs to confine, feed, and guard one delinquent in one year. As LaMar Empey astutely concludes:

> Jobs, in short, might not only be less costly in economic terms but in terms of the destruction wreaked on the unemployed in terms of a loss of self-esteem and self-worth. When these are lacking, young people have little to lose by becoming delinquent. That is why punishment alone is not likely to deter them from criminal behavior.[71]

THE NEED FOR A THIRD REVOLUTION

The prevention of juvenile delinquency is obviously not the concern solely of the juvenile court. All of society must help in this endeavor. Families, schools, businesses, governments, and communities must all pitch in. Perhaps what is needed is a third revolution in American juvenile justice. This revolution would put the responsibility for the care, protection, and education of children back where it belongs—with the people themselves and with private organizations created by the people.

Let the juvenile court deal with serious offenders, and let the people and their communities sort out the other problems of youth. The general public, of course, must first acknowledge and confront these problems. Covering their eyes or removing from their sight all of the unpleasant aspects of troubled juveniles solves nothing. It merely aggravates the problem. Once the public squarely faces the problems and consequences of juvenile delinquency—and this is by far the biggest hurdle—they will arrive at solutions, for the American people have great depths of care, concern, and ingenuity. Until then, the juvenile court must continue to evolve, must continue to balance the rights of children against the interests of society, and must—against all odds—survive.

NOTES
CHAPTER TWELVE

1. *In re Gault,* 387 U.S. 1 (1967). Also see President's Commission on Law Enforcement and Administration of Justice, *Task Force Report: Juvenile Delinquency and Youth Crime* (Washington, D. C., 1967.

2. See *In re Winship,* 397 U. S. 358 (1970).

3. *Breed* v. *Jones,* 421 U.S. 519 (1975).

4. See H. Ted Rubin, "Retain the Juvenile Court? Legislative Developments, Reform Directions, and the Call for Abolition," *Crime and Delinquency* 25 (July, 1979): 281–87.

5. See *McKeiver* v. *Pennsylvania,* 403 U.S. 528 (1971).

6. The right to a public hearing is denied in every state except Kansas, where in August of 1980 a judge in the 8th Judicial District opened all juvenile proceedings and records except psychiatric and social evaluations to the public. "It is my feeling," the judge pointed out, "that the best protection for a juvenile's rights is to have proceedings that are open to the public and to public scrutiny. I think too many abuses can transpire under closed proceedings. And secret proceedings prevent public concern for the problems of the system—because if no one knows what is going on in juvenile court, nobody cares." See the *Kansas City Times* (August 7, 1980).

7. Frances Barry McCarthy, "Should Juvenile Delinquency Be Abolished," *Crime and Delinquency* 23 (April, 1977): 198.

8. Rubin, "Retain the Juvenile Court?" p. 282.

9. Sanford J. Fox, "Abolishing the Juvenile Court," *Harvard Law School Bulletin* 28 (1977): 22–26.

10. Ibid.

11. McCarthy, "Should Delinquency Be Abolished," pp. 196–202.

12. See Frances B. McCarthy, "Delinquency Dispositions under the Juvenile Justice Standards: The Consequences of a Change of Rationale," *New York University Law Review* (November, 1977): 1093–1118.

13. See Rubin, "Retain the Juvenile Court?" p. 294; and Stephen Wizner and Mary F. Keller, "The Penal Model of Juvenile Justice: Is Juvenile Court Delinquency Jurisdiction Obsolete?" *New York University Law Review* (November 1977): 1120–34.

14. Ibid.

15. Martin Guggenheim, *A Call to Abolish the Juvenile Justice System,* Children's Rights Report II (New York, June 1978).

16. Ibid.

17. Rubin, "Retain the Juvenile Court," p. 283.

18. Ibid.

19. Ibid., p. 284.

20. *Virginia Juvenile and Domestic Relations District Court Law,* sec. 16.1-227.4. Also see the *California Welfare and Institutions Code,* sec. 202, which states, "The purpose of this chapter . . . includes the protection of the public from the consequences of criminal activity, and to such purpose probation officers, peace officers,

and juvenile courts shall take into account such protection of the public in their determinations under this chapter." Also see Washington Juvenile Justice Act of 1977, sec. 55.

21. New Jersey and Connecticut are states that have lowered the certification age to fourteen. See New Jersey Assembly Bill No. 1641 (1978). Also see *Connecticut General Statutes Annotated*, sec. 17-60b. For the expansion of the waiver process in other states, see *California Welfare and Institutions Code*, sec. 707d; *Virginia Juvenile and Domestic Relations District Court Law*, sec. 16.1-296 (3) (b); and Washington Juvenile Justice Act of 1977, sec. 65 (1) (a) and (b). Also see Rubin, "Retain the Juvenile Court," p. 286.

22. See *Alabama Juvenile Code*, art. 5, sec. 129 (1977); West Virginia Senate Bill No. 364, sec. 49-5-10 (1978); and Idaho House Bill 188, sec. 16-1806 (1977).

23. See New York Juvenile Justice Reform Act of 1976, Amendments to the Family Court Act, secs. 753-a, 515a, and 516. Also see *Colorado Revised Statutes*, sec. 19-1-103.

24. State of Washington, Department of Health Services, Bureau of Juvenile Rehabilitation, *Sentencing Standards* (1977).

25. Rubin, "Retain the Juvenile Court," p. 287.

26. Ibid., p. 288.

27. Ibid.

28. Ibid., pp. 288–99. Also see Barbara D. Flicker, *Standards for Juvenile Justice: A Summary and Analysis*, Institute of Judicial Administration–American Bar Association Juvenile Justice Standards Project (Cambridge, Mass., 1977), pp. 22–23.

29. See Rubin, "Retain the Juvenile Court," pp. 283–89.

30. Ibid., p. 289.

31. See IJA-ABA Juvenile Justice Standards Project, *Standards Relating to Transfer Between Courts; Standards Relating to Court Organization and Administration; Standards Relating to Corrections Administration; Standards Relating to Interim Status; Standards Relating to Prosecution; Standards Relating to Pretrial Court Proceedings; Standards Relating to Counsel for Private Parties; Standards Relating to Dispositional Procedures; Standards Relating to Dispositions; Standards Relating to Juvenile Delinquency and Sanctions;* and *Standards Relating to Disposition.*

32. Twentieth Century Fund Task Force on Sentencing Policy Toward Young Offenders, *Confronting Youth Crime* (New York, 1978), pp. 6–17. Also see Rubin, "Retain the Juvenile Court," p. 291.

33. See McCarthy, "Should Juvenile Delinquency be Abolished," pp. 196–202; Wizner and Keller, "The Penal Model of Juvenile Justice," pp. 1120–34; Fox, "Abolishing the Juvenile Court," pp. 22–26; and Guggenheim, *A Call to Abolish the Juvenile Justice System.*

34. See Steven L. Schlossman, *Love and the American Delinquent,* (Chicago, 1977).

35. Rubin, "Retain the Juvenile Court," p. 295.

36. Ibid.

37. Ibid., p. 296. Also see Russell R. Wheeler and Howard R. Whitcomb, *Judicial Administration: Text and Readings* (Englewood Cliffs, N. J., 1976), Ch. 6.

38. Rubin, "Retain the Juvenile Court," p. 296.

39. See Sheldon Krantz et al., *Right to Council in Criminal Cases: The Mandate of Argersinger v. Hamlin* (Cambridge, Mass., 1976).

40. See Raymond T. Nimmer and Patricia Ann Krauthaus, "Pretrial Diversion: The Premature Quest for Recognition," *University of Michigan Journal of Law Reform* (Winter, 1976): 206–30; and Franklin E. Zimring, "Measuring the Impact of Pretrial Diversion," *University of Chicago Law Review* (Winter, 1974): 205–95. Also see Rubin, "Retain the Juvenile Court," p. 297.

41. Rubin, "Retain the Juvenile Court."

42. Ibid., p. 298.

43. Ibid.

44. Ibid.

45. Ibid., p. 298.

46. Ibid.

47. See Milton G. Rector and David Gilman, "The Future of the Juvenile Court," *Criminal Justice Review* 1 (Spring, 1976): p. 88.

48. Ibid.

49. Ibid. Also see M. E. Frankel, *Criminal Sentences: Law without Order* (New York, 1973); W. Gaylin, *Partial Justice: A Study of Bias in Sentencing* (New York, 1974); J. Monahan, "The Prediction of Violence," in D. Chappell and J. Monahan, eds., *Violence and Criminal Justice* (Lexington, Mass., 1975); National Criminal Justice Information and Statistics Service, Law Enforcement Assistance Administration, *Children in Custody: A Report on the Juvenile Detention and Correctional Facility Census of 1971* (Washington, D. C., 1974); Pennsylvania Program for Women and Girl Offenders, *Child Abuse at Taxpayers' Expense* (Media, Pa., 1974); Rosemary C. Sarri, "Under Lock and Key," in *Juveniles in Jails and Detention* (Detroit, 1974); and E. Wenk et al., "Can Violence be Predicted," *Criminal Delinquency* 18 (1972): 392–402.

50. See Philip Slater, *The Pursuit of Loneliness: American Culture at the Breaking Point* (Boston, 1970).

51. Rector and Gilman, "The Future of the Juvenile Court," p. 88.

52. Ibid.

53. See Monahan, "The Prediction of Violence," and Wenk et al., "Can Violence be Predicted," pp. 393–402. Also see Rector and Gilman, "The Future of the Juvenile Court," p. 89.

54. Rector and Gilman, "The Future of the Juvenile Court," p. 89.

55. See P. Lejins, "The Field of Prevention," in W. Amos and C. Wellford, eds., *Delinquency Prevention* (Englewood Cliffs, N. J., 1967).

56. Richard J. Lundman et al., "Delinquency Prevention: A Description and Assessment of Projects Reported in the Professional Literature," *Crime and Delinquency* 22, (July, 1976): 300. Also see J. Stratton and R. Terry, *Prevention of Juvenile Delinquency* (New York, 1968), and M. Dixon, *Juvenile Delinquency Prevention Programs* (Washington, D. C., 1974).

57. See S. Lutzin and R. Orem, "Prevention through Recreation," in W. Amos and C. Wellford, eds., *Delinquency Prevention* (Englewood Cliffs, N. J., 1967).

58. See R. MacIver, *The Prevention and Control of Delinquent Behavior* (New York, 1967), p. 52ff.

59. Lundman et al., "Delinquency Prevention," p. 307.

60. Ibid., p. 308.

61. Ibid.

62. Ibid.

63. R. J. Lundman and F. R. Scarpitti, "Delinquency Prevention: Recommendations for Future Projects," *Crime and Delinquency* 24 (April, 1978): 220.

64. Ibid., pp. 212–13, 220.

65. LaMar T. Empey, *American Delinquency: Its Meaning and Construction* (Homewood, Ill., 1978), p. 591.

66. Ibid.

67. Ibid., p. 596.

68. Ibid., pp. 596–97.

69. See *Time* (August 29, 1977).

70. Empey, *American Delinquency*, p. 598.

71. Ibid.

APPENDIX:
FBI UNIFORM CRIME REPORTS FOR THE UNITED STATES, 1978

List of Tables from
FBI Uniform Crime Reports
For the United States, 1978

TABLE 24.
Total Estimated Arrests[1], United States, 1978

TOTAL[2]	10,271,000
Murder and nonnegligent manslaughter	19,840
Forcible rape	29,660
Robbery	148,930
Aggravated assault	271,270
Burglary	511,600
Larceny-theft	1,141,800
Motor vehicle theft	161,400
Violent crime[2]	469,700
Property crime[2]	1,814,700
Crime index total	2,284,400
Other assaults	468,600
Arson	19,000
Forgery and counterfeiting	77,200
Fraud	262,500
Embezzlement	8,100
Stolen property; buying, receiving, possessing	118,200
Vandalism	235,300
Weapons; carrying, possessing, etc.	157,900
Prostitution and commercialized vice	94,200
Sex offenses (except forcible rape and prostitution)	69,100
Drug abuse violations	628,700
Opium or cocaine and their derivatives	83,100
Marijuana	445,800
Synthetic or manufactured narcotics	17,200
Other dangerous nonnarcotic drugs	82,500

Gambling	55,800
Bookmaking	5,400
Numbers and lottery	8,200
All other gambling	42,200
Offenses against family	56,900
Driving under the influence	1,268,700
Liquor laws	376,400
Drunkenness	1,176,600
Disorderly conduct	715,200
Vagrancy	49,300
All other offenses (except traffic)	1,883,800
Suspicion (not included in total)	22,900
Curfew and loitering law violations	83,100
Running away	182,100

[1]Arrest totals based on all reporting agencies and estimates for unreported areas.
[2]Because of rounding, items may not add to totals.

Appendix

TABLE 25.
Arrest, Number and Rate, Population Group, 1978

Offense Charged	Total (11,872 agencies; total population 207,060,000)	Total city arrests (8,705 cities population 144,062,000)	Group I (55 cities 250,000 and over; population 40,619,000)	Group II (115 cities 100,000 to 249,999; population 16,483,000)
TOTAL	9,753,437	7,304,389	2,701,720	839,770
Rate per 100,000 inhabitants ...	4,710.4	5,070.3	6,651.4	5,094.9
Murder and nonnegligent man-				
slaughter	18,755	12,755	7,338	1,617
Rate per 100,000	9.1	8.9	18.1	9.8
Forcible rape	28,257	20,093	10,718	2,439
Rate per 100,000	13.6	13.9	26.4	14.8
Robbery	141,481	108,666	66,042	11,658
Rate per 100,000	68.3	75.4	162.6	70.7
Aggravated assault	257,629	180,349	74,037	23,213
Rate per 100,000	124.4	125.2	182.3	140.8
Burglary	485,782	345,808	124,988	43,554
Rate per 100,000	234.6	240.0	307.7	264.2
Larceny-theft	1,084,088	891,623	285,014	120,418
Rate per 100,000	523.6	618.9	701.7	730.6
Motor vehicle theft	153,270	110,960	48,549	12,050
Rate per 100,000	74.0	77.0	119.5	73.1
Violent crime[2]	446,122	321,863	158,135	38,927
Rate per 100,000	215.5	223.4	389.3	236.2
Property crime[3]	1,723,140	1,348,391	458,551	176,022
Rate per 100,000	832.2	936.0	1,128.9	1,067.9
Crime Index total	2,169,262	1,670,254	616,686	214,949
Rate per 100,000	1,047.6	1,159.4	1,518.2	1,304.1

See footnotes at end of table.

	Cities				Counties	
	Group III (275 cities 50,000 to 99,999; population 18,847,000)	Group IV (647 cities 25,000 to 49,999; population 22,145,000)	Group V (1,559 cities 10,000 to 24,999; population 24,246,000)	Group VI (6,054 cities under 10,000 population 21,723,000)	Suburban counties[1] (819 agencies; population 34,100,000)	Rural counties (2,348 agencies; population 28,898,000)
	848,132	943,437	984,811	986,519	1,518,325	930,723
	4,500.2	4,260.3	4,061.7	4,541.4	4,452.5	3,220.7
	1,254	989	906	651	3,695	2,305
	6.7	4.5	3.7	3.0	10.8	8.0
	2,105	2,011	1,564	1,256	5,476	2,688
	11.2	9.1	6.5	5.8	16.1	9.3
	11,142	9,553	6,535	3,736	28,121	4,694
	59.1	43.1	27.0	17.2	82.5	16.2
	21,508	21,102	20,736	19,753	50,740	26,540
	114.1	95.3	85.5	90.9	148.8	91.8
	48,289	49,240	43,692	36,045	93,766	46,208
	256.2	222.4	180.2	165.9	275.0	159.9
	128,590	140,471	128,101	89,029	140,530	51,935
	682.3	634.3	528.3	409.8	412.1	179.7
	14,001	13,438	12,063	10,859	29,634	12,676
	74.3	60.7	49.8	50.0	86.9	43.9
	36,009	33,655	29,741	25,396	88,032	36,227
	191.1	152.0	122.7	116.9	258.2	125.4
	190,880	203,149	183,856	135,933	263,930	110,819
	1,012.8	917.4	758.3	625.8	774.0	383.5
	226,889	236,804	213,597	161,329	351,962	147,046
	1,203.9	1,069.3	881.0	742.7	1,032.1	508.8

TABLE 25
Arrest, Number and Rate, Population Group, 1978—Continued

Offense charged	Total (11,872 agencies; total population 207,060,000)	Total city arrests (8,705 cities population 144,062,000)	Group I (55 cities 250,000 and over; population 40,619,000)	Group II (115 cities 100,000 to 249,999; population 16,483,000)
Other assaults	445,020	338,187	115,639	46,795
Rate per 100,000	214.9	234.8	284.7	283.9
Arson	18,114	12,450	4,030	1,574
Rate per 100,000	8.7	8.6	9.9	9.5
Forgery and counterfeiting	73,269	50,238	15,009	6,749
Rate per 100,000	35.4	34.9	37.0	40.9
Fraud	249,207	122,794	33,924	24,502
Rate per 100,000	120.4	85.2	83.5	148.7
Embezzlement	7,670	5,022	1,587	708
Rate per 100,000	3.7	3.5	3.9	4.3
Stolen property; buying, receiving, possessing	112,317	81,871	28,792	9,526
Rate per 100,000	54.2	56.8	70.9	57.8
Vandalism	223,391	175,979	42,305	19,190
Rate per 100,000	107.9	122.2	104.2	116.4
Weapons; carrying, possessing, etc.	149,957	118,815	54,221	13,677
Rate per 100,000	72.4	82.5	133.5	83.0
Prostitution and commercialized vice	89,365	83,564	68,091	7,372
Rate per 100,000	43.2	58.0	167.6	44.7
Sex offenses (except forcible rape and prostitution)	65,666	50,483	22,865	6,314
Rate per 100,000	31.7	35.0	56.3	38.3
Drug abuse violations	596,940	440,235	161,392	52,038
Rate per 100,000	288.3	305.6	397.3	315.7
Gambling	53,066	46,839	34,347	4,657
Rate per 100,000	25.6	32.5	84.6	28.3
Offenses against family and children	54,014	22,092	5,986	3,238
Rate per 100,000	26.1	15.3	14.7	19.6
Driving under the influence	1,204,733	752,822	195,082	79,920
Rate per 100,000	581.8	522.6	480.3	484.9
Liquor laws	357,450	286,604	42,107	18,465
Rate per 100,000	172.6	198.9	103.7	112.0
Drunkenness	1,117,349	911,992	292,348	137,126
Rate per 100,000	539.6	633.1	719.7	831.9
Disorderly conduct	679,112	601,536	238,197	55,648
Rate per 100,000	328.0	417.6	586.4	337.6
Vagrancy	46,896	39,794	25,932	2,989
Rate per 100,000	22.6	27.6	63.8	18.1
All other offenses (except traffic)	1,788,757	1,291,831	643,217	111,457
Rate per 100,000	863.9	896.7	1,583.6	676.2
Suspicion (not included in totals)	21,650	18,532	5,702	2,911
Rate per 100,000	10.5	12.9	14.0	17.7
Curfew and loitering law violations	78,986	73,484	28,744	3,697
Rate per 100,000	38.1	51.0	70.8	22.4
Running away	172,896	127,503	31,219	19,179
Rate per 100,000	83.5	88.5	76.9	116.4

[1]Includes only suburban county law enforcement agencies and is not comparable to suburban area totals found in other arrest tables.
[2]Violent crimes are offenses of murder, forcible rape, robbery, and aggravated assault.
[3]Property crimes are offenses of burglary, larceny—theft, and motor vehicle theft.

Population figures rounded to the nearest thousand. All rates were calculated on the population before rour.ding.

Cities				Counties	
Group III (275 cities 50,000 to 99,999; population 18,847,000)	Group IV (647 cities 25,000 to 49,999; population 22,145,000)	Group V (1,559 cities 10,000 to 24,999; population 24,246,000)	Group VI (6,054 cities under 10,000 population 21,723,000)	Suburban counties[1] (819 agencies; population 34,100,000)	Rural counties (2,348 agencies; population 28,898,000)
43,112	48,423	46,560	37,658	67,390	39,443
228.8	218.7	192.0	173.4	197.6	136.5
1,667	1,776	1,845	1,558	3,656	2,008
8.8	8.0	7.6	7.2	10.7	6.9
6,778	7,644	7,373	6,685	13,961	9,070
36.0	34.5	30.4	30.8	40.9	31.4
14,803	16,928	20,212	12,425	71,906	54,507
78.5	76.4	83.4	57.2	210.9	188.6
735	838	631	523	1,582	1,066
3.9	3.8	2.6	2.4	4.6	3.7
11,672	12,141	11,340	8,400	21,953	8,493
61.9	54.8	46.8	38.7	64.4	29.4
23,876	29,870	31,148	29,590	32,242	15,170
126.7	134.9	128.5	136.2	94.6	52.5
13,738	13,395	12,552	11,232	21,587	9,555
72.9	60.5	51.8	51.7	63.3	33.1
4,695	1,838	912	656	5,351	450
24.9	8.3	3.8	3.0	15.7	1.6
6,194	6,445	4,751	3,914	11,703	3,480
32.9	29.1	19.6	18.0	34.3	12.0
57,110	55,327	57,067	57,301	99,127	57,578
303.0	249.8	235.4	263.8	290.7	199.2
2,605	2,715	1,373	1,142	4,706	1,521
13.8	12.3	5.7	5.3	13.8	5.3
2,437	3,282	3,992	3,157	18,461	13,461
12.9	14.8	16.5	14.5	54.1	46.6
89,300	107,996	127,743	152,781	246,499	205,412
473.8	487.7	526.9	703.3	722.9	710.8
30,657	50,702	59,645	85,028	31,520	39,326
162.7	229.0	246.0	391.4	92.4	136.1
110,229	101,233	124,974	146,082	89,832	115,525
584.9	457.1	515.4	672.5	263.4	399.8
59,455	75,825	83,259	89,152	42,071	35,505
315.5	342.4	343.4	410.4	123.4	122.9
3,976	2,221	2,355	2,321	5,839	1,263
21.1	10.0	9.7	10.7	17.1	4.4
108,940	135,215	141,925	151,077	343,761	153,165
578.0	610.6	585.4	695.5	1,008.1	530.0
3,170	1,741	2,999	2,009	1,969	1,149
16.8	7.9	12.4	9.2	5.8	4.0
8,889	10,906	11,049	10,199	3,861	1,641
47.2	49.2	45.6	47.0	11.3	5.7
20,375	21,913	20,508	14,309	29,355	16,038
108.1	99.0	84.6	65.9	86.1	55.5

Appendix

TABLE 26.
Total Arrest Trends, 1969–1978
(3,608 agencies; 1978 estimated population 114,764,000)

Offense charged	Total all ages		
	1969	1978	Percent change
TOTAL	4,854,724	5,342,246	+10.0
Murder and nonnegligent manslaughter	9,230	10,570	+14.5
Forcible rape	11,705	16,018	+36.8
Robbery	59,361	79,774	+34.4
Aggravated assault	90,839	135,667	+49.3
Burglary	207,497	278,610	+34.3
Larceny—theft	427,333	684,111	+60.1
Motor vehicle theft	102,566	86,269	−15.9
Violent crime[1]	171,135	242,029	+41.4
Property crime[2]	737,396	1,048,990	+42.3
Crime index total	908,531	1,291,019	+42.1
Other assaults	220,086	264,056	+20.0
Arson	6,886	10,145	+47.3
Forgery and counterfeiting	29,953	40,728	+36.0
Fraud	53,525	109,317	+104.2
Embezzlement	4,903	4,162	−15.1
Stolen property; buying, receiving, possessing	32,363	62,572	+93.3
Vandalism	87,445	134,202	+53.5
Weapons; carrying, possessing, etc.	73,738	92,177	+25.0
Prostitution and commercialized vice	35,315	60,394	+71.0
Sex offenses (except forcible rape and prostitution)	41,976	38,651	−7.9
Drug abuse violations	174,926	349,405	+99.7
Gambling	54,376	36,221	−33.4
Offenses against family and children	45,753	23,790	−48.0
Driving under the influence	297,268	549,469	+84.8
Liquor Laws	176,820	184,550	+4.4
Drunkenness	1,267,672	678,154	−46.5
Disorderly conduct	488,604	456,972	−6.5
Vagrancy	75,123	20,725	−72.4
All other offenses (except traffic)	555,720	767,964	+38.2
Suspicion (not included in totals)	85,499	11,752	−86.3
Curfew and loitering law violations	86,980	56,854	−34.6
Running away	136,761	110,719	−19.0

[1]Violent crimes are offenses of murder, forcible rape, robbery, and aggravated assault.
[2]Property crimes are offenses of burglary, larceny—theft, and motor vehicle theft.

Number of persons arrested					
Under 18 years of age			18 years of age and over		
1969	1978	Percent change	1969	1978	Percent change
1,227,852	**1,371,241**	**+11.7**	**3,626,872**	**3,971,005**	**+9.5**
930	1,057	+13.7	8,300	9,513	+14.6
2,355	2,691	+14.3	9,350	13,327	+42.5
18,981	25,480	+34.2	40,380	54,294	+34.5
14,393	23,541	+63.6	76,446	112,126	+46.7
112,837	148,498	+31.6	94,660	130,112	+37.5
222,961	293,787	+31.8	204,372	390,324	+91.0
59,858	45,648	−23.7	42,708	40,621	−4.9
36,659	52,769	+43.9	134,476	189,260	+40.7
395,656	487,933	+23.3	341,740	561,057	+64.2
432,315	540,702	+25.1	476,216	750,317	+57.6
38,701	55,198	+42.6	181,385	208,858	+15.1
4.421	5,319	+20.3	2,465	4,826	+95.8
3,523	5,833	+65.6	26,430	34,895	+32.0
2,305	3,799	+64.8	51,220	105,518	+106.0
188	579	+208.0	4,715	3,583	−24.0
11,333	22,580	+99.2	21,030	39,992	+90.2
63,771	78,669	+23.4	23,674	55,533	+134.6
13,037	15,467	+18.6	60,701	76,710	+26.4
853	2,562	+200.4	34,462	57,832	+67.8
9,210	7,202	−21.8	32,766	31,449	−4.0
45,257	87,168	+92.6	129,669	262,237	+102.2
1,353	1,365	+.9	53,023	34,856	−34.3
712	1,841	+158.6	45,041	21,949	−51.3
3,250	12,671	+289.9	294,018	536,798	+82.6
59,311	70,337	+18.6	117,509	114,213	−2.8
37,332	25,065	−32.9	1,230,340	653,089	−46.9
100,835	86,356	−14.4	387,769	370,616	−4.4
7,378	3,306	−55.2	67,745	17,419	−74.3
169,026	177,649	+5.1	386,694	590,315	+52.7
18,379	3,785	−79.4	67,120	7,967	−88.1
86,980	56,854	−34.6	....	....	....
136,761	110,719	−19.0	....	....	....

TABLE 27.
Total Arrest Trends, Sex, 1969–1978
(3,608 agencies; 1978 estimated population 114,764,000)

Offense charged	Total			Males
	1969	1978	Percent change	1969
TOTAL	4,195,086	4,424,628	+5.5	975,556
Murder and nonnegligent manslaughter	7,777	8,988	+15.6	845
Forcible rape	11,705	15,877	+35.6	2,355
Robbery	55,827	74,035	+32.6	17,833
Aggravated assault	79,565	117,849	+48.1	12,718
Burglary	198,496	261,321	+31.7	108,128
Larceny—theft	312,139	459,261	+47.1	169,722
Motor vehicle theft	97,101	78,724	−18.9	56,705
Violent crime[1]	154,874	216,749	+40.0	33,751
Property crime[2]	607,736	799,306	+31.5	334,555
Crime index total	762,610	1,016,055	+33.2	368,306
Other assaults	193,664	226,830	+17.1	31,438
Arson	6,280	8,881	+41.4	4,076
Forgery and counterfeiting	22,895	27,621	+20.6	2,721
Fraud	39,467	64,514	+63.5	1,850
Embezzlement	3,839	3,050	−20.6	131
Stolen property; buying, receiving, possessing	29,562	55,350	+87.2	10,514
Vandalism	81,028	122,801	+51.6	59,703
Weapons; carrying, possessing, etc.	68,936	84,753	+22.9	12,441
Prostitution and commercialized vice	7,816	19,588	+150.6	236
Sex offenses (except forcible rape and prostitution)	36,044	35,154	−2.5	7,020
Drug abuse violations	145,864	298,220	+104.5	35,182
Gambling	50,010	32,928	−34.2	1,309
Offenses against family and children	41,521	20,638	−50.3	531
Driving under the influence	277,972	500,299	+80.0	3,112
Liquor laws	153,995	155,295	+.8	49,182
Drunkenness	1,178,850	626,369	−46.9	32,652
Disorderly conduct	422,959	380,070	−10.1	84,138
Vagrancy	67,818	16,633	−75.5	6,279
All other offenses (except traffic)	468,358	637,951	+36.2	129,137
Suspicion (not included in totals)	72,802	10,070	−86.2	15,805
Curfew and loitering law violations	69,788	45,499	−34.8	69,788
Running away	65,810	46,129	−29.9	65,810

[1]Violent crimes are offenses of murder, forcible rape, robbery, and aggravated assault.
[2]Property crimes are offenses of burglary, larceny—theft, and motor vehicle theft.

			Females				
Under 18			Total			Under 18	
1978	Percent change	1969	1978	Percent change	1969	1978	Percent change
1,074,142	+10.1	659,638	917,618	+39.1	252,296	297,099	+17.8
960	+13.6	1,453	1,582	+8.9	85	97	+14.1
2,643	+12.2	....	141	....	....	48	....
23,773	+33.3	3,534	5,739	+62.4	1,148	1,707	+48.7
20,082	+57.9	11,274	17,818	+58.0	1,675	3,459	+106.5
139,524	+29.0	9,001	17,289	+92.1	4,709	8,974	+90.6
209,342	+23.3	115,194	224,850	+95.2	53,239	84,445	+58.6
41,202	−27.3	5,465	7,545	+38.1	3,153	4,446	+41.0
47,458	+40.6	16,261	25,280	+55.5	2,908	5,311	+82.6
390,068	+16.6	129,660	249,684	+92.6	61,101	97,865	+60.2
437,526	+18.8	145,921	274,964	+88.4	64,009	103,176	+61.2
43,942	+39.8	26,422	37,226	+40.9	7,263	11,256	+55.0
4,800	+17.8	606	1,264	+108.6	345	519	+50.4
4,058	+49.1	7,058	13,107	+85.7	802	1,775	+121.3
2,669	+44.3	14,058	44,803	+218.7	455	1,130	+148.4
434	+231.3	1,064	1,112	+4.5	57	145	+154.4
20,545	+95.4	2,801	7,222	+157.8	819	2,035	+148.5
72,645	+21.7	6,417	11,401	+77.7	4,068	6,024	+48.1
14,546	+16.9	4,802	7,424	+54.6	596	921	+54.5
814	+244.9	27,499	40,806	+48.4	617	1,748	+183.3
6,515	−7.2	5,932	3,497	−41.0	2,190	687	−68.6
72,412	+105.8	29,062	51,185	+76.1	10,075	14,756	+46.5
1,297	−.9	4,366	3,293	−24.6	44	68	+54.5
1,109	+108.9	4,232	3,152	−25.5	181	732	+304.4
11,370	+265.4	19,296	49,170	+154.8	138	1,301	+842.8
54,268	+10.3	22,825	29,255	+28.2	10,129	16,069	+58.6
21,399	−34.5	88,822	51,785	−41.7	4,680	3,666	−21.7
71,301	−15.3	65,645	76,902	+17.1	16,697	15,055	−9.8
2,733	−56.5	7,305	4,092	−44.0	1,099	573	−47.9
138,131	+7.0	87,362	130,013	+48.8	39,889	39,518	−.9
3,232	−79.6	12,697	1,682	−86.8	2,574	553	−78.5
45,499	−34.8	17,192	11,355	−34.0	17,192	11,355	−34.0
46,129	−29.9	70,951	64,590	−9.0	70,951	64,590	−9.0

TABLE 28.
Total Arrest Trends, 1974–1978
(7,056 agencies; 1978 estimated population 153,356,000)

Offense charged	Total all ages		Percent change
	1974	1978	
TOTAL	6,989,947	6,838,286	−2.2
Murder and nonnegligent manslaughter	14,818	12,780	−13.8
Forcible rape	18,467	19,873	+7.6
Robbery	103,147	91,228	−11.6
Aggravated assault	161,486	173,877	+7.7
Burglary	372,778	352,447	−5.5
Larceny—theft	796,010	836,639	+5.1
Motor vehicle theft	112,825	109,641	−2.8
Violent crime[1]	297,918	297,758	−.1
Property crime[2]	1,281,613	1,298,727	+1.3
Crime index total	1,579,531	1,596,485	+1.1
Other assaults	294,959	328,385	+11.3
Arson	11,710	12,901	+10.2
Forgery and counterfeiting	44,722	51,361	+14.8
Fraud	111,923	140,185	+25.3
Embezzlement	4,756	5,259	+10.6
Stolen property; buying, receiving, possessing	79,379	77,764	−2.0
Vandalism	154,893	174,400	+12.6
Weapons; carrying, possessing, etc.	124,926	110,230	−11.8
Prostitution and commercialized vice	51,883	69,022	+33.0
Sex offenses (except forcible rape and prostitution)	46,366	47,795	+3.1
Drug abuse violations	525,975	434,541	−17.4
Gambling	54,203	41,183	−24.0
Offenses against family and children	48,713	36,050	−26.0
Driving under the influence	785,996	878,384	+11.8
Liquor laws	218,963	269,008	+22.9
Drunkenness	1,103,463	809,825	−26.6
Disorderly conduct	522,528	540,358	+3.4
Vagrancy	40,214	25,579	−36.4
All other offenses (except traffic)	890,162	984,467	+10.6
Suspicion (not included in totals)	36,130	14,515	−59.8
Curfew and loitering law violations	115,076	66,474	−42.2
Running away	179,606	138,630	−22.8

[1]Violent crimes are offenses of murder, forcible rape, robbery, and aggravated assault.
[2]Property crimes are offenses of burglary, larceny—theft, and motor vehicle theft.

Number of persons arrested Under 18 years of age			18 years of age and over		
1974	1978	Percent change	1974	1978	Percent change
1,905,102	**1,711,079**	**−10.2**	**5,084,845**	**5,127,207**	**+.8**
1,459	1,190	−18.4	13,359	11,590	−13.2
3,615	3,240	−10.4	14,852	16,633	+12.0
33,571	28,631	−14.7	69,576	62,597	−10.0
28,486	29,006	+1.8	133,000	144,871	+8.9
201,377	187,957	−6.7	171,401	164,490	−4.0
384,928	360,644	−6.3	411,082	475,995	+15.8
64,458	57,891	−10.2	48,367	51,750	+7.0
67,131	62,067	−7.5	230,787	235,691	+2.1
650,763	606,492	−6.8	630,850	692,235	+9.7
717,894	668,559	−6.9	861,637	927,926	+7.7
60,101	66,306	+10.3	234,858	262,079	+11.6
6,872	6,607	−3.9	4,838	6,294	+30.1
6,060	7,462	+23.1	38,662	43,899	+13.5
5,116	4,725	−7.6	106,807	135,460	+26.8
473	712	+50.5	4,283	4,547	+6.2
28,351	27,587	−2.7	51,028	50,177	−1.7
106,072	101,887	−3.9	48,821	72,513	+48.5
20,439	18,256	−10.7	104,487	91,974	−12.0
2,327	2,942	+26.4	49,556	66,080	+33.3
10,777	8,995	−16.5	35,589	38,800	+9.0
140,268	109,077	−22.2	385,707	325,464	−15.6
2,285	1,566	−31.5	51,918	39,617	−23.7
3,934	2,140	−45.6	44,779	33,910	−24.3
12,214	19,726	+61.5	773,782	858,658	+11.0
90,612	100,529	+10.9	128,351	168,479	+31.3
35,463	31,327	−11.7	1,068,000	778,498	−27.1
114,135	100,731	−11.7	408,393	439,627	+7.6
5,681	3,956	−30.4	34,533	21,623	−37.4
241,346	222,885	−7.6	648,816	761,582	+17.4
10,588	4,195	−60.4	25,542	10,320	−59.6
115,076	66,474	−42.2	....	....	....
179,606	138,630	−22.8	....	....	....

Appendix

TABLE 29.
Total Arrest Trends, Sex, 1974–1978
(7,056 agencies; 1978 estimated population 153,356,000)

Offense charged	Total			Males	
	1974	1978	Percent change	Under 18 1974	Under 18 1978
TOTAL	5,913,437	5,695,159	−3.7	1,497,831	1,342,821
Murder and nonnegligent manslaughter	12,616	10,876	−13.8	1,342	1,073
Forcible rape	18,301	19,692	+7.6	3,554	3,175
Robbery	96,278	84,599	−12.1	31,283	26,677
Aggravated assault	140,488	151,650	+7.9	24,015	24,681
Burglary	352,395	330,360	−6.3	190,715	176,408
Larceny—theft	548,371	564,818	+3.0	275,053	258,012
Motor vehicle theft	105,403	99,945	−5.2	60,077	52,118
Violent crime[1]	267,683	266,817	−.3	60,194	55,606
Property crime[2]	1,006,169	995,123	−1.1	525,845	486,538
Crime index total	1,273,852	1,261,940	−.9	586,039	542,144
Other assaults	254,361	282,623	+11.1	47,613	52,894
Arson	10,495	11,333	+8.0	6,228	5,967
Forgery and counterfeiting	31,913	35,008	+9.7	4,253	5,175
Fraud	74,487	84,312	+13.2	3,974	3,325
Embezzlement	3,830	3,889	+1.5	375	536
Stolen property; buying, receiving, possessing	71,085	68,836	−3.2	25,943	25,135
Vandalism	142,621	159,838	+12.1	98,273	94,121
Weapons; carrying, possessing, etc. ...	115,033	101,502	−11.8	19,282	17,177
Prostitution and commercialized vice	12,926	22,376	+73.1	754	945
Sex offenses (except forcible rape and prostitution)	42,521	43,669	+2.7	9,356	8,154
Drug abuse violations	451,248	372,147	−17.5	116,201	90,474
Gambling	49,419	37,500	−24.1	2,195	1,493
Offenses against family and children .	43,289	32,017	−26.0	2,534	1,358
Driving under the influence	724,510	800,264	+10.5	11,321	17,691
Liquor laws	186,267	227,777	+22.3	72,495	78,084
Drunkenness	1,024,287	749,179	−26.9	30,810	26,784
Disorderly conduct	448,679	452,591	+.9	94,564	83,536
Vagrancy	34,740	18,908	−45.6	4,759	3,263
All other offenses (except traffic)	745,642	818,847	+9.8	188,630	173,962
Suspicion (not included in totals)	31,293	12,465	−60.2	8,970	3,557
Curfew and loitering law violations ...	92,447	52,449	−43.3	92,447	52,449
Running away	79,785	58,154	−27.1	79,785	58,154

[1]Violent crimes are offenses of murder, forcible rape, robbery, and aggravated assault.
[2]Property crimes are offenses of burglary, larceny—theft, and motor vehicle theft.

Percent change	1974	Total 1978	Females Percent change	1974	Under 18 1978	Percent change
−10.3	1,076,510	1,143,127	+6.2	407,271	368,258	−9.6
−20.0	2,202	1,904	−13.5	117	117	....
−10.7	166	181	+9.0	61	65	+6.6
−14.7	6,869	6,629	−3.5	2,288	1,954	−14.6
+2.8	20,998	22,227	+5.9	4,471	4,325	−3.3
−7.5	20,383	22,087	+8.4	10,662	11,549	+8.3
−6.2	247,639	271,821	+9.8	109,875	102,632	−6.6
−13.2	7,422	9,696	+30.6	4,381	5,773	+31.8
−7.6	30,235	30,941	+2.3	6,937	6,461	−6.9
−7.5	275,444	303,604	+10.2	124,918	119,954	−4.0
−7.5	305,679	334,545	+9.4	131,855	126,415	−4.1
+11.1	40,598	45,762	+12.7	12,488	13,412	+7.4
−4.2	1,215	1,568	+29.1	644	640	−.6
+21.7	12,809	16,353	+27.7	1,807	2,287	+26.6
−16.3	37,436	55,873	+49.2	1,142	1,400	+22.6
+42.9	926	1,370	+47.9	98	176	+79.6
−3.1	8,294	8,928	+7.6	2,408	2,452	+1.8
−4.2	12,272	14,562	+18.7	7,799	7,766	−.4
−10.9	9,893	8,728	−11.8	1,157	1,079	−6.7
+25.3	38,957	46,646	+19.7	1,573	1,997	+27.0
−12.8	3,845	4,126	+7.3	1,421	841	−40.8
−22.1	74,727	62,394	−16.5	24,067	18,603	−22.7
−32.0	4,784	3,683	−23.0	90	73	−18.9
−46.4	5,424	4,033	−25.6	1,400	782	−44.1
+56.3	61,486	78,120	+27.1	893	2,035	+127.9
+7.7	32,696	41,231	+26.1	18,117	22,445	+23.9
−13.1	79,176	60,646	−23.4	4,653	4,543	−2.4
−11.7	73,849	87,767	+18.8	19,571	17,195	−12.1
−31.4	5,474	6,671	+21.9	922	693	−24.8
−7.8	144,520	165,620	+14.6	52,716	48,923	−7.2
−60.3	4,837	2,050	−57.6	1,618	638	−60.6
−43.3	22,629	14,025	−38.0	22,629	14,025	−38.0
−27.1	99,821	80,476	−19.4	99,821	80,476	−19.4

Appendix

TABLE 30.
Total Arrest Trends, 1977–1978
(10,319 agencies; 1978 estimated population 179,569,000)

Offense charged	Total all ages			Number of persons arrested Under 15 years of age		
	1977	1978	Percent change	1977	1978	Percent change
TOTAL	7,953,397	8,073,735	+1.5	649,283	623,105	−4.0
Murder and nonnegligent manslaughter	14,798	14,970	+1.2	198	187	−5.6
Forcible rape	22,318	22,794	+2.1	925	867	−6.3
Robbery	95,307	95,839	+.6	7,099	7,041	−.8
Aggravated assault	185,352	197,882	+6.8	8,477	8,503	+.3
Burglary	400,698	401,959	+.3	79,048	79,301	+.3
Larceny—theft	917,707	935,921	+2.0	175,431	170,229	−3.0
Motot vehicle theft	112,915	118,120	+4.6	16,421	16,433	+.1
Violent crime[1]	317,775	331,485	+4.3	16,699	16,598	−.6
Property crime[2]	1,431,320	1,456,000	+1.7	270,900	265,963	−1.8
Crime index total	1,749,095	1,787,485	+2.2	287,599	282,561	−1.8
Other assaults	369,721	385,347	+4.2	25,373	24,585	−3.1
Arson	14,868	15,186	+2.1	4,633	4,536	−2.1
Forgery and counterfeiting	60,566	61,308	+1.2	1,314	1,372	+4.4
Fraud	182,837	205,126	+12.2	1,099	984	−10.5
Embezzlement	6,063	6,644	+9.6	115	142	+23.5
Stolen property; buying, receiving, possessing	90,526	89,643	−1.0	8,954	8,842	−1.3
Vandalism	182,066	194,623	+6.9	59,309	58,338	−1.6
Weapons; carrying, possessing, etc. ...	122,340	125,905	+2.9	4,710	4,802	+2.0
Prostitution and commercialized vice	65,121	68,779	+5.6	336	289	−14.0
Sex offenses (except forcible rape and prostitution)	52,703	51,941	−1.4	3,778	3,595	−4.8
Drug abuse violations	499,995	496,029	−.8	16,952	18,374	+8.4
Gambling	402	41,348	−4.7	249	214	−14.1
Offenses against family and children	51,427	50,296	−2.2	1,431	1,134	−20.8
Driving under the influence	1,015,004	1,085,544	+6.9	352	467	+32.7
Liquor laws	306,589	319,895	+4.3	9,417	8,850	−6.0
Drunkenness	1,088,656	994,097	−8.7	4,467	3,797	−15.0
Disorderly conduct	584,256	618,321	+5.8	32,466	31,959	−1.6
Vagrancy	26,274	25,046	−4.7	1,291	1,261	−2.3
All other offenses (except traffic)	1,184,407	1,221,938	+3.2	92,010	85,224	−7.4
Suspicion (not included in totals)	22,173	18,075	−18.5	1,825	1,560	−14.5
Curfew and loitering law violations ...	81,919	72,735	−11.2	22,942	19,052	−17.0
Running away	175,562	156,499	−10.9	70,486	62,727	−11.0

[1]Violent crimes are offenses of murder, forcible rape, robbery, and aggravated assault.
[2]Property crimes are offenses of burglary, larceny—theft, and motor vehicle theft.

Under 18 years of age			18 years of age and over		
1977	1978	Percent change	1977	1978	Percent change
1,959,833	1,917,915	−2.1	5,993,564	6,155,820	+2.7
1,456	1,346	−7.6	13,342	13,624	+2.1
3,702	3,584	−3.2	18,616	19,210	+3.2
29,438	29,257	−.6	65,869	66,582	+1.1
30,219	31,070	+2.8	155,133	166,812	+7.5
211,524	212,175	+.3	189,174	189,784	+.3
401,319	398,210	−.8	516,388	537,711	+4.1
62,219	62,452	+.4	50,696	55,668	+9.8
64,815	65,257	+.7	252,960	266,228	+5.2
675,062	672,837	−.3	756,258	783,163	+3.6
739,877	738,094	−.2	1,009,218	1,049,391	+4.0
70,684	70,966	+.4	299,307	314,381	+5.1
7,548	7,585	+.5	7,320	7,601	+3.8
7,627	8,254	+8.2	52,939	53,054	+.2
5,513	5,622	+2.0	177,324	199,504	+12.5
735	781	+6.3	5,328	5,863	+10.0
30,594	30,581	....	59,932	59,062	−1.5
110,275	112,798	+2.3	71,791	81,825	+14.0
19,832	19,917	+.4	102,508	105,988	+3.4
2,882	2,922	+1.4	62,239	65,857	+5.8
10,248	9,850	−3.9	42,455	42,091	−.9
121,086	122,629	+1.3	378,909	373,400	−1.5
1,855	1,621	−12.6	41,547	39,727	−4.4
3,018	2,664	−11.7	48,409	47,632	−1.6
23,101	25,221	+9.2	991,903	1,060,323	+6.9
115,793	115,383	−.4	190,796	204,512	+7.2
46,042	39,330	−14.6	1,042,614	954,767	−8.4
111,835	113,034	+1.1	472,421	505,287	+7.0
5,239	4,657	−11.1	21,035	20,389	−3.1
268,568	256,772	−4.4	915,839	965,166	+5.4
5,868	5,083	−13.4	16,305	12,992	−20.3
81,919	72,735	−11.2	....	....	....
175,562	156,499	−10.9	....	....	....

Appendix

TABLE 31.
Total Arrest Trends, Sex, 1977–1978
(10,319 agencies; 1978 estimated population 179,569,000)

Offense charged	Total			Males Under 18	
	1977	1978	Percent change	1977	1978
TOTAL	6,657,275	6,755,387	+1.5	1,530,909	1,507,287
Murder and nonegligent man-slaughter	12,558	12,736	+1.4	1,321	1,197
Forcible rape	22,087	22,608	+2.4	3,618	3,526
Robbery	88,123	88,928	+.9	27,294	27,272
Aggravated assault	161,795	172,849	+6.8	25,669	26,452
Burglary	376,233	376,982	+.2	198,758	199,105
Larceny—theft	626,194	636,550	+1.7	287,981	285,416
Motor vehicle theft	103,413	107,690	+4.1	56,423	56,121
Violent crime[1]	284,563	297,121	+4.4	57,902	58,447
Property crime[2]	1,105,840	1,121,222	+1.4	543,162	540,642
Crime index total	1,390,403	1,418,343	+2.0	601,064	599,089
Other assaults	318,511	332,081	+4.3	56,144	56,607
Arson	13,231	13,400	+1.3	6,853	6,866
Forgery and counterfeiting	42,753	42,682	−.2	5435	5,734
Fraud	113,120	122,039	+7.9	3,962	3,941
Embezzlement	4,698	4,951	+5.4	576	574
Stolen property; buying, receiving, possessing	80,577	79,367	−1.5	27,887	27,762
Vandalism	166,698	178,336	+7.0	101,924	104,265
Weapons; carrying, possessing, etc. ...	112,339	115,927	+3.2	18,564	18,727
Prostitution and commercialized vice	19,366	21,967	+13.4	895	891
Sex offenses (except forcible rape and prostitution)	48,039	47,825	−.4	9,195	8,953
Drug abuse violations	430,585	426,682	−.9	101,000	101,855
Gambling	39,426	37,566	−4.7	1,756	1,547
Offenses against family and children	46,211	45,127	−2.3	1,887	1,711
Driving under the influence	930,421	993,468	+6.8	20,986	22,789
Liquor laws	261,068	272,604	+4.4	90,724	89,991
Drunkenness	1,008,105	919,200	−8.8	39,706	33,949
Disorderly conduct	485,983	518,816	+6.8	90,655	93,452
Vagrancy	20,125	17,954	−10.8	4,237	3,849
All other offenses (except traffic)	987,070	1,023,489	+3.7	208,913	201,172
Suspicion (not included in totals)	19,012	15,717	−17.3	4,963	4,327
Curfew and loitering law violations ...	64,176	57,048	−11.1	64,176	57,048
Running away	74,370	66,515	−10.6	74,370	66,515

[1]Violent crimes are offenses of murder, forcible rape, robbery, and aggravated assault.
[2]Property crimes are offenses of burglary, larceny—theft, and motor-vehicle theft.

		Total		Females		Under 18	
Percent change	1977	1978	Percent change	1977	1978	Percent change
−1.5	1,296,122	1,318,348	+1.7	428,924	410,628	−4.3
−9.4	2,240	2,234	−.3	135	149	+10.4
−2.5	231	186	−19.5	84	58	−31.0
−.1	7,184	6,911	−3.8	2,144	1,985	−7.4
+3.1	23,557	25,033	+6.3	4,550	4,618	+1.5
+.2	24,465	24,977	+2.1	12,766	13,070	+2.4
−.9	291,513	299,371	+2.7	113,338	112,794	−.5
−.5	9,502	10,430	+9.8	5,796	6,331	+9.2
+.9	33,212	34,364	+3.5	6,913	6,810	−1.5
−.5	325,480	334,778	+2.9	131,900	132,195	+.2
−.3	358,692	369,142	+2.9	138,813	139,005	+.1
+.8	51,210	53,266	+4.0	14,540	14,359	−1.2
+.2	1,637	1,786	+9.1	695	719	+3.5
+5.5	17,813	18,626	+4.6	2,192	2,520	+15.0
−.5	69,717	83,087	+19.2	1,551	1,681	+8.4
−.3	1,365	1,693	+24.0	159	207	+30.2
−.4	9,949	10,276	+3.3	2,707	2,819	+4.1
+2.3	15,368	16,287	+6.0	8,351	8,533	+2.2
+.9	10,001	9,978	−.2	1,268	1,190	−6.2
−.4	45,755	46,812	+2.3	1,987	2,031	+2.2
−2.6	4,664	4,116	−11.7	1,053	897	−14.8
+.8	69,410	69,347	−.1	20,086	20,774	+3.4
−11.9	3,976	3,782	−4.9	99	74	−25.3
−9.3	5,216	5,169	−.9	1,131	953	−15.7
+8.6	84,583	92,076	+8.9	2,115	2,432	+15.0
−.8	45,521	47,291	+3.9	25,069	25,392	+1.3
−14.5	80,551	74,897	−7.0	6,336	5,381	−15.1
+3.1	98,273	99,505	+1.3	21,180	19,582	−7.5
−9.2	6,149	7,092	+15.3	1,002	808	−19.4
−3.7	197,337	198,449	+.6	59,655	55,600	−6.8
−12.8	3,161	2,358	−25.4	905	756	−16.5
−11.1	17,743	15,687	−11.6	17,743	15,687	−11.6
−10.6	101,192	89,984	−11.1	101,192	89,984	−11.1

Appendix

TABLE 32.
Total Arrests, Distribution by Age, 1978
(11,872 agencies; 1978 estimated population 207,060,000)

Offense charged	Grand total all ages	Ages under 15	Ages under 18	Ages 18 and over	10 and under	11–12
TOTAL	9,775,087	728,198	2,279,365	7,495,722	79,007	152,317
Percent distribution[1]	100.0	7.4	23.3	76.7	.8	1.6
Murder and nonnegligent manslaughter	18,755	244	1,735	17,020	26	20
Forcible rape	28,257	1,102	4,517	23,740	75	185
Robbery	141,481	13,086	48,088	93,393	534	2,428
Aggravated assault	257,629	11,508	41,253	216,376	1,014	2,433
Burglary	485,782	93,652	250,649	235,133	9,806	20,012
Larceny—theft	1,084,088	194,680	454,994	629,094	23,850	49,098
Motor vehicle theft	153,270	20,146	77,534	75,736	507	2,409
Violent crime[2]	446,122	25,940	95,593	350,529	1,649	5,066
Percent distribution[1]	100.0	5.8	21.4	78.6	.4	1.1
Property crime[3]	1,723,140	308,478	783,177	939,963	34,163	71,519
Percent distribution[1]	100.0	17.9	45.5	54.5	2.0	4.2
Crime index total	2,169,262	334,418	878,770	1,290,492	35,812	76,585
Percent distribution[1]	100.0	15.4	40.5	59.5	1.7	3.5
Other assaults	445,020	28,496	82,425	362,595	3,181	6,622
Arson	18,114	5,129	8,760	9,354	1,502	1,313
Forgery and counterfeiting	73,269	1,680	9,991	63,278	74	243
Fraud	249,207	7,084	18,874	230,333	293	1,216
Embezzlement	7,670	185	909	6,761	17	37
Stolen property; buying, receiving, possessing	112,317	10,997	37,490	74,827	664	2,029
Vandalism	223,391	66,586	127,973	95,418	14,018	17,635
Weapons, carrying, possessing, etc.	149,957	5,504	23,689	126,268	323	922
Prostitution and commercialized vice	89,365	659	4,212	85,153	33	78
Sex offenses (except forcible rape and prostitution)	65,666	4,427	11,842	53,824	426	892
Drug abuse violations	596,940	20,771	141,186	455,754	430	1,714
Gambling	53,066	300	2,137	50,929	23	42
Offenses against family and children	54,014	1,230	2,871	51,143	671	161
Driving under the influence	1,204,733	513	27,494	1,177,239	142	50
Liquor Laws	357,450	9,761	127,069	230,381	281	656
Drunkenness	1,117,349	4,195	43,210	1,074,139	301	332
Disorderly conduct	679,112	34,978	124,307	554,805	3,695	7,643
Vagrancy	46,896	1,960	6,578	40,318	198	401
All other offenses (except traffic)	1,788,794	96,735	341,579	1,447,215	11,595	19,172
Suspicion	21,650	1,987	6,154	15,496	256	398
Curfew and loitering law violations	78,972	20,723	78,972	....	1,028	3,462
Running away	172,873	69,880	172,873	....	4,044	10,714

See footnotes at end of table.

Juvenile Delinquency and Juvenile Justice

			Age				
13–14	15	16	17	18	19	20	21
496,874	432,078	542,459	576,630	589,767	540,790	499,585	471,078
5.1	4.4	5.5	5.9	6.0	5.5	5.1	4.8
198	281	540	670	931	924	929	933
842	820	1,156	1,439	1,598	1,558	1,593	1,630
10,124	9,835	12,171	12,996	12,511	10,474	8,860	8,192
8,061	7,454	10,135	12,156	12,974	12,564	12,577	12,599
63,834	51,785	54,487	50,725	41,262	30,285	23,926	19,762
121,732	83,888	90,121	86,305	74,182	58,465	49,108	42,584
17,230	19,178	20,660	17,550	12,681	9,524	7,231	6,251
19,225	18,390	24,002	27,261	28,014	25,520	23,959	23,354
4.3	4.1	5.4	6.1	6.3	5.7	5.4	5.2
202,796	154,851	165,268	154,580	128,125	98,274	80,265	68,597
11.8	9.0	9.6	9.0	7.4	5.7	4.7	4.0
222,021	173,241	189,270	181,841	156,139	123,794	104,224	91,951
10.2	8.0	8.7	8.4	7.2	5.7	4.8	4.2
18,693	14,505	18,303	21,121	21,743	22,070	21,894	22,368
2,314	1,412	1,148	1,071	820	804	629	537
1,363	1,741	2,692	3,878	4,170	4,367	4,240	4,369
5,575	5,445	2,228	4,117	7,268	9,190	10,980	12,557
131	109	226	389	411	385	383	445
8,304	7,686	9,047	9,760	9,273	7,642	6,544	5,655
34,933	21,038	21,037	19,312	14,006	10,529	8,439	7,440
4,259	4,286	6,059	7,840	9,084	8,498	7,843	7,950
548	735	851	1,967	5,390	7,837	8,128	8,945
3,109	2,248	2,444	2,723	2,829	2,774	2,846	2,853
18,627	26,312	41,602	52,501	57,933	53,621	48,395	42,895
235	360	606	871	1,253	1,331	1,346	1,458
398	476	530	635	2,442	2,265	2,241	2,420
321	1,062	7,002	18,917	42,789	50,673	53,636	57,936
8,824	18,149	39,840	59,319	54,695	41,337	30,406	12,895
3,562	6,136	11,995	20,884	40,430	40,113	40,527	45,808
23,640	21,844	29,040	38,445	47,321	45,361	42,757	40,573
1,361	1,353	1,499	1,766	2,578	3,071	2,840	3,179
65,968	57,833	93,590	93,421	107,562	103,590	100,009	97,648
1,333	1,110	1,388	1,669	1,631	1,538	1,278	1,197
16,233	17,446	22,950	17,853	....	....	....	....
55,122	47,551	39,112	16,330	....	....	....	....

Appendix

TABLE 32.
Total Arrests, Distribution by Age, 1978—Continued

Offense charged	22	23	24	25–29	30–34	35–39
TOTAL	420,821	382,602	352,854	1,283,448	827,948	586,293
Percent distribution[1]	4.3	3.9	3.6	13.1	8.5	6.0
Murder and nonnegligent man-						
slaughter	925	892	867	3,445	2,237	1,575
Forcible rape	1,558	1,452	1,325	5,308	3,207	1,916
Robbery	6,963	6,176	5,429	18,139	8,384	3,909
Aggravated assault	12,142	11,553	10,823	43,173	28,934	19,545
Burglary	16,228	13,784	11,864	38,562	17,595	8,937
Larceny—theft	36,992	32,644	29,059	108,186	61,392	38,235
Motor vehicle theft	5,079	4,358	3,793	12,430	6,138	3,326
Violent crime[2]	21,588	20,073	18,444	70,065	42,762	26,945
Percent distribution[1]	4.8	4.5	4.1	15.7	9.6	6.0
Property crime[3]	58,299	50,786	44,716	159,178	85,125	50,498
Percent distribution[1]	3.4	2.9	2.6	9.2	4.9	2.9
Crime index total	79,887	70,859	63,160	229,243	127,887	77,443
—Percent distribution[1]	3.7	3.3	2.9	10.6	5.9	3.6
Other assaults	21,073	20,156	18,924	73,738	48,372	31,873
Arson	569	506	443	1,600	1,051	804
Forgery and counterfeiting	4,292	3,861	3,868	14,746	8,320	4,468
Fraud	12,722	12,997	13,078	53,775	37,426	23,845
Embezzlement	366	337	355	1,294	936	648
Stolen property; buying, receiv-						
ing, possessing	4,850	4,383	3,700	13,346	7,480	4,417
Vandalism	5,994	5.267	4,681	15,577	8,903	5,199
Weapons; carrying, possessing,						
etc.	7,339	6,754	6,241	23,864	15,568	10,598
Prostitution and commercialized						
vice	8,408	7,392	5,990	16,612	7,001	3,471
Sex offenses (except forcible rape						
and prostitution)	2,814	2,543	2,398	9,826	7,573	5,356
Drug abuse violations	36,433	30,739	27,151	85,515	37,318	16,613
Gambling	1,470	1,407	1,246	6,592	6,247	5,616
Offenses against family and						
children	2,489	2,948	2,628	11,231	8,395	5,830
Driving under the influence	54,819	51,059	48,655	197,230	148,257	118,872
Liquor laws	9,898	7,578	6,303	19,589	11,614	8,752
Drunkenness	40,748	37,558	35,397	142,636	116,635	105,446
Disorderly conduct	34,821	30,550	27,542	96,624	57,494	38,628
Vagrancy	2,879	2,749	2,109	7,185	3,972	2,774
All other offenses (except						
traffic)	87,922	82,027	78,144	260,351	166,006	114,754
Suspicion	1,028	932	841	2,874	1,493	886
Curfew and loitering law						
violations	....	....	....	....	....	....
Running away	....	....	....	....	....	....

[1]Because of rounding, the percentages may not add to total.
[2]Violent crimes are offenses of murder, forcible rape, robbery, and aggravated assault.
[3]Property crimes are offenses of burglary, larceny—theft, and motor vehicle theft.
[4]Less than one-tenth of 1 percent.

40–44	45–49	50–54	55–59	60–64	65 and over	Not known
450,570	**366,798**	**302,276**	**199,119**	**113,311**	**99,564**	**8,898**
4.6	**3.8**	**3.1**	**2.0**	**1.2**	**1.0**	**.1**
1,095	786	602	360	224	285	10
1,055	676	398	224	104	126	12
1,919	1,127	646	304	107	212	41
13,565	9,498	7,090	4,255	2,470	2,457	157
5,210	3,324	2,057	1,054	433	572	278
26,613	21,015	17,747	12,637	8,357	11,279	599
1,958	1,309	808	415	160	194	81
17,634	12,087	8,736	5,143	2,905	3,080	220
4.0	2.7	2.0	1.2	.7	.7	(4)
33,781	25,648	20,612	14,106	8,950	12,045	958
2.0	1.5	1.2	.8	.5	.7	.1
51,415	37,735	29,348	19,249	11,855	15,125	1,178
2.4	1.7	1.4	.9	.5	.7	.1
22,004	15,023	10,588	6,063	3,240	3,106	360
566	410	264	163	92	85	11
2,773	1,748	1,101	503	168	167	118
15,193	9,410	6,061	3,106	1,480	1,216	29
496	324	185	111	47	18	20
2,886	1,957	1,275	729	353	294	43
3,304	2,319	1,584	940	454	511	271
7,383	5,414	4,150	2,581	1,414	1,512	75
2,115	1,402	1,018	662	353	390	39
3,698	2,819	2,186	1,485	874	920	30
8,369	5,013	2,827	1,355	596	648	333
5,270	5,208	4,442	3,243	2,221	2,572	7
3,562	2,178	1,357	631	257	205	64
98,527	84,862	71,342	48,436	27,047	20,034	3,065
7,356	6,184	5,057	3,732	2,248	2,084	653
100,501	97,544	93,747	66,096	39,696	31,106	151
28,614	22,682	17,509	11,092	6,085	6,624	528
1,970	1,658	1,419	936	462	521	16
83,992	62,473	46,486	27,844	14,250	12,302	1,855
576	435	330	162	119	124	52
....	....	....	....	....	....	....
....	....	....	....	....	....	....

Appendix

TABLE 33.
Total Arrests of Persons under 15, 18, 21, and 25 Years of Age, 1978
(11,872 agencies; 1978 estimated population 207,060,000)

Offense charged	Grand total all ages	Number of persons arrested	
		Under 15	Under 18
TOTAL	9,775,087	728,198	2,279,365
Murder and nonnegligent manslaughter	18,755	244	1,735
Forcible rape	28,257	1,102	4,517
Robbery	141,481	13,086	48,088
Aggravated assault	257,629	11,508	41,253
Burglary	485,782	93,652	250,649
Larceny—theft	1,084,088	194,680	454,994
Motor vehicle theft	153,270	20,146	77,534
Violent crime[1]	446,122	25,940	95,593
Property crime[2]	1,723,140	308,478	783,177
Crime index total	2,169,262	334,418	878,770
Other assaults	445,020	28,496	82,425
Arson	18,114	5,129	8,760
Forgery and counterfeiting	73,269	1,680	9,991
Fraud	249,207	7,084	18,874
Embezzlement	7,670	185	909
Stolen property; buying, receiving, possessing	112,317	10,997	37,490
Vandalism	223,391	66,586	127,973
Weapons; carrying, possessing, etc.	149,957	5,504	23,689
Prostitution and commercialized vice	89,365	659	4,212
Sex offenses (except forcible rape and prostitution) ..	65,666	4,427	11,842
Drug abuse violations	596,940	20,771	141,186
Gambling	53,066	300	2,137
Offenses against family and children	54,014	1,230	2,871
Driving under the influence	1,204,733	513	27,494
Liquor laws	357,450	9,761	127,069
Drunkenness	1,117,349	4,195	43,210
Disorderly conduct	679,112	34,978	124,307
Vagrancy	46,896	1,960	6,578
All other offenses (except traffic)	1,788,794	96,735	341,579
Suspicion	21,650	1,987	6,154
Curfew and loitering law violations	78,972	20,723	78,972
Running away	172,873	69,880	172,873

[1]Violent crimes are offenses of murder, forcible rape, robbery, and aggravated assault.
[2]Property crimes are offenses of burglary, larceny—theft, and motor vehicle theft.
[3]Less than one-tenth of 1 percent.

		Percent of total all ages			
Under 21	Under 25	Under 15	Under 18	Under 21	Under 25
3,909,507	**5,536,862**	**7.4**	**23.3**	**40.0**	**56.6**
4,519	8,136	1.3	9.3	24.1	43.4
9,266	15,231	3.9	16.0	32.8	53.9
79,933	106,693	9.2	34.0	56.5	75.4
79,368	126,485	4.5	16.0	30.8	49.1
346,122	407,760	19.3	51.6	71.3	83.9
636,749	778,028	18.0	42.0	58.7	71.8
106,970	126,451	13.1	50.6	69.8	82.5
173,086	256,545	5.8	21.4	38.8	57.5
1,089,841	1,312,239	17.9	45.5	63.2	76.2
1,262,927	1,568,784	15.4	40.5	58.2	72.3
148,132	230,653	6.4	18.5	33.3	51.8
11,013	13,068	28.3	48.4	60.8	72.1
22,768	39,157	2.3	13.6	31.1	53.4
46,312	97,666	2.8	7.6	18.6	39.2
2,088	3,591	2.4	11.9	27.2	46.8
60,949	79,537	9.8	33.4	54.3	70.8
160,947	184,329	29.8	57.3	72.0	82.5
49,114	77,398	3.7	15.8	32.8	51.6
25,567	56,302	.7	4.7	28.6	63.0
20,291	30,899	6.7	18.0	30.9	47.1
301,135	438,353	3.5	23.7	50.4	73.4
6,067	11,648	.6	4.0	11.4	22.0
9,819	20,304	2.3	5.3	18.2	37.6
174,592	387,061	(3)	2.3	14.5	32.1
253,507	290,181	2.7	35.5	70.9	81.2
164,280	323,791	.4	3.9	14.7	29.0
259,746	393,232	5.2	18.3	38.2	57.9
15,067	25,983	4.2	14.0	32.1	55.4
652,740	998,481	5.4	19.1	36.5	55.8
10,601	14,599	9.2	28.4	49.0	67.4
78,972	78,972	26.2	100.0	100.0	100.0
172,873	172,873	40.4	100.0	100.0	100.0

Appendix

ANNOTATED BIBLIOGRAPHY

This bibliography was compiled to provide students of juvenile delinquency and juvenile justice, as well as the general reading public, with a select list of recent and classic works in the field. All of the books and articles cited were consulted or used in the preparation of this book, and, although the list is not inclusive, we believe it is representative of the available literature. Especially evident in this compilation are contrasting points of view reflecting the volatile state of contemporary thinking on the nature of delinquency, the juvenile court process, and the future of the juvenile justice system.

ARTICLES

Adamson, LeMay and H. Warren Dunham, "Clinical Treatment for Male Delinquents: A Case Study in Effort and Result," *American Sociological Review* 21 (1956): 312–20.

A report on an evaluative study of the Wayne County Clinic for Child Study in Detroit, Michigan. An attempt was made to determine whether or not the prevention of crime was increased through appropriate treatment of juvenile delinquents in a clinic setting. The results indicated that clinic treatment did not change delinquent behavior.

Bailey, Walter C., "Correctional Outcome: An Evaluation of 100 Reports," *Journal of Criminal Law, Criminology and Police Science* 57 (June 1966): 153–60.

A presentation of selected results of a content analysis of 100 reports of empirical evaluations of correctional treatment. Results indicated that "a slight majority of the correctional treatment programs evaluated in the reports was carried out in 'forced treatment' settings as compared with correctional treatment programs carried out in 'voluntary treatment' settings."

Berger, Alan S., and William Simon, "Black Families and the Moynihan Report: A Research Evaluation," *Social Problems* 22 (December, 1974): 145–61.

A study of 14 to 18 year old children in Illinois which examines the joint effects of race, gender, social class, and family organization on a number of indicators of family interaction, antisocial behavior patterns, educational aspirations, and gender role conceptions. "Few differences were found in the ways that families treat their children, and these differences were not concentrated in the lower class."

Briar, Scott, and Irving Piliavin, "Delinquency, Situational Inducements, and Commitment to Conformity," *Social Problems* 12 (Summer, 1965): 35–45.

An argument that the subculture theses of delinquency causation, as well as the general class of theories of which it is a part, "are unable to account satisfactorily for crucial aspects of the phenomenon of delinquency." Social control theories have more substance.

Dahrendorf, Rolf, "Out of Utopia: Toward a Reorientation of Sociological Analysis," *American Journal of Sociology* 64 (September, 1958): 115–27.

An outline of the common elements of construction in utopian societies. The author suggests that "overconcern with the social system—in the structural-functionalist approach—has led contemporary sociology to a loss of problem consciousness," and he urges that "a conflict model be adopted for the explanation of sociological problems."

Demos, John and Virginia, "Adolescence in Historical Perspective," *Journal of Marriage and the Family* 31 (November, 1969): 632–638.

An examination of various written materials from the period 1800–1875 uncovers (1) almost no usage of the word "adolescence" and (2) only a limited degree of concern with adolescence and its characteristic behaviors. The "discovery" of adolescence, according to the authors, "can be related to certain broad changes in American life," especially in the structure of the family as part of the new urban and industrial order.

Erickson, Maynard L. and LaMar T. Empey, "Court Records, Undetected Delinquency, and Decisionmaking," *The Journal of Criminal Law, Criminology, and Police Science* 54 (December, 1963): 456–69.

A discussion of two problems related to the practical and theoretical decisions made concerning the use of official statistics. (1) The currently increasing emphasis on preventing delinquency, and (2) research on delinquency. The authors conclude that "official records seemed more accurate in reflecting an individual's single most *serious* violation than the pattern of offenses, either *serious* or *nonserious* which he most commonly commits."

Erickson, Maynard, Jack P. Gibbs, and Garry F. Jensen, "The Deterrence Doctrine and the Perceived Certainty of Legal Punishments," *American Sociological Review* (April, 1977): 305–17.

The authors focus on the perceived properties of legal punishments rather than objective properties. Their findings indicate that "the perceived certainty of punishment and perceived seriousness are so highly collinear that their effects on the rates cannot be differentiated." Thus the findings "raise doubts about previous interpretations of the inverse relation among states between the objective certainty of imprisonment and crime rates."

Erickson, Maynard and Jack P. Gibbs, "The Deterrence Question: Some Alternative Methods of Analysis," *Social Science Quarterly* 54:3 (December, 1973): 534–551.

An argument that numerous criminologists have dismissed the deterrence principle prematurely. According to the authors, "they have done so for humanitarian reasons and/or by considering findings limited largely to the death penalty." Humanitarian reasons are relevant, the authors assert, but "it is premature to declare that evidence *refutes* the deterrence principle."

Erickson, Maynard, and Jack P. Gibbs, "Objective and Perceptual Properties of Legal Punishment and the Deterrence Doctrine," *Social Problems* (February, 1978): 253–64.

Unlike most previous deterrence investigations which examine the relation between the objective probability of arrest or imprisonment and the official crime rate among states or counties, this is an examination of the same relation among ten types of crimes in the same jurisdiction—Tucson, Arizona. "The findings indicate that the objective certainty of punishment is not related to the crime rate *through* perceived certainty."

Fox, Richard G., "The XYY Offender: A Modern Myth?" *The Journal of Criminal Law, Criminology and Police Science* 52:1 (March, 1971): 59–70.

An examination of the literature and research on the connection between criminals and an extra Y chromosome in their genetic makeup. The author concludes that "in the present state of knowledge, no one should be subjected to any additional sanction or suffer any other disability on account of the finding in that person of an XYY chromosome abnormality."

Franklin, Jerry and Dan C. Gibbons, "New Directions for Juvenile Courts—Probation Officers' Views," *Crime and Delinquency* 19 (October, 1973): 508–18.

An examination of attitudes of juvenile court counselors in a Pacific Northwest metropolitan community toward due process and restrictions upon the powers of the juvenile court and correctional workers. The workers expressed relatively positive views, and few differences existed between social workers and persons with other training and between supervisors and other workers.

Frease, Dean, "Delinquency, Social Class and the Schools," *Sociology and Social Research* 57 (July, 1973): 443–59.

An argument that social class and social class perceptions on the part of teachers and school administrators foster a delinquent mentality in those who feel rejected, alienated, and outside of "mainstream America."

Gibbs, Jack P., "Another Rush to Judgment on the Deterrence Question," *Criminology* 16 (May, 1978): 22–30.

A comment on Henry N. Pontell's article opposing deterrence theory. The author believes that Pontell was too hasty in his judgment about deterrence theory and that "premature judgments of the deterrence doctrine are not conducive to marshalling compelling evidence."

Gibbs, Jack P., "Conceptions of Deviant Behavior: The Old and the New," *Pacific Sociological Review* 9 (Spring, 1966): 9–14.

A brief history of criminology and the changing conceptions of crime, criminals, deviants, and deviation. According to the author, the most current deviation theory postulates that the actions of a person (or a person himself) are labeled delinquent, criminal, or deviant because of the reactions of the public and/or officials. Many questions remain, however, with this theory.

Gibbs, Jack P., "Crime, Punishment, and Deterrence," *Southwest Social Science Quarterly* 48 (1968): 515–30.

A suggestion that "opinions on punitive reactions to crime reflect an excessive concern with capital punishment and a premature rejection of the deterrence argument." The author presents findings which question "the common assertion that there is no relation between legal reactions to crime and the crime rate."

Goldman, Nathan, "The Differential Selection of Juvenile Offenders for Court Appearance," *The Ambivalent Force*, Arthur Neederhoffer and Abraham S. Blumberg, eds. (Hensdale, Ill., 1976): 183–87.

A study which tested the general hypothesis of the differential selection, by police, of juvenile offenders for court referral. The study also investigated this process of selection.

Goode, Erick, "On Behalf of Labeling Theory," *Social Problems* 22 (June, 1975): 570–83.

An argument in favor of labeling theory and the ways in which delinquency is found to be consistently related to a stigmatization process.

Gottheil, Diane L., "Pretrial Diversion: A Response to the Critics," *Crime and Delinquency* 25 (January, 1979): 65–75.

An examination of pretrial diversion programs and their critics. The author defends diversion and concludes that "what we need are sound evaluation techniques that are workable in the community setting and constructive analyses to advance the knowledge of this relatively new field and to provide models for practitioners and decision makers."

Haller, Mark, "Urban Crime and Criminal Justice: The Chicago Case," *Journal of American History* 57 (1970).

A study of the informal system of criminal justice in Chicago in the period 1900–30 that largely came to replace the formal system of strict law enforcement and due process.

Hellum, Frank, "Juvenile Justice: The Second Revolution," *Crime and Delinquency* 25 (July, 1979): 299–317.

An analysis of the major forces for institutional change confronting the juvenile courts, and a review of recent federal and state responses likely to promote further modifications in the present system. The author also discusses a modified system capable of accommodating demands for basic alterations of juvenile justice.

Henshel, Richard L., "Considerations on the Deterrence and System Capacity Models," *Criminology* 16 (May, 1978): 35–46.

A comment on Henry N. Pontell's article opposing deterrence theory. The author points out that although Pontell's methodology has serious flaws, he should be commended, because "by grappling with the reciprocal relationship of crime rate and criminal justice practice, he has pioneered in an area of the greatest theoretical and practical importance: the manifold relationships holding between crime rate and criminal justice practices."

Jensen, Gary and Raymond Eve, "Sex Differences in Delinquency," *Criminology* 13 (February 1976): 427–48.

An exploration of the relationship between sexual status and self-reported delinquent action. Utilizing questionnaire data from a large sample of black and white adolescents, females were found to report less delinquent activity than males.

Kituse, John I. and Aaron V. Cicourel, "A Note on the Uses of Official Statistics," *Social Problems* II (1963): 131–39.

An attempt to answer two questions: (1) How is "deviant behavior" to be defined sociologically, and (2) what are the relevant rates of deviant behavior which constitute "the facts to be explained"? The authors propose that "these difficulties arise as a consequence of the failure to distinguish between the social conduct which produces a *unit* of behavior and organizational activity which produces a unit in the rate of *deviant* behavior." Official statistics, as a consequence, are unreliable.

Lemert, Edwin M., "Juvenile Justice—Quest and Reality," *Trans-action* 4 (July, 1967): 30–40.

An argument that humanitarian concerns have led to faulty justice for children. According to the author it is the family—even one disturbed by conflict, morality problems, divorce, or death—that is the institution best suited for nurturing children into stable adults. Thus the flow of cases into the juvenile courts must be stopped somehow.

Liazos, Alexander, "School, Alienation, and Delinquency," *Crime and Delinquency* 24 (July, 1978): 355–70.

An argument that schools create delinquents because of their success, not their failure. Under the present economic system, the author insists, schools must prepare youths, especially of the lower classes, for alienated work and lives, and youths become delinquent when they reject this destiny. The author concludes that before schools can prepare people for liberated lives, the society and economy must change first.

Logan, Charles H., "Arrest Rates and Deterrence," *Social Science Quarterly* (December, 1975): 376–89.

A study which finds a negative relation between certainty of legal sanctioning (arrest) and rates of major felony offenses. Nevertheless, according to the author, common sense tells us that legal sanctions do in fact deter many people from committing criminal acts. We must not, however, "make estimates as to the marginal effects on crime rates that will result from given increases or decreases in some form of the criminal sanction."

Logan, Charles H., "Evaluation Research in Crime and Delinquency," *Journal of Criminal Law, Criminology and Police Science* 63 (September 1972): 378–87.

An evaluation of available research on the effectiveness of specific correctional or preventive practices in terms of certain specific methodological criteria. Some obstacles to evaluational research in corrections are reviewed.

Lundman, Richard J., et al., "Delinquency Prevention: A Description and Assessment of Projects Reported in the Professional Literature," *Crime and Delinquency* 22 (July, 1976).

An attempt to solve some of the practical problems associated with describing and assessing efforts at delinquency prevention. Following a search of the professional literature, previous efforts are described and evaluative criteria are suggested and then applied. The authors conclude that it is unlikely that any of these projects successfully prevented delinquent behavior.

Lundman, Richard J., and F. R. Scarpitti, "Delinquency Prevention: Recommendations for Future Projects," *Crime and Delinquency* 24 (April, 1978): 219–225.

A review of forty past or continuing attempts at the prevention of juvenile delinquency. The authors conclude that none of these projects has successfully prevented delinquency, and they discuss a series of nine recommendations for future projects.

McCarthy, Frances B., "Delinquency Dispositions under the Juvenile Justice Standards: The Consequences of a Change of Rationale," *New York University Law Review* (November, 1977): 1093–1118.

An examination of standards promoted by the Joint Commission on Juvenile Justice Standards under the supervision of the Institute of Judicial Administration and the American Bar Association (IJA-ABA), specifically delinquency dispositions. The author concludes that "if one accepts the premises of the juvenile standards, one must reach the inevitable conclusion that juvenile courts should no longer possess jurisdiction over children who commit criminal acts."

McCarthy, Francis B., "Should Juvenile Delinquency Be Abolished?" *Crime and Delinquency* 23 (April, 1977): 196–203.

An argument that criminal courts do a better job of protecting the rights of juveniles than do juvenile courts. Because of this, and for many other substantial reasons, the junveile courts should be abolished.

Martinson, Robert, "What Works—Questions and Answers About Prison Reform," *The Public Interest* (Spring 1974): 22–54.

An intensive examination of the literature on rehabilitative efforts between 1945 and 1967 in a variety of settings and countries. The authors concluded that "with few and isolated exceptions, the rehabilitative efforts that have been reported so far have had no appreciable effect on recidivism."

Merton, Robert K., "Social Structure and Anomie," *American Sociological Review* 3 (October, 1938): 672–82.

An attempt to determine the nonbiological conditions which induce deviations from prescribed patterns of conduct. The author suggests that "certain phases of social structure generate the circumstances in which infringement of social codes constitutes a 'normal' response."

Miller, Walter B., "Lower Class Culture as a Generating Milieu of Gang Delinquency," *Journal of Social Issues* 14 (No. 3, 1958): 5–19.

The author selects one particular kind of "delinquency"—law-violating acts committed by members of adolescent street corner groups in lower-class communities—and attempts to show that "the dominant component of motivation underlying these acts consists in a directed attempt by the actor to adhere to forms of behavior, and to achieve standards of value as they are defined within that community."

Nimmer, Raymond T., and Patricia Ann Krauthaus, "Pretrial Diversion: The Premature Quest for Recognition," *University of Michigan Journal of Law Reform* (Winter, 1976): 206–30.

An argument that current data do not support the belief that diversion achieves its stated goals, and that diversion may in fact be detrimental to defendant's interests. Thus "pretrial diversion data must be critically reassessed and reevaluated."

Noblit, George W., and Thomas W. Collins, "Order and Disruption in a Desegregated High School," *Crime and Delinquency* 24 (July, 1978): 277–289.

A demonstration of the interrelationship among school administrative styles, deterrence, commitment, and disruption. According to the author, "it appears that legitimacy of rules even within a school's bureaucracy needs to be developed through negotiating order with students."

Nye, Ivan F., James F. Short, Jr., and Virgil J. Olson, "Socioeconomic Status and Delinquent Behavior," *American Journal of Sociology* 63 (January, 1958): 381–89.

A questioning of the assumptions frequently made concerning "the differential status distribution of delinquent behavior." Data collected by the authors indicate no significant difference in the amount of delinquent behavior of boys and girls in different socioeconomic strata.

Palmer, Ted, "Martinson Revisited," *Journal of Research in Crime and Delinquency* 12 (July, 1975): 133–52.

A critical examination of the earlier findings of Robert Martinson who postulated that "with few and isolated exceptions, the rehabilitative efforts that have been reported so far have had no appreciable effect on recidivism."

Pontell, Henry N., "Deterrence: Theory Versus Practice," *Criminology* 16 (May, 1978): 3–21.

An anti-deterrence theory paper that argues that increases in crime "may overburden existing legal machinery, and thus cause decreases in the certainty of punishment as a result." The author asserts that "crime may affect certainty of punishment more strongly than certainty of punishment affects the crime rate." Thus legal threats probably do not deter crime.

Quay, Herbert C., "What Corrections Can Correct and How," *Federal Probation* 37 (June, 1973): 3–5.

Quay argues that "under current conditions corrections can only be evaluated on the basis of changes it can demonstrate to have brought about in the social, academic, and vocational behavior of offenders." Community treatment is not necessarily the panacea some would believe, and meaningful correctional reform should continue.

Rector, Milton, and David Gilman, "How Did We Get Here and Where Are We Going?—The Future of the Juvenile Court System," *Criminal Justice Review* 1 (Spring, 1976): 77–90.

A history of the juvenile justice system in the United States and a discussion of the current state of juvenile justice. Suggestions are offered for improving the system.

Rubin, H. Ted, "Retain the Juvenile Court? Legislative Development, Reform Directions, and the Call for Abolition," *Crime and Delinquency* 25 (July, 1979): 281–98.

An analysis of the several trends discernible in today's juvenile court including a more punitive approach to recidivists, an easing of punitiveness toward status offenders, and an expansion of the prosecutor's role. According to the author, although reform is needed, abolition would create massive problems.

Scioli, Frank P., Jr., and Thomas J. Cook, "How Effective are Volunteers?—Public Participation in the Criminal Justice System," *Crime and Delinquency* 22 (April, 1976): 192–200.

A review of the major findings on formal methods of rehabilitation in the courts and correction, and a comparison of the findings with ratings of effectiveness assigned to an informal method—the use of volunteers.

Serrill, Michael S., "Harvard Recidivism Study," *Corrections Magazine* II (November/December 1975): 21–23.

This article is one of several in a special edition of *Corrections Magazine* devoted to a review of Jerome Miller's impact on juvenile corrections in Massachusetts.

Tappan, Paul, "Who is the Criminal?" *American Sociological Review* 12 (1947): 96–102.

An examination of the post World War II protests that orthodox conceptions of crime and the criminal are unfair and antiquated. The author concludes that crime "as legally defined, is a sociologically significant province of study."

Tittle, Charles R., "Comment on Deterrence Theory Versus Practice," *Criminology* 16 (May, 1978): 31–34.

A comment on Henry N. Pontell's article opposing deterrence theory. According to the author, Pontell's work "is seriously out of date, its methodology does not solve the underlying problem it identifies and it is addressed to a straw man."

Tittle, Charles R., "Crime Rates and Legal Sanctions," *Social Problems* 18 (1970): 200–17.

An argument that when all crimes are considered together, strong and consistent negative associations appear between certainty of punishment and crime rates. Thus, increasing the severity of punishment may be useful only in a few very select circumstances.

Tittle, Charles R., and Charles H. Logan, "Sanctions and Deviance: Evidence and Remaining Questions," *Law and Society Review* (Spring, 1973): 371–92.

A review of the deficiencies of capital punishment research and recidivism research. According to the authors, it is now necessary to undertake careful research in an attempt to specify the conditions under which sanctions are likely to be important influences on behavior.

Tomaino, Louis, "The Five Faces of Probation," *Federal Probation* 39 (December, 1975).

Tomaino adapts the Managerial Grid developed by Blake and Mouton to a probation department context. Probation officers are classified into five categories, according to their style of interaction with clients.

Vanagunas, Stanley, "Police Diversion of Juvenile Offenders: An Ambiguous State of the Art," *Federal Probation* 43 (September 1979).

An analysis of juvenile diversion practices of 34 municipal police agencies in order to determine the extent to which juvenile diversion has been formally integrated in contemporary police operations. Results suggest that juvenile diversion has been only partially "institutionalized" within contemporary police practice.

Voss, Harwin, L., "Socioeconomic Status and Reported Delinquent Behavior," *Social Problems* 13 (Winter, 1966): 314–24.

An attempt to locate significant differences in the incidence of delinquent behavior by socioeconomic status. The results of the study indicate that boys "in the higher and lower strata respond differentially to the presentation of delinquent patterns of behavior."

Weiner, Norman C., and Charles V. Willie, "Decisions of Juvenile Officers," *American Journal of Sociology* 77 (September, 1971): 199–21.

An examination of decision making by juvenile officers. The authors look at the effect that race and socioeconomic status, as well as the racial composition and socioeconomic status of the neighborhood, have on juvenile police disposition. The data gathered indicate little, if any influence of any of these factors.

Wenk, E., et al., "Can Violence be Predicted?," *Criminal Delinquency* 18 (1972): 392–402.

A study seeking to develop a classification device for estimating assaultive potential with sufficient accuracy to be useful in correctional program decisions. The attempt was unsuccessful because much of the violent behavior we would wish to predict probably never comes to the attention of researchers, and the part that does is not a representative sample.

Williams, Jay R., and Martin Gold, "From Delinquent Behavior to Official Delinquency," *Social Problems* 20 (Fall, 1972): 209–29.

The authors make a conceptual distinction between delinquent behavior and official delinquency. They examine data from a national sample of 13- to 16-year-old boys and girls for empirical evidence of this conceptual distinction. Their findings indicate that "the distribution of official delinquency among categories of sex, age, race, and socio-economic status does not parallel the distribution of delinquent behavior."

Wizner, Stephen and Mary F. Keller, "The Penal Model of Juvenile Justice: Is Juvenile Court Delinquency Jurisdiction Obsolete?" *New York University Law Review* (November, 1977): 1120–34.

An examination of the new juvenile court standards proposed by the Institute of Judicial Administration–American Bar Association (IJA-ABA) Joint Commission on Juvenile Justice Standards, specifically sanctions, dispositions, and dispositional procedures. The authors argue that "juvenile court delinquency jurisdiction should be abolished and the jurisdiction of the juvenile court reserved for the protection of abused, neglected, and emotionally disturbed children."

Zimring, Franklin, "Measuring the Impact of Pretrial Diversion," *University of Chicago Law Review* (Winter, 1974): 224–42.

An effort to describe the effects of the Manhattan Court Employment Project "after-the-fact matching exercise" in diversion, the current state of knowledge of the impact of diversion programs, and the impressions held by the Project's staff and the general public regarding the Project's goals. According to the author this paper "is a plea for experimentation in law reform."

BOOKS

Abbott, Grace, *The Child and the State*, 2 vols. (Chicago, 1938).

A collection of original documents and source material from the late eighteenth century to the present time which give a realistic picture of family relationships, the role of children in industrial development, and the effects of changing society upon children.

Abell, Aaron I., *American Catholicism and Social Action: A Search for Social Justice, 1865–1950* (South Bend, Ind., 1963).

A comprehensive study of the Catholic social movement in the United States from 1865 to 1950. The author discusses the "dynamic interplay of 'charity' or social service, labor association, and state action as the great propulsive influences in social reform."

Addams, Jane, *The Spirit of Youth and the City Streets* (New York, 1909).

An examination of a city's obligation to concern itself with the insatiable desire that children have for play. Her thesis is that if this desire is recognized and subsequently satisfied by cities, the numbers of children who fall victim to "evil ways" will diminish astonishingly.

Amos, William E. and Charles F. Wellford, eds., *Delinquency Prevention: Theory and Practice* (Englewood Cliffs, N.J., 1967).

A summary of developments in delinquency prevention and an indication of the direction of future trends. The editors emphasize the sociological implications of prevention programs, but they do discuss other perspectives.

Aries, Phillipe, *Centuries of Childhood* (New York, 1962).

A study of the development of ideas about children and child care between the Middle Ages and the early nineteenth century.

Bailyn, Bernard, *Education in the Forming of American Society* (Chapel Hill, N.C., 1960).

An analysis of the roots of American education and a clear picture of the processes by which the public school was eventually singled out to be the dominant institution of education.

Ban, John R., and Lewis M. Ciminillo, *Violence and Vandalism in Public Education* (Danville, Ill., 1977).

An overview of violence and vandalism in the schools as well as an examination of the numerous elements allied with school violence. The authors also present a "blueprint for action that schools can follow as they pursue measures of crime prevention and control."

Becker, Howard S., *Outsiders: Studies in the Sociology of Deviance* (New York, 1966).

A compilation of articles from the *Journal of the Society for the Study of Social Problems* which defines deviancy by "the audience which eventually determines whether or not any episode of behavior or any class of episodes is labeled deviant."

Blumberg, Abraham, *Criminal Justice: Issues and Ironies*, 2nd ed. (New York, 1979).

A "radical criminology" view of the criminal justice system. Adult and juvenile courts are seen as bureaucracies with judges, prosecutors, defense attorneys, probation officers and defendants all playing prescribed roles.

Breckenridge, Sophonisba P., ed., *Family Welfare in a Metropolitan Community: Selected Case Records* (Chicago, 1924).

Forty-four cases are selected from the records of two social agencies in Chicago in the field of family welfare work as typical of social agency problems. The complete history of each case is given as well as the method of treatment.

Bremner, Robert H., et al., eds., *Children and Youth in America: A Documentary History,* 2 vols. (Cambridge, Mass., 1970).

A history of public policy toward children and youth in America from Colonial times to the present.

Carter, Robert M., and Malcolm W. Klein, *Back on the Street: The Diversion of Juvenile Offenders* (Englewood Cliffs, N.J., 1976).

A collection of statements, essays, and discussions on diversion, its effectiveness, its desirability, labeling theory, police discretion, and youth service bureaus.

Cavan, Ruth Shonle, and Theodore N. Ferdinand, *Juvenile Delinquency,* 3d ed. (New York, 1975).

An attempt to relate the evidence of delinquency to four broad perspectives in sociological theory. The authors integrate recent advances in the typological description of delinquency into their argument, and they briefly examine psychological and social psychological interpretations of delinquency. They also integrate into the narrative recent statistics from state and federal agencies.

Chambliss, William J., and Milton Mankoff, eds. *Whose Law? What Order?* (New York, 1976).

A "conflict criminology" approach that presents a critical analysis of functional and conflict theories in criminology. The book examines the development of legal norms in Western society, and discusses the economic and political context within which legal categories and specific legislation have evolved. The authors also consider law enforcement and its selective nature, and the nature of the American crime problem.

Chappell, Duncan, and John Monahan, *Violence and Criminal Justice* (Lexington, Mass., 1975).

Nine articles that focus on particular facets of violence felt to present immediate and significant problems for the criminal justice system in the Pacific Northwest. The authors focus on three principal issues facing the criminal justice system in the future: (1) victims of violence, (2) violence committed by the criminal justice system in the name of justice, and (3) the beneficial consequences of the politicization of offenders.

Cicourel, Aaron V., and John I. Kitsuse, *The Educational Decision Makers* (Indianapolis, 1963).

An analysis of the strategies by which teachers, counselors, and other school personnel discourage upward mobility of students from the underclass. One strategy is the use of tests designed to convince certain students that they are intellectually deficient.

Clark, Kenneth B., *Dark Ghetto: Dilemmas of Social Power* (New York, 1965).

An analysis of the pathologies of Harlem and of the poverty, crime, low aspirations, family instability, and exploitation of the "social victims of a world for which they are not responsible."

Clemmer, Donald, *The Prison Community,* 3d ed. (Indianapolis, 1971).

Classic study of the formal and informal social organization of a prison in the 1930s.

Annotated Bibliography

Cloward, Richard A., and Lloyd E. Ohlin, *Delinquency and Opportunity: A Theory of Delinquent Gangs* (New York, 1960).

Opportunity, meaning a differential access throughout the social structure, is the basic variable used by the authors to account for a set of experiences they consider indispensable to the onset of sustained patterns of delinquent conduct.

Cohen, Albert K., *Delinquent Boys: The Culture of the Gang* (New York, 1955).

A diagnostic analysis of working-class and middle-class subcultures of society and of how their differing standards affect youth. The author promotes the theory that the frustrations of working-class children are reinforced by middle-class standards that most under-class youth cannot meet. Accordingly, a hostile subculture of delinquency is created, a subculture that must be understood to be remedied.

Cortes, J. B., and F. N. Gatti, *Delinquency and Crime: A Biopsychosocial Approach* (New York, 1972).

A review and analysis of the biological, psychological, and social factors associated with juvenile delinquency and crime.

Cressey, Donald R., and Robert A. McDermott, *Diversion for the Juvenile Justice System* (Ann Arbor, Mich., 1973).

A detailed review of a 1972 summer project on diversion of youth from the California juvenile justice system. The mission of the project was "to explore, probe, and define issues and research problems likely to arise in a wider-range study of diversion processes taking place after juveniles first come into contact with juvenile court officials."

Davenport, Charles B., *Heredity in Relation to Eugenics* (New York, 1911).

A treatment of the meanings, nature, importance, and aims of eugenics. The author also describes eugenics methods, how family traits are inherited, the geographical distribution of inheritable traits, migrations and their eugenic significance, the study of American families, and the organization of applied eugenics.

Davies, John D., *Phrenology: Fad and Science* (New Haven, Conn., 1955).

An examination of the original, scientific aspects of phrenology rather than of its tangential evolution into a cult of personal involvement and social reform. Davies demonstrates that the now-disdained movement permeated and influenced many currents of American thought between 1825 and 1860.

de Mause, Lloyd, *The History of Childhood* (New York, 1974).

Ten authoritative and original essays covering a history of child rearing in the Western world from the late Roman period to the nineteenth century.

Demos, John, *A Little Commonwealth: Family Life in the Plymouth Colony* (New York, 1970).

A history of the Plymouth Colony with an account of the physical setting of family life. Demos portrays the family as a structure of roles and relationships emphasizing those of husband and wife, parent and child, master and servant.

Dixon, Michael, and William E. Wright, *Juvenile Delinquency Prevention Programs: An Evaluation of Policy Related Research on the Effectiveness of Prevention Programs* (Nashville, Tenn., 1975).

A survey of approximately 6,600 abstracts of studies published between 1965 and 1975 which describe delinquency prevention services that do not remove youth from their home community. The overview revealed that certain types of prevention and treatment projects—recreational programs, guided group interaction, social casework, and detached worker projects—have failed to show evidence of effectiveness and should be discarded. Community treatment programs, on the other hand, as well as the use of volunteers, diversion, youth service bureaus, and special school projects were successful and should be continued.

Donovan, Frank R., *Wild Kids: How Youth Has Shocked Its Elders—Then and Now* (Harrisburg, Pa., 1967).

A history of juvenile delinquency from the dawn of civilization to the present. According to Donovan, "todays 'wild kids' are no wilder than those of previous generations."

Duffee, David, Frederick Hussey, and John Kramer, *Criminal Justice: Organization, Structure and Analysis* (Englewood Cliffs, N.J., 1978).

A discussion of "related but different views of the criminal justice 'system': the network of agencies and processes that are responsible for certain types of crime prevention, investigation, apprehension, prosecution, defense, conviction, and sentencing and the implementation of dispositional alternatives."

Eisner, Victor, *The Delinquency Label: The Epidemiology of Juvenile Delinquency* (New York, 1969).

An examination of the findings of a series of delinquency studies in San Francisco between 1963 and 1967. Eisner concludes that a delinquent is "any person whom society labels as delinquent" and juvenile delinquency is a phenomenon that "cannot be equated with deviant behavior."

Eissler, K. R., ed., *Searchlights on Delinquency* (New York, 1949).

A collection of articles which represent a cross-section of psychoanalytic theory and treatment of delinquency.

Empey, Lamar T., *American Delinquency: Its Meaning and Construction* (Homewood, Ill., 1978).

A clearly stated discussion of the theories of delinquency causation including control, cultural deviance, strain, symbolic interaction, and labeling. The evolution of the American response to delinquency is also detailed as is the ongoing revolution of the juvenile court system.

Empey, Lamar T., *Explaining Delinquency: Construction, Test, and Reformation of a Sociological Theory* (Lexington, Mass., 1971).

An attempt to test the class-biased sociological theory which views official delinquency as a lower-class phenomenon.

Empey, Lamar T., and Maynard L. Erickson, *The Provo Experiment: Evaluating Community Control and Delinquency* (Lexington, Mass., 1972).

An analysis of one of the first attempts to provide a community alternative to incarceration for recidivists. The experiment's assumptions are explained first and this is followed by a discussion of the program's impact.

Empey, Lamar T., and Steven Lubeck, *The Silverlake Experiment: Testing Delinquency Theory and Community Intervention* (Chicago, 1971).

Tests a number of postulates and theorems from sociological delinquency theory by comparing two samples of male youth drawn from the Los Angeles Boys' Republic. The control group remained in the Republic, the experimental group lived with a resident staff in a community location.

Erikson, Erik H., "Identity and the Life Cycle," *Psychological Issues* (New York, 1959).

A clear and persuasive statement of Erikson's theories of delinquency formation.

Erikson, Kai, *Wayward Puritans: A Study in the Sociology of Deviance* (New York, 1966).

Erikson uses the Puritan settlement in seventeenth-century Massachusetts as a setting in which to examine several ideas about deviant behavior in society. Combining sociology and history he draws on the records of the Bay Colony to illustrate how deviant behavior fits into the texture of social life generally.

Eysenck, Hans, *Crime and Personality* (Boston, 1964).

The author attempts to "work out a theory of antisocial conduct, relate this to personality, and indicate some of the biological factors underlying both personality and criminality," which he assumes to be "the most widespread expression of antisocial conduct."

Faris, Robert E. L., *Chicago Sociology 1920–1932* (Chicago, 1970).

This history of the Chicago school of sociology and its rivals describes the severing of relationships between the schools of sociology and social welfare.

Fisher, Berenice, *Industrial Education: American Ideals and Institutions* (Madison, Wis., 1967).

An exposition of the main approaches to, and ideals of, the education of the working man in this country.

Flicker, Barbara D., *Standards for Juvenile Justice: A Summary and Analysis,* Institute of Judicial Administration–American Bar Association Juvenile Justice Standards Project (Cambridge, Mass., 1977).

Contains lists of proposed changes in the areas of juvenile court process and delinquency prevention. The author provides extensive commentary on each of the proposed standards.

Frankel, M. E., *Criminal Sentences: Law Without Order* (New York, 1973).

A criticism of the manner in which prisoners are sentenced, and a description of existing and possible remedies. The author discusses proposals for tribunals and councils on sentencing, and for controlling extreme and emotional judicial sentences.

Gaylin, Willard, *Partial Justice: A Study of Bias in Sentencing* (New York, 1974).

The author seeks to document disparities in sentencing theory and practice that pervade the legal system. He urges several reforms including follow-up reports to teach educable judges how to sentence more fairly; statements of sentencing reasons in each case; appellate review of sentences; and consideration that long sentences breed more crime.

Giallombardo, Rose, ed., *Juvenile Delinquency: A Book of Readings* (New York, 1966).

A collection of articles on juvenile delinquency designed for college students. The perspective is sociological, and the articles "either are important research contributions or provide valuable theoretical analysis and description."

Gibbens, T.C.N., and R. H. Ahrenfeldt, *Cultural Factors in Delinquency* (Philadelphia, 1966).

A discussion of the contribution of cultural factors to juvenile delinquency. Definitions of delinquency are offered and the factors of sex, age, social class, role of the police, subcultures, internal controls, statistics, research, and deterrence programs are examined.

Gibbons, Don. C., *Delinquent Behavior*, 2nd ed. (Englewood Cliffs, N.J., 1976).

A general overview of the delinquency problem. The author emphasizes sociological factors, but does discuss psychological factors leading to delinquent behavior as well. He points out the troublesome nature of defining delinquency and asks for more research.

Glaser, Daniel, *The Effectiveness of a Prison and Parole System* (Indianapolis, 1964).

An attempt to achieve three broad objectives: "1. to determine specifically the failure rates of different types of offenders released from prison; 2. to determine the factors involved in their reversion or non-reversion to crime . . . ; 3. to determine what practicable measures and programs are best suited to reduce recidivism."

Glasser, William, *Reality Therapy: A New Approach to Psychiatry* (New York, 1965).

A discussion of the many uses to which reality therapy can be put in the area of psychiatry, especially when the patients are teenage girls.

Glueck, Sheldon and Eleanor, *Physique and Delinquency* (New York, 1956).

An attempt to establish physical criteria for distinguishing delinquent from non-delinquent youths. According to the authors, a large number of delinquent boys are of the "mesomorph" (muscular) group and relatively few are "ectomorphs" (thin) or "endomorphs" (fat) or "balanced."

Goddard, Henry H., *The Kallekak Family* (New York, 1912).

A study of the hereditary characteristics of feeble-mindedness, which considers the relation of feeble-mindedness to crime and immorality as well as the question of how to care for "defectives."

Goffman, Erving, *Asylums* (New York, 1962).

Four essays which describe the social situations common to total institutions; that is, institutions which provide for the essential needs of the individuals entrusted by society to their maintenance and control such as mental hospitals, long-term care facilities, and correctional institutions.

Gold, Martin, *Delinquent Behavior in an American City* (Belmont, Calif., 1970).

A study of delinquency in Flint, Michigan, which stresses the difference between delinquency and delinquent behavior. The author concludes that the idea of "the delinquent" is invalid because almost everyone breaks the law and because uniform delinquency does not exist.

Gossett, Thomas F., *Race: The History of an Idea in America* (Dallas, 1963).

A historical survey of the evolution of ideas about race in American history.

Gove, Walter R., ed., *The Labeling of Deviance: Evaluating a Perspective,* 2nd ed. (Beverly Hills, Calif., 1980).

An attempt to empirically assess labeling theory by carefully examining the empirical evidence bearing on the labeling perspective in the eight areas of deviant behavior to which the perspective has been most commonly applied.

Grob, Gerald N., *The State and the Mentally Ill* (Chapel Hill, N.C., 1966).

A study of a pioneer state hospital for the mentally ill and of the interacting evolution of psychiatric theory and practice, state policy, and public attitudes with respect to mental illness.

Guggenheim, Martin, *A Call to Abolish the Juvenile Justice System,* Children's Rights Report II (New York, 1978).

A strong argument for the abolition of the juvenile court. The author claims that the court neither protects children nor adheres to the rule of law. Moreover, the system harms more children than it helps.

Hahn, Paul H., *The Juvenile Offender and the Law* (Cincinnati, 1971).

An attempt to provide police officers with the background and information "necessary to understand from a legal and a behavioral standpoint the phenomenon that is so commonly called juvenile delinquency." The author believes that "the good enforcement officer must understand juvenile delinquency and the law applying to it just as much if not more than judges, lawyers, and court personnel."

Hasenfeld, Yeheskel, and Richard A. English, eds., *Human Service Organizations: A Book of Readings* (Ann Arbor, Mich., 1974).

A collection of articles that examines some of the key dimensions of human service organizations and their interrelationships, and provides "a unique conceptual framework for the analysis and understanding of these organizations."

Haskell, Martin R., and Lewis Yoblonsky, *Crime and Delinquency* (Chicago, 1970).

A description of the nature and extent of crime and delinquency in America with specific recommendations for reducing the rates of both problems. Causes of delinquency, the juvenile court, the socialization process, gangs and subcultures, and treatment and control are discussed.

Hawes, Joseph M., *Children in Urban Society: Juvenile Delinquency in Nineteenth Century America* (New York, 1971).

A history of juvenile delinquency in nineteenth-century America which emphasizes the role of the city and the views that Americans of the last century had of juvenile delinquency.

Hewitt, John P., *Social Stratification and Deviant Behavior* (New York, 1970).

An explanation of social stratification and deviant behavior and a demonstration of the relationship between the two concepts as explained by a third concept, self-esteem.

Higham, John, *Strangers in the Land* (New York, 1955).

An examination of the lot of the immigrants arriving in America in successive population shifts, and more particularly of the varying reactions of "native" Americans to the newcomers. The author dissects the various elements which formed this hostility to the immigrants—the fear of Anglo-Saxon tradition, anti-Semitism, and the suspicion of the European radical.

Hirchi, Travis, *Causes of Delinquency* (Berkeley, 1969).

The author attempts to state and test the theory of delinquency that postulates that delinquents are youths who are relatively free of the intimate attachments, aspirations, and moral beliefs that bind most people to life within the law.

Hooten, Ernest A., *Crime and the Man* (Cambridge, 1939).

A study of the physical characteristics of criminals, which attempts to discover whether these characteristics are related to antisocial conduct. He concludes that they are.

Jessor, Richard, et al., *Society, Personality and Deviant Behavior: A Study of a Tri-Ethnic Community* (New York, 1968).

An interdisciplinary field research project conducted in a small tri-ethnic (Anglo, Spanish, Indian) community in southwestern Colorado. The investigation focused on drinking problems and other patterns of deviant behavior.

Johnson, Richard E., *Juvenile Delinquency and Its Origins* (Cambridge, 1979).

This monograph reports the evolution of a new theoretical model for the explanation of juvenile delinquency. The author reviews contemporary and past theoretical models of delinquency and then presents his new model which is based on balance theory.

Johnson, Thomas A., *Introduction to the Juvenile Justice System* (St. Paul, Minn., 1975).

An overview of the juvenile justice system which provides discussions of the development, jurisdiction, role, responsibilities, administration, and organization of the juvenile court. The author also examines the role of the probation officer, court services, strategies of treatment, the police, the schools and the future.

Kassebaum, Gene, *Delinquency and Social Policy* (Englewood Cliffs, N.J., 1974).

A sociological approach to the phenomena of juvenile delinquency and the policies of control that confront it. The author's intent is to provide materials for a critical perspective on juvenile crime prevention and control programs. The emphasis is on programs—what thinking a program is based on, who is included, how it operates, and its measurable effects.

Kassebaum, Gene, David Ward and Daniel Wilner, *Prison Treatment and Parole Survival* (New York, 1971).

A report on research undertaken in a California State Prison. Group counseling was undertaken to determine its effect upon parolee performance. The report concluded that group counseling did not affect parole performance.

Katkin, Daniel, et al., *Juvenile Delinquency and the Juvenile Justice System* (North Scituate, Mass., 1976).

A thorough examination of delinquency and the often astonishingly inequitous juvenile justice system.

Katz, Michael, *The Irony of Urban School Reform* (Cambridge, Mass., 1968).

An examination of the failure of educational reformers due to their increasing isolation from society and their growing bureaucratization.

Killinger, George G. and Paul F. Cromwell, Jr., eds., *Corrections in the Community: Alternatives to Imprisonment—Selected Readings* (St. Paul, Minn., 1974).

Analyses of probation, parole, diversion and community based corrections which provide a comprehensive view of corrections outside the prison.

Klein, Malcolm and Kathie S. Teilmann, *Pivotal Ingredients of Police Juvenile Diversion Programs* (Washington, D.C., 1976).

A discussion of the elements, factors, personnel and policies needed by the police to implement a successful diversion program.

Knight, Edgar W., *A Documentary History of Education in the South Before 1860,* 5 vols. (Chapel Hill, N.C., 1949 53).

An examination of European influences on the education of the South, from the founding of Jamestown to the Civil War.

Kvareceus, William C., and Walter Miller, *Delinquent Behavior: Culture and the Individual* (Washington, D.C., 1959).

A broadly based analysis of the influences of culture on the individual and on the principles and practices of delinquent behavior.

Kvaraceus, William C., *Juvenile Delinquency* (Washington, D.C., 1958).

An attempt to draw from research material on juvenile delinquency that which seemed to the author to give the most help to classroom teachers in their day-to-day dealings with troubled youths.

Laslett, Peter, *Household and Family in Past Time* (Cambridge, 1972).

Comparative studies in the size and structure of the domestic group over the last three centuries in England, France, Serbia, Japan, and colonial North America, with further materials from Western Europe. Also contains an analytical introduction on the history of the family.

Laslett, Peter, *The World We Have Lost: England Before the Industrial Age* (New York, 1965).

A sociological history of the English seventeenth century using demographic techniques.

Lefcourt, Robert, *Law Against the People* (New York, 1971).

A collection of essays arguing that the legal system of the United States is bankrupt and that the law "is against 'the people'; that law schools only turn out capitalist lawyers; and that the underclass can never hope to win lawsuits." Thus, a traumatic break with the jurisprudence of the past is needed.

Levin, Mark M. and Rosemary C. Sarri, *Juvenile Delinquency: A Comparative Analysis of Legal Codes in the United States* (Ann Arbor, Mich., 1974).

A report by the National Assessment of Juvenile Corrections which documents many contemporary issues and problems in juvenile law and identifies areas of considerable change. The results of the study help make it possible to efficiently compare the patterns and directions of statutory change in all the states.

Lipton, Douglas, Robert Martinson and Judith Wilks, *The Effectiveness of Correctional Treatment* (New York, 1976).

A critical review of many correctional research projects undertaken between 1945 and 1967. The authors concluded that few if any correctional programs contributed significantly to rehabilitation of offenders.

Lou, Herbert H., *Juvenile Courts in the United States* (Chapel Hill, N.C., 1927).

A history of the development of the juvenile courts and the fight to maintain their status. The organization of the courts, as well as the processes before hearing, and the working of the courts during the 1920s is described in detail.

Lubove, Roy, *The Professional Altruist: The Emergence of Social Work as a Career 1880–1930* (Cambridge, 1965).

An analysis of the way in which the traditional practices of private charity organizations became outmoded as the process of urbanization changed family and neighborhood life, and as newer knowledge in the behavioral and social sciences gave deeper insight to understanding and influencing human behavior.

McCary, James, *Human Sexuality*, 2nd ed. (New York, 1973).

A consideration of every aspect of sex from sex education, through conception, pregnancy, and birth, with detailed material on sexual aberrations and disorders and a comprehensive section on the techniques of sexual intercourse.

McDermott, M. Joan, *Criminal Victimization in Urban Schools* (Washington, D.C., 1979).

A victimization survey involving students 12 years of age or older and teachers or other school personnel inside schools in 26 American cities. Most of the in-school crime was either petty theft or assault resulting in minor injury to the victim. The majority of in-school victimizations were reported by students.

McEachern, Alexander, and Edward Taylor, *SIMBAD: Simulation as a Basis for Social Agent's Decisions* Rev. (Los Angeles, 1967).

A report on large scale research to determine the effects of probation treatment on a large population of juveniles. A model was developed to predict outcomes for delinquents who were subjected to various treatment strategies.

MacIver, Robert M., *The Prevention and Control of Delinquency* (New York, 1966).

A discussion of the conditions under which juvenile delinquency is most likely to occur, and suggestions of various strategies for better prevention and control of this social problem.

March, James G. and Herbert Simon, *Organizations* (New York, 1958).

The seminal work on modern organization theory. The authors translate various concepts, approaches, and "proverbs" into operational terms, which can be tested by hypothetical research methods.

Matza, David, *Becoming Deviant* (Englewood Cliffs, N.J., 1969).

An examination of the main themes of deviant behavior as interpreted by three major sociological viewpoints: the Chicago school, the functionalists, and a contemporary neo-Chicagoan approach. The author also describes the process of becoming deviant and shows various ways deviancy has been conceived.

Matza, David, *Delinquency and Drift* (New York, 1964).

Matza formulates a general theory of delinquency which postulates that the most important) conditions involve the relationship of the drifting adolescent to the legal system. Most delinquency occurs, Matza claims, because the ordinary code of criminal justice does not apply to children and they cannot claim its safeguards.

Mennel, Robert M., *Thorns and Thistles: Juvenile Delinquents and the United States 1825–1940* (Hanover, N.H., 1973).

An analysis of society's changing perception and changing solutions to the problem of delinquency. Those perceptions and solutions, according to Mennel, became integral parts of class conflict in American society and must be understood in that context.

Motley, Willard, *Knock on Any Door* (New York, 1947).

This is the case history of a Chicago boy whose early tendencies toward decency were slowly beaten down by his contacts with life along Chicago's streets. Eventually he became a killer and died in the electric chair.

National Advisory Commission on Criminal Justice Standards, *Corrections* (Washington, 1973).

An extensive report dealing with the problems and prospects of corrections including the setting for corrections, the rights of offenders, diversion, principles of sentencing, classification of offenders, the need for changes, elements basic to improvement, and the priorities and strategies needed to reduce crime and protect the community.

National Advisory Committee on Criminal Justice Standards, *Juvenile Justice and Delinquency Prevention: Report of the Task Force on Juvenile Justice and Delinquency Prevention* (Washington, 1976).

A presentation of the national standards for juvenile justice and delinquency prevention as developed by a task force working for the Law Enforcement Assistance Administration. The task force believed that their task "represented an outstanding opportunity to establish standards that would insure fairness and consistency and assure adequate levels of service to deal with the problems of juvenile justice throughout the nation."

National Institute of Law Enforcement and Criminal Justice, *The Deterrent Effectiveness of Criminal Justice Sanction Strategies: Summary Report* by Solomon Kobren and others (Washington, D.C., 1972).

An initial effort to measure the relationship between the sanctioning activities of criminal justice and the magnitude of the crime problem. The findings indicated that higher sanction levels were almost uniformly associated with lower crime levels but that social factors had considerably greater effect on crime levels than did the operations of criminal justice.

Newman, Graeme, *The Punishment Response* (New York, 1978).

An examination of various theories and philosophies that attempt to define the use of punishment throughout history.

Niederhoffer, Arthur, and Abraham S. Blumberg, eds., *The Ambivalent Force: Perspectives on the Police,* 2nd ed. (Hinsdale, Ill., 1976).

A collection of articles which brings together the "variegated approaches of the academic behavioral scientist, the journalist, the psychiatrist, the lawyer, the policeman, the historian, and the administrator in their assessments of some major features of the police occupation and role."

Ohlin, Lloyd, et al., *Juvenile Correctional Reform in Massachusetts* (Washington, D.C., 1977).

A description of the conditions in Massachusetts correctional institutions that led to the Massachusetts experiment in deinstitutionalization. The possibility of other states adopting the plan is also discussed.

Park, Robert E., and Ernest W. Burgess, eds., *The City* (Chicago, 1925).

Annotated Bibliography

Various sociological papers which study human nature and social life under modern city conditions including the growth of the city, an ecological approach to the study of the human community, and community organization and juvenile delinquency.

Pinchbeck, Ivy and Margaret Hewitt, *Children in English Society*, 2 vols. (London, 1969).

A study of the social concern for children in England, from the Tudor paternalism of the mid-sixteenth century to the legislation of the welfare state of the mid-twentieth century.

Platt, Anthony M., *The Child Savers: The Invention of Delinquency* (Chicago, 1969).

An analysis of the early "child savers" who helped found professional social work, this book also surveys delinquency from the nineteenth century to the present and emphasizes the major role played by women. The changing philosophy and accompanying legislation relating to the underage lawbreaker is also discussed.

The President's Commission on Law Enforcement and Administration of Justice, *Juvenile Delinquency and Youth Crime: Report on Juvenile Justice and Consultants Papers* (Washington, D.C., 1967).

A collection of articles by the country's top authorities on juvenile delinquency covering such topics as prevention, juvenile courts and probation services, male delinquency, delinquency trends, affluence and crime, delinquent careers, methods of prediction, and the role of the family, schools, religion, and the community.

Presthus, Robert, *The Organizational Society*, 2d ed. (New York, 1978).

An analysis of the varieties of methods of individual adaptation to organizational life, and the consequences of such adaptations for the organization.

Quay, Herbert C., *Juvenile Delinquency: Research and Theory* (Princeton, N.J., 1965).

A critical survey of theory, research, and research method in juvenile delinquency. The book serves as a handbook of theory and research and also provides a summing up of the past and offers guidelines for future investigations.

Reeves, Margaret, *Training Schools for Delinquent Girls* (New York, 1929).

A study by the Russell Sage Foundation of state, county, and municipal training schools and a few private training schools for delinquent girls throughout the United States.

Ridgway, V. F., "Dysfunctional Consequences of Performance Measurements," *Some Theories of Organization*, Albert H. Rubenstein and Chadwick J. Haberstroh, eds. (Homewood, Ill., 1960).

A discussion of goal displacement and of the behavioral consequences of instruments designed to measure performance.

Rogers, Carl, *Carl Rogers on Encounter Groups* (New York, 1970).

A history of encounter groups as well as a discussion of the author's experiences in encounter groups. The author presents examples to demonstrate how a person experiences change after time in an encounter group and how a person combats loneliness through group life.

Romig, Dennis A., *Justice for Our Children* (Lexington, Mass., 1978).

A study of what rehabilitates delinquent children and what does not, and why, in each case. "Recommendations are made in every area of delinquency programming for the upgrading of existing treatment approaches." Moreover, an ideal program is developed and offered for consideration.

Rosen, George, *Madness in Society: Chapters in the Historical Sociology of Mental Illness* (New York, 1969).

Studies of the mentally ill, however defined, in societies at different historical periods, and the social, psychological, and cultural factors that have determined or caused madness.

Ross, Dorothy, G. *Stanley Hall: The Psychologist as Prophet* (Chicago, 1972).

A biographical study of the man who is often credited with being cofounder with William James of academic psychological disciplines in America.

Rowles, Burton J., *The Lady at Box 99* (Greenwich, Conn., 1962).

A biography of Miriam Van Waters which details her association with Massachusetts' only minimum, medium, and maximum security institution for female offenders. The book dwells on Water's belief that the re-education and redemption of girl and women prisoners was the best reason for the Reformatory's existence.

Rubin, H. Ted, *The Courts: Fulcrum of the Justice System* (Pacific Palisades, Calif., 1976).

An attempt "to describe contemporary courts, their progress, problems, and processes. Its basic focus is the state and local court system. Its emphasis is a wide search for policies and strategies to enhance the administration of justice. It describes, criticizes, prescribes."

Sanders, Wiley B., ed., *Juvenile Offenders for a Thousand Years* (Chapel Hill, N.C., 1970).

Readings from Anglo-Saxon times to 1900 which make rare and valuable books, pamphlets, and other data more accessible to teachers, social scientists, judges, and the general public. According to Sanders "as far back as written records go, children who have broken the law have been treated...more leniently than have adult offenders."

Sarri, Rosemary, and Yaheskel Hasenfeld, eds., *Brought to Justice? Juveniles, the Courts and the Law* (Ann Arbor, Mich., 1976).

A survey of structure and practice in a large national sample of courts. It is directed to judges and juvenile court staff, legislators, other juvenile justice personnel, researchers interested in youth and justice, and interested laypersons.

Schlossman, Steven L., *Love and the American Delinquent* (Chicago, 1977).

Annotated Bibliography

An examination of the early application of the child-saving philosophy as reflected in the operations of institutional facilities. The author focuses on the period from 1825 to 1920. He suggests that this philosophy had relatively little impact on the day-to-day operations of residential facilities.

Schrag, Clarence, *Crime and Justice: American Style* (Washington, D.C., 1971).

An examination of "the results of a literature search on crime and justice in American society." According to the author, "an attempt was made to deal with this material by identifying major assumptions, frames of reference, and lines of reasoning." The author concluded that "the term system when applied to the field of justice is mainly a euphemism."

Schur, Edwin M., *Labeling Deviant Behavior* (New York, 1971).

An assessment of the labeling approach to deviance and social control: "what it does and does not assert, its actual and potential contributions, its limitations, and how it fits in with other major approaches to the analysis of deviance and control."

Schur, Edwin M., *Radical Nonintervention: Rethinking the Delinquency Problem* (Englewood Cliffs, N.J., 1973).

An attack on current juvenile delinquency policy. According to the author, a radical change of major institutions and prevailing cultural values and an acceptance of greater diversity of behavior is necessary.

Shaw, Clifford R., *The Jack Roller: A Delinquent Boy's Own Story* (Chicago, 1930).

An extensive case study of a single delinquent boy who robs drunks and homosexuals. It begins with his social and cultural background, continues with the boy's own story as he wrote it, and concludes with a discussion of the case.

Shaw, Clifford R., and Henry D. McKay, *Social Factors in Juvenile Delinquency* (Washington, D.C., 1931).

An examination of the environmental factors contributing to juvenile delinquency which leads the authors to conclude that delinquents "tend to be concentrated in areas adjacent to the central business district and to heavily industrial areas."

Sheldon, William H., *Varieties of Delinquent Youth* (New York, 1949).

An argument that juvenile delinquency is caused solely by "biological irresponsibility," that delinquency is the outgrowth of the weakening of the human stock, and that "our whole society is delinquent in that it is allowing bad reproduction to drive out good."

Slater, Philip, *The Pursuit of Loneliness: American Culture at the Breaking Point* (Boston, 1970).

A depiction of Americans as a disturbed and unhappy people engaging in intergroup struggles that are sapping their energies even while real needs, psychic as well as physical, are being ignored.

Sloan, Irving J., *Youth and the Law: Rights, Privileges and Obligations* (New York, 1970).

An attempt to give young people "an opportunity to gain some measure of knowledge about their legal rights in a democratic society."

Stevenson, George S., and Gesses Smith, *Child Guidance Clinics: A Quarter Century of Development* (New York, 1934).

A depiction of the roots of the child-guidance movement, the development of clinics from 1921–1933, the general pattern of their operation and influence, and the problems of the future.

Stinchcombe, Arthur, *Rebellion in a High School* (Chicago, 1964).

The author argues that the causes of rebellious students lie partly in the educational system itself. He demonstrates that the basic problem is one of distortion between the students' own knowledge of our society and the image of that society which the school presents. Pressures to succeed, moreover, create the tensions which produce violence.

Stratton, John R. and Robert M. Terry, eds., *Prevention of Delinquency: Problems and Programs* (New York, 1968).

A comprehensive overview of the nature of prevention and an illustration of issues and problems confronting those concerned with the control and prevention of delinquency.

Street, David, Robert T. Vinter, and Charles Perrow, *Organization for Treatment* (New York, 1966).

A study of the characteristics of six juvenile institutions and their various treatment strategies, and of the apparent effects these strategies had upon the inmates.

Sutherland, Edwin H., and Donald R. Cressey, *Criminology* (Philadelphia, 1974).

The classic criminology textbook which analyzes crime and criminals, criminal psychology, punishment, and prisons.

Sykes, Graham, *The Society of Captives* (Princeton, N.J., 1958).

An analysis of a maximum security prison in New Jersey which probes the social structure, functions, and collective values of the two caste-like strata of 300 bureaucratized prison personnel and 200 inmates.

Tappan, Paul, *Juvenile Delinquency* (New York, 1949).

Tappan analyzes the nature, cause, and extent of delinquency; the role of the juvenile and adolescent courts; the various methods of treatment including probation, casework, detention, and institutional care.

Taylor, Ian, et al., eds., *Critical Criminology* (Boston, 1975).

A collection of articles which "place on record some of the early attempts that are now being made, by radical thinkers and activists in North America and Europe, to transcend . . . the 'hip concerns' of the sociology of deviance, and to confront the facts of extension of law and the ensuing political dilemmas of the radical criminologist."

Taylor, Ian, et al., *The New Criminology* (New York, 1973).

An attempt to fit criminology into a general theory of social deviance. The authors do this by a comparative analysis of traditional, positivistic, and psychological theories of criminal deviance, as well as by giving the same treatment to sociological theories of deviance.

Thrasher, Frederick M., *The Gang* (Chicago, 1927).

In this analysis of 1,313 gangs in the city of Chicago, the author describes where and under what conditions the gangs flourished, who were the members and why, their gang activities, and what efforts had been made by social and other agencies to attack the problem.

Trattner, William I., *Homer Folks: Pioneer in Social Welfare* (New York, 1968).

A study of Homer Folks which depicts him as standing between nineteenth-century charity organizations and later developments in the 1930s.

Trojanowicz, Robert C., *Juvenile Delinquency: Concepts and Control* (Englewood Cliffs, N.J., 1973).

The author provides "an overview of the juvenile delinquency phenomenon and the process involved in its causation, prevention, control, and treatment." He also analyzes the many variables related to delinquency, and the "orientation, duties, responsibilities, and functions of the agencies in the juvenile justice system that deal with the juvenile delinquent."

Two Hundred Years of American Criminal Justice, an LEAA Bicentennial Study (Washington, D.C., 1976).

A historical view of the origins and development of American criminal justice. The study also frames the Law Enforcement Assistance Administration's work in a larger historical context and provides a measure of the Agency's accomplishments since it was established in 1968.

United States Department of Justice, *FBI Uniform Crime Reports: Crime in the United States 1978* (Washington, 1979).

A collection of crime-related statistics submitted voluntarily by the law enforcement agencies of the United States. The information is correlated and published "for the information of the American people and to provide law enforcement and other areas of the criminal justice community with both an insight to criminality throughout the United States and a sound basis for studies of criminal activity."

van den Haag, Ernest, *Punishing Criminals* (New York, 1975).

A discussion of society's right to expect that criminals will be punished. The author analyzes the means by which crime may be controlled, who commits crimes and why, and whether punishment does in fact deter the commission of any crime.

Van Waters, Miriam, *Youth in Conflict* (New York, 1925).

A study of twelve cases from the Los Angeles Juvenile Court analyzes the forces which cause conflict for juveniles. The author traces juvenile delinquency back to parental indifference and a social indifference to the value of childhood.

Vinter, Robert D., *Juvenile Corrections in the United States* (Ann Arbor, Mich., 1975).

Analyses of the residential services provided by state agencies for young offenders in their care and custody. Nothing revealed in this study challenges the criticisms leveled against traditional institutions or the argument that community-based corrections are more economical and probably at least as effective.

Vold, George B., *Theoretical Criminology* (New York, 1958).

An attempt to deal "with the explanations that contemporary society has given in the past, and continues to give today, to the enigmatic question of why there is so much crime."

Voss, Harwin, *Society, Delinquency and Delinquent Behavior,* 2nd ed. (Englewood Cliffs, N.J., 1976).

A selection of articles dealing with sociological aspects of juvenile delinquency. Particular attention is given to contemporary theories and controversies.

Wade, Louis C., *Graham Taylor, Pioneer for Social Justice, 1851–1938* (Chicago, 1964).

A biography of the founder and director of the Chicago Commons Settlement House. The author develops the thesis that Taylor's contribution as a "pioneer for social justice" was that of an organizer and propagandist.

Walker, Nigel, *Crime and Punishment in Britain* 2nd. ed. (Edinburgh, 1968).

A discussion of contemporary formulas for delinquency and relapse prediction. The author is primarily concerned with the sentencing process and the effectiveness of present-day penal measures in Britain.

West, D. J., *The Young Offender* (Baltimore, 1967).

An analysis of the delinquency problem in both its historical and international perspectives. The author presents statistical data and examines all major sociological, biological, and psychological theories of delinquency.

Wheeler, Gerald R., *Counter-Deterrence: A Report on Juvenile Sentencing and Effects of Prisonization* (Chicago, 1978).

A presentation of the theory and results of current juvenile sentencing and parole practices, including the social effects of the "revolving door" and prisonization. The book also focuses on social policy issues, juvenile justice reform, and strategies of decriminilization.

Wheeler, Russell R., and Howard R. Whitcomb, *Judicial Administration: Text and Readings* (Englewood Cliffs, N.J., 1976).

An examination of the problems afflicting the criminal justice system in America today. Overcrowding, racism, incompetence, citizen apathy, and antiquated methods are a few of the problems examined.

Wicks, Robert J., *Correctional Psychology: Themes and Problems in Correcting the Offender* (San Francisco, 1974).

A comprehensive study in the area of correctional psychology that attempts to supply "social workers, nurses, correction officers, psychological interns, parole officers, and other correctional personnel with sound, practical advice."

Wilson, James Q., *Varieties of Police Behavior* (Cambridge, Mass., 1968).

An examination of the role of the police patrolman in eight communities, with special emphasis on the differences between the law enforcement and order maintenance functions of the patrolman and his discretion with respect to whether or how to intervene in various situations. The role of the influence of the political culture of a community on its style of law enforcement is also examined.

Wilson, James Q., *Thinking About Crime* (New York, 1975).

A suggestion that sociologists and professional criminologists have been overly preoccupied with unraveling and attempting to solve the underlying "causes" of crime. According to the author, faulty conclusions concerning crime causation have prevented the adoption of practical remedial policies. He recommends that more attention be paid to the question of deterrence, especially to the certainty and severity of sentencing.

Witmer, Helen L., *Psychiatric Clinics for Children* (New York, 1940).

A review of the philosophy, practices, objectives, and achievements of clinical child psychiatry in the United States. Part one gives the background of the child psychiatry movement; part two gives the results of an extensive survey of clinics; and part three describes the principles underlying the development of future programs.

Wolfgang, Marvin E., Robert Figlio, and Thorsten Sellin, *Delinquency in a Birth Cohort* (Chicago, 1972).

An analysis of all available official data on nearly 10,000 boys from the time they were 10 until they turned 18. Those who became delinquent were compared systematically to those who did not. Thus a statistical description of juvenile delinquency of both the official and unofficial variety is presented.

Zimring, Franklin M., and Gordon J. Hawkins, *Deterrence* (Chicago, 1973).

The authors contend that the question of whether punishment deters crime is unanswerable unless one specifies the situation, the offense, the penalty, the way in which the threat of penalty is communicated, and the audience of the communication. In short, the deterrent effect is not absolute.

INDEX

Victim accounts, 83–86, 152
Victimology, 117
Vinter, 202, 206
VISTA, 39
Vocational and work programs,
211–212
Vocational training, 202–203
Voluntary admissions, 198

Waivers, 158–162
Ward, 208
Wards of the court, 148, 155, 157,
170, 172, 183, 185

Waters, Miriam Van, 34, 36
Wilderness camping, 214
Winship decision, 41, 144, 273
Wirt, Robert, 238
Wizner, Stephen, 276
Work programs, 211–212, 296
Work project, 177–178
YINS, 148, 252
Youth Control Act, 38
Youth Correction Authority Act, 37
Youth Home Admissions statistics, 89
Youth Services Bureau, 134–135, 252
Youth Services Department, 39